AMERICAN STATES OF NATURE

THE ORIGINS OF INDEPENDENCE, 1761–1775

MARK SOMOS

OXFORD
UNIVERSITY PRESS

Oxford University Press is a department of the University of Oxford. It furthers
the University's objective of excellence in research, scholarship, and education
by publishing worldwide. Oxford is a registered trade mark of Oxford University
Press in the UK and certain other countries.

Published in the United States of America by Oxford University Press
198 Madison Avenue, New York, NY 10016, United States of America.

© Oxford University Press 2019

CIP data is on file at the Library of Congress
ISBN 978–0–19–046285–7

1 3 5 7 9 8 6 4 2

Printed by Sheridan Books, Inc., United States of America

CONTENTS

8

ON SLAVERY AND RACE 314

9

CONCLUSION 330

FIGURES

ACKNOWLEDGMENTS

The debts contracted between the first framing of the research question and the completion of this book are too numerous to acknowledge. It is my pleasure to try. I am grateful to the American Society for Eighteenth-Century Studies for a W. Jackson Bate/Douglas W. Bryant fellowship at the Houghton Library in 2010, to the Jack Miller Center for two fellowships at the Huntington Library (in 2012 and 2014) and one at the Center for the Study of Representative Institutions at Yale University (in 2016), the Edmond J. Safra Center for Ethics for a fellowship in 2014–15, to the British School at Rome for a Balsdon fellowship, and the Alexander von Humboldt Foundation for a fellowship at the Max Planck Institute for Comparative Public Law and International Law in Heidelberg. In 2015–16, when my Harvard posts were over but I still needed access to that great university's resources, Harvey Mansfield secured a visiting fellowship that proved vital to finishing the archival work. Researching and writing this book have been a joyful and rewarding part of my life, and I am grateful to Professor Mansfield, and to these organizations, for the opportunity.

I also wish to thank Richard Bell, Hans Blom, Pamela Edwards, Ioannis Evrigenis, John Ford, Renaud Gagné, Ash Cesia Gallwey, George Gallwey, Jonathan Gienapp, David Grewal, Tara Helfman, Béla Kapossy, Alexandra Kemmerer, Joseph Kochanek, László Kontler, Dániel Margócsy, Chris Moore, James Russell Muirhead, Isaac Nakhimovsky, Anne Peters, Andrew Sartori, and Brandon Turner, who improved a succession of drafts over the years with invaluable comments. In the final round of editing, Daniela Cammack, David Grewal and Tom Sparks were extraordinarily generous with their help. All these colleagues and friends opened up new avenues and saved me from innumerable mistakes. I am privileged and lucky to have had their advice. Remaining errors are my own.

I first presented the central thesis concerning a distinctive American state of nature in September 2008 at a conference in Vadstena, Sweden, organized by Koen Stapelbroek. I gave papers on the work in progress at the University of Bayreuth (2012), Chiba University in Japan at the gracious invitation of Mon-Han Tsai (2013), the Huntington Library in San Marino, California (2014), the University of Dundee on the kind invitation of James Livesey (2014), the John Carter Brown Library in Providence, Rhode Island (2015), the University of Heidelberg (2015), the New York University Intellectual History Workshop thanks to the encouragement of Andrew Sartori and Stefanos Geroulanos (2016), and the University of Basel (2016) on the generous invitation of Anna Becker. Questions and comments from organizers and participants at these events have considerably shaped and enriched this book. The manuscript was submitted in July 2017 and revised by July 2018 in the light of constructive and incisive reviews. An early draft of sections 3.1 to 4.1 appeared as "Boston in the State of Nature: The Birth of an American Constitutional Trope," *Jus Gentium: Journal of International Legal History* 3:1 (2018), 63–113. I am grateful to the editor and anonymous reviewers of this article, as well as to the Houghton Library, the Boston Public Library, the Massachusetts Historical Society, the Royal Archives, the American Philosophical Society, Harvard Law School's Historical & Special Collections, the Manuscripts and Archives Division of the New York Public Library, the Library Company of Philadelphia, and the Library of Congress, for their kind permission to reproduce images.

My curiosity about the state of nature was sparked in 2003 in the basement of Harvard's Littauer Building, still home to Government PhD candidates' tiny cubicles at the time. To prepare for general examinations I was encouraged to survey and memorize the history of Western political thought. Every time I was stuck, whether on Aristotle or Hegel, a concept or a text, I turned to Ioannis Evrigenis. We sat in Littauer, or outside when it was sunny, as with infinite skill and patience he explained things to me. The state of nature was the topic that excited us the most. It's been fifteen years; and my life and my work have been so much better for his friendship. In 2005 Russ Muirhead hired me as a teaching fellow for his course on the history of American political thought. There was profound knowledge, combined with a playfulness and a rare ability to move between the lowest and highest vantage points to find the most original angles and lines. Ioannis and Russ have been looking after me since. I hope they don't mind if I thank them here at the end of the acknowledgments, conventionally reserved for family.

I am fortunate beyond words and measure to have my beautiful wife, Marketa Klicova, and daughter, Emma Eva Meike Somos, keep me company on this trip. Our son, Philip Hunter Somos, was born half-way through this book project, which shaped his life to an unfair degree. He was six weeks old when we started traveling to San Marino, CA, Philadelphia, PA, Providence, RI, Chicago IL, Washington, DC, New Haven, CT, New York City, Scotland, Cambridge in Massachusetts and Cambridge in the UK, and wherever archival work needed to be done. He sat or slept through my presentations, and my colleagues played with him and fed him at two dozen conferences while we exchanged stories and ideas about the Old and the New Worlds. Philip is a natural citizen of the United States and Europe, but he is the best of all worlds. This book is for him.

ACKNOWLEDGMENTS

INTRODUCTION

If you pursue your design of writing an History of the "glorious Struggle" . . . you will no doubt produce a Work of much Value to the Public. Certainly I Should read it with high Expectations. But, give me leave to Suggest that the Period you have defined from 1775 to 1783 was by no means the most important nor the most interesting Eight Years of the Revolution. The Revolution was indeed effected in the Period from 1761 to 1775. I mean a compleat Revolution in the Minds of the People. A total Change of the Opinions and Affections of The People, and a full Confidence in the practicability of a Union of the Colonies. All this was done and the Principles all established and the System matured before the year 1775. The War and the Peace followed of Course.

—John Adams to Richard Sharp, February 27, 1811

For over fifty years, John Adams repeatedly described a 1761 speech by James Otis, Jr. as the start of the American Revolution. Adams summarized this speech as "a dissertation on the state of nature." When the First Continental Congress convened in Philadelphia on September 5, 1774, the delegates spent the first day agreeing on procedure. The next day, the first day of substantial business in Congress, began with Patrick Henry's dramatic announcement that the colonies were in a state of nature, government was dissolved, and a new state and government must therefore be formed. Adams was present and recorded Henry's conclusion: "I am not a Virginian, but an American."

Between what Adams called the beginning of the American Revolution and the first day of business in the new American Congress, the colonists used the phrase "state of nature" thousands of times. They used it to claim a set of fundamental rights: the right to protest, to be represented, to resist, to property and life, to freedom of conscience, speech, and assembly, and to self-defense. They debated whether the state of nature was a condition of war, sin, violence, and bare survival; or of sociability, benevolence, and true religion—or a rich interaction of individuals and states following moral and natural laws. In these debates the revolutionary generation forged a shared and original meaning of the state of nature, unique to them, and later adopted in Europe, Latin America, and wherever people looked to the American Revolution for inspiration.

In this book, I contend that the state of nature is one of the most important concepts in the history of the Revolution, a cardinal point comparable to rights, liberty and property on the compass that American patriots, radicals, loyalists, and those who changed positions used to structure their thoughts and guide their actions. From their uses of this term, a distinctive American state of nature discourse emerged. Without understanding it, we cannot accurately interpret revolutionary and founding texts, nor properly gauge their impact on late eighteenth- and early nineteenth-century revolutions and reforms in the United States and in the Latin American and European countries that they influenced.[1]

---

1. As I show below, discussion of this distinctively American state of nature discourse is almost entirely absent from the historiographical literature. Although the revolutionary generation used and debated the technical sense of this precise term (as opposed, for instance, to "human nature" or "state of natural liberty"), "state of nature" does not occur once in Sally E. Hadden and Alfred L. Brophy (eds.), *A Companion to American Legal History* (Wiley-Blackwell, 2013) and appears only once in Michael Grossberg and Christopher Tomlins (eds.), *The Cambridge History of Law in America*, vol. 1, *Early America (1580–1815)* (Cambridge, 2008). This is not a comment on these volumes, but an indication of the gap in the literature that these works survey. A notable exception to this neglect, which is strikingly at odds with the frequency and importance of the state of nature in the primary sources, is a chapter in Thomas

The revolutionary meaning of the state of nature is important to get right partly because of its inherent historical interest. It is also important because the concept continues to be used—and often, as I will show, misused—in constitutional debates and decisions today. Recovering the interpretations and uses of the state of nature in revolutionary ideology should help to improve current and future constitutional interpretation and dispel the widespread and obstructive misunderstanding of revolutionary-era state of nature arguments that continues to distort judicial opinions concerning legal remedy, adverse possession, proportional justice, same-sex marriage, parental rights, and other issues.[2]

The distinctive American state of nature discourse that I describe emerged in several stages, beginning in the 1760s and ending a half-century later, with a new concept of American nature and its political and social significance that endures with some variation down to the present day. This book explores the first two stages, concentrating on how a specifically *revolutionary* state of nature discourse was fashioned.

The first stage I identify is 1761–1772, when the state of nature discourse served mostly to ground an independent source of rights, in order to support the colonists' grievances and remonstrations. The starting point of 1761 is not an arbitrary historiographical device, but comes directly from the primary sources I examine, such as the letter by John Adams quoted in the epigraph, and his insistence that Otis's speech in *Paxton's Case* signaled the start of the Revolution that year. These texts also invite us to reassess established intellectual genealogies of the American Revolution that propose a later starting date, whether in 1763 with the end of the Seven Years' War; in 1765–1769 under the influence of Blackstone's *Commentaries*; or as late as 1773 or even 1776.

From 1772 to 1775, the second stage I identify, the discourse shifted to a sense of the state of nature as the site of an inalienable right to self-defense. On this basis the revolutionaries built a new constitutional

G. West, *The Political Theory of the American Founding: Natural Rights, Public Policy, and the Moral Conditions of Freedom* (Cambridge, 2017), 96–111.

2. See the index for such cases, and appendix 2.

identity for the American colonies as a "natural" community that had effectively been abandoned by Britain, but had yet to become an independent republic. During this stage, a common Patriot defense of using the state of nature, and a common Loyalist objection to it, was that it had become such a radical concept that its invocation drastically reduced the possibility of any compromise with Britain.

The third stage, 1775–1789, was a period of putting the new, American state of nature concept to work in constitution-making and consolidation. This stage saw constitutional conventions and debates at both the federal and the state levels, draftings, redraftings and ratifications, all of which drew on the state of nature as much as they contested and reframed the meaning of "liberty." While legal and intellectual historians over the past few decades have made great efforts to recover the conceptual building-blocks of the American founding, they have largely neglected this central feature of constitutional discourse, which ties the American experiment, in complex and ongoing ways, to the much longer tradition of social-contractarian thought.

In the final stage, from 1789 to roughly 1811, the state of nature discourse was adapted to the tasks of state-building in the newly federal United States of America. During this time, constitutional, economic, and cultural programs developed a usefully ambivalent image and self-image of the United States as a natural community of autonomous individuals possessed of a virtually endless capacity for material and moral growth, animated and sustained by the country's inexhaustible natural potential. The meaning of the state of nature in international relations also came to the foreground in this period. Diverse uses of the state of nature now appeared in scientific debates over the European thesis that the American climate produced a pervasive degeneracy, which was contested by the first group of publicly funded American museums as well as the first constitutional textbooks, which put an emphasis on the optimistic revolutionary version of the state of nature. Several enduring tropes of continuing interest emerged at this time, from the vision of the "wild West" as an abundant frontier able to absorb natural growth and sustain a virtuous farming citizenry, to the assumption that technological progress and innovation predicated on the country's vast natural and intellectual resources would solve the same environmental, public health, and sociological problems that such exploitation entailed. Again, while my focus remains on the revolutionary articulation of the state of nature, I hope that this examination will prove useful to scholars interested in the development of an array of nature discourses in American history that go beyond the political and juridical uses of the colonial and revolutionary eras.

None of these stages was monolithic. Revolutionary or constitutive usages can be found in each stage. Nevertheless, the dominant sense that defines each stage of the American state of nature discourse can be established by paying attention to political context and rhetorical method, which often combined to refute or marginalize rival meanings. There were techniques and key moments that shaped the American reconceptualization of the state of nature. For instance, Loyalists tended to argue that the state of nature was a harmful constitutional fiction, or that its only valid meaning was a state of war. Patriots countered with formulations in which the state of nature was a condition of natural sociability among those whom Britain had pushed into a state of imperial lawlessness, where they found themselves surprisingly stable and harmonious. In the wake of the 1765 Stamp Act, both Loyalists and Patriots sought to refute the meaning that their opponents ascribed to the state of nature. In 1774, the First Continental Congress struck Galloway's plan for imperial reconciliation from its records, based on a non-revolutionary view of the state of nature as limited to interstate relations. Such episodes during which one party tried to seize or recapture control over the emergent American discourse worked to determine the acceptable semantic range of "state of nature" at each stage.

In the history that follows, I will show that the Founders read and debated, but did not endorse Locke's, Montesquieu's, Blackstone's, and others' arguments concerning the trade-off between natural and civil liberty. Instead, they formulated an original discourse in which the natural rights of individuals, collected in the American state of nature where the unjust and unconstitutional measures of the British government had pushed them, transformed into a set of collective and co-ordinated rights and obligations robust and rich enough not only to justify protest, and later revolution, but eventually to constitute a new polity. The distinctly American, constitutive state of nature—tied to the geography, climate, land, and natural resources of the continent—served as a bridge between the Revolution's constitutional stages, from dissenting colonies to a functioning new state with a federal government and sovereignty recognized by international treaties. Before the United States became an internationally acknowledged state, it was seen as a natural community, in a state of nature viewed as irreducibly and unexchangeably American.[3]

1.1 THE BACKGROUND AND VARIETIES OF STATE OF NATURE THEORIZING

The state of nature, man's pre-political condition, has long been a key concept in the history and philosophy of law. Its influence extends from ancient accounts of the Golden Age and Paradise to currently prevailing paradigms of constitutionalism and international ethics. Legal historians focus on a range of state of nature theorists: medieval theologians such as Thomas Aquinas and William of Ockham; early modern thinkers including Hugo Grotius, Thomas Hobbes, John Locke, and Samuel von Pufendorf, who redefined the concept partly to accommodate advances in anthropology; the reprioritization of natural over divine law in Enlightenment state of nature accounts by Montesquieu, Rousseau, Hume, and Vattel; and near-contemporary figures such as Carl Schmitt, Robert Nozick, and John Rawls, who used the trope to elaborate their constitutional theories.[4] Critical legal scholars take encounters with "the

3. As Donald Lutz pointed out in the context of local constitutionalism, "[s]ometimes a document of foundation will create a people but not a government." *Colonial Origins of the American Constitution: A Documentary History* (Liberty Fund, 1998), xxiv. This book aims to show that this is also true for revolutionary federal and state-level constitutionalism.
4. See two excellent recent books: Ioannis Evrigenis, *Images of Anarchy: The Rhetoric and Science in Hobbes's State of Nature* (Cambridge, 2014), and Benjamin Straumann, *Roman Law in the State of the Nature: The Classical Foundations of Hugo Grotius'*

other" as their starting point and have charted how state of nature theories were used to justify conquest and subordination. Historians of science have produced relevant studies, seldom invoked in legal historiography, on a sub-tradition that regarded American flora and fauna as essentially inferior to Europe's—which, as I discuss subsequently, provoked an important response from American thinkers.[5]

But what is the "state of nature"? At least since Thomas Aquinas, the state of nature has combined historical and analytical dimensions, often with intended and useful ambiguity. Did such a state ever exist? Does it continue to exist? Some writers proposed that it did, among peoples at an early stage of social development.[6] Others saw it everywhere, as a permanent background to established polities, in the form of threats of anarchy or as repositories of natural, pre-, and supra-political laws and rights, such as the right to property, representation, resistance, freedom of conscience, religion, and speech, and a condition one could reactivate or reprioritize when politics failed.

Does it matter whether the state of nature ever existed? Can the state of nature set legal and moral baselines and norms irrespective of whether its historical existence is accepted, denied, or bracketed? These are not only retrospective questions by intellectual historians, but were often raised by contemporaries baffled by the deliberately ambiguous use of the term. Among state of nature thinkers, perhaps Hobbes and Rousseau are best known for their use of the state of nature's strategic ambiguity.[7]

Natural Law (Cambridge, 2015). Law students are also likely to know the state of nature from the lively Lon L. Fuller, "The Case of the Speluncean Explorers," *Harvard Law Review* 62:4 (1949), 616–45.

5. Although it does not address the state of nature, one relevant work that transcends disciplinary boundaries is Antonello Gerbi, *La disputa del Nuovo mondo: storia di una polemica, 1750–1900* (Ricciardi, 1955; 2nd ed. 1983, tr. as *The Dispute of the New World: The History of a Polemic, 1750–1900*, Pittsburgh, 2010). Also see J. G. A. Pocock, *Barbarism and Religion*, vol. 4, *Barbarians, Savages and Empires* (Cambridge, 2008), chapters. 1, 4, 5, 9–12, 15–17.

6. Ronald L. Meek, *Social Science and the Ignoble Savage* (Cambridge, 1976).

7. Ioannis Evrigenis, "Freeing Man from Sin: Rousseau on the Natural Condition of Mankind," in Christie McDonald and Stanley Hoffmann (eds.), *Rousseau and Freedom* (Cambridge, 2010), 9–23.

Positions concerning the epistemic and polemical value, meaning, and status of the state of nature show important variation. Some writers imagined states of nature that were idyllic and irrecoverable, or a condition of justice and equality that we could and ought to restore. Others saw it as a violent place that we escaped and must stay away from, or a condition that applied to interstate relations, but remained unacceptable within the state. In addition to the range of positions that various thinkers took on the character and value of the state of nature, certain topics were strongly and regularly associated with it. Descriptions of savages, noble or otherwise, situated them in a state of nature. Stadial theories of progress, and attempts to justify slavery and the occupation of uncultivated lands, often involved a state of nature theory. Ancient constitutionalism is another allied political language, advocating a legal position or reform based on a mythical or pseudo-historical pristine condition.[8]

Moreover, the direct human control of nature, as a historical enterprise, prominently features the notion and explicit language of the state of nature. For centuries, alchemists, natural historians, theologians, breeders, and agrarian improvers have debated whether nature can be improved, or if its state is perfect as it is. Can art improve on nature, is art always inferior, or can art restore degenerated nature to its paradisiacal

8. J. G. A. Pocock, *The Ancient Constitution and the Feudal Law: A Study of English Historical Thought in the Seventeenth Century* (Cambridge, 1957); Jacob T. Levy, "Montesquieu's Constitutional Legacies," in R. E. Kingston (ed.), *Montesquieu and His Legacy* (New York, 2008), 115–38; Matthew Crow, "Jefferson, Pocock, and the Temporality of Law in a Republic," *Republics of Letters* 2:1 (2010), 55–81. Another instance is James Otis Jr., *Rights of the British Colonies Asserted and Proved* (Boston, 1764) , 47, where Otis dismissed Magna Carta as less important than the liberty enjoyed by the Saxons before 1066. Bernard Bailyn, *The Ideological Origins of the American Revolution* (Belknap, 1967; enlarged ed. 1992), 81–82; John P. Reid, "The Jurisprudence of Liberty: The Ancient Constitution in Legal Historiography of the Seventeenth and Eighteenth Centuries," in Ellis Sandoz (ed.), *The Roots of Liberty: Magna Carta, Ancient Constitution, and the Anglo-American Tradition of Rule of Law* (Liberty Fund, 1993), 147–231; John P. Reid, *The Ancient Constitution and the Origins of Anglo-American Liberty* (Wisconsin, 2005); Matthew Crow, *Thomas Jefferson, Legal History, and the Art of Recollection* (Cambridge, 2017).

condition?[9] An intellectual history of the state of nature needs to trace shifts in the perceived degree and domains of malleability, and therefore potential human control, in both nature and society.[10]

Constitutional models that relied on the idea of a social contract, whether the original, a particular historical one, a possible new one (usually for self-defense), or one that is re-enacted daily—for instance by the tacit enjoyment of the government's protection of property—drew both their overall shape and specific provisions from the version of the state of nature that their authors endorsed. These thinkers normally derived from a fundamental definition of the state(s) of nature several further positions, including theories of resistance, the diversity of nations and races, natural slavery and natural aristocracy, and limits on private property before and after the polity's establishment.

Most of these theories shared the assumption that man is unique, and differs from animals. This was not to deny all commonality. Some animals were considered gregarious, even "political," with bees and ants the classical examples.[11] Other animals were understood to show affection for their offspring or parents that seems to transcend their self-interest. The care of storks for their aged parents was a commonplace and emblematic

9. Lorraine Daston and Katherine Park, *Wonders and the Order of Nature* (MIT Press, 1998). William R. Newman, *Promethean Ambitions: Alchemy and the Quest to Perfect Nature* (Chicago, 2004); Pamela H. Smith, *The Body of the Artisan: Art and Experience in the Scientific Revolution* (Chicago, 2004); Smith, "Making as Knowing: Craft as Natural Philosophy," in P. H. Smith, A. R. W. Meyers, and H. J. Cook (eds.), *Ways of Making and Knowing: The Material Culture of Empirical Knowledge* (Bard, 2014).

10. Joyce Chaplin, *Subject Matter: Technology, the Body, and Science on the Anglo-American Frontier, 1500–1676* (Harvard, 2003); Lorraine Daston, "Nature's Custom versus Nature's Laws," Tanner Lectures on Human Values, II, delivered at Harvard, November 6, 2002. Lorraine Daston and Fernando Vidal (eds.), *The Moral Authority of Nature* (Chicago, 2003). Lorraine Daston and Michael Stolleis (eds.), *Natural Law and Laws of Nature in Early Modern Europe: Jurisprudence, Theology, Moral and Natural Philosophy* (Ashgate, 2008).

11. See the references in David J. Depew, "The Ethics of Aristotle's *Politics*," in Ryan K. Balot (ed.), *A Companion to Greek and Roman Political Thought* (Wiley-Blackwell, 2009), 399–418, at 402–3, and in Evrigenis, *Images*, 99–101.

reference.[12] Most famously, in and following Aristotle's *Politics*, man was described as a political animal. In all these cases, however, something else was in turn offered to distinguish men from beasts, be it reason, speech, conscience, bipedalism, erect posture, abstract thought, toolmaking, corruption, a divine origin or likeness, or the necessity of sociability for surviving in or leaving the state of nature. Such is the package and range of concerns, and the intricate and rich connections between them, that shaped the mental world of the colonists and serve as background to the following history of the American state of nature.

1.2 THE DISTINCTIVE AMERICAN STATE
OF NATURE DISCOURSE

In this book, I contend that a distinctive American state of nature discourse was at the heart of the American Founding. Much of the intellectual foundation of the American colonies, and later the United States, was debated and framed in state of nature terms. The phrase, "state of nature," was used thousands of times in the British colonies between 1630 and 1810, in theological, scientific, economic, political, and other senses. By the 1760s a distinct constitutional usage and meaning started to emerge. It combined already existing semantic ranges, excluded others in clear and specific contestation over the term's use, and it gained specifically American connotations while it was used to justify independence at least as much as American formulations of liberty, property, and individual rights did. The state of nature framework could accommodate a wide range of legal, religious, economic, and scientific concerns in varied

---

12. Notable moral discussions of this animal emblem of sociability, with direct legal implications for regulating commonwealths, appear in storks' piety toward parents in James I, "The Trew Law of Free Monarchies" (1598) in *Political Writings* (ed. Johann P. Sommerville, Cambridge, 1994), 62–84, at 77; Hugo Grotius, *De iure belli ac pacis* (Paris, 1625), Prolegomena; and *The Pennsylvania, Delaware, Maryland, and Virginia almanack and ephemeris, for the year of our Lord, 1783* (Baltimore, 1782), which intriguingly cites Samuel Bochart's *Hierozoicon* (London, 1663). A related sentimental-political commonplace held that storks only live in republics. E.g., James Harrington, *The Censure of the Rota* (London, 1660), 8–9.

combinations. The specific formulation of the state of nature chosen by an author, and the relationship between natural philosophy and law in this formulation, are among the vectors that enable the reconstruction of what the state of nature meant for the American Founding, and how this meaning shifted and evolved.

It may be difficult today, when the state of nature is usually encountered only in political and legal philosophy, to recognize how much this discourse relied on arguments concerning the actual natural world, particularly in the context of the settling of a new continent. As I mentioned earlier, one of the claims of European observers was that American nature was corrupt: Spanish, Portuguese, British, and French conquests were accompanied by arguments for the natural inferiority of the whole continent, including its native inhabitants. Enlightenment natural philosophers and historians such as the Comte de Buffon, the Abbé Raynal, William Robertson, and Cornelius de Pauw extended this tradition by positing a natural, inevitable process of degeneration in the Americas.[13]

Against this view, Benjamin Franklin, Thomas Paine, J. Hector St. John de Crèvecœur, Thomas Jefferson, Charles Willson Peale, and others passionately defended American nature and character—though their views on the state of nature have been widely neglected. Consequently, it has become difficult to appreciate the impact of the American state of nature discourse on European reforms and revolutions, despite the wealth and clarity of primary sources. Among other benefits, recovering this colonial intellectual tradition will help to correct Eurocentric accounts of the Enlightenment, and legal histories that regard pre-revolutionary colonial constitutional thought as either nonexistent or fully derivative.

Recovering the colonial state of nature tradition should also help to foreground the relationship between science and law as another vector

13. Jan Golinski, "American Climate and the Civilization of Nature," in J. Delbourgo and N. Dew (eds.), *Science and Empire in the Atlantic World* (Routledge, 2007), 153–74; Lee A. Dugatkin, *Mr. Jefferson and the Giant Moose: Natural History in Early America* (Chicago, 2009); Andrew J. Lewis, *A Democracy of Facts: Natural History in the Early Republic* (Pennsylvania, 2011), with relevant sensibilities, but focusing on the early nineteenth century.

along which the shifting meaning of the state of nature can be traced. Some state of nature writers paid close attention to scientific discoveries; others, less so. But one striking feature of the American state of nature discourse in particular is its close connection to science. The reason this scientific connection matters even to traditional political and juridical concerns is that if the scientific evidence available to the Founders suggested that human nature was essentially good or perfectible, or (relatedly) common sense and sympathy were biologically determined, reliable aspects of moral psychology, then specific institutional features of the new republic could be expected to follow.

For example, as a typical argument might run, good and perfectible citizens deserve publicly funded education, a constitution that provides for the periodic expansion of suffrage, public participation in municipal deliberations, a directly elected president, and a low barrier to passing new legislation, as opposed to the stabilizing but demeaning intergenerational dead weight of accumulating laws. However, men with natural and insurmountable selfishness, driven by passion, would require a powerful state, a government with separation of powers and checks and balances, a strict rotation of offices, and a political rhetoric that supplied a working illusion of direct participation. By contrast, men whose greed and ambition are demonstrably constant and rational would be best ruled through mechanisms, including commerce and a system of public honors, that put their private vices to public benefit.

Similarly, if scientific observation showed that the family was the natural unit of human sociability, then one could not rely on unenlightened self-interest to keep families united in polities. In this case, either a stadial theory of progress, or a process of artificially creating powerful new needs by demonstrating the benefits of civilization, commerce, and the division of labor, was required to ensure that the new state would not lapse into anarchy. Whether property, happiness, freedom of religion, and other rights should be regarded as grounded in a state of nature, and whether or not they can be alienated, were questions with a direct correlation to views on what government could and should regulate. (A vivid American example is the set of debates about whether a separate Bill of Rights was needed.) If studies of the state of nature showed that man's empathy naturally weakened as his circles of identity expanded, from himself through his family and town to his class, state, and nation, then ties of enforceable allegiance, including financial and military contributions, had to similarly vary in strength. Whether scientific evidence suggested that races have disparate natural capacities, or differences between them are due to historical accidents and stages of development, also made a considerable difference to the design of the young, independent state, including but not limited to the constitutional framework for chattel slavery and relations with Native Americans.

Yet the depth and breadth of this engagement with the state of nature remains missing from our secondary literature. The absence is all the more striking given the prevalence of state of nature arguments throughout this period in sermons, pamphlets, letters, resolutions, and declarations.[14] Gordon Wood identified sovereignty, Morgan emphasized equality, and Joseph Ellis named individualism as the central concept that the Founders had to redefine.[15] Yet none of these terms is used in the primary sources as frequently and creatively as the "state of nature."

Not only is the American state of nature tradition missing from our understanding of legal and scientific history, but our political and economic history cannot be complete without it. The state of nature debates concerning the character of the new republic had direct but now largely neglected practical implications. Franklin, Jefferson, Paine, Coram,

14. Many of these are discussed below. For federalism and the state of nature see Noah Webster, *An Examination of the Leading Principles of the Federal Constitution* (Philadelphia, 1787); James Madison, *Federalist Papers* No. 51 (1788), in Clinton Rossiter (ed.), *The Federalist Papers*, Penguin, 1961); James Wilson's 1790–91 *Lectures on Law* in Wilson, *Collected Works* (ed. Kermit L. Hall and Mark D. Hall, Liberty Fund, 2007); David Ramsay, *History of the American Revolution* (Philadelphia, 1789). Education: Robert Coram, *Political Inquiries . . .* (Wilmington, 1791).

15. Gordon S. Wood, *The Creation of the American Republic, 1776–1787* (Chapel Hill, NC, 1969), 345; Edmund S. Morgan, *The Birth of the Republic, 1763–89* (Chicago, 1956, revised ed. 1977); Joseph Ellis, *American Sphinx: The Character of Thomas Jefferson* (Knopf, 1997), 300–301 and *Founding Brothers: The Revolutionary Generation* (Knopf Doubleday, 2000).

Hamilton, Benjamin Rush, and others wrote essays and manuals on the advantages of American nature and character, to convince Europeans to immigrate. To secure Dutch and French loans, Franklin, Adams, and Jefferson had to counter the degeneracy theses of de Pauw, Robertson, Raynal, and Buffon, the latter two being both scientists and advisors to the French court. Historians of science today occasionally recount Jefferson's sending a moose to Buffon, and his quasi-Darwinian and athe-istic passages on mammoths and the age of the Earth in the *Notes on the State of Virginia* (1781, 1784). Yet the significance of such actions and writings that countered the degeneracy thesis in constitutional design remains underexamined, even though they framed debates concerning independence and the desirable form of government, the optimal fran-chise, the choice between militias or a standing army, religious liberty, church-state relations, and the education and potentials of an American citizenry.[16]

In addition to recovering a distinctive American state of nature dis-course, a close reading of the sources, combined with a broad survey of how often the "state of nature" occurs in seventeenth- and eighteenth-century texts, leads to a startling conclusion about its significance. All major constitutional arguments during the Revolution touched on the state of nature, and the Founders returned to it as the first principle from which both particular and general constitutional designs and ar-rangements flowed. Prominent examples include Otis's 1761 rejection of taxation without consent as an offense against property rights; John Adams's frequent elaborations of the state of nature foundation of Otis's argument between 1765 and 1819; Joseph Warren's and Samuel Adams's founding charter of the Committee of Correspondence, which grew quickly into the first shadow government of the thirteen colonies; John Adams's, Patrick Henry's, and others' starting and continuing the First Continental Congress with state of nature arguments; the influential 1786 pamphlet by "Amicus Republicae"; the state of nature references in

16. I am grateful to Russell Muirhead for insights into the political context of Jefferson's *Notes*.

Webster's 1787 *Examination* and in James Wilson's speeches at the 1787 Federal Convention and in his 1791 *Lectures on Law*; Madison's uses of the state of nature in the *Federalist Papers*; Coram's advocacy of universal education based on state of nature principles in his 1791 *Political Inquiries*; and Timothy Ford's *The Constitutionalist* pamphlets. All these texts contain specifically constitutional uses of the concept that have seldom, if ever, been treated carefully and in conjunction before.

1.3 METHOD, SCOPE, AND OUTLINE

From the thousands of surviving state of nature discussions in colonial America, this book focuses on the brief but pivotal period from 1761 to 1775. There are several reasons for the starting date. John Adams thought that James Otis Jr.'s 1761 state of nature speech in *Paxton's Case* marked the birth of American independence. This striking claim from an influential participant and astute observer is in itself worth further exploration, especially as the fullest version of Adams's courtroom notes on the case may have only now come to light.[17] Starting with 1761 also highlights the extent to which the beginning of the distinctly American state of nature discourse predated Blackstone's 1765–1769 *Commentaries*, which many historians regard as a defining stimulus to American revolutionary ideology. The little literature that exists on the American state of nature neglects this earlier period, which helps to obscure the significance of this discourse even before Blackstone's *Commentaries* reached American shores.[18]

17. See appendix 1.
18. Focusing on 1761–1775 does not mean that no state of nature arguments appeared in the colonies before or after this period. There were thousands of relevant state of nature texts, a few of which are discussed in the secondary literature. Shipton describes the significance of the state of nature in John Bulkley's 1725 preface to Roger Wolcott's *Poetical Meditations* (*Sibley's Harvard Graduates*, vol. 4, Cambridge, MA, 1933, 451). In *Settlers, Liberty, and Empire: The Roots of Early American Political Theory, 1675–1775* (Cambridge, 2011), Craig Yirush discusses the state of nature in Bulkley's preface as well as in Daniel Dulany's 1728 *The Right of the Inhabitants of Maryland to the Benefit of the English Laws*, and in the 1747 *An Address to the Inhabitants of the Province of Massachusetts Bay*, probably by Samuel

A starting date of 1761 also allows us to challenge several mistaken presuppositions in the historiography. These include the thesis that nobody contemplated independence before 1773, as well as the historiographical convention of beginning accounts of the Revolution with 1763, the end of the Seven Years' War, which intensified the British policy of colonial extraction. Indeed, examining the sources before 1763 proves useful for comparing explanations of why and how the North American colonies moved from the allegedly loyal formulation of grievances in 1763 to the 1776 Declaration of Independence in a mere thirteen years.[19] It is also salutary to challenge this convention a little, and start with 1761 in order to get a sharper perspective on the difference that the end of the Seven Years' War made.[20]

A final reason comes from British events and texts related to the American colonies after 1761. The twelfth parliament, one of the most tumultuous, opened in 1761. By the time the next parliament was elected in May 1768, the Sugar and Stamp Acts had been passed and repealed, Massachusetts' Circular Letter against taxation without representation had been banned by royal decree and endorsed by New York, Connecticut, and New Hampshire, and a British warship had sailed into Boston harbor. The reason for the *terminus ad quem* of 1775 is perhaps more obvious: it allows us assess the state of nature literature in the aftermath of the First Continental Congress of September 5–October 26,

Adams. For relevant uses after 1775 see Wood, *Creation*, chapter 7, section 4, "The Social Contract," 282–91, and Eric Slauter, *The State as a Work of Art: The Cultural Origins of the Constitution* (Chicago, 2009). For some uses after 1780 see Philip A. Hamburger, "Natural Rights, Natural Law, and American Constitutions," *Yale Law Journal* 102:907 (1993), 907–60.

19. Merrill Jensen, *The Founding of a Nation: A History of the American Revolution, 1763–1776* (1968, repr. Hackett, 2004); Morgan, *Birth of the Republic*; Jack P. Greene, *The Constitutional Origins of the American Revolution* (Cambridge, 2011), chap. 2; Steven Pincus, *The Heart of the Declaration: The Founders' Case for an Activist Government* (Yale, 2017).

20. Peter N. Miller, *Defining the Common Good: Empire, Religion and Philosophy in Eighteenth-Century Britain* (Cambridge, 2004), 170–72, describes American historiographical problems for which "1763 was an ill-chosen landmark in an already confused terrain," 171.

1774, at the very end of the colonial era and before the birth of the new nation.

The approach adopted in this book has limitations, both intended and accidental. One intentional limit is the scope of the material, which focuses on American uses of the state of nature. European invocations are brought in only as background. Deciding how to select the material, my first thought was that a less than exhaustive study of concurrent usages in Britain would ignore the important fact that there was a transatlantic English-language political discourse, in which the state of nature played a key role. Further research showed that the Swiss and French connections, and the German, Italian, and Latin American reception of evolving American state of nature ideas, also offer source materials rich enough to have made a British-American focus similarly biased. Given the aim of recovering the American revolutionary state of nature discourse, it seemed more appropriate to focus on texts written in the colonies, placed in conversation with British and European texts when appropriate. The American revolutionaries' use of Locke's state of nature is extensively discussed, but so are Montesquieu, Rousseau, Burlamaqui, and Vattel, without trying to comprehensively connect the American state of nature discourse to its British, French, or Swiss counterparts.

Choosing to focus on American texts, and thereby creating an asymmetry of sources in which a comprehensive survey of American texts is contextualized through a selective use of British and European texts, is not to deny that there were Tories and Whigs on both sides of the Atlantic, or that there were similarities between the way writers on every side of the imperial conflict—for instance, American revolutionaries and English radicals—thought about constitutional issues. Nor does this approach imply that the historiographical method of distinguishing between British and American texts, and comparing and contrasting them to arrive at ideological mechanisms of the Revolution, is preferable to the method of historians such as Craig Yirush or Daniel Hulsebosch, who convincingly challenge the conventional British-American dualism by describing the transatlantic identities of creole elites, merchants, colonial agents, and others who understood themselves as members of an empire, and were forced to balance conflicting identities only when metropolitan and colonial allegiances increasingly came into conflict.

Instead, the present approach begins with where the texts were produced, and prioritizes American over other texts in order to trace the rise of a distinctive discourse that drew on but transformed European ideas of the state of nature. It brings in other texts as and when they help to clarify the American meaning.[21] Another reason for this localizing priority is that the American revolutionaries' use of the state of nature topos relied on the particular territory of North America, its flora, fauna, inhabitants, customs, past constitutions, and future potential. Anchoring American independence and identity closely to the land makes it possible and rewarding to examine the emergence and revolutionary role of this discourse without a comprehensive comparison with its extra-American equivalents.

An accidental limitation is the preponderance of New England, particularly Massachusetts, in the archival material. Scholarly and public search engines are powerful tools but cannot locate much of the material required for reconstructing the American state of nature discourse. There is a vast amount of material that has not yet been digitized, although terrific projects, such as the continuing edition of John Adams's papers at the Massachusetts Historical Society, the Georgian Papers online, and the Bentham Project at University College London, continue to reveal exciting state of nature documents. Another limitation of digitization is that a considerable proportion of digitized and potentially digitizable material has been erroneously or incompletely cataloged and described. Furthermore, some sources, including manuscript revisions, the probable dating of undated texts based on their location, arrangement, and other contextual evidence garnered from physical records, are difficult or impossible to digitize. Archival work remains necessary and delightful.

---

21. Locke features in this book extensively, but only in relation to American state of nature texts. Francis Hutcheson in chapter 2, Montesquieu, Rousseau, and Thomas Pownall in chapter 3, William Blackstone in chapter 4, together with Grotius, Hobbes, Pufendorf, Vattel, and others mentioned throughout, are similarly brought in only when they shed light on the American discourse.

I was fortunate to pursue extensive archival research in New England, but with only a few trips to research libraries and archives in Virginia, California, and Illinois. There is a great deal more American state of nature to find even for the 1761–1775 period, let alone for subsequent stages of the Revolution and constitution-making; but the materials presented and analyzed here are sufficient to demonstrate its importance and provide a general explanatory framework.[22]

Another limitation is a strict focus on the phrase, "state of nature." The few scholars who discuss this constitutional device tend to confuse or uncritically equate it with the domain of natural law. For instance, in a 1967 article on Blackstone, Finnis elides natural law and state of nature references as if they were substantively the same.[23] Hamburger's seminal 1993 article on natural rights treats the state of nature, natural rights, and the sphere of natural law interchangeably, and uses the "state of nature" at least twenty-six times to characterize natural law texts and debates in which the state of nature was not mentioned.[24] The primary sources suggest that the revolutionary generations had a more precise meaning of the state of nature in mind, and it rarely overlapped with natural law. The "state of nature" could mean the domain of natural law, but also lawless war, the realm of sin, the relationship between states, a domain for divine, natural, and even civil law put together, nudity, and other referents that natural law does not have. Similarly, the thousands of uses of "human nature" and the "state of natural liberty" are sometimes, for instance in Hamburger's article, taken to be identical with state of nature references; but they should not be. In the context of colonial education, the latter phrase represents Francis Hutcheson's attempt to revisit the same

22. This may not be a critical bias. Contemporaries, for instance in reaction to the Boston Port Act, praised or condemned Massachusetts for taking the lead in the Revolution. Morgan (in *Birth of the Republic*) is one of many historians who make the same point.

23. John M. Finnis, "Blackstone's Theoretical Intentions," *Natural Law Forum* 13 (1967), 163–83, 175–76.

24. The clear and emphatic distinction between natural rights and state of nature rights goes back at least as far as Anthony Ascham's *Of the Confusions and Revolutions of Government* . . . (London, 1648).

notion of man's pre-political condition that we find in Hobbes, Locke, Pufendorf, and others, and reclaim it as a condition not of war or untenable atomism, but of natural sociability.[25]

This book's thesis concerning the significance of the state of nature for American colonial history is therefore built on a robust but narrow lexical foundation. The primary sources abound with invocations of human nature and natural law, but the focus of this study is on explicit uses of the term, "state of nature." Limiting this book's primary sources to "state of nature" references sometimes means that the broader context, including debates about human nature, are sidelined. However, given this focus, some of the current confusion can be dispelled and the historical meaning more accurately captured. The best way to dispel the neglect and misunderstanding of revolutionary references to the state of nature is to survey explicit uses, explain their significance, and explore state of nature thinking more broadly on this clear foundation.

In this sense, this book follows the model of Bailyn's attempt to place uses of the term "corruption" in a rich pre-revolutionary context in order to arrive at the revolutionaries' narrow, technical sense, and Hamburger's attempt to do the same with "natural rights." As both scholars point out, the historical meanings they recover sound all the more strange to us as we are accustomed to a broader semantic range for both terms.[26] Balkin and Levinson employ the same method to recover the eighteenth-century meaning of "slavery" as broader than our current notion, which is mostly limited to chattel slavery. Similarly, Steilen examines over seven hundred American texts produced between 1764 and 1788 and concludes that contrary to prevailing assumptions, "prerogative" was not used in Locke's sense, and Blackstone's influence has also been overstated.[27]

25. István Hont, *Jealousy of Trade: International Competition and the Nation-State in Historical Perspective* (Belknap, 2005), and chapter 2, section 2.4 in this volume.

26. Bailyn, *Ideological Origins*; Hamburger, "Natural Rights."

27. Jack M. Balkin and Sanford Levinson, "The Dangerous Thirteenth Amendment," *Columbia Law Review* 112 (2012), 1459–99; Matthew Steilen, "How to Think Constitutionally about Prerogative: A Study of Early American Usage," *Buffalo Law Review* (forthcoming, April 11, 2018 SSRN version). See also Thomas H. Lee,

Although eighteenth-century authors sometimes combine them, for analytical purposes it is useful to distinguish five senses of the state of nature in the texts examined here. The first set of texts comprises denials and denunciations of the state of nature by writers who, for illuminatingly diverse reasons, regarded the state of nature as chimerical, a dangerous instance of abstract theorizing, and an invalid legal fiction. The second semantic range is theological. It runs from the state of nature as the Kingdom of Satan, the condition opposed to the state of grace, the post-lapsarian condition that must be redeemed through right Christianity, the postlapsarian condition as simply the historical period we live in, and, at the other end of the spectrum, as right Christianity.

The third sense applies to places, peoples, animals, and other entities that are uncultivated and uncivilized. The fourth is the state of nature as a locus of pre- or supra-political rights. Many writers claimed that these rights, such as equality, property, the right to judge and punish injuries, the freedom of conscience and religion, the right to create, enter, or leave a polity, the right to resist oppression, the right to inherit rights, or the "right to rights" (in Hannah Arendt's and John Phillip Reid's felicitous phrase), survive the transition to civil society and persist under the surface of political life either as rights that civil laws must harmonize with, or as rights that can be recalled under special circumstances, including the natural, organic growth of colonial autonomy, or emergencies such as civil war and tyranny. An allied meaning is independence, the spirit and love of which was often thought to be integral to the state of nature. This could be a good thing, insofar as it kept people free. Others thought it was a bad thing, acting as an impulse for licentiousness and a systemic barrier to collective action. The fifth meaning considered in this book is the state of nature as a defining conceptual hinterland to race.

When reconstructing the origins, significance, and evolution of the American state of nature discourse, we must avoid oversimplification. Some intellectual shifts were simultaneous yet contrary, or at least

"Natural Born Citizen," *American University Law Review* 67 (2017), 327–411 for a similar exercise.

discordant. For instance, a straight line connects early seventeenth-century colonists' deprecatory views of Native Americans with eighteenth-century European charges of pan-American degeneracy. Another line that runs in the opposite direction connects two positive assessments. Seventeenth-century hired pens working as corporate and imperial propagandists developed state of nature tropes about friendly, hard-working, and noble natives, who inhabit a fertile and free American paradise. Perhaps paradoxically, the same tropes reappear in texts by their colonial readers' eighteenth-century descendants, as they reinvent themselves as a people of hard-earned pride, exceptional promise, and fierce independence. Challenging reductionist etiologies of the invention of subaltern races, the primary state of nature sources reveal similar lines connecting the European theme of the American noble savage (which runs uninterrupted at least from the sixteenth to the eighteenth century) to the inversion and adaptation of the same features into a white American self-identity that stands in contrast with savages and natives, but which is identically ennobled by simplicity, and purified by a return to American nature and redemptive hard work. The explicit state of nature values, originally associated with noble savages, were appropriated to create a new and self-justifying American ideal, sometimes in tandem with replacing the noble savage ideal with similarly long-established stereotypes of indolent and retrograde Native Americans. This normative inversion is the key to texts ranging from *An Historical Account of the Expedition against the Ohio Indians* by Thomas Hutchins and William Smith (1765), through Crèvecœur's *Letters from an American Farmer* (1782), to Thoreau's *Walden* (1854) and beyond.[28]

The book hopes to survey a representative sample of the abundant primary sources and convey their arguments in support of the overdue recognition of a distinctive American state of nature discourse. It

28. For the state of nature in Melville see Isaac Schapira and Mark Somos, "'Bonapartes and Sharks': The Political Philosophy of Herman Melville," *Storia del pensiero politico* 1:2 (2012), 239–74. The idea of "normative inversion" comes from Jan Assmann, *Moses the Egyptian: The Memory of Egypt in Western Monotheism* (Harvard, 1997).

proceeds as follows. As background, chapter 2 provides a sketch of the various meanings and uses of the state of nature in relation to the British American colonies until the early 1760s, including the significance of the state of nature theme in the colonial education of the founding generation. Chapter 3 examines Otis's speech in *Paxton's Case* to understand why John Adams regarded it as the start of the American Revolution and follows the strands of state of nature interpretation that emerged before the 1765 Stamp Act. Chapter 4 reveals the cardinal importance of the state of nature in colonial reactions to the Stamp Act, and how these reactions stood in contrast to Blackstone's conceptualization of the state of nature in his *Commentaries,* which is often but mistakenly seen as shaping the earliest stage of American revolutionary ideology. By the time the Stamp Act was repealed, the state of nature was a standard and un-avoidable trope in American formulations of rights and remonstrations. Chapter 5 describes the consolidation of this trope, and the beginning of its transformation from a vindication of protest into the foundation of an American natural community.

Chapter 6 shows that as tensions with the mother country escalated in the early 1770s, the second stage in the evolution of the American state of nature endowed this natural community with the collective right to self-defense, also grounded in the state of nature. Moderates and loyalists vehemently contested revolutionary state of nature arguments for a natural community of American settlers separate from Britain, and for this community's right to self-defense. Following overviews of revolutionary, moderate, loyalist, and shifting usages, chapter 7 introduces state of nature arguments during and around the First Continental Congress in order to reconstruct the process of contestation and consolidation that led to a relatively stable, and distinctly American concept of the state of nature by 1776. Finally, chapter 8 offers an overview of the increasing role of the state of nature in American thinking about race and slavery.

2

THE STATE OF NATURE
Sources and Traditions

In framing the state of nature as an analytical device, Hobbes, Locke, and Rousseau agreed that (as Locke put it) "in the beginning all the World was America, and more so than that is now."[1] Likewise, Voltaire asserted in *La philosophie de l'histoire* (1765) that the state of nature actually existed in America. The claim of this book is that the founding generation of Americans drew on these and other European state of nature discourses but put them to new effect in developing a distinctive constitutional trope of the "state of nature." To understand exactly what the founding generation did with their inherited versions of the state of nature, we need to know their actual sources and intellectual building blocks.

In this chapter I examine four such building blocks: the "state of nature" as applied to locations that were considered uncultivated or uncivilized,

---

1. John Locke, *Second Treatise*, §49; Evrigenis, *Images of Anarchy*; Evrigenis, "The State of Nature," in A. P. Martinich and Kinch Hoekstra (eds.), *The Oxford Handbook of Hobbes* (Oxford, 2016), 221–41.

often in the context of imperial planning; metropolitan portrayals of American state of nature as a fertile environment full of promise and potential for new settlers; a widely read American formulation of the optimistic state of nature theme in an almanac; and teaching materials and exams in colonial colleges. Together, these four strands give us a cross-section of the state of nature trope shortly before the Revolution in horticultural, political, and juridical uses, from metropolitan and colonial perspectives, in academic and everyday contexts.

2.1 THE UNCIVILIZED STATE OF NATURE

Readers today may find it striking that writers in the sixteenth to eighteenth centuries used the state of nature to characterize theological and abstract philosophical conditions, scientific principles and observations, and actual places and people, with equal ease. In the short period between 1761 and 1775, a wide variety of locations were described as being in an uncultivated, rude state of nature. For example, in his 1773 *Voyage à l'Ile de France, à l'Ile Bourbon et au cap de Bonne-Espérance,* two years after he and Jean-Jacques Rousseau had become friends and started studying plants together, the botanist Jacques-Henri Bernardin de Saint-Pierre described the black slaves he encountered in Mauritius as raising their children in an awful state of nature.[2] A 1774 description of the Caribbean as an uncultivated state of nature was probably written by Sir William Young, and used as evidence in geopolitical calculations during the war.[3]

2. Jacques-Henri Bernardin de Saint-Pierre, *A Voyage to the Island of Mauritius* (tr. John Parish, London, 1775), 96–97. Also see the introduction and notes in *Journey to Mauritius* (tr. and notes by Jason Wilson, Signal, 2002). In his 1784 *Études de la nature,* in the eighth study concerning Providence, Bernardin de St. Pierre employed the term in a Rousseauvian sense, describing the character and travails of either a historical or a theoretical figure living before and outside society.

3. [Sir William Young?], *Authentic papers relative to the expedition against the Charibbs, and the sale of lands in the island of St. Vincent* (London, 1773); Jack Greene, *Evaluating Empire and Confronting Colonialism in Eighteenth-Century Britain* (Cambridge, 2013), 4–10; and Brooke N. Newman, "Identity Articulated: British Settlers, Black Caribs, and the Politics of Indigeneity on St. Vincent, 1763–1797," in

The same year, in his massive *Political Survey of Britain*, a celebration of the British Empire and a detailed blueprint for agricultural, infrastructural, economic, and military improvement, John Campbell described Siberia and Ireland, and the lands and ports in both, as in a rude, uncultivated state of nature.[4]

John Gray described Ireland in similar terms in *A Comparative View of the Public Burdens of Great Britain and Ireland* (1772). This influential work argued that Ireland should be allowed to trade on the same terms as Britain, thereby removing animosity and incentivizing Ireland to support the war in America. Amplifying its reception on both sides of the Atlantic, it was summarized, extracted and reviewed in the *Critical Review*, which praised its proposals to bring more Irish land in "a state of nature" into settled agriculture.[5] In a 1771 sermon John Freebairn applied the term to Scotland before anybody thought it worthwhile to considerably extend its agriculture.[6] Likewise, the 1775 *Concise Historical Account of all the British Colonies in North-America, Comprehending Their Rise, Progress, and Modern State; Particularly of the Massachusets-Bay (the Seat of the Present Civil War)*, probably by Paul Wein, described Labrador and its inhabitants as living in an uncultivated state of nature.[7]

G. D. Smithers and B. N. Newman (eds.), *Native Diasporas: Indigenous Identities and Settler Colonialism in the Americas* (Nebraska, 2014), 109–50.

4. John Campbell, *A Political Survey of Britain: Being a Series of Reflections on the Situation, Lands, Inhabitants, Revenues, Colonies, and Commerce of this Island* (London, 1774).

5. John Gray, *A Comparative View of the Public Burdens of Great Britain and Ireland; with Aproposal [sic] for Putting Both Islands on an Equality in regard to the Freedom of Foreign Trade* (London, 1772), summary, extracts, and review in Tobias George Smollett (ed.), *The Critical Review: Or, Annals of Literature*, 33:462–68 (London, 1772). Vincent Morley suggests that the review's author may have been English. Morley, *Irish Opinion and the American Revolution, 1760–1783* (Cambridge, 2002), 220.

6. John Freebairn, *A Caution against False Teachers: a Sermon, Preached before The Society in Scotland for Propagating Christian Knowledge, At their Anniversary Meeting, In the High Church of Edinburgh, On Friday, June 7, 1771* (Edinburgh, 1771).

7. [Paul Wein?], *A Concise Historical Account of all the British Colonies in North-America, Comprehending Their Rise, Progress, and Modern State; Particularly of the Massachusets-Bay (the Seat of the Present Civil War): together with the other*

The state of nature was indeed the device of choice for connecting distinct uncultivated lands or peoples deemed uncivilized. In 1768, Pierre Poivre, the *Intendant* of Mauritius who smuggled nutmeg, cloves and other spices to break the Dutch monopoly, claimed that the Chinese considered all lands not under agricultural cultivation as in a state of nature.[8] In his widely read *A Tour in Scotland* (1771), Thomas Pennant recounted coming across old Scottish canoes, the kind made when Scotland's inhabitants were "in the same state of nature as *Virginia*, when first discovered by Captain *Philip Amidas*." Pennant cited Theodore De Bry's illustrations in Thomas Harriot's *Briefe and True Report of the New Found Land of Virginia* (1588) as visual evidence for the parallel between the canoes of Native Americans and his ancient Scots', both in the state of nature. Pennant also applied the term to uncultivated land, to Samoyeds and the Eskimo, the natives of California, all mankind before the domestication of animals, and the wild men of Ceylon, known as Wedas

provinces of New-England: to which is annexed, an accurate descriptive table of the several countries ... (London, 1775).

8. Pierre Poivre, *Voyages d'un philosophe ou observations sur les moeurs et les arts des peuples de l'Afrique, de l'Asie et de l'Amérique* (Yverdon, 1768). Emma Spary, *Utopia's Garden: French Natural History from the Old Regime to the Revolution* (Chicago, 2000); Richard Grove, *Green Imperialism: Colonial Expansion, Tropical Island Edens, and the Origins of Environmentalism, 1600–1860* (Cambridge, 1995), including 238–40 on Philibert Commerson comparing Tahiti to both More's utopia and Rousseau's state of nature. Poivre also claimed that free labor is so much more productive that slavery makes no sense. The Founder, physician, and abolitionist Benjamin Rush and others cited this passage to buttress their moral argument. E.g. Benjamin Rush, *An address to the inhabitants of the British settlements in America, upon slave-keeping* (Philadelphia, 1773) 4–7. I am grateful to Hans Blom for pointing out that the same argument about slaves' low productivity appears in Willem Usselincx, *More excellent obseruations of the estates and affairs of Holland* (London, 1622), 15–16. On Jefferson reading and thinking about Poivre: *Thomas Jefferson Encyclopedia*, s.v. "Rice." http://www.monticello.org/site/house-and-gardens/rice. Poivre's *Voyages* was published the year that Bernardin de St. Pierre first arrived in Mauritius. On the relationship between Bernardin and Poivre, see Jean E. Luck, "Science and Knowledge in Bernardin de Saint-Pierre's 'Etudes de la nature' (1784)," PhD diss., Exeter (2013), 15.

or Bedas.[9] Bougainville's widely read *Voyage autour du monde* (1771), which famously portrayed Tahitians as living in blissful innocence, likewise described the Pécherais (Fugians) as living in the state of nature. Diderot's 1772 *Supplément* used the same term for Tahiti.

The characterization of a place or people as being in the state of nature was not necessarily disparaging. In some cases, the state of nature as an uncultivated condition carried positive connotations. A whole semantic range of the state of nature clusters around the notion of innocence. Thomas Newburgh was one of several writers who compared the Christian vision of paradise as a state of nature with pagan tales of a golden age.[10] Another thread described rural life as an innocent and virtuous state of nature.[11] John Gordon, archbishop of Lincoln, mused in his discourse on Rousseau about childhood as the true state of nature, innocent while it lasts, but not a condition that one should seek to perpetuate.[12] John Wilkes's morally innocent state of nature could not accommodate the distinction between right and wrong.[13] In *A New Inquiry into the Causes, Symptoms, and Cure, of Putrid and Inflammatory Fevers* (1774), the Scottish physician William Fordyce praised the state of nature as a healthier human habitat than cities. The Reverend Samuel

9. Thomas Pennant, *A Tour in Scotland, and Voyage to the Hebrides* (Chester, 1771). Samoyeds and Eskimo: Thomas Pennant, *The British Zoology* (London, 2nd ed., 1768), 1:142, s.v. "Kite." Probably paraphrasing without acknowledgment Eusebio Kino, S.J.'s 1708–11 account, Pennant asserts that the inhabitants of California, "the most innocent of people, are in a state of paradisaical nature, or at least were so before the arrival of the *European* colonists among them." *Arctic Zoology . . . Introduction*, Class I, Quadrupeds (London, 1784–85), 1:cxxxvi. Mankind in the state of nature uninterested in domesticating animals: *Arctic Zoology*, s.v. "Bison," 1:6. The wild men of Ceylon, Wedas or Bedas, who speak Cingalese, live in woods and mountains, they trade but have no laws: *The View of Hindoostan* (London, 1798), 191–93.
10. Thomas Newburgh, *Essays Poetical, Moral and Critical* (Dublin, 1769).
11. Arthur Young, *Rural Oeconomy: or, Essays on the Practical Parts of Husbandry* (London, 1770).
12. John Gordon, *A New Estimate of Manners and Principles: or a Comparison between Ancient and Modern Times, in the Three Great Articles of Knowledge, Happiness, and Virtue* (Cambridge, 1760).
13. John Wilkes, *The Works of the Celebrated John Wilkes, Esq; Formerly Published under the Title of The North Briton, in Three Volumes* (London, 1765?).

Ward pointed out in his monumental *A Modern System of Natural History* (1775–76) that some animals are still in a state of nature, while others, such as sheep, used to be much tougher and independent before domestication. Simultaneously and contrary to this meaning, others asserted that uncultivated land, plants, and animals in the state of nature were inferior.

Alongside positive and negative connotations of the state of nature as an uncultivated condition were texts that attached little or no moral quality or value judgment to their characterization of uncultivated lands, plants, and animals as being in a state of nature. Thomas Pennant's *British Zoology* (1766), William Hanbury's *A Complete Body of Planting and Gardening* (1773), a bulky book on botany and gardening that often features the term, and William Boutcher's *A Treatise on Forest-Trees* (1776), discussing unpruned trees as in a state of nature, are cases in point. Even Lord Kames, whose moral and legal views influenced the Founders, especially Jefferson, used the state of nature in a neutral sense in his 1776 *The Gentleman Farmer*. This is not to say that in some texts the value-free state of nature is not invoked to support a morally charged issue. Nathaniel Forster in his 1767 *An Enquiry into the Causes of the Present High Price of Provisions* matter-of-factly described uncultivated land as being in a state of nature, but remained passionate about the welfare provisions of his proposed agrarian reform based on the moral and economic potential of such lands.

2.2 ADVERTISING AMERICA

While Hobbes, Locke, Voltaire, and others depicted a free but backward American state of nature, one of the most pervasive tropes was a more exuberant praise of the American environment than the applications of state of nature terminology to the Caribbean, Siberia, Ireland, and other places mentioned above.[14] The exuberant genre included advertisements

---

14. Also see the *Sailor's Letters* of Edward Thompson, a navy officer later known as Poet Thompson for his literary work, containing a 1756 letter in which Thompson describes New York as a lovely and rough place, a state of nature like the mythical golden age or Paradise must have been. On early modern and eighteenth-century

and propaganda aimed at buyers and settlers of American lands, which normally described the environment, and sometimes Native Americans, as being in an unusually productive state of nature, already yielding above-average material and moral benefits, and waiting for the right settlers to harness their full potential.

For instance, the lead item in the January 10, 1765, issue of the *Georgia Gazette* was a piece by George Johnstone, Governor of West Florida from 1763 to 1767, who arrived in the provincial capital of Pensacola on October 21, 1764. He signed and sent out the article in question ten days later, on November 1, 1764. Johnstone hoped to turn West Florida into "the Emporium of the New World."[15] To that end, he needed to attract immigrants and cultivate good relations with Native Americans. (Frustrated, he left the colony in January 1767.) In the early piece that reached the *Georgia Gazette*, Johnstone addressed potential settlers.

> The produce of the country in its present state of nature is valuable: *live-oak, cedar, pines of the best kind* cover the banks of every river and bay; those can with great advantage be transported to all the West-Indies, and some of our northern colonies.

An even better part of West Florida's nature, he continued, was the commercial potential afforded by its bays, harbors, and favorable tides and winds. "Nature seems to have intended" Pensacola to become the center of trade, partly because of its location and natural bay, and partly because the relatively lower fertility of the lands around it should incentivize commerce. It was the same combination of natural advantage

adaptations of ancient accounts of the Golden Age to a state of nature discourse see Jacob Bryant, *A New System, or, an Analysis of Ancient Mythology*, vol. 2 (London, 1775), 349–50; vol. 3 (London, 1776), 35–36; Evrigenis, "Sovereignty, Rebellion, and Golden Age: Hesiod's Legacy," in David Matthew Carter, Rachel Foxley, and Liz Sawyer (eds.), *The Brill Companion to the Legacy of Greek Political Thought* (Brill, forthcoming).

15. Robin F. A. Fabel, "Johnstone, George," *Oxford Dictionary of National Biography* online.

in commerce and disadvantage in agriculture that made Tyre, Sidon, Carthage, Colchis, Palmyra, Wisby, Amsterdam, Venice, and Genoa rich and populous.[16] Moreover, the whole colony's settlers could depend on trade to reinforce peaceful relations with Native Americans, who "have those ideas of justice, which are only universal in society, before an advanced state of civility has corrupted the manners of individuals." The benefits of the American state of nature for enterprising settlers therefore accrue from the natural fertility and produce of the province; the commercial value of its natural resources; the suitability of its capital for commerce; and the natural sense of justice that makes the natives reliably co-dependent on peaceful trade and coexistence.[17] Johnstone's paper was followed by royal instructions to settlers that specified the terms of land grants and emphasized the inconvenience "in many of our colonies in America, from the granting excessive quantities of land to particular persons who never cultivated or settled it, and have thereby prevented others more industrious from improving the same."

We find a similar template in the March 1, 1765 proclamation of James Murray, Governor of Quebec.[18] Settlers should come, he stated, having understood that they would receive generous land grants on the strict condition of building a permanent residence, cultivating the arable portions, and improving barren and infertile plots by clearing rocks and draining swamps. Feeling that this may not be sufficient inducement, the Governor added that as Quebec had been misrepresented as "barren, and incapable of Improvement, from the Length and Severity of the Winter, it becomes necessary in this Proclamation to remove these Errors."

16. For the same argument in Cunaeus and Harrington see Somos, *Varieties of Secularisation in English and Dutch public international law* (Leiden PhD, 2014), 105, 286–87; and "Harrington's Project: The Balance of Money, a Republican Constitution for Europe, and England's Patronage of the World" in Béla Kapossy, Isaac Nakhimovsky, and Richard Whatmore (eds.), *Commerce and Peace in the Enlightenment* (Cambridge, 2017), 20–43.

17. Johnstone's article appeared in *The Gentleman's and London Magazine* (where it was called a "Proclamation") and *The Scots Magazine* only in February 1765.

18. Published in the May 16 and July 18, 1765, issues of the *Pennsylvania Gazette* and the May 27, 1765, *Boston-Gazette*.

Potential settlers should know that Quebec's "Meadows in a State of Nature, yield amazing Quantities of Hay; and the Droughts, so frequent in the more southern Colonies, are not known here."

Britain created the province of Quebec in 1763 when France ceded the region as part of the settlement of the Seven Years' War. Despite pressure from colonists and merchants, the government refused to replace the French civil code in Quebec with the common law, or to exclude Catholics from local government by other means. Murray was particularly despised by British merchants and colonists for what they regarded as his partiality toward French Canadians. In addition, long before the 1774 *Quebec Act* further expanded the province and guaranteed freedom of worship to Catholics, the thirteen British American colonies already regarded the new Province of Quebec as a threat and a provocation. Murray's invitation to settle in Quebec's idyllic state of nature was bound to irritate some readers of the May 27, 1765 *Boston Gazette*—especially given the context created by the editors, who firmly tied in the Stamp Act. Parliament passed the Stamp Act on March 22, scheduled to come into effect on November 1. The Act, discussed in more detail below, stipulated that a range of documents, including pamphlets and newspapers, court documents, professional licenses and playing cards, had to be printed on paper manufactured in London, and carrying an embossed stamp.

At the time the *Boston Gazette* was published by Benjamin Edes and John Gill, undoubtedly among the most influential revolutionary printers and publishers.[19] They will reappear throughout this book, reprinting strategically chosen texts from the English Civil War, publishing Locke's *Second Treatise* without chapter 1, starting instead with chapter 2 on the state of nature, or receiving praise from John Adams for their revolutionary allegiance. There is extensive and excellent secondary literature on their work, but perhaps insufficient attention has been paid to how

---

19. See the literature in Jeffrey L. Pasley, *The Tyranny of Printers": Newspaper Politics in the Early American Republic* (Virginia, 2001), 37–40, and Eric Slauter, "Reading and Radicalization: Print, Politics, and the American Revolution," *Early American Studies* 8:1 (2010), 5–40, at 7 n. 22.

they shaped their newspaper's message through subtle clues, including layout and juxtaposition. Their framing of Governor Murray's invitation to British settlers to leave drought-stricken southern colonies for Canada is a good example. After the proclamation, the next page of the *Boston Gazette* carried an unsigned May 10, 1765, letter from Jared Ingersoll, Sr., the Loyalist Stamp Master for Connecticut (whose son of the same name became a leading Patriot). Ingersoll, Sr.'s letter reported just a few words from Charles Townshend's speech in support of the Stamp Act, followed by a long extract from the speech of Isaac Barré, MP, a fierce opponent of taxing the colonies, and author of the phrase "Sons of Liberty." Barré declared that the American colonists had received no support from England, yet they embodied the best of English liberty when they "fled from your Tyranny, into a then uncultivated Land, where they were exposed to almost all the Hardships, to which human Nature is liable . . . and yet actuated by the Principles of true *English* Liberty; they met all these Hardships, with Pleasure, compared with those they suffered in their own Country, from the Hands of those that should have been their Friends." Then came an announcement that the Stamp Act had come into effect in Boston, followed by the former colonial agent William Bollan's thorough criticism of Britain's misguided economic calculus and of the Stamp Act's erroneous premise that the colonists owed Britain for defense. Not for the first time, the *Boston-Gazette*'s editors, Edes and Gill, co-opted the metropolitan praise of the Canadian state of nature as evidence for the American colonists' complaint.

2.3 NATHANIEL AMES'S ALMANAC (1763)

A particularly vivid example of the optimistic American state of nature genre comes from a colonial almanac of great popularity. Almanacs were among the most widely owned texts. Their usual format consisted of a small page for every month with weather forecasts, times of the rising and setting of the sun and the moon, sowing dates for farmers, tide information, a chart of distances between nearby towns, dates of circuit courts, and the like. They also included blank pages for the owner's own notes, and short philosophical, political, and moral texts that the readers could work their way through, revisit, ponder, and discuss with others throughout the year.

From 1725 until his death in 1764, Nathaniel Ames, Sr., physician and almanac-maker, published in Dedham, Massachusetts the most popular almanac throughout New England. His son, Nathaniel Jr., carried on the tradition until 1775. The almanac was among the few printed texts in truly wide circulation and regular use in New England households. The last essay that Nathaniel Ames, Sr. wrote, published in 1763 in *An astronomical diary: or, almanack for the year of our Lord Christ, 1764.... Calculated for the meridian of Boston, New-England*, and promptly reprinted in Massachusetts, Connecticut, Rhode Island, New Hampshire and New York, was the remarkable "An Introduction to Agriculture."[20] It may seem similar to the advertisements mentioned above, but it was written from a crucially different perspective. Unlike European corporate and imperial propaganda to attract settlers, charter rights, and investment, Ames's essay exemplifies the American praise of the continent's potential using the state of nature trope:

> If we may judge by Analogy, and the progressive Increase of the Inhabitants of this Continent, the Kingdoms of the Earth, and the Glory of the World will be transplanted into AMERICA: But the Study and Practice of Agriculture must go Hand in Hand with our Increase; for all the Policy and Learning in the World will not enable us to become a rich, flourishing and happy People, without the Knowledge and Practice of Agriculture. The vast and noble Scenes of Nature infinitely excel the pitiful Shifts of

20. Under the name of Nathaniel Low, Boston; Newport, RI, reprinted and sold by Samuel Hall; in Portsmouth, NH, by D. Fowle; in New Haven, CT, by Benjamin Mecom[?]. Pirated by Timothy Green in New London, CT. These versions are somewhat different in layout, but they all conclude with this essay. The introduction was reprinted with slight variations in the 1764 *Poor Thomas improved: being More's country almanack for the year of Christian account, 1765 ... Calculated according to art; and, without any sensible error, may serve all the northern colonies ...*, the almanac for New York by Thomas More. That this was Nathaniel, Sr.'s last essay: William A. Pencak, *Essays in American History* (Lehigh, 2011), 191.

Policy. The Lands here are taken from a State of Nature, and we may improve them by the Strength of Nature.

Perhaps partly in defiance of the degeneracy thesis, here the American state of nature became a potential ally and autonomous agent of independence. Practical advice on improvements followed this declaration of imminent superiority, with exhortations to American nature and colonists to work together to harness its potential. Nathaniel, Jr. wrote an introduction for this almanac to make the political stakes involved clear. After describing his dear father's death and his own decision to finish the issue in his father's memory, he noted the importance of his father's essay on agriculture, given that "it is now become absolutely necessary that we begin to cultivate every Art and Manufacture" to improve the colonies' balance of trade with Britain, and pay the "heavy Duties" recently laid upon them.[21]

It is hard to assess the impact of the essay by Nathaniel Sr., but the wide dissemination of copies and reprints, together with the evidence of reading practices, suggest that it was considerable. Most colonial households may not have owned many books, but almanacs were cheap and useful publications that often doubled as diaries and notebooks. A range of owners, from semi-literate and otherwise unknown farmers to Founders like Jefferson, left notes that relate to the printed text in interesting ways. For instance, the entries that Edward Marrett, a soldier and farmer in Cambridge, made in his copies of Ames's almanacs offer a glimpse into local government, local opinion about the Stamp Act, its repeal, unrest in Boston, and, strikingly, the degree of confusion and

21. Nathaniel Jr.'s introduction is missing from some exemplars, but can be found, inter alia, in the John Carter Brown Library, DD Drake 3142 copy. In locating the potential for liberty and greatness in the fertility of the American soil, Nathaniel Sr. followed a tradition going back at least to Fortescue, *De laudibus legum Angliae*, cited in Jack Greene, "Empire and Identity from the Glorious Revolution to the American Revolution," in P. J. Marshall (ed.), *The Eighteenth Century* (Oxford, 1998, repr. 2006), 208–30, 211.

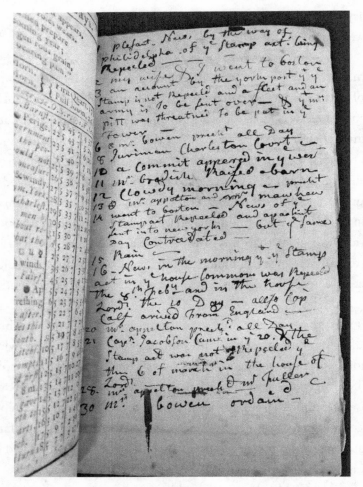

Fig. 2.1 Edward Marrett, diary, April 1766. Ms Am 1171, Houghton Library, Harvard University.

contradiction concerning British plans and policies toward Massachusetts (see fig. 2.1).[22]

The morally and constitutionally charged uses of the state of nature never crowded out the descriptive meaning of uncultivated or wild lands—even as these lands took on increasing political importance. In

22. Also see Jonathan Sayward's diary entries condemning revolutionary events in Boston as they occurred (American Antiquarian Society, e.g., vol. 6 for 1765).

1767 the Massachusetts House of Representatives set up a committee at the request of Asa Douglas, ancestor of the Stephen A. Douglas who debated Lincoln in 1858, to establish the value of the lands "as in a State of Nature" on the contentious Massachusetts–New York border.[23] On June 25, 1771, the House instructed Benjamin Franklin, as colonial agent for the province, to request the King's approval for the General Court's grant of township status to settlements east of the Penobscot River. The House suggestively invoked the precedent of Francis Bernard, Governor of New Jersey from 1758 to 1760 and of Massachusetts from 1760 until 1769, who in 1762 invested heavily in settlements that received the status of townships from the court, with later approval from the King. Although Bernard left as Governor under a cloud in 1769, the House now tendered the same reasons, namely expense and intention to settle, to obtain the same grant.

> These Circumstances it is apprehended will serve to place the Grantees in a favorable Light with his Majesty; especially if it be further considered, that they have most of them laid out their whole Substance on those Lands, and been clearing and improving them for divers Years past with great Labor, whereby from a State of Nature they are coming to be a well inhabited, and valuable Part of his Majesty's Dominions.[24]

Not granting township would ruin "a very great Number of His Majesty's Subjects," many of whom were tempted to migrate to Canada, and without whom the eastern settlements could not be extended and defended from Native Americans.

The next year, though in less detail, the House built a similar case for settlers who spent decades bringing lands "out of a State of Nature" as

23. *Journals of the House of Representatives of Massachusetts, 1767,* Massachusetts Historical Society (Boston, 1974), vol. 43, pt. 2, 356.
24. Benjamin Franklin, *Papers,* vol. 18 (ed. William B. Willcox et al., Yale, 1974), 138–44.

the reason for granting them titles in Lunenburgh and Fitchburgh.[25] As late in the British-American conflict as May 1774, when John Adams had already published a dozen texts in which he used the constitutional sense of the state of nature, as a practicing lawyer he could still describe land in Charles Phelps's case as sold for a dollar an acre "in the State of Nature," without any moral connotation.[26]

2.4 THE STATE OF NATURE IN PRE-REVOLUTIONARY COLONIAL EDUCATION

Alongside the previously mentioned uses of the state of nature to describe uncultivated or wild lands, colonial teachers lectured and examined students on juridical and political texts that featured the concept prominently. The state of nature appears on the earliest surviving curricula and examinations. Examples relevant to the 1761–1775 period, when erstwhile Harvard students became active in public affairs, include Theses Ethicae #4 from 1756, "Leges Naturae in Statu naturali sunt Regula et Modus Libertatis naturalis"; Theses Theologicae #11 from 1766, "Omnibus hominibus in statu naturali est saluti jus aequale"; #8 of the 1768 Quaestiones, "An homo in statu naturali, majori voluptate, quam in statu civili, fruitur" (argued in the negative by Belcher Noyes, nephew of Governor Jonathan Belcher); #13 of the 1769 Quaestiones, "An Homo in statu naturali ad Bonum et Malum sit indifferens," argued in the negative by Samuel Morrill; the 1771 Theses Physicae #30, "Radii solares trigintaquinques densiores quam in Statu naturali eorum apud Superficiem Terrae aequalem efficiunt calorem ac Ignis ligneus," Quaestiones #22, "An alicui in Statu Naturae competat Jus gubernandi," which Peleg Wadsworth, later Revolutionary War officer, congressman from 1793 to 1803, and grandfather of Henry

25. 1772 An Act for Confirming the Titles . . . in *Massachusetts Session Laws* (Boston: Draper and Green & Russell), chapter 9, 636.
26. "Charles Phelps' State of His Case, March–May 1774," *Founders Online*, National Archives, last modified March 30, 2017, http://founders.archives.gov/documents/Adams/06-02-02-0007-0002.

Wadsworth Longfellow, answered in the negative as part of his 1772 MA exam; and so on.[27] We should remember that the surviving material is incomplete, and that printed theses circulated outside the university. Diaries show that not only scholars, but interested members of the public also attended commencements, listened to students' and professors' declamations, and discussed them at home and in their correspondence. Newspapers often reported commencement exercises. Harvard elaborations on the state of nature theme, which contributed greatly to the revolutionary state of nature discourse, were publicly disseminated through several channels.

As early as 1760, Benjamin Rush's graduating class at Princeton (then College of New Jersey) had a commencement thesis, Ethics #9: "In statu naturae, id suum cuique fuit, quod prae omnibus aliis occupaverat." Dartmouth's commencement records go back to 1771 and also contain state of nature theses and declamations before the end of the century.[28] While evidence at Yale is also fragmentary, it is clear that the state of nature was also taught there by the early 1760s. Ebenezer Baldwin, who died in the defense of New York City in 1776, graduated in 1763. His student notes discuss equality in the state of nature, based on Locke's *Two Treatises*.[29] Among the few known printed lists of early Yale theses, the 1765 Theses Ethicae #6 is "Omnes Homines, in Naturae Statu, quoad Dominium sunt aequales."[30] Full declamations that predate the 1780s rarely survive. They are full of expositions on the state of nature and

27. *Commencement Theses, Quaestiones, and Orders of Exercises, 1642–1818*, Harvard University Archives, HUC 6642.
28. In 1772 Bezaleel Woodward, professor of mathematics and natural philosophy, gave a valedictory discourse to two graduates setting out to preach to the Delaware Indians in Muskingum Country, Ohio, describing ignorance in the state of nature as one of Satan's strongholds. Rauner Library, MS 772269. For the state of nature in theses and exams see Commencement Parts Records, Rauner Library, DA-43; Abijah Bisco, Student Papers, 1795–1798, Rauner Library, MS 003125.
29. Baldwin Family Papers, Yale University Archives, MS 55, Box 63, Folder 818.
30. Connecticut Historical Society, Yale Ephemera, Oversize.

its relation to happy ignorance, man's pre-political condition, idleness, stadial theory, the benefits of literature, and other themes.[31]

The College of Philadelphia was chartered in 1755. Newspaper reports and undergraduate notes show that state of nature topics and texts had been taught there from the start.[32] Francis Alison (1705–79), student of Francis Hutcheson (1694–1746) in Glasgow, later tutor to John Dickinson (1732–1808) in Philadelphia, and in 1755 vice-provost of the new college, gave a course on ethics, economics, natural law, and politics, in which he criticized Hobbes and Pufendorf for exaggerating the inconvenience of the state of nature. He taught students that remedy for harm is a universal ethical principle that applies to interpersonal as well as interstate relations. He proposed that the best proof of the analogy between the relationship between individuals, and the relationship between states, comes from comparing them in their "state of natural liberty." According to Alison, Hobbes and Pufendorf were wrong about the state of nature: among friendly states, and among friendly individuals, it can even serve as a framework for sophisticated dispute settlement based on natural, not civil laws. Hutcheson made the same points as early as his 1730 Glasgow inaugural lecture.[33] He derived enduring legal principles, such as restitution for harm, from the state of nature. Hutcheson presented the state of nature as a condition that would not need to be abandoned for the polity if people in the state of nature remained friends, and had a natural sense of justice.

A student notebook for Alison's course, shared by the three sons of Chief Justice William Allen, is preserved in the archives of the University of Pennsylvania.[34] The same view of a benign state of nature, which both

31. Student Declamations, Yale University Archives, RU 145 and Theses and Quaestiones, Yale University Archives, RU 146. Early Yale Documents, Beinecke GEN MSS 856.
32. The 1755 exercises already included a debate on "Whether a State of Nature (so called) Be a State of War," discussed "in a forensic manner" by the students Samuel Magaw, Hugh Williamson, and Jacob Duché. *Pennsylvania Gazette,* July 31, 1755.
33. Francis Hutcheson, *Two Texts on Human Nature* (ed. Thomas Mautner, Cambridge, 1993), 135.
34. UPA 3, Box 23, Folder 1642.

constitutes a pre-political community and demonstrates legal principles that endure after the exit from the state of nature to the polity, can be found in William Kinnersley's 1759 lecture notes.[35] The state of nature here is a condition of liberty, equity, peace, friendship, and benevolence, and emphatically not of war. It is also the sphere of domestic rights and, by extension, of economic rights such as those between masters and servants in the household. While these records of Alison's early courses suggest that he drew primarily on Hutcheson, already in 1760–1761 he seems to start incorporating into his courses the work of another, younger Hutcheson student, namely Adam Smith's 1759 *Theory of Moral Sentiments*.[36]

The student notebooks show a fascinating trend. They increasingly took Hutcheson's "state of natural liberty," which Hutcheson preferred in order to distinguish his sociable state of nature from Hobbes's and Pufendorf's warlike one, and changed it to the "state of nature" while keeping and developing Hutcheson's sense, thereby adapting it to the American discourse. Hutcheson and his students who taught in colonial

35. UPA 3, Box 26, Folder 1647.
36. See Samuel Jones's notebooks from 1760 and 1761, UPA 3, Box 25, Folders 1645 and 1646. Smith's reception in the colonies before 1776 is a significant but somewhat neglected topic. Libraries such as the Providence Library Company (later Athenaeum) acquired *Theory of Moral Sentiments* shortly after it was published (*Catalogue of All the Books belonging to the Providence Library*, Providence, 1768, 16). Arthur Lee, born in Virginia, studied in Eton, graduated in medicine from Edinburgh in 1764, and published "An essay in vindication of the continental colonies of America, from a censure of Mr. Adam Smith, in his Theory of moral sentiments" the same year. Here the twenty-four-year-old Lee, who later played an important if chequered role in the Revolution, described life and liberty as "the gifts of God. In a state of nature they were both equally sacred" (32). It remains to be examined which sources Lee drew on for this positive, if simple formulation, and how it fit into his criticism of Smith, who rejected Hobbes's state of nature in *Theory of Moral Sentiments* (TMS), VII.iii.ii. Benjamin Rush's citation from TMS in his February 1774 oration is discussed below. Student notes from his classes strongly suggest that he drew on TMS in his teaching, as well. Benjamin Rush Lectures, University of Chicago, Regenstein Library, Crerar Ms 277. For a later part of Smith's American reception, focusing on *The Wealth of Nations*, see Samuel Fleischacker, "Adam Smith's Reception among the American Founders, 1776–1790," *William and Mary Quarterly* 59:4 (2002), 897–924.

colleges were a major source of the constitutive sense of the state of nature in American revolutionary discourse.

The three Glaswegians, Hutcheson, Alison and Adam Smith, shared the benign, constitutive sense of the state of nature. Another Scotsman, William Smith from Aberdeen, first provost of the College of Philadelphia from 1755 to 1779, brought a different range of meanings to Philadelphia. In 1759, Smith published *Discourses on Several Public Occasions during the War in America*. In this book he discussed the state of nature in several contexts, including the virtue of ancient Britons, the origin of civil society, the relationship between law-abiding citizens and criminals, and despotism. That the state of nature was also on the curriculum is clear from the surviving archival material. The College's 1762 commencement thesis #12 in the "De jurisprudentia naturali" category is "In statu naturae unicuique jus non competit in omnia."[37] A comparison of surviving student notebooks shows that Hutcheson's brief treatment of the dissolution of states began to receive more and more attention in the Philadelphia classroom during the 1750s–1760s. One example of this trend is in Jasper Yeates's 1760 student notes on the course, "A brief compendium of the law of nature, with politicks & oeconomicks," based on Hutcheson's 1747 *Short Introduction to Moral Philosophy*.[38]

Soon after he graduated, Yeates moved to Lancaster, Pennsylvania. The small town had a wonderful subscription library, called Juliana,

37. University of Pennsylvania Archives, UPA 3, Box 30, item 1677. Smith moved to Maryland and became the first president of Washington College, established in 1782 largely from George Washington's financial support. As in Philadelphia, he immediately placed the state of nature on the curriculum. At the College's first commencement, four of its five graduates participated in the "English Forensic Debate" on the topic, "Whether the state of nature be a state of war?" Horace W. Smith et al., *Life and Correspondence of the Rev. William Smith, DD* (Philadelphia, 1880), 2:88.

38. University of Pennsylvania, Kislak Library Special Collections, Ms Coll. 600. Also see the diary of Solomon Drowne at the Rhode-Island College on studying Hutcheson's *Ethics* in 1772 (John Hay Library, Ms. Drowne Papers 1767–1792, Box 24).

founded in late 1759.[39] Its 1766 charter is unusually high-brow even for this location and kind of enterprise. One cannot help but wonder if the newly graduated and arrived Yeates had a hand in prefacing the library's charter with the thought,

> The Human Mind, in a State of Nature, may be justly compared to the Soil:—By the Improvement of the one, and the Cultivation of the other, both are rendered highly advantageous to Mankind, for Want whereof Error and Barbarity spring up in the first, and Briars and Thorns choak the latter.—We come into the World inveloped in a Cloud of Ignorance: Nature places almost all upon a Level, and makes no very material Difference in dispensing her Gifts.—Of all Endowments of the Mind, then, *Knowledge* is undoubtedly, on every civil, as well as moral, Consideration, the greatest.

This is a sentiment and definition that a College of Philadelphia student would have learned and propagated. Yeates went on to serve as delegate to the Pennsylvania Convention that ratified the Constitution in 1787, and as Federalist judge on the state's Supreme Court from 1791 to 1817. Despite his meteoric rise to power, Yeates ended up leaving his books to Lancaster's local library, which serves as some, if slight, corroboration of the conjecture that he authored the new proclamation of the town's public library shortly after his arrival.

Another intriguing Scottish source of the revolutionary state of nature is David Fordyce's *The Elements of Moral Philosophy*, first published as a free-standing book by R. and J. Dodsley in London in 1754, with further

39. Charles I. Landis and Thomas Penn, "The Juliana Library Company in Lancaster," *Pennsylvania Magazine of History and Biography* 43:1 (1919), 24–52, 25. For the Library Company's 1763 address to John Penn, similar in eloquence and spirit but without using the term "state of nature," see 32. The 1766 charter's state of nature passage, probably by Yeates, features radical, natural equality. The library was named in honor of Julia, wife of William Penn, Jr., son of the founder. There is a ca. 1772–75 memorandum detailing some of the books they donated. When the Declaration of Independence dissolved all corporations that depended on the Crown, the Juliana was refounded by the General Assembly on September 6, 1783.

editions in 1758 and 1769. An unsigned version was printed in Robert
Dodsley's *The Preceptor*, a phenomenally successful set of textbooks that
first appeared in 1748. Fordyce's text was section IX of *The Preceptor*, "On
Ethics, or Morality." In the *Elements*, Fordyce described Hobbes's state of
nature and objected that in a Hobbesian state nothing stops people from
looking for ways to renege on their original promise. Hobbes also fails
to take sociability into account, or acknowledge the plain facts that we
are born into families and societies and we honor moral ties. According
to Fordyce, these facts render Hobbes's state of nature "a mere Chimera,
a Vision of his own Brain."[40] To fulfil our human nature, we follow our
"social principle" as it expands from the circle of family to friends to the
neighborhood and

> spreads into wider Systems, and draws Men into larger Confederacies,
> Communities, and Commonwealths.—It is in these only that the higher
> Powers of our Nature attain the highest Improvement and Perfection
> of which they are capable. These Principles hardly find Objects in the
> solitary State of Nature.[41]

Fordyce concludes that society is man's "Natural State."[42] Those, including colonial students and readers, who saw Fordyce's treatment of the
state of nature in section IX of *The Preceptor*, could continue to section X,
"On Trade and Commerce," and section XI, "On Laws and Government."
In section X they read that without industry, Native Americans are in
a state of nature, satisfying their basic needs with hunting, gathering,
and minimal agriculture. They are not idle, but they are wrong to imagine that without constant improvement their way of life is better than
Europeans'. Given their harsher environment, Hottentots, by contrast,

40. 1754 *Elements*, 51–55, quotation from 55. In 1758 *Preceptor*, 264–65.
41. 1754 *Elements*, 190. 1758 *Preceptor*, 326.
42. 1754 *Elements*, 193. 1758 *Preceptor*, 327. This passage also appears in the
Encyclopaedia Britannica entry on Moral Philosophy, which was adapted from
Fordyce, in the first few editions from 1771 until at least 1817. In the 1771 edition,
this passage is in vol. 3, 294.

turn bestial without industry. Another telling contrast is between the Native Americans' state of nature and the British settlers in America, whose participation in imperial industriousness and commerce raises them above the rest.[43] In section XI, they read a summary of Hobbes's state of nature (not dismissed as resolutely as in Fordyce's section) and a long explanation that rights are useless in the state of nature that is the original condition of absolute equality, because only the polity can offer effective protection of rights, even when they are transformed from un-limited state of nature rights into limited civil rights.[44]

It is probable that Fordyce's *Elements*, and the state of nature discus-sions in *The Preceptor*, were part of the educational background story of the revolutionary American state of nature discourse. Fordyce grad-uated from Marischal College in Aberdeen with an MA in 1728. After working in Glasgow, England, France, and Edinburgh, he settled down as professor of moral philosophy in his old alma mater in 1742. His 1745 *Dialogues concerning Education* was instrumental in Aberdeen's educational reform. William Smith left Aberdeen without receiving his degree in 1747, and started working as a tutor in America in 1751. In 1753 he published a plan for an ideal curriculum and school, "A general idea of the College of Mirania," indebted to Fordyce's *Dialogues*.[45] Smith emphasized the importance of shaping the moral and civil character of students, and turning them into productive and virtuous citizens. It was on the strength of this pamphlet that Benjamin Franklin and Richard Peters, another prominent Pennsylvania politician, invited Smith to join the new College of Philadelphia and work with Francis Alison. It has been suggested that the 1754 edition of *The Preceptor* was published partly with Smith's American students in mind. In any case, there is little doubt that Smith's Mirania, and work at the College, were inspired by

43. 1758 *Preceptor*, 427–28.
44. 1758 *Preceptor*, 468–71.
45. Princeton also had a copy of Fordyce's *Dialogues* by early 1760. *A Catalogue of Books in the Library of The College of New-Jersey* (Woodbridge, NJ, 1760), 15.

Fordyce and the reforms at Marischal College.[46] Moreover, Hornberger shows that Smith relied heavily on *The Preceptor* and recommended Fordyce's section on moral philosophy.[47]

Fordyce's treatments of the state of nature were on the curricula in other colonial colleges and libraries, as well. The previously mentioned Juliana owned the 1754 *Preceptor*.[48] *The Elements of Moral Philosophy* was the standard textbook on ethics at Harvard before the Revolution.[49] William Small, another Marischal College graduate (1755), taught at the College of William & Mary from 1758 to 1764. Howell shows that Small used William Duncan's textbook on logic to teach Thomas Jefferson between 1760 and 1762. Duncan's *The Elements of Logick* was included in the same volume of *The Preceptor* as Fordyce's *Ethics*, and Howell suggests that *The Preceptor* became part of Small's curriculum reform at William & Mary as soon as he started teaching in 1758.[50] If Howell is correct, then Fordyce was probably one of Jefferson's sources on the state of nature. Howell intricately reconstructs the likely impact of Duncan's logic on the Declaration of Independence; one could perhaps find a similarly attenuated but nonetheless probable and important connection between Fordyce's view of expanding circles of affinity

46. Franklin E. Court, *The Scottish Connection: The Rise of English Literary Study in Early America* (Syracuse, 2001), 17–21. Harry M. Solomon, *The Rise of Robert Dodsley: Creating the New Age of Print* (Southern Illinois University Press, 1996), 125–26. Knud Haakonssen, "From Natural Law to the Rights of Man: A European Perspective on American Debates," in Michael James Lacey and Knud Haakonssen (eds.), *A Culture of Rights: The Bill of Rights in Philosophy, Politics and Law 1791 and 1991* (Cambridge, 1992), 19–61, at 38–39; William A. Clebsch, "William Smith on Education: Religion, 'The Soul of the Whole'," *Historical Magazine of the Protestant Episcopal Church* 52:4 (1983), 369–90, at 380.

47. Theodore Hornberger, "A Note on the Probable Source of Provost Smith's Famous Curriculum for the College of Philadelphia," *Pennsylvania Magazine of History and Biography* 58:4 (1934), 370–77.

48. Charles I. Landis, "The Juliana Library Company in Lancaster (continued)," *Pennsylvania Magazine of History and Biography* 43:2 (1919): 163–81, at 170.

49. David W. Robson, *Educating Republicans: The College in the Era of the American Revolution* (Greenwood, 1985), 82.

50. William Howell, "The Declaration of Independence and Eighteenth-Century Logic," *William and Mary Quarterly* 18 (1961), 463–84.

and the Declaration's Preamble, including the need to justify secession to humankind. In 1762 Donald Robertson, who moved from Aberdeen and Edinburgh to Virginia in 1753, taught James Madison, the future President, from Dodsley's *Preceptor*, though it is unclear which edition they used.[51] Brown's 1843 catalog shows the 1758 *Preceptor*, probably acquired early.[52] In 1763 David Hall, who ran Franklin's printing and book trading firm in Philadelphia, was importing the 1758 or 1763 edition of *The Preceptor*.[53] Queen's College (Rutgers) used the 1763 *Preceptor*.[54] In sum, there is a strong case that Fordyce was one source of state of nature thinking at Harvard, William & Mary, Rutgers, and Philadelphia, via Franklin's bookstore; and probably at Brown.

However, Hutcheson is a more important source for three reasons. First, his treatment of the state of natural liberty had a formative influence on the constitutive American state of nature, which the brief and fragmented passages in Fordyce's *Elements* or *The Preceptor* could hardly have. Second, as shown, the extent and pace of the colonial reception of Fordyce and *The Preceptor* is unclear. This is not to say that Fordyce and *The Preceptor* did not shape the American discussion of the state of nature; only that Hutcheson had a greater impact. Furthermore, while these colonial sources are very useful in reconstructing the sources of the American state of nature, they have limits. James Otis, Jr., for instance, graduated from Harvard in 1743, before Burlamaqui, Hutcheson, Vattel, Fordyce, and the other classroom texts discussed here. He used Hobbes,

51. Ralph Ketcham, *James Madison: A Biography* (Virginia, 1971; 1st paperback 1990), 19–20. At William & Mary, the notes of St. George Tucker and his son, and orations by Samuel Henley and James Madison in 1772 (all discussed in detail below) suggest that the state of nature continued to play at least a comparable role in the curriculum in Virginia as it did in Massachusetts and Connecticut.
52. Charles Coffin Jewett, *A Catalogue of the Library of Brown University* (Providence, RI, 1843), 126.
53. Richard B. Sher, "Transatlantic Books and Literature Culture," in Eve Tavor Bannet and Susan Manning (eds.), *Transatlantic Literary Studies* (Cambridge, 2012), 10–27, at 18–19.
54. Dale Randall, "Dodsley's Preceptor—a Window into the 18th Century," *Rutgers University Library Journal* 22:1 (1958), 10–22.

Locke, Mandeville, Montesquieu, Rousseau, Vattel, and others in his state of nature texts in the 1760s, but he encountered and adapted them as an already established lawyer.

Principles of Natural and Politic Law by the Genevan theorist Jean-Jacques Burlamaqui was another item on the curricula of colonial colleges that provided building blocks for the American state of nature discourse. Originally published in French in 1747, the 1748 English translation of *The Principles of Natural Law* by Thomas Nugent (also the translator of Montesquieu and Rousseau), and his 1752 translation of the *Principles of Politic Law*, re-edited and first published together in 1763, became a standard textbook. Section II.VI.ii of *The Principles of Natural Law*, summarized on the margin as "The civil state does not destroy but improve the state of nature," argues that far from replacing civil society, as Hobbes and Rousseau would have it, government gives "the primitive state of union and society . . . a new degree of force and consistency."[55] However, in I.III of *The Principles of Politic Law*, Burlamaqui changed his mind. Here the state of nature is an idyllic condition of natural equality, but given man's passions, it cannot last. As Montesquieu and Rousseau also believed, people cannot stay in the state of nature, and need to exit into the polity that has a common arbiter. Civil liberty gained in the state is superior to natural liberty.[56] Nevertheless, even though Burlamaqui's state of nature is not a persisting community or locus of rights, it remains a boundary condition for politics. Originally created radically equal, no man in the state of nature had sovereignty over others. When sovereignty comes into existence, it can only derive from the people united in civil society; not from an individual, not from God (as Grotius has shown), and not from God appointing any individual.[57] The July 1774 Pennsylvania

55. Burlamaqui, *The Principles of Natural and Politic Law* (tr. Thomas Nugent, ed. and introduction by Peter Korkman, Liberty Fund, 2006), 173.
56. Peter Korkman, a modern editor, draws attention to Barbeyrac's comment on this chapter, namely that the state can in fact be worse than the state of nature (281 n. 3).
57. Burlamaqui, *Principles*, VIII.iii–xvi.

committee's instructions extensively cite Burlamaqui, including this state of nature passage.[58]

There are several reasons to suppose that the Scottish state of nature influenced the American revolutionary constitutive state of nature more than Burlamaqui did. First, there is little resemblance between colonial uses and Burlamaqui's. Unlike the constitutive state of nature in John Adams, Samuel Adams and others, Burlamaqui's state of nature in *Principles of Natural Law* is not prior and superior to, but harmonious with, the state. By contrast, in *Principles of Politic Law*, the state of nature and the state are antithetical. (As we will see, this is the passage that Galloway invokes in 1775, and in their rejoinder Dickinson and Thomson chose to ignore.) Even in the first work, Burlamaqui does not develop the constitutive state of nature, and does not locate rights or mechanisms of resistance in it. Second, Nugent's 1763 combined edition seems to have been used more widely than the 1748 and 1752 translations, and many of the key revolutionaries who developed a constitutive American state of nature text had left school by 1763. Third, a partial survey of surviving copies and student notebooks in colonial universities' archives suggests that Burlamaqui was read and studied, but less than Hutcheson and the other Scots.

Alongside the Scottish and Swiss notions of a sociable state of nature between individuals and among nations, there may have been a distinct Oxbridge tradition that had some formative influence on the American revolutionary discourse. It defined the state of nature in mechanistic terms, combining natural philosophy with constitutional thought. The 1757–1760 Massachusetts Governor, Thomas Pownall's 1750 Harringtonian *Treatise* and criticism of Hobbes's state of nature, of which he donated an expanded 1752 version to Harvard in 1764, and Samuel Henley's combination of scientific and political states of nature, both of which are discussed in this book in detail, are examples of the Oxbridge

---

58. John Dickinson, *An Essay on the Constitutional Power of Great-Britain over the Colonies* (Philadelphia, 1774), 308–10. On Blackstone and Burlamaqui see Finnis, "Theoretical," 171.

view that had a demonstrable influence in the colonies. Another case may be a sermon "on the wisdom of providence in the administration of the world" that John Rotheram, who was born and later taught in Barbados, gave at Oxford in 1762. Rotheram set out to prove that fluctuations and patterns in history are meaningless without revelation. History and revelation together teach valuable lessons, notably that divine providence trumps human design. His first step was to show that the co-existence of multiple states is a providential arrangement. Anarchy, which is not the state of nature, is as untenable as the other extreme possibility: a universal government. The half-way point between these two extremes, namely the state system, is the real state of nature—just as bodies, not atoms, are the natural form in which matter exists.[59]

A survey of state of nature sources used in colonial education shortly before the Revolution highlights the importance of Scottish texts and teachers, in addition to the influence of Grotius, Hobbes, Locke, Pufendorf, Rousseau, Vattel, and Blackstone that emerges from the revolutionary texts examined in the next chapters. It also shows how state of nature ideas were adapted already before the Revolution, notably Hutcheson's "state of natural liberty," with which he aimed to replace Hobbes's state of nature, becoming gradually equated with a constitutive, morally charged state of nature that could be directly and constructively reconnected with Grotius's, Locke's, Rousseau's and others' usage, instead of accepting Hutcheson's terminological gambit. The increasing attention that colonial education paid during the 1750s–1760s to Hutcheson's account of the dissolution of states is another sign that the conceptual toolkit that allowed the Founders to invoke the state of nature in Hobbes, Locke, Rousseau, and Vattel in arguments for independence neither arose *ex nihilo* nor was it merely imported from British Whigs and radicals.

This is not to say that Scottish doctrines of the state of nature were introduced and transformed with the intention to prepare an American

---

59. John Rotheram, *A Sermon on the Wisdom of Providence* ... (London, 1762), 5–11. It was reissued with two other sermons in 1766.

Revolution; but the evidence shows that the revolutionary generation that studied at Harvard, Philadelphia, Yale, William & Mary, or the College of New Jersey entered their professional careers with a notion of a state of nature that was the sphere of liberty, morality, self-constituting community, and sufficiently self-sufficient to resist attempts by established polities to encroach on these values. The process whereby Rousseau, Vattel, and other state of nature theorists were incorporated into the emerging American state of nature topos was inflected by the Scottish formulation of a constitutive state of nature, able to resist such encroachment.

3

RIGHTS AND CONSTITUTIONS
From *Paxton's Case* to the Stamp Act

In this chapter I suggest that Otis's 1761 speech in *Paxton's Case* marked the turning point when the European state of nature theories turned into a revolutionary American discourse. In Otis's system, the state of nature is a source of substantive rights that endure the transition to the polity. Such rights include life, liberty, and property, and they are inalienable (in Otis's formulation) for both white colonists and enslaved African Americans. Newly discovered archival evidence about this key speech is introduced.

The immediate political context of Otis's speech was partisan controversy between Hutchinson and Otis's father, and their supporters. Commenting on this rivalry, Abraham Williams's 1762 election sermon placed civil laws in the framework of natural laws which, crucially, he understood as the rules that "the God of Nature" imposes on the state of nature. Freedom of religion and conscience are therefore state of nature rights protected by the God of nature both outside and within the polity, while the God of revelation—the same God considered under a different aspect—remains suprapolitical.

In a series of publications between 1762 and 1765 Otis further elaborated his theory, developing the start of an American doctrine of judicial review, a juridical account of the state of nature as a condition triggered by major failures of the justice system (including the Glorious Revolution and the Stamp Act) in which communities are not destroyed but reconstitute themselves at will, and a range of applications of his conceptual innovation to the conventional state of nature doctrine obtaining between states, and its explanatory role for the history of colonial North America. Finally, the chapter compares the emerging American state of nature discourse with that of Thomas Pownall, a governor, administrator, and theorist sympathetic to colonial grievances. Pownall even shared some of Otis's theoretical commitments. Yet he regarded not the colonies, but the whole British empire as a natural, self-constituting community and considered the state of nature to be a useful constitutional fiction but not a condition that ever existed in reality, for instance among the first British settlers.

3.1 JOHN ADAMS, JAMES OTIS, AND *PAXTON'S CASE* (1761)

For over fifty years, over and over again John Adams described James Otis's concluding speech in *Paxton's Case* as the beginning of the Revolution. In a letter, one in a series he sent in 1816–1819 to William Tudor, his former clerk who was now preparing a biography of Otis, Adams announced, "Then and there, the child Independence was born. In fifteen years, i.e. in 1776, he grew up to manhood and declared himself free."[1]

---

1. "Child independence": Adams to Tudor, March 29, 1817, Charles F. Adams (ed.), *Works of John Adams* (Boston, 1850–56), 10:247–48. On the impact of Adams's account on the historiography of the Revolution see James M. Farrell, "The Child Independence Is Born: James Otis and Writs of Assistance," in Stephen E. Lucas (ed.), *A Rhetorical History of the United States*, vol. 2 (forthcoming), though Farrell does not discuss the state of nature. Also see Adams's letter to his wife, Abigail, on the auspicious day of July 3, 1776 concerning the causal link between Otis's 1761

The background to this critical speech can be summarized briefly. Smuggling was rampant in the colonies. One attempt to curtail smuggling was to issue writs of assistance that allowed customs officers to search ships, shops and houses without giving a reason and without liability for damage. In August 1760, William Pitt the Elder, at the time Secretary of State for the Southern Department and leader of the House of Commons, instructed colonial governors to clamp down on contraband naval stores that could aid Britain's enemies. Francis Bernard, the new Governor of Massachusetts, who arrived in Boston only that month, assured Westminster that no smuggling took place in Massachusetts. Bernard also appointed Thomas Hutchinson (1711–1780) as Lieutenant Governor, although the post had been promised to James Otis, Sr.

George II died in October 1760. Writs of assistance had to be reissued under the new royal authority within six months. News of the king's death reached Boston in December, and a group of sixty-three merchants instructed Oxenbridge Thacher (1719–1765) and the disgruntled James Otis, Jr. (1725–1783) to challenge the writs in court. The dispute is known as *Paxton's Case*, after the British customs agent who obtained such a writ in 1755, and now filed a countersuit.[2]

---

speech and the Revolution; and Adams to William Wirt, January 5, 1818, in *Works*, 10:272.

2. Maurice H. Smith, *The Writs of Assistance Case* (University of California Press, 1978); William J. Cuddihy, *The Fourth Amendment: Origins and Original Meaning, 602–1791* (Oxford, 2009), chap. 17. For a brief overview of the history and types of writs of assistance, see Horace Gray in Josiah Quincy Jr., in Samuel M. Quincy (ed.), *Reports of Cases Argued and Adjudged in the Superior Court of Judicature of the Province of Massachusetts Bay, Between 1761 and 1772* (Boston, 1865), Appendix I, section A, 395–400. In Gray's reading, Adams intentionally and repeatedly misconstrued Pitt's instructions and inquiries as orders to start strictly enforcing the Acts of Trade and Navigation, as encouragement to customs officers to apply for writs of assistance, and as the direct reason for Hutchinson's appointment. *Quincy's Reports*, 407–11. Even if this were the case, and Otis, Adams and others misrepresented events as more provocative toward the colonists than they were, the merchants still had a point. The writs of assistance, issued at least since 1755, had an overly broad remit. *Quincy's Reports*, 405.

To fulfil his clients' instructions and plead that such writs cannot be issued again, Otis did not need to deny the legitimacy of the writs issued by George II. That he did so, and refused to accept a fee, shows that George II's death produced a contestable constitutional moment, not far from a state of nature.[3] When Otis challenged the legality of the writs, he created one of the most important cases in pre-revolutionary America.

Even though the state of nature component of the case is front and center, it is seldom discussed in contemporary legal historiography. The beginning of Adams's summary of Otis's speech is worth citing at length.

2. A dissertation on the rights of man in a state of nature. He asserted that every man, merely natural, was an independent sovereign, subject to no law, but the law written on his heart, and revealed to him by his Maker in the constitution of his nature and the inspiration of his understanding and his conscience. His right to his life, his liberty, no created being could rightfully contest. Nor was his right to his property less incontestable. The club that he had snapped from a tree, for a staff or for defence, was his own. His bow and arrow were his own; if by a pebble he had killed a partridge or a squirrel, it was his own. No creature, man or beast, had a right to take it from him. If he had taken an eel, or a smelt, or a sculpion, it was his property. In short, he sported upon this topic with so much wit and humor, and at the same time so much indisputable truth and reason, that he was not less entertaining than instructive. He asserted that these rights were inherent and inalienable. That they never could be surrendered or alienated but by idiots or madmen, and all the acts of idiots and lunatics were void, and not obligatory by all the laws of God and man. Nor were the poor negroes forgotten. Not a Quaker in Philadelphia, or Mr. Jefferson, of Virginia, ever asserted the rights of negroes in stronger terms. Young as I was, and ignorant as I was, I shuddered at the doctrine he taught; and I have all my lifetime shuddered, and still shudder, at the

3. L.Kinvin Wroth and Hiller B. Zobel (eds.), *Legal Papers of John Adams* (Belknap, 1965), introduction, 106–23, especially 112–13 on the ramifications of the death of George II.

consequences that may be drawn from such premises. Shall we say, that the rights of masters and servants clash, and can be decided only by force? I adore the idea of gradual abolitions! But who shall decide how fast or how slowly these abolitions shall be made?

3. From individual independence he proceeded to association. If it was inconsistent with the dignity of human nature to say that men were gregarious animals, like wild horses and wild geese, it surely could offend no delicacy to say they were social animals by nature, that there were mutual sympathies, and, above all, the sweet attraction of the sexes, which must soon draw them together in little groups, and by degrees in larger congregations, for mutual assistance and defence. And this must have happened before any formal covenant, by express words or signs, was concluded. When general counsels and deliberations commenced, the objects could be no other than the mutual defence and security of every individual for his life, his liberty, and his property. To suppose them to have surrendered these in any other way than by equal rules and general consent was to suppose them idiots or madmen, whose acts were never binding. To suppose them surprised by fraud, or compelled by force, into any other compact, such fraud and such force could confer no obligation. Every man had a right to trample it under foot whenever he pleased. In short, he asserted these rights to be derived only from nature and the author of nature; that they were inherent, inalienable, and indefeasible by any laws, pacts, contracts, covenants, or stipulations, which man could devise.[4]

To my knowledge, it has not been noted before that the substance and thrust of this section of Otis's speech resemble not only Locke's *Second Treatise* but, in terms of both argument and language, it recalls Rousseau's *Discourse on the Origin and Basis of Inequality among Men* (1755).[5] Otis's

4. Adams to William Tudor, June 1, 1818.

5. John Locke, "An Essay concerning the True Original, Extent, and End of Civil Government," in Locke, *Two Treatises of Government* . . . (London, 1689), chapter 5, §§ 28, 30. Also compare Adams's summary with Rousseau, *A Discourse upon the Origin and Foundation of the Inequality among Mankind* (London, 1761), 100–101. This translation appeared too late to inform Otis's speech in February 1761. It also translated terms like bow, arrow, staff, and partridge differently than Otis, according

account of a state of nature right to property in weapons and necessities, his comparison of animal with human sociability, and postulating sexual attraction as the first step in gradual, widening association, resemble Rousseau's *Second Discourse* more than any well-known state of nature text by Hobbes, Locke, or Montesquieu. Recovering Rousseau's influence on the state of nature arguments of Otis and John Adams helps to achieve a faithful and balanced view of the revolutionary generations' sources. Among other things, it shows that Locke played an important, but not a predominant role.

Some scholars have noted Rousseau's influence on Otis, but they either left the matter vague or named the *Social Contract* (1762), seldom substantiating the connection with textual evidence. An important source of this nebulous claim is William Tudor's loose remark in the introduction to his 1823 biography of Otis, where he connected the spirit of American and French liberty by mentioning Otis's revolutionary pamphlets in conjunction with the *Social Contract*.[6] However, it is probable that Otis knew and drew on the *Second Discourse* when he made his state of nature speech in *Paxton's Case* and combined it with other state of nature discussions. As shown below, this has important implications for the American state of nature discourse and the American Revolution.

To understand how Otis crafted his influential state of nature theme, it helps to reconstruct part of his working environment. John Adams had already studied state of nature texts at Harvard for both his undergraduate (1755) and graduate (1758) degrees by the time he was admitted to the Suffolk bar, on Gridley's recommendation, in November 1758. In Gridley's circle, Adams worked with Joseph Dudley, Oxenbridge Thacher,

---

to Adams's much later letter. Otis may have read the *Second Discourse* in French, or came across its state of nature arguments in one of the numerous English-language commentaries, or reviews and summaries in learned journals, that appeared between 1755 and 1761.

6. William Tudor, *The Life of James Otis, of Massachusetts: Containing also, Notices of Some Contemporary Characters and Events, from the Year 1760 to 1775* (Boston, 1823), preface, viii–ix.

Josiah Quincy II, and Otis.[7] Adams's diaries record numerous extensive state of nature discussions with Otis over the years. They analyzed state of nature theories in Grotius and Hobbes, Justice Holt and Montesquieu, Pufendorf, Pollexfen, and Vattel. Many of the arguments they prepared later appear in their legal orations and revolutionary publications.

In a letter drafted in summer 1759, but probably never sent, to Col. Josiah Quincy, father of Josiah Quincy II, Adams reflects on his state of nature readings in Hobbes and Montesquieu's *Spirit of the Laws*. He sketches a thought experiment.[8] What would happen if a child was isolated in a room and grew to age twenty supplied with all necessities except for human contact? Would he feel powerless and weak, and be frightened by everything when he finally left the room, as Montesquieu suggests in *Spirit of the Laws*, I.2? Would Hobbes's state of nature apply if "a whole Army of Persons, trained up in this manner in single separate Cells" were brought together? Would they flee, fight, or feel sympathy and begin to collaborate? Adams could not resolve these questions and wrote a note to himself to think through the state of nature systematically when he was able.[9]

From his diary we know that in June 1760 Adams returned to Montesquieu, "resolved to read that Work, thro, in order and with

---

7. Adams formally trained with James Putnam in Worcester, but learned little from him. Instead, he studied Justinian, Grotius, Pufendorf, Van Muyden, and other civil, canon, and common law sources under Gridley. See Shipton, *Biographical Sketches...*, Classes 1722–1725, 7:523–24. Coquillette is also right to include Adams among Gridley's students, alongside Thacher and Otis, in Daniel R. Coquillette and Neil L. York (eds.), *Portrait of a Patriot: The Major Political and Legal Papers of Josiah Quincy Junior* (6 vols., Boston 2005–14), 2:76–77. He provides details of Adams's training under "the informal tutelage of Jeremiah Gridley, a great teacher," in "Justinian in Braintree: John Adams, Civilian Learning, and Legal Elitism, 1758–1775" in Coquillette (ed.), *Law in Colonial Massachusetts, 1630–1800* (Boston, 1984), 359–418. Adams continued to discuss ideas and texts with Gridley in 1765 in the Junto, a reading club that also included Samuel Fitch, Otis, Thacher, and Robert Auchmuty.
8. On the young lawyers who frequented the Quincy household see David McCullough, *John Adams* (Simon & Schuster, 2001), 50–51.
9. John Adams, *Diary and Autobiography* (ed. Butterfield, 1961), 1:115–16.

Attention," compiling "a sort of Index to every Paragraph" to help sharpen his attention. His copy of the two-volume 1752 second edition by Thomas Nugent (now at the Massachusetts Historical Society) shows Adams valiantly working through the first six hundred pages or so, including Montesquieu's passages on the state of nature. He gave up indexing and, perhaps, reading, for the last two hundred pages.

From internal evidence it is difficult to establish when Adams first read through his copy of the 1761 translation of Rousseau's *Second Discourse*.[10] Adams's account of the savage state of man in his August 1, 1763 essay on private revenge strongly resembles the *Second Discourse*.[11] If he read it soon after the translation appeared in 1761, and while he was still following the course of close study of Montesquieu that he set for himself in 1760, then a possible reason why he stopped taking notes on Montesquieu is that Rousseau made Adams doubt the premise he sketched in 1759, namely that the behavior of such a child would be analogous to behavior in the state of nature (see fig. 3.1).

Another circumstance to suggest that Rousseau's 1755 *Second Discourse* was known in Gridley's circles by 1761 is that they picked up the *Social Contract* very soon after its English translation appeared in 1764. In his February 21, 1765 diary entry Adams recalls a session of the Junto, the lawyers' reading club that gathered around Gridley, where Adams mentioned Rousseau's condemnation of feudalism and praise of representation in the *Social Contract*, chapter 15. Gridley replied that "the observation you quote proves that Rousseau is shallow."[12] Fortunately, the conversation did not end there. These Junto meetings became the source of Adams's four letters, later collectively known as the *Dissertation on the Canon and Feudal Law*.[13] In the second letter, first published on

---

10. While it is unclear when Adams read his copy, he did read it several times. One note, on 38, is dated 1791 and blames Rousseau for the French Revolution. Other marginalia are dated 1794 (x), and 1800 (x, xiii, xxiv).

11. Ed. C. Bradley Thompson, *The Revolutionary Writings of John Adams* (Liberty Fund, 2000), 4.

12. *Works of John Adams*, 2:148–49.

13. Shipton, *Harvard Graduates*, 7:524.

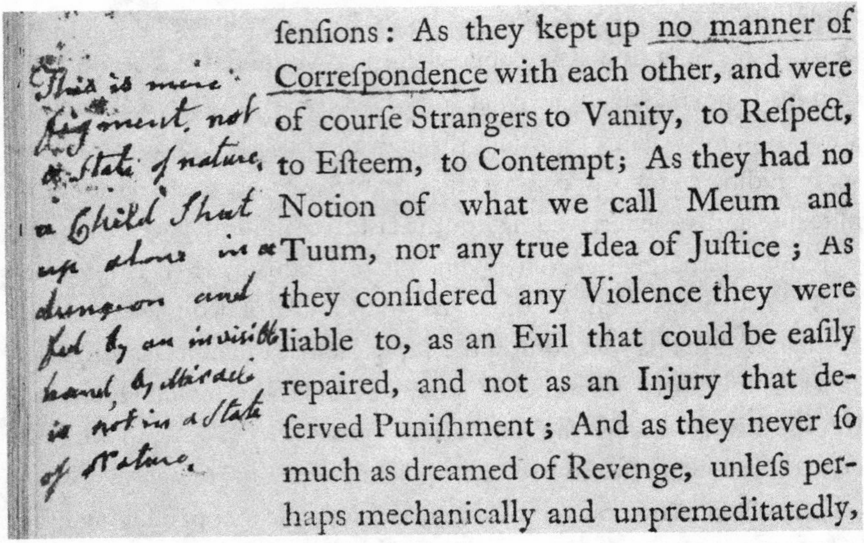

This is mere figment, not a State of nature, a Child shut up alone in a dungeon and fed by an invisible hand, by Miracle, is not in a State of Nature. fensions: As they kept up no manner of Correspondence with each other, and were of course Strangers to Vanity, to Respect, to Esteem, to Contempt; As they had no Notion of what we call Meum and Tuum, nor any true Idea of Justice; As they considered any Violence they were liable to, as an Evil that could be easily repaired, and not as an Injury that deserved Punishment; And as they never so much as dreamed of Revenge, unless perhaps mechanically and unpremeditatedly,

Fig. 3.1 John Adams's annotations in John James Rousseau [sic], *A Discourse upon the Origin and Foundation of the Inequality among Mankind* (London, 1761), 78. Boston Public Library.

August 19, 1765, Adams indeed cites the 1764 translation of Rousseau's *Social Contract.*[14] At Thomas Hollis's instigation, the letters were reprinted in the November 23 and 28, and December 3 and 26, 1765 issues of the *London Chronicle,* where Hollis mistakenly attributed them to Gridley.[15] (Adams's letter was also reprinted in another influential

14. Adams may have also read the *Social Contract* in French. He owned several versions of Rousseau's works, including a set assembled from various French-language editions published between 1764 and 1768, now at the Boston Public Library (Adams 184.10). It contains extensive and important annotations by Adams. Harvard's Phi Beta Kappa society started their own library in 1766. It contains the 1767 two-volume London edition of Rousseau's *Works* (Harvard Archives, HU 255.914.133 Box 8). Though only donated to PBK in 1790, the donor was a Harvard graduate, and the marginal notes and emphases next to the state of nature passages probably predate the donation.

15. Even though there is no comprehensive study of the political impact of the younger Thomas Hollis's projects, his contributions to Boston's state of nature discourse in the 1760s are remarkable. Republishing Adams's essays is only one instance. In June 1764 he donated a first edition of Locke's *Two Treatises* to Harvard (now Houghton *EC75.H7267.Zz7641 Lobby IV.2.2), inscribed "Thomas Hollis, an Englishman, a Lover of Liberty, the principles of the Revolution, & the Protestant

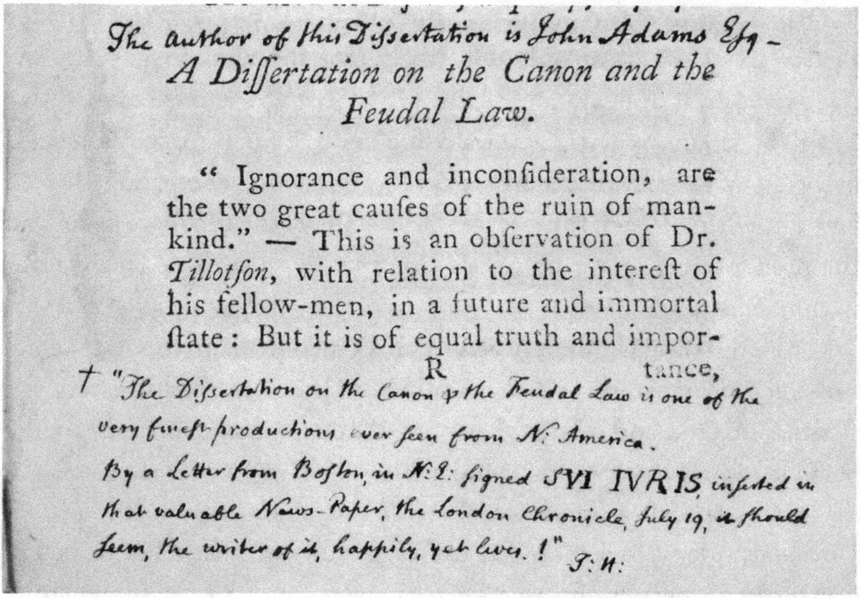

The author of this Dissertation is John Adams Esq

A Differtation on the Canon and the
Feudal Law.

" Ignorance and inconfideration, are
the two great caufes of the ruin of mankind." — This is an obfervation of Dr.
Tillotfon, with relation to the intereft of
his fellow-men, in a future and immortal
ftate : But it is of equal truth and impor-
R   tance,

† "The Differtation on the Canon & the Feudal Law is one of the very finest productions ever seen from N. America. By a Letter from Boston, in N. E: signed SVI IVRIS, inserted in that valuable News-Paper, the London Chronicle, July 19, it should seem, the writer of it, happily, yet lives !" T: H:

Fig. 3.2 Thomas Hollis's annotations in *True Sentiments*, 111. *AC7 M382G 768t(B),
Houghton Library, Harvard University.

state of nature text, the 1768 collection entitled *The True Sentiments of America*, discussed below.) Hollis donated a copy of *True Sentiments* to Harvard and another to the Congregational minister Andrew Eliot, who first informed him that the letters were written by Adams.[16] Hollis left marginalia in both copies. In the Eliot copy (now also at Harvard), Hollis notes that the *Dissertation* is "one of the very finest productions ever seen from N. America." Although he first thought its author was Gridley, who died in 1767, he now knew that it was written by Adams, who "happily, yet lives!" (fig. 3.2).[17]

Succession in the House of Hanover, Citizen of the World [...]." Many of Locke's state of nature passages are highlighted and annotated in this copy, whether by Hollis or an early Harvard reader.

16. Andrew Eliot to Thomas Hollis, October 17, 1768, in *Collections of the Massachusetts Historical Society*, 4th series (1858), 4:434.

17. Houghton, *AC7.M382G.768t (B). Harbottle Dorr was similarly enthusiastic, but knew the author. He wrote in his copy of August 12, 1765, *Boston Gazette*, under Adams's first letter: "By John Adams Esq. of Braintree Attorney at Law. An

Otis also cited the *Social Contract* in his 1764 *The Rights of the British Colonies.*[18] Not only is it likely that the almost six years between the first appearance of the 1755 *Second Discourse* and Otis's 1761 speech in *Paxton's Case* was time enough for Rousseau's second prize essay for the Academy of Dijon to reach these young Boston lawyers with a special interest in the state of nature—we also find them adapting Rousseau's *Social Contract* to colonial legal disputes within a year.

Given the similarities between Adams's own work on the state of nature, records of extensive discussions about the state of nature between Adams and Otis, and Adams's early use of Rousseau's *Social Contract*, the balance of probability is that similarities between the *Second Discourse* and Otis's speech are not accidental. In his marginalia to the *Second Discourse*, Adams in fact objects to Rousseau's formulation of weak and transitory property rights that savage man acquired in a state of nature, and assigns strong property rights in his club, stone hatchet, and bow and arrow, prior to the acquisition of property rights in land, and transition to civil society (see fig. 3.3).[19] If Adams and Otis discussed this passage as thoroughly as they did Grotius, Hobbes, Pufendorf, Locke,

Excellent peice this, and does great Honour to the Worthy Author!" http://www.masshist.org/dorr/volume/1/sequence/164. Dorr's other comments on the August 19 letter refer to events in 1768, so it is unclear whether he correctly identified the author as early as 1765, or later.

18. James Otis, Jr, *The Rights of the British Colonies Asserted and Proved* (Boston, 1764), 11, citing p. 5 of the same 1764 translation of the *Social Contract* as Adams.

19. Adams's combination of admiration for Rousseau's rhetoric and contempt for his abstractions is matched by James Kent, *Dissertations: Being a Preliminary Part of a Course of Law Lectures* (New York, 1795), esp. 5–7. Adams and Kent also agree that the sense and desire of property are so intrinsic to man that Rousseau, and state of nature theorists in general, are wrong about property's correlation with the emergence of society. James Kent, *Commentaries on American Law* (New York, 1826–30), based on his Columbia lectures starting in 1794. The idea that Adams changed his mind about the state of nature after the French Revolution began is worth pursuing. It is unclear when Adams wrote the criticism on the margin of p. 124 of his copy of the English translation of the *Second Discourse*, but as some marginalia date from 1794, it is possible that Adams and Kent raised this objection at roughly the same time. The contempt for Rousseau's high theory remained widespread,

> *A Club, an hatchet* To the tilling of the Earth the Diftri-
> *of Stone, a Bow* bution of it neceſſarily ſucceeded, and to
> *an arrow was* Property once acknowledged the firſt
> *property before* Rules of Juſtice : for to ſecure every Man
> *land. So was* his own, every Man muſt have ſome-
> *the dry ones Skin* thing. Moreover, as Men began to ex-
> *of Hercules.* tend their Views to Futurity, and all

Fig. 3.3 John Adams's annotations in Rousseau, *A Discourse upon the Origin and Foundation of Inequality*, 124. Boston Public Library.

and Montesquieu, it would explain why Otis used Rousseau's state of nature to claim strong pre- and supra-political property rights for the colonists.

Strikingly, Otis adapts Rousseau's reasoning to the colonists' agenda. As we saw, he summarizes Rousseau's account of property in the state of nature, down to the club that the savage snaps from a tree, his bow and arrow, and his unquestionable property in the animals he kills for food. Otis anchors colonists' rights in this state of nature, and characterizes the same state of nature as one that bestows inherent and inalienable rights on everyone, including black people currently in slavery. The strong connection Otis created between equality and property rights in the state of nature as both a justification for resisting British authority, and the source of an abolitionist imperative, was to echo down and haunt the

evinced for instance in Timothy Field's 1797 English Oration (Yale, Manuscripts and Archives, College Commencement Orations and Poems, RU 140, Box 4, Folder 35) and George Ticknor's 1816–17 student notebooks from Göttingen (Dartmouth, Rauner, ms983, Box 5, Folder 4: *Spirit of the Times*, and Box 5, Folder 7: *Progress of Politicks or History of the Theory of Constitutions*). Friedrich Saalfeld, Ticknor's lecturer, argued that the French Revolution was caused by a misguided attempt to reconcile Montesquieu with Rousseau, and analyzed the state of nature in both, as well as in the writings of Hobbes and Locke. See introduction in Somos (ed.), "George Ticknor's *Progress of Politicks* (1816): An American Reception of German Comparative Constitutional Thought," Max Planck Institute for Comparative Public Law and International Law Working Papers, 2017-20.

next three decades. It fostered the notion that slave-holding Americans themselves deserved slavery, or through their slave-holding they debased and enslaved themselves.[20] The double-edged nature of this formulation of American liberty was not lost on Adams, as he described Otis's speech. "Not a Quaker in Philadelphia, or Mr. Jefferson of Virginia, ever asserted the rights of Negroes in stronger terms."[21] Adams recalled being torn. He found Otis's argument compelling, but the foundational anti-slavery principle Otis drew from the state of nature was too categorical to allow for practical solutions, such as "gradual abolitions."[22]

Otis is unlikely to have drawn much from Montesquieu for his state of nature. Montesquieu's state of nature houses an equality that is lost on entering society but can be restored by the civil laws (fig. 3.4).[23] However, Montesquieu's sense of the state of nature guides "Of Laws relative to Government in general," an unpublished essay that George III wrote and revised. It begins with the state of nature as a condition of equality and

20. E.g. Thomas Paine, "African Slavery in America," *Pennsylvania Journal and Weekly Advertiser*, March 1775. During the 1776 drafting of the Virginia Declaration of Rights, which famously influenced the US Declaration of Independence, Edmund Pendleton added the clause, "when they enter into a state of society" to the declaration that "all men are by nature equally free and independent." This allowed slaveholders to support the Virginia Declaration on the assumption that slaves are excluded from society. Pendleton probably had in mind the well-established contrast between the "state of society" and the "state of nature". In any case, the Virginia Declaration's relocation of equality from nature, as found in Otis's formulation, to society, was a telling sign of the tension that Adams drew attention to. Brent Tarter, "The Virginia Declaration of Rights," in Josephine F. Pacheco (ed.), *To Secure the Blessings of Liberty: Rights in American History, The George Mason Lectures* (George Mason University Press, 1993), 37–54.

21. Tudor, *Life of Otis*, 18.

22. Anthony Benezet, *A Short Account of that Part of Africa Inhabited by the Negroes* (Philadelphia, 1762), makes the same case for abolition based on supra-political equality in the state of nature. Here he draws on p. 7 of the 1760 *Two Dialogues on the Man-Trade*, published in London under the pseudonym J. Philmore. Rush based his anti-slavery argument on the same reading of the state of nature as a condition of equality in *An Address to the Inhabitants of the British Settlements* (Philadelphia, 1773).

23. Adams notes this on 162–63 of his copy. Mass. Hist. Soc., Special Colls. John Adams Annotated Books.

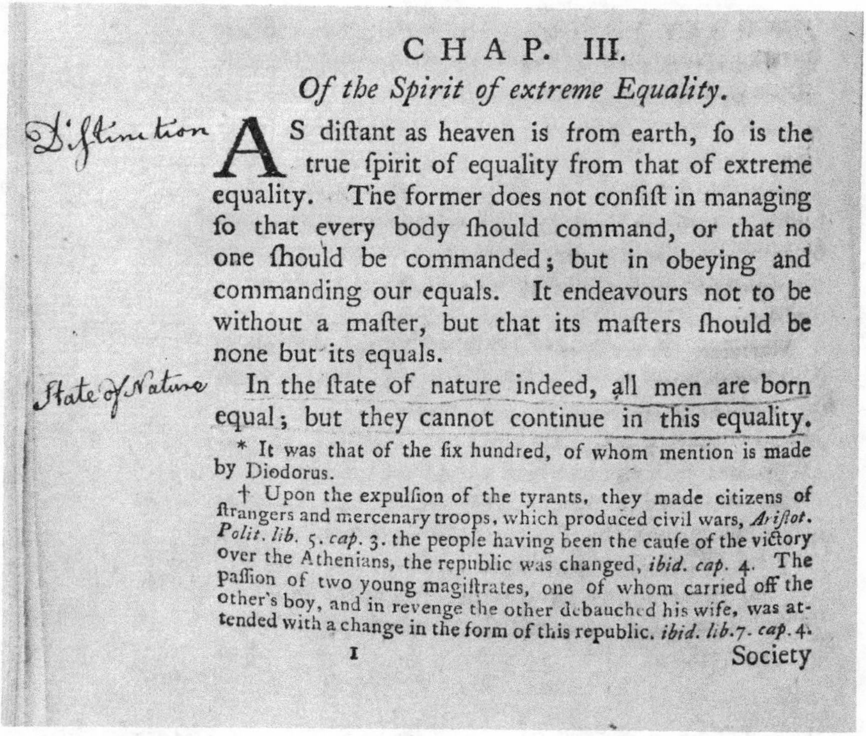

C H A P. III.

Of the Spirit of extreme Equality.

Diſtinction

AS diſtant as heaven is from earth, ſo is the true ſpirit of equality from that of extreme equality. The former does not conſiſt in managing ſo that every body ſhould command, or that no one ſhould be commanded; but in obeying and commanding our equals. It endeavours not to be without a maſter, but that its maſters ſhould be none but its equals.

State of Nature

In the ſtate of nature indeed, all men are born equal; but they cannot continue in this equality.

* It was that of the ſix hundred, of whom mention is made by Diodorus.

† Upon the expulſion of the tyrants, they made citizens of ſtrangers and mercenary troops, which produced civil wars, *Ariſtot. Polit. lib.* 5. *cap.* 3. the people having been the cauſe of the victory over the Athenians, the republic was changed, *ibid. cap.* 4. The paſſion of two young magiſtrates, one of whom carried off the other's boy, and in revenge the other debauched his wife, was attended with a change in the form of this republic. *ibid. lib.*7. *cap.* 4.

I   Society

Fig. 3.4 John Adams's annotations in Montesquieu, *The Spirit of Laws*, 162. Collection of the Massachusetts Historical Society.

weakness. Both were given up when people formed societies. There they recognized their combined force; nations turned against each other; and the law of nations became as necessary as national governments (fig. 3.5).

If the laws permit slavery, a follower of Montesquieu cannot argue on a state of nature basis that slaves have a natural right to resist, or that the civil laws regulating slavery are no laws at all. In Montesquieu, abolition is essential in republics (as opposed to monarchies) because of their constitutional character, not because of any radical human equality grounded in a state of nature that survives the transition to the polity.[24] Rousseau is a more likely source for Otis's equality and for the link between the state of nature defenses of American liberty, and of abolition.

24. Noted by Adams in his copy, XV.xvii, 354–56.

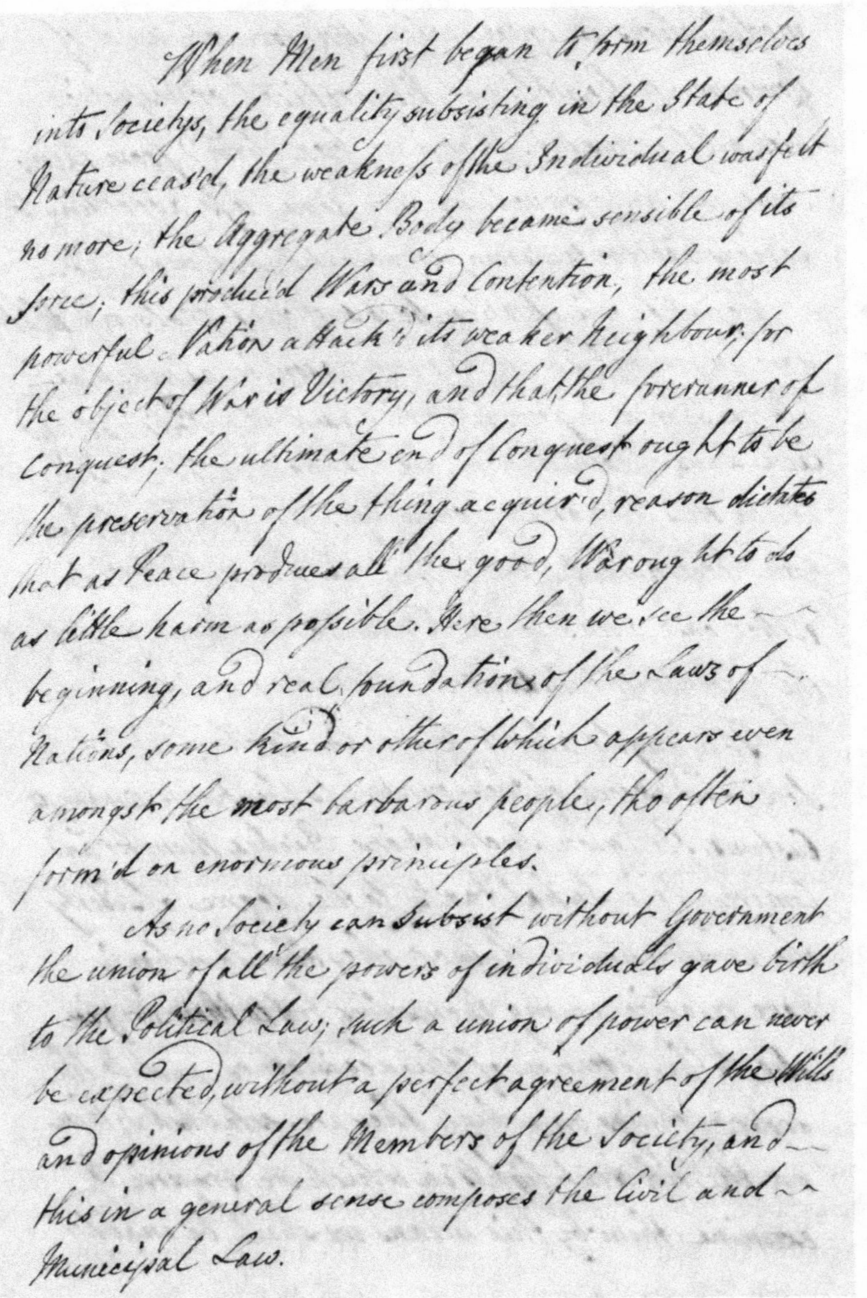

When Men first began to form themselves
into Societys, the equality subsisting in the State of
Nature ceased, the weakness of the Individual was felt
no more; the Aggregate Body became sensible of its
force; this produc'd Wars and Contention, the most
powerful Nation attack'd its weaker Neighbour; for
the object of War is Victory, and that the forerunner of
conquest; the ultimate end of Conquest ought to be
the preservation of the thing acquir'd, reason dictates
that as Peace produces all the good, War ought to do
as little harm as possible. Here then we see the
beginning, and real foundation of the Laws of
Nations, some kind or other of which appears even
amongst the most barbarous people, tho often
form'd on enormous principles.

    As no Society can subsist without Government
the union of all the powers of individuals gave birth
to the Political Laws; such a union of power can never
be expected, without a perfect agreement of the Wills
and opinions of the Members of the Society, and
this in a general sense composes the Civil and
Municipal Laws.

Fig. 3.5 George III, "Of Laws relative to Government in general." RA GEO ADDL
MSS 32, 1072. Royal Archives/© Her Majesty Queen Elizabeth II 2018.

Otis's reformulation of the state of nature as a font of substantive rights that endures after the state is created is a vital intellectual move for American resistance. In principle, the common law does not allow for *non liquet*, a situation in which no clear law applies.[25] If statute law and precedent fail to provide an answer, lawyers can render existing statute law and precedent relevant by offering agonistic interpretations, or rather constructions, to the court and the jury; or they can appeal to equity, or to the principle of progress that is inherent in common law, in order to show that they are perfecting the common law, not departing from it.[26] As many of the texts discussed in this book will show, by formulating state of nature rights for the colonists, Otis opened the door to using the state of nature in the dispute between Britain and the American colonies the same way that progress and equity had been used, namely as a corrective or catalyst to the common law's progress. Dickinson's 1774 *Essay* is one of many American rejections of British policy that follow the *non liquet* line of reasoning opened by Otis, and pitch state of nature rights

25. Roscoe Pound, "Hierarchy of Sources and Forms in Different Systems of Law," *Tulane Law Review* 7:4 (1933), 475–87, at 483–84 and *passim*. For an eighteenth-century state of nature example see the 1759 *Astley v. Younge*, 2 Burr. 807, where Serjeant William Davy argued that defamation laws must extend to protecting the reputation of the plaintiff, Sir John Astley, because "if he could not be protected by legal methods, he might (as in a state of nature) be driven to revenge himself." 2 Burr 809. The Boston Public Library has John Adams's copy of James Burr, *Reports of Cases Adjudged in the Court of King's Bench since the Death of Lord Raymond* (London, 1766), vol. 2. A relevant twentieth-century US case is the 1975 *Davis v. Richmond*, 512 F. 2d 201, in which the US Court of Appeals for the First Circuit ruled that a landlord lawfully seized the possessions of a tenant who failed to pay rent while he was hospitalized, because "in either a state of nature or an organized society without an applicable law, a boardinghouse keeper might reasonably assert the right to hold a guest's property within the premises until the rent is paid."

26. On appeals to equity in the absence of statute of law or precedent see Kames, discussed at the end of this chapter. Appeals to equity as common ground for reconciliation plans: Reid, *Authority to Tax*, 239. On appeals to progress see John Selden, *Notes on Fortescue*, in Sir John Fortescue, *De laudibus legum Angliæ* (London, 1616) and Geoffrey Robertson, *The Tyrannicide Brief* (Chatto, 2005). Blackstone supplies an elegant inversion: "The WRITTEN or STATUTE Laws, are the Acts which are made by the King, Lords, and Commons, in Parliament; to supply the Defects, or amend what is amiss, of the unwritten Law." *Analysis*, I.ii.4.

and equity against the common law as understood by Blackstone and Parliament.[27]

Otis's adaptation of Rousseau shaped the Massachusetts House of Representatives' January 12, 1768 letter to Dennys DeBerdt, their colonial agent in London.[28] Here the House anchored property in the state of nature, and recognized the "American savage" to have property in his "bow, the arrow, and the tomahawk," as well as in his hunting and fishing grounds. Property must survive the transition to civil society; therefore the Crown has no claims on the colonists' property without their consent.[29] The House, like Otis in 1761, cited Rousseau's imagery of property in the state of nature, adapted it to America, and offered it in defense of the colonists' property rights. The letter, which Otis drafted in part, concludes with instructions for DeBerdt to make these sentiments known to his Majesty's ministers.

The counter-theory to the authenticity and content of Otis's speech in *Paxton's Case* is that Adams made it all up. The state of nature is absent from the known fragments of Adams's 1761 Abstract of Otis's

27. Dickinson, *Essay*, 330–37, 399–400.
28. Published in Boston papers as well as in the April 4 *New-York Gazette* and the April 11 *Pennsylvania Chronicle*. For a very detailed account of Otis's influence on this text see John Adams, letter to William Tudor, Sr., March 7, 1819. https://founders.archives.gov/?q=Recipient%3A%22Tudor%2C%20William%2C%20Sr.%22&s=1111311111&r=78.
29. "It is observable, that though many have disregarded life, and contemned liberty, yet there are few men who do not agree that property is a valuable acquisition, which ought to be held sacred. Many have fought, and bled, and died for this, who have been insensible to all other obligations. Those who ridicule the ideas of right and justice, faith and truth among men, will put a high value upon money. Property is admitted to have an existence, even in the savage state of nature. The bow, the arrow, and the tomahawk; the hunting and the fishing ground, are species of property, as important to an American savage, as pearls, rubies, and diamonds are to the Mogul, or a Nabob in the East, or the lands, tenements, hereditaments, messuages, gold and silver of the Europeans. And if property is necessary for the support of savage life, it is by no means less so in civil society. The Utopian schemes of levelling, and a community of goods, are as visionary and impracticable, as those which vest all property in the Crown, are arbitrary, despotic, and in our government unconstitutional." Samuel Adams, *Writings*, ed. Harry A. Cushing (New York, 1904–8), I.134–52, at 137. Printed in the *Boston Gazette*, April 4, 1768.

argument, based on minutes that Adams took in court. The Abstract was lost early on, and only survives in conjectural reconstructions. According to Adams's letter to Tudor, it was "carried off by some individual, who 'interpolated them, with some bombastic expressions of his own.'"[30] Adams accused Jonathan Williams Austin of the theft, embellishments, and publication. Tudor probably understood that Adams was referring to Austin, as Tudor and Austin both graduated from Harvard in 1769 and started clerking for Adams the same year.[31] One source of historical reconstructions of the Abstract is Hawley's commonplace book, which contains a version of Gridley's and Otis's speeches.[32] This is followed by Hawley's notes on *Rex v. Hamilton* from March 1771, and another case from 1771 that Hawley copies from Quincy. Although dating sections of a commonplace book is uncertain, it would be remiss not to note the possibility that Hawley copied his records on *Paxton's Case* directly from Adams's Abstract or from another intermediary source, not from the April 29, 1773 *Massachusetts Spy* (the second source of Adams's Abstract), which misdated the case to 1771 instead of 1761. The third source is George Richards Minot, *Continuation of the History of the Province of Massachusetts Bay*.[33] The fourth source is a slightly redacted version by Charles Francis Adams in Adams's *Works*, based on Minot's, and Adams's own annotations in his copy of Minot's *History*, pointing out passages that Adams thought were not written by him but interpolated by others in the *Massachusetts Spy* and Minot's versions.

The known version of the Abstract is not only indirect, but also incomplete. First of all, it started as a mere abstract. Second, it was redacted during its adventurous transmission. Hawley's version ends with the note, "I have omitted many authorities; also many fine touches in the order of reasoning, and numberless Rhetorical and popular flourishes." Minot seems to respond to this directly in his reprint: "Mr. Otis appeared for

30. Tudor, *Life of Otis*, 62–63n.
31. Shipton, *Harvard Graduates*, vol. 17.
32. Joseph Hawley Papers, New York Public Library, MssCol 1360, Box 2, Folder 7. Gridley is on 9–12, Otis on 12–18.
33. Boston, 1803, 2:91–99.

the inhabitants of Boston, who had presented a counter-petition. As his plea discloses several curious facts, presents a striking picture of the spirit of the times, and in some measure portrays the manner of that ardent patriot and well-read lawyer, we shall insert more at large such minutes as we possess; lamenting that we cannot recover at this day many elegant rhetorical touches and weighty arguments, which were unavoidably omitted."[34] Charles Francis Adams, Sr. also explained that the published versions reflect merely a part of Otis's speech. In addition, Israel Keith's manuscript, now also lost, but presumed to be a direct copy that Keith made from Adams some time after he graduated from Harvard in 1771, contains a summary of Gridley's and Thacher's statements. It was printed by Horace Gray in 1865.[35]

An exciting possibility is that in addition to Adams's lost Abstract, Hawley's commonplace book, and the 1773 *Spy*, 1803 Minot and 1865 *Works* printed versions, another near-contemporary manuscript source of Adams's Abstract is at the American Philosophical Society (Sol Feinstone Collection #1045 Mss. B. F327). The Society's catalog dates it to 1772 and attributes it to the otherwise unknown Elisha Mayer. However, the corner of the flyleaf with the author's name inscribed is torn, obscuring the supposed "M." Even if the "M" is correct, it is possible that someone else mistook "Th" for "M," and noted the owner's name incorrectly (fig. 3.6). Elisha Thayer was one of Adams's clerks from May 1771 to February 1773, when he was excused from law studies due to ill health.[36] He died in 1774. Although in his 1759 diary Adams called Col. Ebenezer Thayer, Jr., Elisha's father, one of the "pettifogging Dabblers in Iniquity and Law" in Braintree[37] and lost an election to the General Court to Thayer in 1766,[38] he accepted his son as a clerk in 1771 and sent

---

34. Minot, *Continuation*, 91.
35. Appendix 1 of *Quincy's Reports*, 479–82. For a summary of versions see Wroth and Zobel, *Legal Papers of Adams*, 2:134–35 n. 103.
36. Wroth and Zobel, *Legal Papers of Adams*, 1:lxxxi.
37. *Founders Online*, National Archives, last modified March 30, 2017, http://founders.archives.gov/documents/Adams/01-01-02-0004-0005-0001.
38. John Ferling, *John Adams: A Life* (University of Tennessee Press, 1992, repr. Oxford, 2010), 54.

Fig. 3.6 Elisha Thayer's legal notebook. Sol Feinstone Collection of the David Library of the American Revolution, #1045 Mss. B.F327, on deposit at the American Philosophical Society.

his condolences to the Colonel on Elisha's death.[39] While still based on a mere abstract, pages 6–14 of this notebook contain more details than any of the other known versions, including at least some of the legal authorities Otis cited, and Hawley or his source chose to redact. It may be the best and least-used source for the speech that, Adams insisted for over fifty years, started the Revolution.

There are major and minor differences between the Feinstone manuscripts and the other four sources. A detailed comparison can be made on the basis of appendix 1. Among minor variations are single terms, phrases, and short clauses in the Feinstone manuscript that the other sources are lacking. More rarely, a phrase is absent from the Feinstone. The longest such lacuna is Otis's prediction that if the writ of assize were granted, "every man may reign in his petty tyranny, and spread terror and desolation around him, until the trump of the arch angel shall excite different emotions in his soul." John Adams told his grandson, Charles Francis, that he did not write this passage. Gray took this statement as evidence that Adams was wrong, and in this case "was guided by his taste rather than his notes or his memory."[40] The Feinstone manuscript raises the possibility that Adams was right about his own lost Abstract—and

39. April 25, 1774, letter in *Papers of John Adams*, ed. Taylor et al. (Belknap, 1977), 84.
40. *Quincy's Reports*, 479.

if that is the case, the absence of this passage corroborates the value of Thayer's copy.

The manuscript also contains sentences and paragraphs that are missing from Hawley's notes, the 1773 *Massachusetts Spy* article, Minot's version, and Charles Francis Adams's corrections. Some of these are Otis's citations, for instance from Cicero's *Pro Archia*, and references to authorities, including Viner. Other passages enrich the case. For instance, in every version, Otis complains about the political context of the lawsuit. In a sentence, also present in the other sources, the Feinstone version has an additional clause, according to which Otis complained of being "represented as a seditious person: a stirrer of uneasiness & rebellion." The other surviving versions end abruptly, either with a reference to a law from Queen Anne's reign or, as in Hawley's case, the copyist's note about abridging their source for Otis's speech. By contrast, the Feinstone version ends with Otis proclaiming that liberty is dear to Englishmen, and if officers illegally entered the houses of colonists, all would probably end in violence. In the known versions Otis argues that Parliament cannot make writs of assistance binding, even if it passed a law that verbatim included the writ as granted to particularly named customs officers, because "[a]n act against the constitution is void." Feinstone has this, and adds, "an act against natural equity is void." Moreover:

And with all due regard to precedents, authorities, parliaments & positive institutions of every kind, one good reason is a better foundation for any court or private person to build on, than all the learning of that kind that ever was wrote.

The parliament of England has treated her plantations with more rigour than was perhaps needful. The restrictions laid upon us have been vastly severe—so severe that a Noble Lord who it seems had some feeling for us, was heard to say, of the rigid prohibitions of iron manufactures here, that he wondered they did not by an act of parliament oblige us to send our horses across the atlantic to be shorn. They seem to have considered us as a kind of cattle, not intitled to the common privileges of humanity, or at least as savages with neither the understanding nor the feeling of civilized nations:—They have bound us with acts of trade that are every one of them inconsistent with common right & that nothing but absolute necessity can justify. And they send over unto us officers to inspect our trade & collect the customs, who seem to consider us in the same light as a people without sense or resentment. They assume important airs & pretend to high powers & vast authority. They are the representatives of royal majesty. The management of the sacred, important revenue is in their hands. They are to be feared & reverenced. We to be dispised & trampled on, tamely suffering the worst of insolence. As if a birth or a year's residence in England had given them all knowledge & all power: & as if a birth & education in this country, had deprived us of human senses. But it is high time that they in England & their emissaries here, know that we have at least the sense of feeling: That we know a little both of natural justice & common law. We have the same Books & the same order of Ideas, excepting the common differences between man & man, in New England as they have in old. And for my own part who know of no title to respect in any man but what his understanding & goodness give him. I never will regard an old Englishman—no nor a custom house officer, without either of those titles to respect, at all the more, for the place of his birth, or the office he sustains.

These paragraphs are absent from the other versions, which, as mentioned, depend closely on each other. They are internally coherent, insofar as other variations, such as Otis's complaint that he is accused of sedition and rebellion, confirm the radicalism of this passage. They also match the tone that Adams ascribed to Otis's 1761 speech and Otis's later writings, discussed below. The Feinstone manuscript should join the exegetical tradition that aims to reconstruct the speech that Adams consistently hailed as the start of the Revolution.[41]

41. Another source that one day might be found is an account of Otis's speech, possibly a manuscript copy of Adams's Abstract (though possibly only the *Massachusetts Spy* version) that the Massachusetts Committee of Correspondence sent to its Connecticut counterpart in August 1773 in response to Connecticut's request for arguments against writs of assistance. Smith, *Writs*, 239.

Another theory queries the reliability of Adams's account of Otis's speech not in the 1810s, but right from the start. Wroth and Zobel speculate that in writing up his rough notes taken in court into the more polished, now lost Abstract, Adams mixed in his own political ideas with Otis's argument.[42] This does not matter much. First, Wroth and Zobel also write that Otis said everything that Adams attributed to him, and more. Second, the state of nature features prominently in Otis's writing in the 1760s, including drafts of texts endorsed by the Massachusetts Assembly. The identical or strongly similar arguments—later enhanced with more authorities—also make it probable that Otis used state of nature arguments already in 1761. Third, from Adams's diary we know that the two of them discussed the state of nature. This makes Otis's use of it more probable, and Adams's possible contribution less of a problem. To the extent that Adams may have augmented Otis's speech in court, their possible but certainly limited co-authorship reflects their shared thinking. Finally, in his letters to Tudor, Adams is clear when he disagrees with Otis and the Assembly in the 1760s, yet he is still able to reproduce their arguments with precision. There is no compelling reason to suppose that Adams augmented Otis's argument, but hid his own contribution.

The complicated condition of the surviving Abstract is not enough to discredit Adams's recollection in his letter to Tudor that Otis started the American Revolution with a "dissertation on the state of nature." Circumstantial evidence, including the collaboration between Adams and Otis on the state of nature, Adams's several diary entries by 1761 concerning the state of nature, and Otis's own direct references to the state of nature in texts that survived in a better condition than his oration in *Paxton's Case*, all support Adams's recollection. Otis references state of nature texts in his 1762 *A Vindication of the Conduct of the House of Representatives of the Province of the Massachusetts-Bay*, such as Mandeville's *Fable of the Bees*, and he chastises "the *Leviathan* in power, or those other overgrown *Animals*" in a December 19, 1761 essay on

42. Wroth and Zobel, *Legal Papers of Adams*, 2:122–23.

currency in the *Boston Gazette*.[43] Yet the 1764 *The Rights of the British Colonies Asserted and Proved* is Otis's first major publication where he uses the term with the sophistication and purpose that Adams attributes to him in his 1817–1819 letters to Tudor.[44]

On balance, it seems unlikely that Adams invented Otis's use of the state of nature in *Paxton's Case*, given his own 1759–1766 diary entries on the state of nature, his discussions with Otis, his notes to Tudor concerning his disagreements with some of Otis's statements, the similarity between the arguments Adams attributes to Otis in 1761 and those that appear in Otis's own writings soon thereafter, and another state of nature source from Gridley's circle, namely Oxenbridge Thacher's 1764 draft, discussed below. The possibility of Adams's retrospective fabrication, however, should be noted. It would make some, though little, difference to the point that a sophisticated state of nature argument against British encroachments existed in the colonies before Blackstone's 1765 *Commentaries*, and blended Grotius, Hobbes, Locke, Montesquieu, Vattel, Rousseau, and other authorities.

3.2 ABRAHAM WILLIAMS, ELECTION SERMON (1762)

In Adams's June 1, 1818 letter to Tudor, the fourth section of Otis's speech in *Paxton's Case* exemplified the connection between the state of nature that a given writer proposed, and his or her view on the

---

43. Adams's discussions of Montesquieu and Rousseau, and Otis's references to them and to Richelieu, seem to question Carl L. Becker's claim in *The Declaration of Independence* (New York, 1922), 27, that Founders did not "read many French books."

44. Andrew C. McLaughlin, *The Foundations of American Constitutionalism* (New York, 1932), 124 writes that Adams's 1818 letter to Tudor is "of little value" and "a compound of the whole Revolutionary argument as it developed after 1761." The point is repeated in milder form by Wroth and Zobel in Adams, *Legal Papers of Adams*, 2:107. Quincy's *Reports* show that his own notes on Otis are incomplete ("but I was absent, while he was speaking . . ."), thus in addition to their obvious importance for American history, Adams's notes also remain essential for bare reconstruction.

traditional problem of the hierarchy of laws. A simplified, four-tier scheme can illustrate the problem. What is the relationship between divine law, natural law, international law, and civil or common law? A view of law in which all other tiers flow or emanate from divine law follows from the premise of an interventionist god. In this case, specifics in international or divine law can be debated on the basis of detailed biblical exegeses. When God is seen as the prime mover with a providential plan for mankind, but no miracles or other direct interventions are admitted after Christ's ascent; and/or it is considered epistemically arrogant for any human to assume they can share God's knowledge in sufficient detail to support forensic reasoning, then the gap between divine and other kinds of law widens.[45]

A similar problem appears in the relationship between common law and equity. In early modern England, equity became a legal principle that created a scope for royal and, increasingly, parliamentary privilege. Benign interpreters of the English legal system saw equity as a complement to the common law, insofar as it allowed the common law to evolve through history (as it was supposed to) in response to being overruled by equity courts when appeals to precedent proved insufficient to make the common law just. Founding figures, including John Adams and Thomas Jefferson, worked hard to redefine equity toward its ancient Roman meaning as the natural law or instinct of fairness, the standard against which civil or common law should improve. They did so in order to move "equity" away from its established common law use in supporting executive or legislative privilege in institutions such as the Court of Chancery, Star Chamber, or the Exchequer.[46]

One of the most striking attempts to combat what was seen as the increasingly arbitrary British government of Massachusetts took the

45. Somos, *Secularisation and the Leiden Circle* (Brill, 2011).
46. Debora Shuger, *Political Theologies in Shakespeare's England: The Sacred and the State in "Measure for Measure"* (Palgrave, 2001), chap. 3; William S. Holdsworth, *A History of English Law* (London, 1903; 7th ed., 1956), 1:398–409, 466–69, 477–516; Mark Fortier, *The Culture of Equity in Early Modern England* (Ashgate, 2005); Crow, *Thomas Jefferson*, 87–104.

form of a political sermon on the hierarchy of laws. This was the election sermon delivered on May 26, 1762, by Abraham Williams (1727–1784).[47] Edmund Morgan described Williams as "not an outstanding thinker" and this sermon as "memorable, not because of any originality or forceful expression, but simply because it illustrates the transformation that had taken place in Puritan ideas." According to Morgan, this transformation consisted of Williams addressing magistrates, rather than the people, when he expounded the conservative Puritan notion of popular sovereignty held in check by the duty to obey magistrates. In Morgan's account, Williams's contribution was merely some sort of unclear shift in emphasis toward the audience.[48] Hyneman and Lutz similarly describe Williams as cautious and rarely political, and this sermon as containing "almost all the basic assumptions underlying American political thinking on the eve of the Stamp Act." They chose it as the first in their collection because it is representative of the mainstream. In the mature Williams's conservatism they saw a departure from his Harvard student days, when he was known as "Grand heretick Williams."[49] Swift, however, suggests that some of Williams's rebellious spirit persisted. She points out that contrary to convention, the sermon's title page omits any reference to the governor or lieutenant-governor, and that it was one of the few sermons that "did not receive the honor of a reprint in London."[50] Freiberg contends that the immediate political context of Williams's

47. Abraham Williams, *A Sermon Preach'd at Boston, Before the Great and General Court or Assembly of the Province of the Massachusetts-Bay in New-England, May 26, 1762. Being the Day Appointed by Royal Charter, for the Election of His Majesty's Council for Said Province* (Boston, 1762). Reprinted in Charles S. Hyneman and Donald S. Lutz (eds.), *American Political Writing during the Founding Era, 1760–1805* (Liberty Fund, 1983), 1:3.
48. Edmund S. Morgan, *Puritan Political Ideas, 1558–1794* (1965, repr. Hackett. 2003), 331.
49. Hymen and Lutz, *American Political Writing*, 1:3.
50. Lindsay Swift, *The Massachusetts Election Sermons: An Essay in Descriptive Bibliography* (Cambridge, 1897, repr. from Publications of the Colonial Society of Massachusetts, vol. 1), 38.

sermon, which included a jeremiad against factionalism, was the contest between the parties of Otis and Hutchinson.[51]

The historians' disagreement about the originality of Williams's sermon touches on a central interpretative problem. Many historians praise the lack of originality and innovation in primary sources as "a blessing," because "platitudinous" texts allow them to capture and reconstruct widely shared assumptions.[52] Much of the substance of the historiographical debate is where the dividing line between everyday and innovative texts runs, and therefore which texts are revolutionary, and which ones are not. This distinction might be important, but it is not obvious why. First, in historical usage, referents and semantic ranges are seldom sufficiently steady to allow a hermeneutically underpowered (e.g., quantitative) aggregation of them to yield so precise an understanding of their original meaning that constitutional interpretation can follow.[53] Second, contextualization seems to be sufficient to render the historiographical debates concerning the dividing line moot. Williams may have used traditional Calvinist tropes about authority. He did so in a particular political context that gave them a specific and localized meaning. Irrespective of the number of times the same point had been made by other Protestant preachers in other contexts, Williams's meaning was part of a story of rising and increasingly better articulated tension between Britain and the American colonies. We will see another election day sermon, delivered in 1774 by Gad Hitchcock on Proverbs 29:2, a conventional trope that Hitchcock gave a fantastically dramatic meaning in front of the newly arrived British troops and General Gage, the latest Governor of Massachusetts. Is an examination of the decontextualized distinction between everyday and innovative meanings useful in such cases?

---

51. *Journals of the House of Representatives of Massachusetts, 1761, 1762 and 1762–63,* vols. 38 and 39 (ed. Malcolm Freiberg, Boston, 1967–69).
52. Hamburger, "Natural Rights," 917.
53. This is Reid's point in *Constitutional History of the American Revolution: The Authority to Tax* (University of Wisconsin Press, 1987), 9, 27. In appendix 2 I argue that Justice Thomas's dissent in *Obergefell v. Hodges* offers a hermeneutically underpowered *and* historically inaccurate reading of "the state of nature."

A close and contextualized reading suggests that Swift's 1897 assessment is more convincing than later interpretations. Williams's sermon is an original exercise in legal systematization, driven by a not wholly orthodox agenda to recalibrate the synthesis between theology and law. The latter is shown by the extent to which Williams relies on biblical citations to establish that "the origin of Government is from God," but the "Constitution, Laws and Sanctions of civil Society respect this World, and are therefore essentially distinct and different from the *Kingdom of Christ*." God instituted and approves government, but gave no specific laws to shape it, only the general mandate that government must "secure and promote the Happiness of Society."[54] The close link between the Bible and politics is missing, but so is the epistemic humility concerning God's detailed plan, which was often invoked to separate politics from theology.[55] According to Williams, the foundation of politics, the place we must explore to find higher laws that shape good politics and override bad politics, is not providence—whether a knowable version, or one in which we must have unknowing faith—but the state of nature.

It is in the state of nature that we see humans acquire, exercise, and protect their rights to property, self-defense, and the punishment of those who threaten or offend against them.[56] In the state of nature, God administers justice through natural laws. For Williams, the state of nature is not a transitory stage that disappears or recedes after people create the polity. It is the sphere where all the laws of nature operate, approved by "the God of Nature." When people enter civil society, they transfer some of their natural rights, including the rights to property and self-defense, to government. The transfer simply aggregates but does not limit or even transform these rights as, for instance, Rousseau would have it. Civil laws are merely explanations and applications of natural laws.[57]

54. Hyneman and Lutz, *American Political Writing*, 1:6–7.
55. Somos, *Secularisation*.
56. Hyneman and Lutz, *American Political Writing*, 1:7–8.
57. Note the contrast with Elisha Williams, *The Essential Rights and Liberties of Protestants . . .* (Boston, 1744), in Ellis Sandoz (ed.), *Political Sermons of the American Founding Era, 1730–1805* (Liberty Fund, 2nd ed. 1998), 1:51–118, at

Some rights, such as the illimitable right of conscience, are never transferred. These are not merely natural rights, but state of nature rights.[58] Government can regulate outward behavior, including public worship; but real religion is a private matter between God and the individual. Williams distinguishes between God and the "God of Nature," a phrase he uses consistently and often.[59] The latter is involved in politics, as prime mover in general, as ruler in the state of nature, and as the author of natural laws that continue to frame and regulate civil laws. God, when considered as supranatural, is apolitical. In Williams's system, suspending, though not wholly eliminating, God's government in the state of nature seems to be the only cost of entering the polity, even when humans do so with God's approval and encouragement. While inalienable rights remain directly in the state of nature, and can be understood and defended there, the polity created by aggregating transferable rights must respect all natural laws and rights, as they obtain and operate in the state of nature. The polity does so by elaborating and implementing *alienable* natural rights and by being careful not to infringe on inalienable rights, such as the freedom of conscience.

In Williams's sermon, the state of nature is the omnipresent and unbreakable link between natural and civil law. In this sense it replaces divine guidance in politics, insofar as Williams's distinction between God and the God of Nature firmly establishes not divine, but natural, laws in the state of

57–60. Elisha Williams also believed that property and punishment were the only two state of nature rights that are surrendered to society, but unlike Abraham, Elisha regarded them as properly delegated, not aggregated. Based on the remaining inalienable state of nature rights, Elisha, judge on the Superior Court of Connecticut, and later Speaker of the Connecticut Assembly, argued in this text for the freedom of religion and speech, against a 1742 Connecticut bill restricting the activities of itinerant preachers. The speech cost Elisha his political position. Nicholas P. Miller, *The Religious Roots of the First Amendment: Dissenting Protestants and the Separation of Church and State* (Oxford, 2012), 95–96.

58. In Williams's phrase, "in a State of Nature prior to Government, every Man has a Right to" property, and self-defense. Hyneman and Lutz, *American Political Writing*, 2:7.

59. "The *Law of Nature*, which is the *Constitution of the God of Nature*, is universally obliging." Hyneman and Lutz, *American Poltiical Writing*, 2:15.

nature as the tier of law above civil laws. Divine laws underpin more than just politics. To assess the righteousness and justice of Massachusetts's government, one must have constant recourse to the standard of the state of nature, not to God, King or Parliament, King-in-Parliament, the common law, colonial custom, or any combination thereof. Thus Williams's sermon, with the snubs to British authority that Swift pointed out, was neither mainstream nor unoriginal for 1762. It is part of the American revolutionary state of nature discourse. Williams anchored only the rights of religion and conscience in the state of nature, protected by Nature's God. He regarded the natural rights of self-defense and property as alienable, necessarily so for the state to function. As we will see, the following years saw the colonists increasingly transfer these and other rights from the purview of the British empire into the state of nature. In tandem with this development, they came to endow the state of nature with natural and historical characteristics that were specifically and uniquely American.

One key to this process was to shift the emphasis from human ingenuity toward nature. Locke thought that mixing one's labor with natural resources creates property in the state of nature. Scottish stadial theorists, including Smith, regarded labor and technological progress as essential for leaving the state of nature behind and advancing to the next stage of development. American Patriots, such as Alexander Hamilton, endorsed this model, and drew attention to the rapidity of progress that the United States could make thanks to industrial and commercial policies that stimulated catch-up with advanced European states, and co-ordinated and optimized the use of resources ranging from raw materials to what is now called human capital.[60] Others, such as Jefferson and Silas Deane, worried about the moral and political corruption that overly rapid material progress was bound to cause. Instead, they preferred a path of progress that coupled American demographic growth with territorial expansion, making it possible for future generations to

---

60. Somos, "'A Price would be Set not only upon our Friendship, but upon our Neutrality': Alexander Hamilton's Political Economy and Early American State-Building," in Koen Stapelbroek (ed.), *War and Trade: The Neutrality of Commerce in the Interstate System* (Helsinki, 2011), 184–211, at 195–99, 204, 208–9.

directly work the land and other natural resources, and cultivate republican virtues without either falling prey to luxury or freezing the new republic at a given stage of development. Again, American nature was unique, and able to underwrite a unique proposition for independence.[61] This is a huge field of scholarship, but the only relevant point here is that both broad contrasting political visions, commonly associated with Hamilton and Jefferson, assumed that the potential of American nature was greater than the Old World's. The belief in a great and largely untapped natural potential was one thing that made the American state of nature discourse distinct from Europe's.

3.3 OTIS, *RIGHTS AND CONSIDERATIONS* (1764–65)

Though I agree with Swift rather than Morgan and Hyneman and Lutz about Williams's radicalism, historians rightly point to Otis's *Rights* as a document that effectively galvanized public opinion in the early 1760s. The state of nature is a defining element in his structure of reasoning. Otis divides the text into five parts: an introduction on the origin of government, a section on colonies in general, one on the natural rights of the colonists, one on "the political and civil rights of the British Colonists," and an appendix.

In the opening, Otis reviews and rejects four common opinions concerning the origin of government: religion, force, contract, and property. He summarily dismisses the first two as obviously unacceptable. Otis's account of the contract theory of government is entertaining and instructive. It is essentially five pages of questions that closely parallel questions that were being asked about the state of nature. Is the original contract historical or analytical? Does it bind posterity? What are the justifications and ramifications of the transition from the pre-contract to the post-contract condition? Are women as free as men in the pre-contract stage? What conditions must be met to justify returning to,

61. See the discussion of Deane's February 7, 1774, letter to William Samuel Johnson in section 6.4 below.

renegotiating, or abrogating the original compact? Can one extrapolate these conditions from the legal principles in current use, for instance when equity overrides the letter of the law? Otis builds up a sequence of these questions, only to put them aside with the instruction that those who wish for answers should consult Locke, Vattel, and their own conscience.

He picks up another thread that applies specifically to Britain and the colonies. Did the original contract provide for the gap between James II's abdication and the accession of William and Mary, perhaps by locating supreme power in Parliament during such a vacuum; or did Britain lapse into a state of nature? Otis heavily hints that the latter was the case and that Parliament had no perfect right to government.

> If on this memorable and very happy event the three kingdoms and the dominions fell back into a state of *nature*, it will be asked, "Whether every man and woman were not then equal? If so, had not every one of them a natural and equitable right to be consulted in the choice of a new king, or in the formation of a new original compact or government, if any new form had been made? Might not the nation at that time have rightfully changed the monarchy into a republic of any form, that might seem best? Could any change from a state of nature take place without the consent of the *majority* of the individuals?" . . . If upon the abdication all were reduced to a state of nature, had not apple-women and orange-girls as good a right to give their respective suffrages for a new king as the philosopher, courtier, petit maitre, and politician? . . . Were not those who did not vote in or for the new model at liberty upon the principles of the compact to remain in what some call the delectable state of nature, to which by the hypothesis they were reduced, or to join themselves to any other state, whose solemn league and covenant they could subscribe? Is it not a first principle of the original compact, that all who are bound should bind *themselves*?[62]

62. Otis, *Rights*, 7–9.

Otis concludes this section by suggesting that those who regard the original compact as "a piece of metaphysical jargon and systematical nonsense" are wrong, and merely by discarding it they already oppose natural equality and liberty. Given the weight he puts on the state of nature in the passages previously mentioned, and the links he establishes between the original compact and the state of nature in this text, it is not a stretch to imagine that Otis would have given the same reply to Governor Hutchinson, Jonathan Boucher, Daniel Leonard, and others who questioned the usefulness of the state of nature as constitutional fiction.[63]

At the same time, the state of nature in this pivotal revolutionary text subsumes the social contract. Here the state of nature is a larger theoretical construct that stands for the absence of government before the first government was formed or when an existing one has failed. The colonists' natural rights grounded in the state of nature would remain effective even if the social contract never took place.[64] Moreover, as the rest of this chapter shows, *Rights* was written in conversation with other colonial texts in which the state of nature, more than the social contract, carried multiple meanings.[65] Such meanings included sin, salvation, the environment, innocence, and others. In the formulation of the American state of nature discourse these meanings interacted with political and legal connotations, thereby further enlarging the state of nature as a semantic field, and dwarfing revolutionary usages of the social contract by comparison.

63. See chapter 5, section 5.5 and chapter 7, section 7.2 on Loyalists below.
64. See Observator, no. VIII, *The Connecticut Courant*, April 30, 1771, which describes the original compact between "men in a state of nature," who are "solitary and defenceless," as "not the origin, but rather the first regulation and form of government, which ever had, and forever will have its rise from necessity." The same structure of the state of nature as the higher-order constitutional condition or fiction in which the social contract may take place features in Thomas Dawes, Jr.'s 1781 oration on the anniversary of the Boston massacre, in which he celebrated the 1780 Massachusetts constitution as passed by the people assembled in the state of nature. Dawes, "An Oration . . .," in Hezekiah Niles (ed.), *Principles and Acts of the Revolution in America . . .* (Baltimore, 1822), 47–52, at 52.
65. See Reid's useful taxonomy of the colonial understanding of contracts (original, social, charter, etc.) in *Constitutional History . . . The Authority to Tax*, chapter 5 and *passim*.

A point we will return to, but worth noting now, is that Otis's exposition in the 1764 *Rights* predates the state of nature discussions in Blackstone's 1765 volume 1 of the *Commentaries*.[66]

Next, Otis turns to property. He acknowledges that it is one of the ends of government in principle, and "the great, the incomparable *Harrington*" is confirmed by experience in that empire follows the balance of property.[67] However, none of this means that "government is *rightfully* founded on *property*, alone."[68] There must be something else.

What, then, is the origin of government? Citing and combining the language and imagery of Harrington's *Oceana* and Rousseau's *Social Contract*, Otis proposes an order both natural and mechanical that encompasses the planets, the attraction between the sexes, and the progression to complex societies that must still rest on "the necessities of our nature."[69] The scientific features of mechanistic nature, including the state of nature and human nature, leave no room for arbitrariness or caprice in government.[70]

Adams described Otis as increasingly incoherent over the course of their friendship.[71] *Rights* has also been characterized as incoherent

66. See chapter 4, section 4.2 below. It is not impossible that Blackstone's Oxford lectures, starting in 1753 and forming the basis of the *Commentaries*, had some sort of effect in the Colonies by 1761. If that were the case, such influence would be minimal, indirect, and would not diminish the remarkable vivacity and multiplicity of sources in the American discourse before the first volume of the *Commentaries* appeared in 1765.

67. On the American reception of Harrington see Somos, "Harrington's Project," 41–43.

68. Otis, *Rights*, 10.

69. Otis, *Rights*, 11, where Otis cites p. 5 of the 1764 translation of Rousseau's *Social Contract*.

70. On the rhetorical purpose of the science of government in Hobbes, with particular focus on the state of nature, see Evrigenis, *Images*. Reid argues that Otis's *Rights* is not "evidence of an emerging colonial political theory," but a case of "American clinging to a common-law definition of liberty" revolving around the security of property. Reid, *The Authority of Rights*, 36. Otis's use of Rousseau and emphatic deprioritization of property are among this text's features that suggest otherwise.

71. John Adams's diary entries for December 23, 1765, in *Works*, 2:163, and January 16, 1770, in *Works*, 2:226.

by later scholars.[72] The latter set of criticisms has its own problems. First, such criticisms seldom take into account the casuistry of forensic reasoning. It was common and normal for a sixteenth- or eighteenth-century legal text to marshall several arguments in support of the same point, even if some of these arguments functioned independently, or could be construed as contradictory. When such an (expected) accusation was made, the person who constructed the argument could discard the weakest part; offer a new synthesis that salvaged all arguments; or trap his opponent in another, more damaging contradiction by shifting the debate to new ground. For instance, if one said that some civil laws said one thing, but divine laws provided for another, and one were criticized for the missing connection and/or the ostensible contradiction between the one thing and the other, then one would offer a synthesis of the two and berate the critic for impiously not assuming that divine and civil laws are always in agreement, even though they do not fully overlap.[73] There are numerous time-honored instances noted in rhetorical and legal scholarship. Holding Otis to standards of twenty-first-century logical coherence instead of eighteenth-century forensic effect has limited rewards. So does faulting him for not prophetically structuring the principles of the American Revolution in accordance with the desires of later historians fixated on property, for instance, to the exclusion of other revolutionary themes. Another problem with existing criticisms of Otis's coherence is that none of them take into account historical shifts in standards of legal coherence, including the rise of alternative pleading in the common law after 1705, and its fall

72. Greene, *Constitutional Origins*; Bailyn, *Ideological Origins*, 177–80. Bailyn's point, namely that Otis confused public and private law by applying a seventeenth-century notion of Parliament as the highest court to eighteenth-century imperial problems, dissolves if we pay attention to Otis's references to the state of nature. Shipton posits that Otis's mental illness began in his early youth and exacerbated continuously. He modifies these statements with admissions that there is no evidence for either the early onset or the continuous decline. *Harvard Graduates*, XI.247–50.

73. One example is Samuel Adams's use of an argument by Hutchinson, his main opponent, in the January 20, 1772, *Boston Gazette* article discussed below.

in 1834.[74] By his contemporary standards, Otis's arguments were not unusually invalid or incoherent in *Rights*, even if reconstructing his sources and the structure of his argument now requires some effort.

This is not to say that the concerns raised by Otis's contemporaries should be disregarded. In his later years (before he died from a lightning strike in May 1783), Otis was increasingly volatile and erratic. However, if the 1764 *Rights* made a few unclear connections, they should be understood in the context of the contested and evolving American state of nature discourse. In addition to the ordinary casuistry and eclecticism of eighteenth-century legal reasoning, in the 1764 *Rights* Otis was synthesizing a range of state of nature arguments into an expansive defense of colonial rights. He was also experimenting with new supporting evidence, some of which found its way into official documents, as we will see in the case of Massachusetts' *True Sentiments*, the 1768 New Jersey petition and the 1772 Boston Pamphlet. Glitches and gaps in *Rights* are not symptoms of Otis's later mental issues, nor evidence of inferior constitutional thought, but part and parcel of the emergence of a distinct American state of nature discourse.

In *Rights*, Otis claimed several times to offer a new natural law stance. He cited with approval Rousseau's verdict on Grotius and Pufendorf as imperfect guides to natural law, merely listing ancient abuses.[75] He expressed his preference for Locke, but nonetheless continued to elaborate the natural law foundation of the colonists' rights based on Grotius and Pufendorf.[76] Otis's system is both a continuation and a reworking of the natural law tradition. A prominent feature of his system is deriving both the definition and limitation of good government from human *debilitas* and sociability.[77] Given that he was writing for forensic and

---

74. Roy W. McDonald, "Alternative Pleading, I," *Michigan Law Review* 48:3 (1950), 311–28. "Alternative Pleading, II," *Michigan Law Review* 48:4 (1950), 429–48. Reid, . . . *The Authority to Tax* (Wisconsin, 1987), 53. Daniel Hulsebosch notes the importance of alternative pleading in New York's October 18, 1764 Humble Petition. *Constituting Empire* . . . (University of North Carolina Press, 2005), 93.
75. Otis, *Rights*, 25–26.
76. Otis, *Rights*, 38–40.
77. *Debilitas* and *sociabilitas*: *Rights*, 13, 15. For background see Hont, *Jealousy*.

public audiences, and that alternative pleading was an accepted method, we should not see Otis's use of Pufendorf's state of nature and his insistence on the themes of *debilitas* and sociability as permanent parts of Otis's grand theory. However, it is also a mistake to give up on coherence entirely, and write off Otis's odd choice in *Rights* to praise Locke, but proceed with Pufendorf, as casuistry or signs of mental disease. The correct interpretation is somewhere in between.

Locke's state of nature offers a powerful protection for individual rights, but his state of nature is untenable and sooner or later must be renounced in favor of a polity with a common arbiter. Humans' natural physical weakness (sometimes called *debilitas*) and natural need to interact with others (*sociabilitas*) never go away. Otis's strategy of combining parts of the state of nature from Pufendorf, Locke, and Rousseau make sense if we remember that his intention was to defend colonial rights in a way that made them hard to dismiss with Lockean points, for instance about the binding consent that was both required for leaving the state of nature, and made a unilateral return to it illegal. It is on this ostensibly eclectic, but in fact experimental and original, natural law foundation that Otis took the next step, namely to justify popular sovereignty by emphasizing that *debilitas* and *sociabilitas* are distributed equally and universally in the state of nature, and remain inalienable human characteristics both in and outside the polity. Among other values, the right to representation and the illegitimacy of slavery are based on these two observably universal and (according to Otis) natural attributes of mankind. The people in turn delegate their divine and natural rights to a ruler, who holds and exercises them in trust.[78]

Otis's tweak of the natural law tradition continues with a particular deployment of *salus populi suprema lex esto*, "the safety of the people

---

78. People delegate but retain and can reclaim natural rights: *Rights*, 13, 17. On trust in the history of political thought see László Kontler and Mark Somos (eds.), *Trust and Happiness in the History of European Political Thought* (Brill, 2018). For a similar combination of Locke and Rousseau from 1766, see section 5.2 below, on the 1766 *British Liberties*.

should be the supreme law." A wide range of political arrangements have been justified by this broadly accepted principle. Some have argued that a single judge is needed to actualize the "should be."[79] Kings can be directly responsible for the people's welfare to God, but cannot be rendered accountable to the people, as that would reduce government to constant (or, what amounts to the same, potentially constant) debate and anarchy. Others have argued that representation, term limits, the separation of powers, or other constitutional arrangements serve this principle best. From the thinkers he cites it is evident that Otis was familiar with much of the spectrum of constitutional theories that were at one point or another supported on this principle. It is against this background that Otis chose neither to relegate this principle to vagueness and irrelevance, as others have done, nor turn it into an argument for a particular political arrangement. Instead, he inferred three general principles from the *salus populi* axiom. The first is that absolute monarchy was unacceptable. As Locke writes, only flatterers pretend that princes have "a *divine right* to absolute power."[80] The other is that the welfare of the people depended on life, liberty, and property. In Otis, the classic political principle becomes constitutive for and of the people, as well as a boundary condition for the legitimacy of governments, which do not have the right to do anything that does not advance the security of these goods. The third is that these goods cannot be secured outside the polity. Since God created mankind's natural sociability as well as our natural debilities that necessitate co-operation, it is unnatural for hermits and misanthropes to

79. E.g. James VI and I, *The True Lawe of Free Monarchies . . .* (Edinburgh, 1598).
80. *Rights*, 13. John Zubly made the same point in his best-known sermon, "The Law of Liberty," preached at the opening of the Provincial Congress of Georgia on July 4, 1775 (printed i.a. in Philadelphia). *Salus populi* is the reason why individuals leave the state of nature; to claim a divine right to rule dishonors God and compared to it "transubstantiation is but a harmless absurdity" (4–5). Partly on the the strength of this pamphlet, Georgia elected Zubly as their representative to the Second Continental Congress, where he opposed independence, resigned in November, and was banished from Georgia as a Loyalist.

try and leave society.[81] Liberty and property are necessary for life and inescapably social.[82]

This is not to say that Otis does not prefer one form of government to others. The *salus populi* axiom belongs to a broad natural law foundation in Otis's scheme, together with other elements. Similarly to Locke and other state of nature theorists, Otis considers the right to choose and change the form of government to be a state of nature right that remains in the individual. Regardless of whether a government takes democratic, aristocratic, or monarchical form, if the "administrators" who run the government violate the laws of nature and reason, they should be opposed, and eventually deposed.[83] The supreme power remains in the people as a "community," even though this community—unlike in Locke—does not exist unless government is dissolved.[84]

For Otis, the state of nature is not lawlessness, but a sphere in which natural law holds sway. Like Rousseau, Otis appreciated the strategic value of ambiguity in deploying the state of nature. Unlike Rousseau, he did not aim to maintain a perfectly balanced ambiguity. In the section on the natural rights of the colonists, Otis brought in cursory references to Locke to show that in resisting injustice and political failure, the state of nature could be brought about in reality. Moreover, this may not be a bad thing. People, Otis asserted, are equal and free by nature. Though valid and useful, this may seem an abstract way to approach the colonists' rights, Otis admits, as men are generally born into society, not nature.

81. Otis, *Rights*, 16. Cicero, *On Duties* (tr. Walter Miller, Harvard, 1913, repr. 1997), III.v.25; Althusius, *Politica* (Herborn, 1603), I.4–5 (Liberty Fund, 1995, 1:22–23); 1599 Geneva Bible, gloss 11 to Eph. 4.15. Linked to Hobbes in Somos, "Bible Interpretation and the Constitution of the Christian Commonwealth in Hobbes's *Leviathan*, Part III," *Storia del pensiero politico* 4:2 (2015), 175–201, at 198. Blackstone describes this as "civil death" in *Commentaries*, I.1.128.

82. Also see "The Preceptor," May 21, 1772, *Massachusetts Spy*: "man is a SOCIAL creature, and formed for a SOCIAL state; and that *society*, being adapted to the higher principles and destinations of his nature, must, of necessity, be his NATURAL state." Hyneman and Lutz, *American Political Writing*, 1:177.

83. Otis, *Rights*, 16–19.

84. Here Otis cites Locke, *Second Treatise*, II.13. Also see Richard Tuck, *The Sleeping Sovereign: The Invention of Modern Democracy* (Cambridge, 2016), chapter 4.

But this hinders not but that the natural and original rights of each individual may be illustrated and explained in this way better than in any other. We see here by the way a probability, that his abstract consideration of men, which has its use in reasoning on the principles of government, has insensibly led some of the greatest men to imagine, some real general state of nature, agreeable to this abstract conception, antecedent to and independent of society. This is certainly not the case in general, for most men become members of society from their birth, though separate independent states are really in the condition of perfect freedom and equality with regard to each other; and so are any number of individuals who separate themselves from a society of which they have formerly been members, for ill treatment, or another. If in such case, there is a real interval, between the separation and the new conjunction, during such interval, the individuals are as much detached, and under the law of nature only, as would be two men who should chance to meet on a desolate island.[85]

This is a sophisticated distinction between senses of the state of nature as the relationship between states, the relationship between men outside the polity, and the locus of inalienable natural rights that continue to operate in the polity. The former meaning, still used today in the academic discipline of international relations, was formulated clearly by Hobbes, and appears in several other American revolutionary texts, including Galloway's writings discussed below. The other meanings of the state of nature that Otis acknowledges in this passage are as an actual condition during the suspension of government or the transition from one state into another, and as a source of natural rights unextinguished by entering the polity. This use prefigures Adams's, Gridley's, and others' discussion

85. Otis, *Rights*, 42–43. Also e.g. 57: "I can see no reason to doubt, but that the imposition of taxes, whether on trade, or on land, or houses, or ships, on real or personal, fixed or floating property, in the colonies, is absolutely irreconcileable with the rights of the Colonists, as British subjects, and as men. I say men, for in a state of nature, no man can take my property from me, without my consent: If he does, he deprives me of my liberty, and makes me a slave. If such a proceeding is a breach of the law of nature, no law of society can make it just."

of Boston and the American colonies being in an orderly, non-anarchical state of nature, waiting for Britain to address the grievances and remedy the abuses that dissolved its government over the colonies after the Stamp Act of 1765. As we will see, the crucial inference they drew from Boston's stability was that the colonists, thrust into a state of nature by Britain but remaining *de facto* non-anarchical, combined themselves into a new polity through their relatively peaceful coexistence without civil law, and through their protestations against British attempts to enslave them. This state of nature is distinctly American partly because it is more expansive than European formulations, and does not defend a troubled polity or people but constitutes a new one; and partly because the revolutionaries explicitly anchored it in the American colonists' natural environment, customs, and constitutional heritage and practice.

Yet as in *Paxton's Case* three years earlier, Otis chose to expand not on these meanings that he clearly distinguished in *Rights*,[86] but on the meaning of the state of nature as a condition of equality. The next sentence reads: "The Colonists are by the law of nature free born, as indeed all men are, white or black," and is followed by a denunciation of chattel slavery. Otis argued that physical differences cannot justify slavery; and the habits of slave-owners makes them careless about their own liberty. As oppressing the colonies corrodes liberty in England (argued famously but not only by Burke in his 1783 speech on Fox's East India Bill), so slaveholding among the colonists, according to Otis, corrupts their right to rights.[87] *Pace* Reid, American nature was fundamental in defending the colonists' rights.[88]

---

86. He recapitulates them in *Rights*, 45.
87. Edmund Burke, *Mr. Burke's Speech* . . . (London, 1784). In "The Dangerous Thirteenth Amendment" Balkin and Levinson show that "slavery" in the Thirteenth Amendment has a broader meaning than chattel slavery. Also see Eric Slauter, *State as a Work of Art*, chapter 4. One should add that the founding generation was not only aware of the distinction between political and chattel slavery, but some of them, including Otis and Rush, deployed ancient moral psychology to argue that slave-owners are also victims of their own practices. Seneca the Younger, *De clementia* (ed. Susanna Braund, Oxford, 2011).
88. Reid, *The Authority of Rights*, 7: "It was much more representative of eighteenth-century legal thought to locate the authority for rights not in nature but in some

It was not the only source. Otis admitted that Parliament could legislate for the American colonies, but proceeded to argue that the common law and the colonists' "political and civil rights" both partly derived from, and set limits to, Westminster's ability to do so.[89] Otis also wished to preserve the colonies' existing charter rights, but, not content with defending them with arguments from royal prerogative, parliamentary statute, or corporate rights, as many of his peers did, he tellingly invoked the state of nature topos in support. The first settlers struggled with nature and savages, and it cannot be just to deprive their posterity from inheriting what they accomplished under their charter rights. The various sources of law combine to support one point.

> Every British Subject born on the continent of America, or in any other British dominions, is by the law of God and nature, by the common law, and by act of parliament (exclusive of all charters from the crown) entitled to all the natural, essential, inherent and inseparable rights of our fellows subjects in Great-Britain.[90]

Otis enumerated six such colonial rights, starting with representation at Westminster and the right to operate subordinate, local legislatures.[91] Moreover, natural law, common law, statutes, and charters also combine to protect the rights of black as well as white free-born colonists.[92]

The harmony between these types of law is unique to Britain, Otis explained. Take the case of the imposition of new taxes. It violates the colonists' rights as British subjects, and as men, "for in a state of nature, no man can take my property from me, without

other theoretical basis, such as ownership or purchase." Reid gives compelling counter-examples on pp. 10, 65–66, and in chapter 11. On p. 93 he explains his frustration that historians he engaged while writing his book (published in 1986) exaggerated the importance of natural law. That may be so; but Reid's overreaction needs to be corrected.

89. Otis, *Rights*, 49–50, 59–60, 66.
90. Otis, *Rights*, 52. To these sources, Otis adds equity on 53–54.
91. Otis, *Rights*, 53–54.
92. Otis, *Rights*, 56–57.

my consent."[93] This natural law, operative in the state of nature, coincides with the right to property granted by the British empire. By contrast, the Dutch and the French enslave their colonists, and their "maxims of state, will never suit with a British constitution."[94] When these laws clash, for instance when Parliament violates equity, and divine and natural laws, the acts of Parliament are void.[95] The judiciary, legislative, and executive "are a perpetual check and balance to each other."[96] This is the glorious constitution that American colonists have spent so much blood and money defending.

It is unclear who first articulated the notion that Britain's imperial legal system is the best because it best protects state of nature rights. It is unlikely that Otis invented it, even in the form of the accusatory demand that appears in his 1764 *Rights*. We find the same soon after, in Blackstone's 1765 *Commentaries* I.1 in the section on absolute rights, but not in earlier texts I know. For Hobbes, the state of nature is antithetical to good government. In Locke, people have to leave the state of nature and delegate the exercise of many of their natural rights. Alongside the state of nature literature, the other avenue, the history of English exceptionalism, also fails to identify the turning point when the state of nature became a standard. In other great milestones in legal history, such as Sir

93. Otis, *Rights*, 57.
94. Otis, *Rights*, 58. Also see 74, and memorandum to Mauduit in *Rights*, appendix, 112–113, restating that British liberties at home and abroad are exceptional.
95. Otis, *Rights*, 71.
96. By 1764, insisting on the separation of powers was a common attack on Hutchinson, who was both Chief Justice of Massachusetts and member of the Massachusetts Council. For Thacher's attack see Clifford Putney, "Oxenbridge Thacher: Boston Lawyer, Early Patriot," *Historical Journal of Massachusetts* 32:1 (2004). See the forceful March 16, 1767 letter from the Massachusetts Assembly to Dennys DeBerdt (Houghton, Arthur Lee Papers, bMS Am 811, folder 33): "The Office of a Chief Justice is most certainly incompatible with that of a Politician. The cool and impartial administration of common Justice can never harmonize with the meanders and Windings of a modern Politician." John Adams carefully and copiously annotated Montesquieu's passages on combining powers as a sign of tyranny in the *Spirit of the Laws*, e.g. I.217, 218, 223, 227–28 (Book XI ch. 6) especially the judiciary with the senate (I.228).

John Fortescue's *De Laudibus Legum Angliae* (written around 1468–71, *editio princeps* around 1543), John Selden's 1635 *Mare clausum*, or even Thomas Smith's 1583 *De Republica Anglorum*, in which Smith is committed to making English law as compatible with continental civil law as possible, English legal exceptionalism rests on particularities of English history, be it extensive maritime navigation, the rise of yeomen, or Saxon liberties. Of course, an accelerating shift from England's historical features toward natural law and rights in the state of nature as a standard for the British empire's exceptional constitutional authority was a sensible strategy for an increasingly revolutionary colonial lawyer who operated far from the metropolis and had to find alternative constitutional grounds for protest; but Otis is an improbable starting point for this shift.

The Assembly's memorandum to the colonial agent Jasper Mauduit, drafted by Otis and printed as an appendix to *Rights*, musters legal authorities for the opinion that statutory laws are invalid if they violate the harmony of laws that makes the English legal system exceptional.

> The judges of England have declared in favour of these sentiments, when they expresly declare, that *acts of parliament against natural equity are void.* That *acts against the fundamental principles of the British constitution are void.* This doctrine is agreeable to the law of nature and nations, and to the divine dictates of natural and revealed religion.[97]

The footnote to this passage cites *Bonham's Case* and Vattel. In the winter of 1610 the Court of Common Pleas, with Sir Edward Coke as Chief Justice, ruled that the College of Physicians wrongfully imprisoned Dr. Thomas Bonham for malpractice, partly because Bonham's lack of a license from the College did not constitute malpractice, and partly because the legislation that empowered the College to both decide and punish malpractice "provided an absurdity." *Bonham's Case* is a landmark in the

97. Drafted by Otis: Adams, letter to William Tudor, August 31, 1818, proceeding to cite the whole text (though with variations, e.g., lifting footnotes in the 1764 *Rights*, appendix, into the running text).

history of judicial review, with competing accounts of its precise role, but a broad consensus about its importance.[98] As far as his 1761 speech can be reconstructed, there Otis cited Coke in *Bonham's Case*: "When an Act of Parliament is against Common Right and Reason, or repugnant, or impossible to be performed, the Common Law will controll it, and adjudge such Act to be Void." Wroth and Zobel argue that Coke referred to the process of construing Parliament's meaning, which must be presumed to be in accordance with reason; and it was Otis who turned Coke's opinion into a constitutional argument concerning the "higher law" that checked Parliament's power.[99] Blackstone, by contrast, rejected interpretations of Coke's opinion in *Bonham's Case* that supported judicial review.[100] At the same time, he left theoretical room for the people (not the judges) to construct a new constitution, if Parliament fatally abused the existing one.[101] Wroth and Zobel point to Locke and Vattel as sources for Otis's

98. Glenn Burgess, *Absolute Monarchy and the Stuart Constitution* (Yale, 1996), 173–94. Hulsebosch, *Constituting*, 30–31. Other positions reviewed in Richard H. Helmholz, "Bonham's Case, Judicial Review, and the Law of Nature," *Journal of Legal Analysis* 1:1 (2009), 325–54.

99. By 1761, the independence of the colonial judiciary from London was one of the colonists' fiercest demands. For later landmarks in the American constitutional history of this issue, and the transformation of the same common law loci that Otis used, see John Adams's argument before Governor Bernard in Council, December 20, 1765; James Wilson, "Comparison of Constitutions" (1791) in *Works* (ed. Robert Green McCloskey, Belknap, 1967), 1:326–31; James Kent, *An Introductory Lecture to a Course of Law Lectures* ... (New York, 1794), 9–10; and Patterson's contrary but interesting opinion in Vanhorne's *Lessee v. Dorrance* (1795). Further cases can be added, and one suspects that Hamburger exaggerated when he wrote that *Bonham's Case* was dropped from the American discourse against Parliament. *Law and Judicial Duty* (Harvard, 2008), 278–79.

100. "But if the parliament will positively enact a thing to be done which is unreasonable, I know of no power that can control it: and the examples usually alleged in support of this sense of the rule do none of them prove, that where the main object of a statute is unreasonable the judges are at liberty to reject it; for that were to set the judicial power above that of the legislature, which would be subversive of all government." Blackstone, *Commentaries*, I.91.

101. Finnis, "Theoretical," 175. Wroth and Zobel's contrast between Blackstone's and Otis's approach to judicial review may overstate the latter's originality. Thomas Wood's *An Institute of the Laws of England* was one of the most influential legal texts in the eighteenth century, undergoing at least nine editions between 1720

transformation of Coke's opinion. However, Vattel does not appear in Otis's writings until 1764.[102]

Given the previously mentioned probability of Otis echoing Rousseau's *Second Discourse*, it is intriguing to consider the possibility

and 1763 (with some editions reissued with emendations and additions substantial enough to warrant considering them as a distinct edition). The Founders referred to Wood very frequently, and annotated copies show long-standing colonial attention to Wood's discussion of the limits of parliamentary authority. See for instance the list on p. 9 of the 1724 edition, including "Acts of Parliament that are against Reason, or impossible to be performed, shall be judged void," marked by Evert Wendell in Albany in 1725, the year after the book appeared in London (author's collection). This is the page John Adams cited in his December 20, 1765, speech in support of reopening the courts of Massachusetts in defiance of the Stamp Act, discussed below. "Notes on the Opening of the Courts, 19 December 1765," *Founders Online*, National Archives, http://founders.archives. gov/documents/Adams/06-01-02-0059. A few pages survive from Otis's copy of the 1734 edition of Wood's *Institute*, which the nineteen-year-old Otis began to annotate at the start of his legal studies in 1744 (Harvard Law School MSS Small Manuscript Collection, fragment). Blackstone and Josiah Quincy Jr. also began studying the law from Wood's *Institute*, following the advice in Sir Thomas Reeve, "Instructions to his Nephew Concerning the Study of the Law," in Francis Hargrave (ed.), *Collectanea Juridica* (London, 1791–92), 1:79–81; Daniel R. Coquillette, "The Legal Education of a Patriot: Josiah Quincy Jr.'s Law Commonplace (1763)," Boston College Law School Legal Studies Research Paper Series, Research Paper 114 (2006); Wilfrid Prest, *William Blackstone: Law and Letters in the Eighteenth Century* (Oxford, 2008), 68.

102. Otis, *Rights*, 118–20. The impact of Vattel's state of nature after 1775 is beyond the scope of this book, but it is worth noting that it became an alternative to Hobbes's state of nature. For Vattel, the moral norms that apply in a state of nature between individuals have an analogous set of moral norms in the state of nature that is the relationship between sovereign states. This is the sense adopted by the Supreme Court, *inter alia*, in the 1781 *Miller v. The Ship Resolution, and Ingersoll*, protecting the state of nature rights of neutrals at sea. John Quincy Adams restricted this sense to the relationship between Christian states in his 1839 *Jubilee of the Constitution*, delivered at the New-York Historical Society to mark the fiftieth anniversary of the inauguration of George Washington. "The Declaration of Independence recognised the European law of nations, as practised among Christian nations, to be that by which they considered themselves bound, and of which they claimed the rights. This system is founded upon the principle, that the state of nature between men and between nations, is a state of peace. But there was a Mahometan law of nations, which considered the state of nature as a state of war—an Asiatic law of nations, which excluded all foreigners from admission

that an early stage in the evolution of the American doctrine of judicial review drew on this text.[103] The separate literatures on American judicial review, and on Rousseau and judicial review, can be reconciled. The evidence of Otis's and Adams's use of Rousseau enriches Wroth and Zobel's point that Otis and others, such as John Adams, were an early source of judicial review. The basic insight is that in Rousseau, the individuals, even the whole society, can err about the general will from time to time. They need a group of independent and wise people to point out the correct course. Rousseau's work on the tribunate is sometimes interpreted as such a group.

In the 1764 *Memorandum* Otis also cites Justice Holt's elaboration of Coke's comment in the 1701 *City of London v. Wood*, that though "an act of parliament can do no wrong, though it may do several things that look pretty odd; for it may discharge one from the allegiance he lives under, and restore him to the state of nature." This passage in the memorandum probably originates from Otis himself, as McLaughlin identifies many of the same sources in Otis's 1761 Paxton speech.[104] Otis takes the *Bonham's*

within the territories of the state—a colonial law of nations, which excluded all foreigners from admission within the colonies—and a savage Indian law of nations, by which the Indian tribes within the bounds of the United States, were *under their protection*, though in a condition of undefined dependance upon the governments of the separate states" (New York, 1839).

103. In tracing judicial review to Rousseau, Freeman points to the well-tempered tribunate in the *Social Contract*, IV.5. Samuel Freeman, "Constitutional Democracy and the Legitimacy of Judicial Review," *Law and Philosophy* 9:4 (1990–91), 327–70. For a philosophical account of Rousseau's incompatibility with judicial review see Jeremy Waldron, "Rights and Majorities: Rousseau Revisited" in John W. Chapman and Alan Wertheimer (eds.), *Nomos XXXII: Majorities and Minorities*, 1990, 44–75. A historical outline is provided in Alec Stone Sweet, "Why Europe Rejected American Judicial Review—and Why It May Not Matter," *Michigan Law Review* 101:8 (2003), 2744–80.

104. McLaughlin, *Foundations*, 124–28. For a historically significant revisitation of this constitutional issue see New York State Bar Association, "Report of the Committee on the Duty of Courts to Refuse to Execute Statutes in Controvention [*sic*] of the Fundamental Law," presented January 22–23, 1915. In US Congressional serial set, issue 6784, *63rd Congress: 3d session, Senate Documents*, 16:3–61. The Committee included McLaughlin.

Case citations from Viner's *Abridgment*.[105] Then remarkably, and unlike in 1761, in 1764 Otis pairs Viner's report on *Bonham's Case* with Vattel's treatment of the colonies in his 1757 *Le droit de gens*.[106] This is how Otis redirects the common law points that reason, natural law, and equity set limits on Parliament's authority, and that ill-founded parliamentary legislation can cause a relapse into the state of nature, to bear on the rights of the American colonies.[107]

Otis seized on the point made in both *Bonham's Case* and Holt's opinion, namely that when Parliament exceeds its authority, it can trigger a lapse into the state of nature. Otis in both *Paxton's Case* and *The Rights of the British Colonies*, and the Massachusetts House of Representatives in various documents, used this connection to hint or explicitly claim that Westminster overstepped its authority vis-à-vis the American colonies. The presentation of the American state of nature as the difficult terrain inhabited by savages and converted into lush, fertile, civilized lands through the work and expense of the first settlers complements this claim. Once again, different state of nature traditions are thoughtfully and strategically mobilized and combined to support colonial claims. Otis adapts English, French, Dutch, German, and Swiss state of nature arguments to colonial America, both as a specific landmass and as an abstract source of rights. Three notable things about Otis's American state of nature innovation are that it invokes natural law, equity, and the law of nations to determine when Parliament exceeded its authority; it predates Blackstone's *Commentaries*; and it forms an important part of the American tradition of at least two legal discourses

---

105. 2nd ed., s.v. "Statutes," 494. The original text, in *English Reports*, 88:1602 (Hilary Term, 13 Will. 3) does not of course refer to Holt.
106. Vattel, *Le droit des gens* . . . ([Neuchâtel, 1757], London, 1758). Introduction and notes by Béla Kapossy and Richard Whatmore (eds.), *The Law of Nations* . . . (Liberty Fund, 2008).
107. Vattel features prominently in the 1764 *Rights* and the 1772 Boston Pamphlet as the preferred authority on the law of nations, and on the binding nature of constitutions. Vattel seems absent from Adams's notes on the 1761 *Paxton's Case*. It is probable that in 1761 Otis has not yet read the first, 1759 English translation of *Le droit de gens*.

that continue to this day, concerning judicial review and the nature of constitutions.[108]

While Blackstone's influence is overstated, what requires further study is the possible impact of Lord Kames's 1760 *Principles of Equity* on Otis's version of judicial review. Benjamin Franklin wrote to Kames as early as May 3, 1760, that he was reading *Principles of Equity*, that colonial judges would greatly benefit from it, and that he sent a copy to a judge on the Pennsylvania Supreme Court.[109] John Adams cites Kames's 1747 *British Antiquities* in the August 19, 1765 second letter in the *Dissertation on the Canon and Feudal Law* series. About the same February 21, 1765 Junto meeting where he cited Rousseau, Adams noted in his diary that he could have quoted Kames as well. Both of Adams's notes refer to *British Antiquities*, not to *Principles*. Otis's knowledge of the 1760 *Principles* by the time he published *Rights* in 1764 is worth pursuing because Kames posits a theory of progress in which the human mind improves, the law of nature and the law of human nature improve with it, and equity is the main judicial principle and source of institutions (notably equity courts)

108. While this genealogy of judicial review builds on Wroth and Zobel's assessment of Otis's contribution, there are colonial precursors. For instance, in an extraordinary letter, probably from 1754, William Kempe, New York's Attorney General, argues that if *Bonham's Case* can help overturn acts of Parliament, it works even better for provincial laws. The common law understands natural right and reason. Every person not legally captured is free, and has natural rights and reason. Therefore provincial laws that make manumission depend on a surety that the freed slave will not cause trouble are void. (Massachusetts Historical Society, Sedgwick Family Papers, Ms. N-851, series XII, section D, Box 115.) Similarly, there were alternatives to Otis's opposition of reason, natural law, equity, and the law of nations, to the doctrine of parliament's omnipotence. Francis Dana rejected Blackstone on this point because, according to Dana, the constitution itself controls Parliament and protects (among other things) the independence of the judiciary. (Massachusetts Historical Society, Dana Family Papers, Ms. N-1088, Box 34.) There are variations on Lord Kames's thesis on judicial review, as well. In Joseph Wimpey's scheme, civilizations improve, governments improve with them, but the state of nature remains the same. *Letters Occasioned by Three Dialogues concerning Liberty; wherein the Author's Doctrine Respecting the State of Nature, is Shewn to be Repugnant to Nature* . . . (London, 1777), 35.

109. *The Papers of Benjamin Franklin*, vol. 9 (ed. Leonard W. Labaree et al., Yale, 1966), 103–6.

that acts as suppletive to the improvable common law that honors progress, but cannot adjust to it without exogenous help. While the corrective
and complementary role of equity is not original, Kames's idea that it is
the progress of natural law that the common law has to adjust to with the
help of equity is a promising potential inspiration for Otis's invocation
of the state of nature to plead the colonists' cause, and for his embryonic
version of judicial review.[110]

According to Wroth and Zobel, Otis's opposition to searches and
warrants fanned but did not kindle the revolutionary spirit in Boston.
More original was his denial of Parliament's sovereignty to do anything
it pleased. I broadly agree with their point that Otis's use of *Bonham's
Case* in 1761 to invoke higher law and thereby expand the limits on the
powers of Parliament marks the beginning of an original American approach to constitutionalism.[111] Yet unlike Wroth and Zobel, I also think
it significant that in *Rights*, which the editors used to reconstruct Otis's
1761 speech, Rousseau was a source for the emergence of the American
doctrine of judicial review; and that one of the higher laws, in addition to
the constitution, natural law, and equity, was the law of nations.[112]

The *Rights of the British Colonies* is an important elaboration of the
theoretical foundations of the same arguments that feature in other revolutionary texts. These include defending the colonists' rights based on
consent, natural rights, the special case of English liberties that approximate the best possible liberties, and the special case of American settlers, who bought and worked lands in the New World. As we saw, each

110. On Kames's view of equity as both a check on Parliament and a mechanism for
legal evolution, see David Lieberman, *The Province of Legislation Determined: Legal
Theory in Eighteenth-Century Britain* (Cambridge, 1989), 159–75.
111. Wroth and Zobel, *Legal Papers of Adams*, 2:117–22.
112. While it has unique and original features, it is useful to place the American
doctrine of judicial review into a broader context. That kings can unking themselves by violating *salus populi* was a well-established trope. See i.m.a. Aquinas,
Summa (written 1265–74, Hackett, 1988), Q92 Reply Obj. 4, p. 28; and
Anon., "Touching the Fundamentall Lawes, or Politique Constitution of this
Kingdome . . ." (London, 1643), in Joyce Lee Malcolm (ed.), *The Struggle for
Sovereignty: Seventeenth-Century English Political Tracts* (Liberty, 1999), 1:261–
79, at 274.

of these arguments, some or all of which appear in most revolutionary texts, mobilizes the state of nature. The debate is about the nature of the state of nature and the implications of differing views for American independence; not about the centrality, let alone relevance, of the state of nature to the debate. At the time that relevance was obvious to all the parties involved.

In addition to rights to property and representation, Otis also anchored equality firmly in the state of nature. In *Considerations on Behalf of the Colonists* (1765), Otis's formulation of the state of nature as a condition of fundamental equality recalls Locke's version in chapter 2 of the *Second Treatise*.[113] Once again, Otis tied the colonists' natural rights and their duty to abolish slavery inextricably together in the natural equality he located in the state of nature. What was new in *Considerations* is that Otis developed parliamentary representation as another corollary of the radical equality in the state of nature that carries over into the polity, and becomes equally inseparable from the right to property and the imperative to abolish slavery.

In Otis's 1761 speech in *Paxton's Case*, the 1762 *Vindication*, the 1764 *Rights of the British Colonies*, the 1765 *Considerations*, and in Thacher's draft and *Warren's Case*, discussed below, we find remarkable sophistication and a multiplicity of state of nature sources that predate Blackstone's treatment of the state of nature in his *Commentaries* (1765–69), often said to be the pre-revolutionary legal source that most influenced the colonists.[114] Samuelson argued that in early 1765 Otis completely changed

---

113. Otis, *Considerations on Behalf of the Colonists. In a Letter to a Noble Lord* (London, 1765).

114. Edmund Burke's March 22, 1775 speech, "Conciliation with the Colonies": booksellers "have sold nearly as many of Blackstone's Commentaries in America as in England," and colonists "had lately fallen into the way of printing them for their own use." Cited in Slauter, "Reading," 7. David Schultz, "Political Theory and Legal History: Conflicting Depictions of Property in the American Founding," *American Journal of Legal History* 37:4 (1993), 464–95, and Steven J. Macias, "Legal Thought from Blackstone to Kent and Story," in Hadden and Brophy, *Companion*, 484–505, at 486–87, survey several decades' scholarship on Blackstone's direct influence on the American Revolution. Additional examples

his mind after reading Blackstone's *Commentaries* (the first volume of which did not appear until late 1765), abandoned the view of natural rights he drew from Locke, and unsuccessfully strove to formulate an imperial constitutionalist compromise acceptable to all sides.[115] Nothing could be further from the truth. Even milder assertions of Blackstone's influence require modification, and the history of the Revolution and early American constitutionalism is better captured through reactions to, and attempts to adapt rather than adopt, the system and substance of the common law presented in Blackstone's *Commentaries*.[116] More relevantly, there were several important colonial engagements with the state of nature before Blackstone.

Moreover, they were already American arguments. The colonists borrowed from Hobbes, Grotius, Pufendorf, Locke, Montesquieu, Rousseau, Burlamaqui, Vattel, and other state of nature thinkers, and adapted them to diverse arguments that all, nonetheless, related specifically to the American colonies' relationship with Britain. One of several ways they did this was to emphasize that it was their ancestors who arrived in America, without the benefit of protection from the Crown, but with chartered, royal, or natural rights; and it was they who bought and tilled

include Stephen M. Feldman, *American Legal Thought from Premodernism to Postmodernism: An Intellectual Voyage* (Oxford, 2000), 49–52 on the uncritical revolutionary adoption of "the Blackstonian faith in natural law as the foundation of the legal system," citation from 52. Horst Dippel's "Blackstone's *Commentaries* and the Origins of Modern Constitutionalism," in Wilfrid Prest (ed.), *Re-interpreting Blackstone's Commentaries: A Seminal Text in National and International Contexts* (Hart, 2014), 199–214, is a more recent example of overstating Blackstone's direct influence, as opposed to adaptations or outright rejections. In Gerald Stourzh, "Wiliam Blackstone: Teacher of Revolution," *Jahrbuch für Amerikastudien* (1970), 184–200, Blackstone is connected to colonial adaptations of the Glorious Revolution to anti-British purposes, in other words in uses of Blackstone as a source of arguments with which he disagreed.

115. Richard A. Samuelson, "The Constitutional Sanity of James Otis: Resistance Leader and Loyal Subject," *Review of Politics* 61:3 (1999), 493–523. Samuelson on the *Commentaries* "published in early 1765": 495. Otis changing his mind due to Blackstone already in "early 1765": 502–3, 505.

116. For further discussion see chapter 4, section 4.2 below.

the soil, defending the corner of civilization they wrested from "savage" natives and natural forces. According to several natural and common law principles, the rights that their ancestors acquired in the state of nature and bestowed on their descendants had endowed the revolutionaries with a legitimacy that was impervious to Parliament's authority.

3.4 THOMAS POWNALL

One of the texts Otis repeatedly but respectfully criticized in the 1764 *Rights* was *The Administration of the Colonies*, first published anonymously the same year by Thomas Pownall and revised and reissued several times until 1777. Pownall had been a friend of Franklin's since the 1754 Albany Congress, served as Lieutenant Governor of New Jersey in 1755–1757, Governor of Massachusetts in 1757–1760, MP in 1767–1780, and according to John Adams he was "the most constitutional and national governor in my opinion, who ever represented the Crown in this province."[117]

Miller shows that to understand Pownall's thinking about empire, it is useful to start with his earliest publications.[118] In 1750 Pownall published *A Treatise on Government*, based on his Cambridge student notes. It is a dialogue, but Pownall usually made it clear which speaker had the stronger argument. Part of his argument was that Harrington's notion of a balance of property was true and useful, but climate, geography and historical circumstances had made each country different. Government abridges state of nature liberties, but when government cannot provide protection, individuals relapse into a state of nature in relation to that government, and become free to choose another. Speaker A** (who in the expanded 1752 *Principles of Polity* became Marcus Licinius Crassus) objects: "All this Confusion and false Application of these Principles arises from our talking too crudely of a State of Nature, as the actual natural State of Man's Existence prior to all Government."[119] Those who, like

---

117. February 4, 1817, letter to William Tudor, *Works*, 10:243.
118. Miller, *Defining the Common Good*, 203, 208.
119. Pownall, *Treatise*, 46.

Hobbes, think that man in a state of nature is fierce, are just as wrong as those who think that he is "God-like." "That which is of Nature is the State of Nature; now that Man should subsist by and exist in Communion is of Nature, therefore the Communion of Mankind is the State of Nature."[120] The state of nature is a useful analytical concept, but the historical fact is that

> the social State or a State of Society is the real State of the Nature of Mankind. To separate and distinguish the Ideas of what is commonly call'd a State of Nature and a State of Government, for the purposes and ease of thinking is just and scientific; but to argue from such a State as an actual existing thing, and to refer to that as a Proof from Matter of Fact, is false and unphilosophical.[121]

Next, Pownall praises Harrington for showing that society and government are natural, not artificial, as Hobbes believed. This makes nature, pre-political community, and government all subject to a unified body of natural laws. "For you see by this how every Man is even from his Birth, and in that State of Nature which we talk of, so connected to the Community, that his Attachment is indissolvable but by the Dissolution of the Community; and you perceive how all those Ties by which he is connectd [sic] and subordinate, spring naturally one from another to the utmost Strictures of Government, and yet all consistent with that Liberty, which is consistent with the natural State of Man, the Social."[122] In 1764, Pownall donated a copy of *Principles of Polity*, a revised and expanded version of his *Treatise*, to Harvard with the inscription,

> As it is the most perfect State of Society, wherein a People enjoy their Rights with Liberty & their Property in Peace, under the Blessings of an enlarg'd Communion: So it is the true End of all Government to protect

120. Pownall, *Treatise*, 48.
121. Pownall, *Treatise*, 47–48.
122. Pownall, *Treatise*, 62.

the Unity of this Communion, in its several conspiring Orders & Powers. Those therefore, who by their Station have a Share in the Lead of, or by the Appointment may be set apart to teach the People, cannot more essentially serve Mankind, than by promoting this *great Truth*. To promote this Truth as arising from Nature & leading to Peace, in Opposition to those erroneous Theories, which, arising from Artificial Invention, lead to Faction, was the following Treatise written & publish'd, & is now put into the hands of the Students of Harvard College, recommending to them to point out all their Studies, & all their Labors, to the Peace of Mankind, as founded in the Universal Law of Nature, & in the positive Command of the Author of Nature.[123]

Pownall's donation note is consistent with the technical terminology and discussion in his treatise. He was asking Harvard professors, clergy, lawyers and other graduates in 1764 to spread the message that the British Empire was a natural community, united in a transatlantic state of nature. It is difficult to establish exactly how much Pownall's notion of the British empire as a natural community in the state of nature influenced Loyalists and Patriots. Many Loyalists certainly appealed to the colonists' natural allegiance to the empire, either as an extended family or as a ring in Pownall's expanding circles of natural allegiance, something larger than a country, but smaller than all mankind. Patriots, on the other hand, presented the colonists *without* Britain as a natural community in the state of nature. Though Pownall's natural community resonated with the revolutionaries, as did his argument that when government fails to protect the individual, a state of nature resumes between them, Pownall also thought that state of nature rights must be given up to government, and do not allow an individual to exempt her- or himself from demands made by the government.

123. Pownall, *Principles of Polity*, Houghton, *EC75.P8758.752.p(A).

THE STAMP ACT AND THE STATE OF NATURE

4.1 *WARREN'S CASE* (1765–67)

The American reconceptualization of the European state of nature ideal charted in the previous chapters went into full swing during the Stamp Act controversy. After months of debate and opposition in the colonies, the Stamp Act came into force on November 1, 1765. It imposed a direct tax on the colonies, ordering that most printed materials be produced on paper bearing an embossed revenue stamp. The stated aim of the tax was to defray the cost of troops stationed in North America after the Seven Years' War. Out of sixty-three articles, the first one takes up about one-third of the whole text of the act and details the types of legal documents that need a stamp. Though colonial objections to the Stamp Act are usually described as focusing on taxation without representation, it is worth noting that in addition to taxing commercial and insurance documents, newspapers, printed colonial laws, playing cards, and the like, the Stamp Act emphatically taxed the provision and administration of justice.

Alongside the high constitutional theory in the colonial reactions detailed above, the everyday experience of resistance and uncertainty continued to generate extraordinary state of nature discussions. On November 6, 1765 John Morse, deputy sheriff for the county of Berkshire, arrested Peter Curtis of Lanesborough for defaulting on a debt and tried to take him to jail. A group of men, including Seth Warren, freed Curtis and explained to Morse that as long as the courts were closed due to the Stamp Act, and writs issued after November 1 remained invalid, no one could be made whole, and no could be arrested. When the supply of legal protection ceases, the civil law cannot make demands. Ten men agreed to free anyone taken to jail as long as these conditions continued, and sought the approval of the other residents of Lanesborough.

On November 26, Morse and his companions tried to arrest Curtis and one of his defenders, John Franklin (who was also in debt) in a tavern.[1] A scuffle ensued. The men paused the fighting, sat Morse down in a chair, and asked him to explain why they were wrong to think that all laws had been effectively suspended. Morse declined to enter the debate, and the men, fifteen at least, promptly resumed the brawl. Eventually the citizens of Lanesborough dragged Morse's party out of the tavern, threatened to throw them on a bonfire, and chased them out of town. They were charged and sentenced. Seth Warren appealed against his fine to the superior court and was heard by a grand jury in Boston in April 1766. He was defended by Joseph Hawley (1723–88), one of the most prominent revolutionary figures in Massachusetts.[2]

Warren pleaded not guilty to some charges and asked for a more lenient sentence for others. He argued that Franklin's arrest was unlawful, as the writ of execution was not stamped, adding, for good measure, "if the stamp-act ever had any force." Another defense was that "as the affair happened in a time of general confusion and distress," the whole

1. For an important analysis of the crippling effect of the Stamp Act on low-cost institutions such as land conveyancing or debt litigation see Justin DuRivage and Claire Priest, "The Stamp Act and the Political Origins of American Legal and Economic Institutions," *Southern California Law Review* 88:4 (2015), 875–905.
2. Ernest Francis Brown, *Joseph Hawley, Colonial Radical* (New York, 1931).

town, usually peaceful, was "driven to a degree of madness and did not perhaps in all things act with prudence and temper." The constitutional uncertainty created by the Stamp Act should be taken into account as extenuating circumstances. "Philanthrop," probably Jonathan Sewall, hitherto a close friend of Adams's and soon to become Attorney General of Massachusetts (in November 1767), began to publish pieces against Warren and his associates in the *Boston Evening-Post*. Hawley's reply was printed in the July 6 and 13, 1767 issues.

Among other remarkable gambits, Hawley accused Governor Thomas Hutchinson, as Chief Justice, of derailing the trial by instructing the grand jury that the Lanesborough group's actions constituted a riot, and therefore they should find Warren guilty. Hawley begged to differ.

> Here it may be proper to mention that in arguing the case for the defendants to the jury, it was twice if not three times observed by me to the jury, that I humbly conceived it ought to be remembered that the time when this affair happened was truly extraordinary; that it was all within that period when there was almost a total blank in the course of law, a chasm and gap in the administration of justice, when the King's writs did not run in the province, which, I conceived, altered the nature of the case almost wholly; and that the same transactions which in ordinary time would have been most criminal, might become so in a low degree, if not wholly justifiable.[3]

3. *Boston Evening Post*, July 13, 1767. The equation between the ineffective administration of justice and the state of nature had a few recent precursors by the time Hawley defended Warren, especially between 1759 and 1762. In *History of Scotland* (1759), William Robertson wondered why assassinations were so frequent in the sixteenth century. After a short stadial theory, Robertson concluded that assassinations are characteristic of weak governments, in an early stage of development, which are able to legislate for a crime but cannot enforce the law, nor stop individuals from judging and punishing crimes as if they still were in a state of nature. In these circumstances some assassinations are just, because they mete out capital punishment according to civil law, even while they draw on the state of nature right to punish to do so. 1:4.311–33 in the 5th edition (London, 1762); restated in *The History of the Reign of the Emperor Charles V...*, vol. 1 (Dublin, 1762), 41. David Hume's *History of England* was not published in chronological sequence, but was rearranged to provide a linear

The jury followed Hutchinson's lead and confirmed Warren's fine. Hawley now came up with an unusual strategy. Before sentence was pronounced the next morning, he interjected that the circumstance of a legal vacuum was so important that *Warren's Case* should be dismissed with a *nolle prosequi*, a notice of no further prosecution, and either the whole thing dropped or, taking Hutchinson's point to its conclusion, a new charge brought against Warren for high treason. The legal vacuum left no middle ground. Next, Hawley launched into a description of the state of Massachusetts in this legal vacuum on the day of the long scuffle in and outside the tavern. It was

indeed little other than a state of absolute outlawry, but in a very different sense from what some have represented—they were outlawed, that is deprived of the benefit of the law, without any crime, offence or default of their own; in the face of Magna Charta, which ordains that no man shall be outlawed, that is as Lord Coke justly says, be deprived of the benefit of the law, unless he be out-lawed according to the laws of the land—And is it not notoriously true and a most plain and evident fact, that at the very time and for months after, all the inhabitants of this province (without any crime or default in forty nine fiftieths of them) were deprived of the benefit of the law, yea put into a state much worse than to be merely deprived of the benefit of the law, or a state of nature—For nothing is plainer or more easily demonstrated, than that the people of a country where civil justice is denied (which is the case where the King's writs, which are to be granted of course, are denied)

historiography in later editions. Hume published the last of the six volumes in 1762, including the reign of Richard III (vol. 2 or 3 in later editions). It ends with a historiographical reflection that has a passage on the absurdity of Saxon and ancient English law. Hume details several absurd legal practices and concludes that the period that ancient constitutionalists regarded as the fountain of the common law was "very little advanced beyond the rude state of nature," given the preponderance of violence, arbitrariness, and a "pretended liberty" that simply meant "an incapacity of submitting to government" (1762 London edition, 2:442–43). More briefly, Hume makes the same point about Anglo-Saxon law and ancient Germans in general, who unfortunately were "very little removed from the original state of nature" (1:153).

and where the courts, which by the constitution have cognizance and jurisdiction of criminal offenses, will continue to exercise their jurisdiction, and will hold and adjudge the same overt acts to be criminal, and in the same degrees so, which the law adjudges criminal at a time when civil justice has its free course and is duly administered; I say nothing is more plain than that the people of such a country are in a worse state than a state of nature.—But every one knows such was the state of this province at the time aforesaid.

Hawley asserted that the colonists were not to blame for the breakdown of law in 1765, "this mischief & calamity, before unheard of, unless in a time of absolute civil war." In fact, resisting writs showed the colonists to have "the principles of the English constitution written on their hearts and interwoven with the constitution of their minds." Echoing Gridley's December 20, 1765 account of the state of nature (discussed below) as better than the aftermath of the Stamp Act, Hawley described the condition created by the cessation of legitimate British authority as worse than the state of nature.[4] In another interesting gambit, he argued that unless the law of nature became operative when civil laws failed, people would sink to the level of mere inanimate existence. The usual recourse people have when the state fails is to return to the state of nature. This is the case in the colonies, because the Stamp Act has abrogated civil laws.

4. Philanthrop (Sewall?) agreed that a breakdown in the provision of justice would throw the colonists into a state of nature, but argued that the Stamp Act created only a partial, not a full breakdown. August 10, 1767 *Boston Evening-Post*. In his charge to the grand jury at the start of the March 1767 term, Hutchinson gave a variation on this theme. Even if the laws are excellent, society falls back into the state of nature if the laws are not executed, and everyone should guard themselves individually. "Let the Body of Laws be ever so good,—if they are not executed, 'tis worse than a State of Nature, because we guard ourselves in a State of Nature, and therefore are more secure than in a Society, where we depend on the Laws for our Protection, which are not put in Force." In this sense Hutchinson agreed with Gridley and Hawley that "there has been a Failure of Law amongst us," and instructed the jury to help execute the law to restore order. *Quincy's Reports*, 234.

This must be true, or else it must be reasonable that mankind at such a season should consent to be in a state worse than brutal, that is, in the same state with inanimate mater, subject to the laws of attraction and repulsion only; or what is a state more confused still, a perfect chaos, which I suppose no one will attempt to maintain—It is therefore to be enquired, whether in a state of nature (which was the state the people of this province were in on the said 26th of November, to say the best of it), it would have been reasonable for Seth Warren to have acted the part he appears to have done at the time.

The state of nature is not simply the domain of natural laws. Laws in the state of nature are, in Hawley's account, distinct from the laws that guide physical existence. They contain rights, such as the right to leave and enter a state, that do not apply to the non-human parts of nature. Moreover, even when civil laws are reinstated, and a criminal case is being tried, it is valid to consider whether the defendant's actions were reasonable in the state of nature. The standard of reasonableness applies across the state of nature—polity divide.

On these foundations, Hawley finds that no debtor can be expected to accept imprisonment in a state of nature, not because property disappears and the debt may not be due, but because the law no longer protects the debtor. Deputy sheriff Morse "in that state of nature undertook to act as an officer, and by colour of law and authority of society (which then was in fact suspended and did not exist) and therefore with great partiality," tried to force one debtor into jail without offering commensurate legal protection, including the right to recover debts owed to the debtor, or to have the debtor's repayment legally recorded. This showed bias and a disregard for justice, and that Warren and his companions acted rightly against Morse. Hutchinson misled the jury as to the facts of the case. Either Warren's sentence should be quashed or, if Hawley's proposition that the colonies were at the time in a state of nature was rejected, Warren should be tried for high treason. Foreshadowing the dynamic of debates about the state of nature at the First Continental Congress, discussed below, in Hawley's defense strategy the state of nature dramatizes, polarizes, and serves to exclude the middle ground and the chance for compromise.

Hutchinson, acting as Chief Justice, disbarred Hawley for publishing his extraordinary state of nature account of the case in the *Boston Evening-Post*. Sewall wrote a long reply in the August 10, 1767 issue, agreeing with Hawley that a dissolution of government would have placed the province in a state of nature, but arguing that as long as some government remained, that condition was averted. Even if some Lanesborough residents were confused, and the courts did not work, government did not cease entirely. Quincy notes that in August 1767 Hutchinson referred to Hawley's account in his instruction to the grand jury at the start of the term; but as Quincy was called out of the room, he only records that he was told that Hutchinson discussed it, not what the substance was.[5]

If the depositions in the original case can be believed, it is remarkable that not only Hawley in 1766–1767, but the good people of the small town of Lanesborough on November 6, 1765, were intimately familiar with the argument that the Stamp Act and the closure of the courts placed them in a state of nature. Presumably they drew their detailed knowledge of state of nature arguments by reading and discussing the newspapers, including the state of nature articles mentioned so far. They also expected it to be widely enough known to challenge the deputy sheriff to debate it. By November 1765, the state of nature permeated public discourse in the colonies. It was only four days earlier that in Oxford, England, William Blackstone finished and dated the preface to the first volume of the *Commentaries*, before sending the manuscript to press.

4.2 ENTER BLACKSTONE

Blackstone's 1762 *Law Tracts in Two Volumes*, and the essays in it that were published separately before 1762, are undoubtedly important for the American Revolution. Blackstone's criticism of inherited titles and privileges, as both unreasonable and causing degeneracy, prefigured Paine's

5. *Quincy's Reports*, 246.

incendiary argument by almost thirty years.[6] His edition of "The Great Charter and the Charter of the Forest" and analysis of England's "antient constitution" influenced Jefferson. However, the notion that American independence owed a substantial intellectual debt to Blackstone is false not only because Otis's speech predates the *Law Tracts*, let alone the later *Commentaries*, but also because the state of nature does not appear in the *Law Tracts* at all and, as we have seen, a lively and rich constitutional discourse concerning the state of nature already existed in the colonies before the first volume of the *Commentaries* appeared.[7] Blackstone dated the preface to November 2, 1765. The first volume is unlikely to have reached the colonies before 1766, long after Otis's *Rights* was read and discussed in England, as shown for instance by Thomas Whately's rejoinder, *The Regulations Lately Made*, published in London still in 1765.

As the *Commentaries* made an impact on later stages of the American state of nature discourse, we should clarify what Blackstone said on this matter. Blackstone effectively questioned the notion of the state of nature as a condition of isolated individuals. Only divine and natural law would exist in this condition, but as man "was formed for society" and cannot live alone, this formulation is implausible.[8] The known accounts of man's earliest existence also contradict it.[9]

Yet Blackstone did not jettison the notion entirely. To form society, people must leave the state of nature by relinquishing natural equality in exchange for justice and arbitration. That powers should be surrendered to wise, good, and competent people, who most approximate God, is an unassailable principle; "but the application of it to particular cases has occasioned one half of those mischiefs which are apt to proceed from misguided political zeal."[10] At first, Blackstone declared that he would

6. Blackstone, *Law Tracts*, 21–22. Thomas Paine, 1791 *Rights of Man*, Part 1, in Paine, *Rights of Man* ... (ed. Mark Philp, Oxford, 1995), 134–35.
7. For views that Blackstone had a formative impact on American revolutionary ideology, see chapter 3, footnote 114 above.
8. Blackstone, *Commentaries*, I §2.43.
9. Blackstone, *Commentaries*, I §2.47.
10. Blackstone, *Commentaries*, I §2.48.

not dispute how various forms of government fit the general principles for constituting a just government. He did, however, deploy the meaning of the state of nature as a locus of rights. In Book I, chapter 1, "The Rights of Persons," Blackstone set out to distinguish between absolute personal rights, which "appertain and belong to particular men, merely as individuals or single persons," and relative rights, "indigent to them as members of society."

> By the absolute rights of individuals we mean those which are so in their primary and strictest sense; such as would belong to their persons merely in a state of nature, and which every man is entitled to enjoy whether out of society or in it. But with regard to the absolute duties, which man is bound to perform considered as a mere individual, it is not to be expected that any human municipal laws should at all explain or enforce them. For the end and intent of such laws being only to regulate the behavior of mankind, as they are members of society, and stand in various relations to each other, they have consequently no business or concern with any but social or relative duties.... For the principal aim of society is to protect individuals in the enjoyment of those absolute rights, which were vested in them by the immutable laws of nature; but which could not be preserved in peace without that mutual assistance and intercourse, which is gained by the institution of friendly and social communities. Hence it follows, that the first and primary end of human laws is to maintain and regulate these *absolute* rights of individuals. Such rights as are social and *relative* result from, and are posterior to, the formation of states and societies: so that to maintain and regulate these, is clearly a subsequent consideration. And therefore the principal view of human laws is, or ought always to be, to explain, protect, and enforce such rights as are absolute, which in themselves are few and simple; and, then, such rights as are relative, which arising from a variety of connexions, will be far more numerous and more complicated.[11]

11. Blackstone, *Commentaries*, I.1.119–21.

Absolute rights are state of nature rights and have force both in and out of society.[12] Human laws concern only the public behavior of members of society and therefore cannot explain or underpin absolute duties. In other words, the state must protect absolute rights as they exist in the state of nature—but it cannot enforce absolute duties. Public sobriety, for instance, can be enforced; but private sobriety, an absolute duty, cannot.[13] In sum, Blackstone gives the state an impossible mission. Just like the common law, the state is both a pragmatic construct and an aspirational embodiment of open-ended progress, and its actions can be tested against both internal coherence (the formal rule of law) and against the mandate for improvement that it received from mankind, or at least the nation, in its natural condition.

Blackstone gave a previous version, without the state of nature, in *An Analysis of the Laws of England* (1756), where he distinguished absolute rights ("such as belong to Individuals") from relative rights ("such as regard Members of Society"). All he wrote there was that

The absolute Rights of Individuals, regarded by the municipal laws, (which pay no Attention to Duties of the absolute Kind) consist in political or civil Liberty. . . . Political or civil Liberty, is the natural Liberty of

---

12. Compare Francis Hutcheson's "imperfect rights," *Short Introduction*, II.ii.iii, 113 in Liberty Fund ed.
13. Drunkenness is also Mill's paradigmatic illustration in *On Liberty* (1859). See, e.g., Mill, *On Liberty and Other Writings* (ed. Stefan Collini, Cambridge, 1989), 82 and *passim*, on why the state cannot punish individuals for exercising their "social right" to private drunkenness but can punish a policeman for being drunk while on duty, anyone for public drunkenness that endangers others, and anyone already convicted for harming others while drunk, if that person gets drunk again. John Cook, Solicitor General of the Commonwealth who prosecuted Charles I, noted that people can corrupt themselves to a state worse than bestial, as animals do not get drunk and do not abide tyranny. *Monarchy No Creature of Gods Making* (Waterford, 1652), 76–79. Hobbes lays out the distinction between natural and civil law, and the state's proper and improper legislative intervention, through drunkenness. A surprising amount of English constitutional thought can be explored through this theme.

Mankind, so far restrained by human Laws as is necessary for the Good of Society.[14]

The absolute rights of Englishmen are personal security, personal liberty, and private property. This equation is familiar from the common law literature well into the eighteenth century. Individual absolute rights exist, but must be limited by the state for the common interest. According to this formula, the legitimacy of acts of Parliament, for instance, would be determined based on balancing the absolute rights of individuals and "the Good of Society." Why Blackstone added the state of nature in the 1765 *Commentaries*, volume I, and why he replaced the *Analysis'* model of restraint and balancing with a scheme in which the state must aim to protect absolute rights, even though it never can, are important questions, but beyond the present scope.

In a case of converging development, in *A Vindication of the British Colonies* (1765), in which he took on Martin Howard Jr.'s *A Letter from a Gentleman at Halifax* (written in Newport, Rhode Island), Otis cited absolute and relative rights in the *Analysis* to build a model quite similar to Blackstone's update in the *Commentaries*. Otis recalled the "shoal of sycophants" that cling to tyrants "like the little wretches in the well known print of Hobbes's Leviathan," and described Howard's work as "truly *Filmerian*." Then he tackled Howard's point that colonists may not claim rights greater than those granted by charter. The laws of God, nature, the common law, and the British constitution all bestow rights on British subjects, Otis explained; charters can only enhance them. "The natural absolute personal rights of individuals, are so far from being opposed to political or civil rights, that they are the very basis of all municipal laws of any great value." Then follows Otis's summary of the aforementioned scheme in Blackstone's "accurate and elegant analysis of the laws of England." Otis emphasized that Britons' "birth-rights" could not be curtailed by charters, as they are granted by "the laws of God and nature, as well as by the common law and the constitution of their

14. Blackstone, *An Analysis of the Laws of England* (2nd ed., Oxford, 1757), I.iv.7.

country."[15] Co-opting Blackstone's *Analysis*, Otis denied that human laws can limit natural rights (which Blackstone explicitly said) and foreshadowed Blackstone's own shift of emphasis in the *Commentaries*, where the quality of human laws is measured by the extent to which they protect state of nature rights.[16]

Though earlier in the *Commentaries* Blackstone declined to measure forms of government against the standard of justice, after he set out the new model of absolute, state of nature rights, Blackstone began to examine how well English laws protected absolute rights as found in the state of nature. On entering society, people must give up parts of their natural, God-given liberty, and promise to obey their particular society's laws. "And this species of legal obedience and conformity is infinitely more desirable, than that wild and savage liberty which is sacrificed to obtain it." Yet political or civil liberty is natural liberty "so far restrained by human laws (and no farther) as is necessary and expedient for the general advantage of the publick."[17] Every restraint on man's power to injure his peers diminishes natural liberty, but "increases the civil liberty of mankind."

15. Otis, *Vindication*, 1–11.

16. In the next edition, Otis added an appendix to reply to criticisms of the *Vindication*. An article in the March 2, 1765 *Providence Gazette* objected to Otis's invocation of natural rights, arguing that natural relations exist only between natural entities, not between mother country and colonies. To counter the natural rights criticism, Otis replied with the state of nature (though unlike in *Paxton's Case* and *Rights*, he did not use the term). The colonists' allegiance is natural in a limited sense that does not extend to all mankind, let alone to all of nature. "Society is certainly natural, and exists prior to, and independent of any form of civil polity." There is a natural relationship within families, between metropolis and colonies, and between sovereign states regulated by the law of nations. *Vindication*, 45–46.

17. *Commentaries*, I.1.121. Blackstone cites Justinian's *Institutes* I.3.i in support: "Facultas ejus, quod cuique facere libet, nisi quid jure prohibetur," "civil liberty as the power to do whatever one pleases, except what is prohibited by law." Alexander M. Burrill points out in his 1850–51 *New Law Dictionary and Glossary . . . Adapted to the Jurisprudence of the United States*, s.v. "Civil liberty" (218), that Blackstone miscites the passage on purpose, omitting "nisi quid *vi aut* jure prohibetur," "except what is prohibited *by force* or law." Bracton and Coke cite the phrase correctly, and Burrill praises Blackstone for the "emendation" that brings the notion of liberty up to date with modern standards, disallowing restraint by force independently from law.

According to Blackstone, every unnecessary restraint, including super-fluous laws, "is a degree of tyranny." Locke is right that "where there is no law, there is no freedom." However, the best constitution is designed to maintain civil liberty while leaving "the subject entire master of his own conduct, except in those points wherein the public good requires some direction or restraint."[18] It is striking how Blackstone's use of the state of nature prefigures the nineteenth-century heyday of liberalism, as well as Hegel and Kant insofar as Blackstone also found that his own country happened to best approximate the ideal standards.

In other words, Blackstone employed the state of nature to transform the way in which constitutions were compared and evaluated. Instead of measuring the excellence of constitutions against more conventional yardsticks, such as agreement with divine laws, the rule of law rather than men,[19] or the extent to which citizens or their interests are well-represented, Blackstone set out to compare and assess constitutions, in-cluding England's, against the standard of their ability to provide *salus populi* with the minimal legal curtailment of individual absolute rights in the state of nature. Blackstone tackled the task of comparing consti-tutions against this new standard with gusto, and shortly declared the

> Taking the passage out of context, Burrill missed the point and extent of Blackstone's preterition. The emphasis of the omission is not on contrasting force and human law, and modernizing civil liberty by expanding human law's purview. Blackstone omitted "force" because the absolute right to use force in the state of na-ture must be restrained when entering society and placing oneself under its human laws. This restriction applies to individuals as well as the government. Blackstone contrasts the legal fiction of the state of nature, a state of "wild and savage liberty," with human society, not pre-modern with modern definitions of civil liberty.

18. *Commentaries*, I.1.122. James Sedgwick, a twenty-five-year old English lawyer and official, published *Remarks Critical and Miscellaneous on the Commentaries of Sir W. Blackstone* (London, 1800), followed by a second edition in 1804. Sedgwick objected to Blackstone's version of the state of nature on two counts: for his un-clear distinction between divine law and natural law in the state of nature, and for the self-contradiction in describing the state of nature as a condition of individual isolation that is unsustainable for any length of time, given man's natural sociability and needs. *Remarks*, 12–14.

19. This ideal runs from Aristotle through Poggio Bracciolini and Harrington uninter-rupted to Blackstone and Adams's draft of the 1780 Constitution of Massachusetts.

superiority of the English constitution over others. This constitution, "very different from the modern constitutions of other states," matches best the ideal combination of public safety with maximum liberty.[20] To epitomize the point, Blackstone invoked slavery, the most profound test of how far natural and civil liberties diverge in a country.

> And this spirit of liberty is so deeply implanted in our constitution, and rooted even in our very soil, that a slave or a negro, the moment he lands in England, falls under the protection of the laws, and with regard to all natural rights becomes *eo instanti* a freeman.[21]

Recall Otis's argument that equality in the state of nature carried over to the American colonies, making slavery unacceptable. Likewise in Blackstone, albeit for a different specific piece of land, the state of nature persists in the constitution and soil of England powerfully enough to void human laws that violate the absolute rights of all men in a state of nature. In the case of Englishmen these absolute rights, Blackstone continued, are "usually called their liberties." This is a valuable remark and confirms that the rights in the state of nature belong to the technical, legal meaning of "liberties," as we encounter them, for instance, in the story of the evolution of the *English Liberties* and *British Liberties* books from 1680 until 1774, discussed in the next chapter.

Blackstone proceeded to evaluate the English constitution against the standards of preserving state of nature rights with minimal and beneficial political restrictions, and enhancing political rights when state of nature

20. This state of nature standard of constitutional excellence had a considerable impact on the second stage of the American state of nature discourse, when it was used to condemn Britain for sacrificing too much colonial liberty for not enough protection. See the discussion of the Boston Pamphlet below. Also see Caleb Evans, a pro-American Nonconformist, in *British Constitutional Liberty* (Bristol and London, 1775), 8–9. For Evans's views see James E. Bradley, *Religion, Revolution and English Radicalism: Non-conformity in Eighteenth-Century Politics and Society* (Cambridge, 1990).
21. Blackstone, *Commentaries*, I.1.123, citing Salkfeld, *Reports* (London, 1717–24), 666.

rights were constrained. He argued that despite historical deviations from this standard, now toward tyranny, now toward anarchy, the vigor of the English constitution saved and continues to save optimal liberty from demise: "As soon as the convulsions consequent on the struggle have been over, the ballance [sic] of our rights and liberties has settled to it's [sic] proper level; and their fundamental articles have been from time to time asserted in parliament, as often as they were thought to be in danger."[22] Among such moments, Blackstone numbered Magna Carta forced from King John and confirmed by Henry III, the 1297 *Confirmatio Cartarum*, the 1628 Petition of Right, the *Habeas Corpus Act* of 1679, the 1688 Bill of Rights, and the 1701 *Act of Settlement*, which recognized liberties as "the birthright of the people of England."[23] Blackstone called these collectively "the *declaration* of our rights and liberties" and asserted that it is in England that the collection of some preserved natural rights, and civil or acquired rights that society substituted for those natural rights that had to be traded in, came closest to the ideal state of nature standard that he proposed.[24]

22. Blackstone, *Commentaries*, I.1.123.
23. Sir John Dalrymple wrote that the Catholics around James II advised him in 1688 not to escape to France because his departure "would reduce all things to a state of nature, and render the re-establishment of the nation impracticable: An argument which weighed much with James, who did not reflect, that convulsions had proved the sources of liberty to the English, ever since the invasion of the Saxons." Dalrymple agreed with Blackstone that 1688 was among the beneficial lurches toward freedom. *Memoirs of Great Britain . . .* (2nd ed., London, 1771), 237.
24. Blackstone, *Commentaries*, I.1.123–25. Often, though not always, it is useful to think about the state of nature in Blackstone and in the American texts discussed here as the standard that regulates the trade-off between natural and civil rights. If a writer regards the state of nature as awful and untenable, then there is a low threshold to giving up natural rights, and a high threshold to preserving natural rights. Conversely, if the state of nature is a condition of independence and/or sociability and benevolence, then the political state has to work harder to remain a preferable proposition. However, this analytical use of the state of nature as the standard for the trade-off does not explain variation in views on whether the state of nature disappears or remains after the state comes into existence. Writers who think the state of nature is terrible, and those who regard it as nice, are equally able to argue that it is ever-present in parallel with the state, or not.

Among the natural rights unaffected by the transition to society, Blackstone counted the rights to life and limb. Limbs "enable man to protect himself from external injuries in a state of nature."[25] This right, effectively a right to the natural means of self-defense, grounded in the state of nature, is highly valued in the common law, and excuses several types of self-defense and other acts that would be otherwise considered misdemeanors. Through these and other rights, the state of nature entered Blackstone's scheme not only as a necessary legal fiction and a constitutional standard, but also a living principle in the common law.

In this context, it is instructive to compare Otis's and Blackstone's views of the Glorious Revolution. They both saw 1688 as a constitutional revolution, but through opposing temperaments of interpretation. Blackstone argued that the dethronement of James II was justified and carried out by the people as a whole, represented by Parliament. Although according to Blackstone the Glorious Revolution could have been less revolutionary, it improved the legal protection of rights, and it remained pervasively valid, given that all posterity, including Blackstone's generation, lived under the protection and benefits of the Glorious Revolution's constitutional settlement. Blackstone praised in particular the wise self-restraint of Parliament for arguing that James tried but failed to subvert the constitution, which would have dissolved government and "reduced the society almost to a state of nature," as Locke described it in *Second Treatise* II.19, "Of the Dissolution of Government." According to Blackstone, instead of such a lapse, the constitution remained intact—only the throne became vacant.[26]

In *Rights*, published more than a year before the first volume of the *Commentaries* appeared, Otis referred to the same Locke chapter in

25. George III copied this phrase in "A Short Abridgment of Mr Blackstone's Commentaries on the Laws of England," RA GEO/32 p. 32.
26. Blackstone, *Commentaries*, I.3.203–6. Compare Locke's *Two Treatises* (London, 1764) that Hollis edited, and a copy of which he donated to Harvard, describing himself as "Thomas Hollis, an Englishman, a Lover of Liberty, the principles of the Revolution, & the Protestant Succession in the House of Hanover, Citizen of the World." Houghton *EC75.H7267.Zz764l Lobby IV.2.2.

relation to James's dethronement. The people, represented by Parliament, turned to natural justice and equity "in all parts of the *British* empire, to put the liberties of the people out of the reach of arbitrary power."[27] In volume I of the *Commentaries* (1765), Blackstone cited a short passage from Parliament's February 12, 1688 proclamation of William and Mary as king and queen. In *Rights*, Otis agreed that the same 1688 proclamation is worth citing, but unlike the few lines in Blackstone's four-volume work, Otis dedicated 10 of his 120 pages to reprinting (in his word, transcribing) strategic selections from the acts of the revolutionary parliamentary session of January 22–February 13, 1688, starting with the *Act for Removing and Preventing All Questions and Disputes Concerning the Assembling and Sitting of this Present Parliament*, and continuing with the Bill of Rights. From both, Otis cited selectively. In the first act he emphasized the authority of Parliament to assemble itself, and omitted sections on the appointment of the monarchs. From the Bill of Rights he cited the twelve charges against James II, including several that also featured in the *Rights* and in colonial grievances against Parliament, such as those concerning the misuse of prerogative to levy money and raising troops without consent; the thirteen "antient rights and liberties" that the 1688 parliament claimed to restore; and provisions for the independence of the judiciary.

Ominously, Otis next invoked chapter 13 from Locke's *Second Treatise*, which concerns not the replacement of the executive (as one would expect, given Otis's previous discussion of the Glorious Revolution), but of the legislative. Otis cited passages from Locke to show that the rights that James II violated, and lost the throne as a result of violating, could not be violated by Parliament, either. Relying on Locke, but creatively playing with the text, Otis explained that the people could never transfer certain natural rights, including the right to decide whether or not the legislative is fulfilling the obligations imposed upon it by the people it was supposed to represent, or their right to constitute a new legislative, should they deem it necessary. The section concludes with Otis's reference to

27. Otis, *Rights*, 22–23.

chapter 9 of the *Second Treatise*, "Of the Ends of Political Society and Government," which anchors the constitutional baseline of representation, trust, and the obligations of the legislative, in Locke's discussion of the state of nature. Otis, in sum, adapted the state of nature apparatus that justified the Glorious Revolution against the monarch to the colonial grievances against Parliament.[28]

Otis in 1764 and Blackstone in 1765 agreed on the historical significance of the Glorious Revolution, that it dissolved the old order and created the one they still lived in, and that it expanded and improved the protection of Englishmen's rights. They differed in that Blackstone, while accepting the legal framework created by the Glorious Revolution as new and binding, praised the 1688 legislature for preserving the continuity of the constitution as far as possible, and for avoiding a lapse into a state of nature in the fashion Locke described in the *Second Treatise*, chapter 19, by pretending that the throne simply became vacant, without a crisis in the underlying constitution. Otis, by contrast, relished the thought that "by the abdication, the original compact was broken to pieces." [29]

Otis then shifted the object of discussion to argue that the legislative can be dismissed for the same reasons as the executive. We can surmise that Blackstone's answer might have drawn on another section of the *Commentaries*, Book I, section 2, where Blackstone suggested that Locke went too far when he wrote that altering the *legislature* would create a state of anarchy in which the people are free "to constitute to themselves

---

28. Dickinson spelled this out in the *Essay*, 366–74, esp. 368–71. "Changing the words *Stuarts* for *parliament*, and *Britons* for *Americans*, the arguments of the illustrious patriots of those times, to whose virtues their descendents owe every blessing they now enjoy, apply with inexpressible force and appositeness, in maintenance of our cause, and in refutation of the pretensions set up by their too forgetful posterity, over their unhappy colonists." Otis's use of the Glorious Revolution as the latest stage of the common law's trajectory of expanding liberties in all of Britain's dominions also offers a revealing contrast with genealogies of resistance that positioned the pre-revolutionary colonies as the heirs of 1649. As we will see, John Adams, for instance, otherwise close to Otis in training, temperament, political allegiances and life experience, preferred 1649 (or, when he was looking at regicide less gleefully, the whole 1642–51 period) to 1688.

29. Otis, *Rights*, 98.

a new legislative power."[30] And while Otis and Blackstone agreed that the Glorious Revolution brought more and better protected individual rights, Otis emphasized that the people's turn to natural justice that Locke described took place throughout the whole empire. Along the same lines, Otis also made it clear that the benefits of the Glorious Revolution applied to "the rights and liberties of the subject in all parts of the dominions," not only in Britain.[31] Blackstone concluded that limited monarchy is the happy medium between the two extremes of a monarchy of "divine indefeasible hereditary right," and the people electing every executive. The Glorious Revolution was a great instance of the common law finding the right path between extreme historical swings.[32] From similar premises and from interpreting the same texts and aspects of the Glorious Revolution, Otis's conclusion was that taxation without representation violated an eternal constitutional principle that was historically enshrined in the Glorious Revolution, which occurred in the first place largely because of a century of Stuart attempts to undermine the principle.[33]

Otis's disagreements with Blackstone on the Glorious Revolution and concerning Parliament's authority shares the tone with much of Blackstone's reception in the American colonies. This chapter aims to show that a substantial body of original constitutional thought emerged in the colonies before the *Commentaries,* and underpinned the Revolution to such an extent that one can plausibly argue that Blackstone's influence has been exaggerated. A corroborating but distinct thesis is that American constitutional theorists and practitioners hardly found Blackstone applicable even after the *Commentaries* reached the colonies. While an exhaustive demonstration of this thesis is beyond this chapter's scope, a few telling examples are worth noting. Edmund Trowbridge (1709–1793) was appointed Attorney General

30. Blackstone, *Commentaries,* I.2.52 in the first American edition (Philadelphia, 1771).
31. Otis, *Rights,* 98.
32. Blackstone, *Commentaries,* I.3.211.
33. Otis, *Rights,* 99.

for Massachusetts in 1749, and replaced in 1767 because of his polit-ical sympathies for the Crown. His reputation for judicial impartiality was such that he became Judge of the Superior Court the same year, and he was one of the presiding judges in the Boston Massacre Trials of 1770. On October 15, 1771, Judge Trowbridge wrote to William Bollan, former Advocate General and colonial agent for Massachusetts, con-cerning the inapplicability of Blackstone in Massachusetts. Trowbridge complained of profound uncertainty about the new structure and hi-erarchy of colonial law. Could anyone, for instance, still appeal against Superior Court decisions to the King in Council? The answer was yes, according to Blackstone, Trowbridge wrote to Bollan (probably refer-ring to Commentaries, I.4), but since Blackstone failed to provide a rea-sonable explanation, he had no authority on this point. Trowbridge then declared that in his own practice, he would assume that Blackstone was wrong on this score.[34]

We find the same view in Virginia. Starting in 1790, St. George Tucker (1752–1827) used the Commentaries as a set text for teaching law at the College of William & Mary in Williamsburg. One of his most insistent arguments was that the Commentaries, though they embodied an admi-rable spirit of laws and ambition to clarify and systematize the law, were inapplicable in America.[35] He emphasized the importance of federal and state law, and accorded even civil law a greater authority than the common law, let alone British statute law. His long 1797 letter to Prof. Christoph Daniel Ebeling on Virginia's legal history mentions Blackstone as the best example of what Americans must replace. It also informed Ebeling that Tucker was preparing an edition of the Commentaries, with comments of his own, though the magnitude of the task and the ex-pense of preparing the edition would probably force him to abandon the

34. Trowbridge, "Letters to William Bollan," Massachusetts Historical Society, Ms. S-813.
35. Klafter reaches the same conclusion based on different evidence. Craig Evan Klafter, Reason over Precedents: Origins of American Legal Thought (Greenwood Press, 1993), chapter 2.

project.[36] Nonetheless, in 1803 Tucker's *Blackstone's Commentaries: with Notes of Reference to the Constitution and Laws of the Federal Government of the United States and of the Commonwealth of Virginia* was published in Philadelphia. Tucker's Note B to volume 1, "Of the Several Forms of Government," begins,

> Government, considered as the administrative authority of a state, or body politic, may, in general, be regarded as coeval with civil society, itself: Since the agreement or contract by which each individual may be supposed to have agreed with all the rest, that they should unite into one society or body, to be governed in all their common interests, by common consent, would probably be immediately followed by the decree, or designation, made by the whole people, of the form or plan of power, which is what we now understand by the constitution of the state; as also of the persons, to whom the administration of those powers should, in the first instance be confided. Considered in this light, government and civil society may be regarded as, generally, inseparable; the one ordinarily resulting from the other: but this is not universally the case; man in a state of nature has no governor but himself: in savage life, which approaches nearly to that state, government is scarcely perceptible. In the epoch of a national revolution, man is, as it were, again remitted to a state of nature: in this case civil society exists, though the constitution or bond of union be dissolved, and the government or administrative authority of the state be suspended, or annihilated. But this suspension is generally of short duration: and even if an annihilation of the government takes place, it is but momentary: were it otherwise, civil society must perish also.

36. Tucker to Ebeling (via William Bentley), June 30, 1797. Houghton GEN MS Am 1855. On Ebeling as integral to the German reception of the American Revolution see Eugene Doll, *American History as Interpreted by German Historians from 1770 to 1815* (Philadelphia, 1949), and the excellent Horst Dippel, *Deutschland und die amerikanische Revolution: sozialgeschichtliche Untersuchung zum politischen Bewusstsein im ausgehenden 18. Jahrhundert* (Cologne, 1972, tr. as *Germany and the American Revolution, 1770–1800: A Sociohistorical Investigation of Late Eighteenth-Century Political Thinking*, North Carolina, 1977).

Even during the suspension, or annihilation of government, the laws of nature and of moral obligation, which are in their nature indissoluble, continue in force in civil society. Hence social rights and obligations, also, are respected, even when there is no government to enforce their observance. This principle, during state convulsions, supplies the absence of regular government: but it cannot long supply its place; government, therefore, either permanent or temporary, results from a state of civilized society.[37]

St. George Tucker's son, the jurist, law professor and Congressman, Henry St. George Tucker, Sr. (1780–1848) continued his father's work in his *Commentaries on the Law of Virginia* (1836–37, with an early version in 1831). There is compelling evidence to connect father's and son's projects to supplant Blackstone. In 1801, the year he concluded his legal studies under his father's tutelage at William & Mary, Henry covered his *Commentaries* with marginalia. In his marginalia, Henry remarked that English common law had been overthrown in America. He wryly added that the principle mentioned by Blackstone, namely that the king can do no wrong, "would be carrying fiction rather too far" in the United States.[38] Other major departures from Blackstone that Henry noted include that in the United States the people, not the Crown, are the source of power, and the judiciary is a check on, not an emanation of, the royal prerogative (fig. 4.1).[39] Still, Blackstone remains useful because he shows the value of reflection and orderly transformation that the chaotic legal system of Virginia, and the United States, should

37. I disagree with Horst Dippel's view that Tucker's 1803 oeuvre was an "Americanised five-volume version of Blackstone's *Commentaries*" and straightforward evidence of Blackstone's influence. Dippel, "Blackstone's *Commentaries*," 200. Similarly, Madison's 1788 reference to Blackstone does not show Blackstone's impact "in the early hours of American constitutionalism" (201).
38. Harvard Law School has volumes 3 and 4. Harvard Law School, Rare Treatises, B: Blackstone, *Commentaries* (London, 1791), III.17.254.
39. Harvard Law School, Rare Treatises, B: Blackstone, *Commentaries*, III.3.24. See also III.7.92 and 106 against Blackstone on ecclesiastical law and admiralty cases; and IV.31.397 against Blackstone on prerogative.

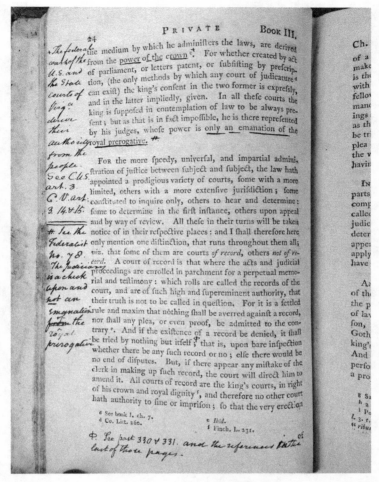

Fig. 4.1 Henry St. George Tucker's annotations in Blackstone, *Commentaries*, III.3.24. Harvard Law School Library, Historical & Special Collections, Rare Treatises, B.

emulate (fig. 4.2).[40] Many of these marginalia are worked out in Henry's *Commentaries on Blackstone's Commentaries*, lecture notes printed for his students in 1826, where Henry explains which parts of Blackstone need the most urgent revision.[41] Building on his father's work, Henry's

40. Harvard Law School, Rare Treatises, B: Blackstone, *Commentaries*, III.17.269. Also see Henry's marginalia on III.23.356, wishing that Virginia's proceedings were more uniform.
41. Harvard Law School, Special Collections, Rare Treatises T.

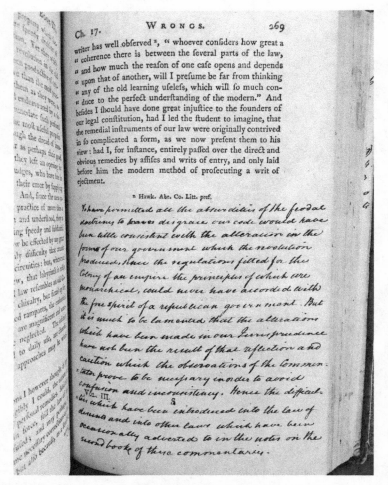

Fig. 4.2 Henry St. George Tucker's annotations in Blackstone, *Commentaries*, III.17.269. Harvard Law School Library, Historical & Special Collections, Rare Treatises, B.

attempt to systematize the laws of Virginia proved successful enough to make his *Commentaries* widely used not only in American legal instruction, but also by legislators, such as Charles J. Faulkner (1806–1884), to record changing and evolving laws.[42] A remarkable line connects

42. See the extensive annotations in Henry St. George Tucker, *Notes on Blackstone's Commentaries: For the Use of Students* (1826) (Virginia Historical Society, K 50 B57 T79 1826). The catalog entry suggests that Faulkner used and annotated this

projects to *replace* Blackstone's *Commentaries* with an American counterpart and with the generation and systematization of a new, independent legal tradition.

Another notable case is Simon Greenleaf (1783–1853), who succeeded
Joseph Story as Dane Professor of Law at Harvard. In 1801, the same
year that twenty-one-year-old Henry St. George Tucker was covering
his *Commentaries* with marginalia in Williamsburg, the eighteen-year-
old Greenleaf embarked on his legal studies with Ezekiel Whitman and
started a commonplace book.[43] Almost all entries cite Blackstone, even
those that no longer applied in the United States in 1801 (forfeiture for
striking a person in the king's presence, the king's pardon, treason, etc.).
One exception is the entry on Statute, where Greenleaf outlined the US
justice system and detailed ways in which it departed from the outline
in Blackstone's *Commentaries*. An important reason for early American
ambivalence toward Blackstone is that Blackstone, as Hulsebosch
points out, was unusually retrograde in claiming that the colonies had
to obey Parliament because they were "conquered or ceded countries."[44]
Interestingly, in his private notes on selected parts of the *Commentaries*,
George III summarized the same position (fig. 4.3).

One thesis of this chapter is that the formative phase of the Revolution
predates the 1765 first volume of the *Commentaries*. The preceding details
illustrate the limits to Blackstone's influence on American constitutional
thought even after 1765. There were also practical barriers. Coquillette
suggests that at least one thousand copies of the *Commentaries* reached

copy when he was a student at Tucker's law school in Winchester, VA. That may
be, but there are also numerous manuscript entries recording changes to Tucker's
notes, for instance from 1829, when Faulkner had already entered the Virginia
General Assembly.

43. Simon Greenleaf, commonplace book, Harvard Law School, Special Collections,
MS 4440.

44. Hulsebosch, *Constituting Empire*, 69–70, 74. Also see Hulsebosch, "An Empire
of Law: Chancellor Kent and the Revolution in Books in the Early Republic,"
Alabama Law Review 60:2 (2009), 377–424, 399–400, on the paradoxical increase
in English law books' and reports' availability in the United States after independence, and their status as guiding but less binding than in England.

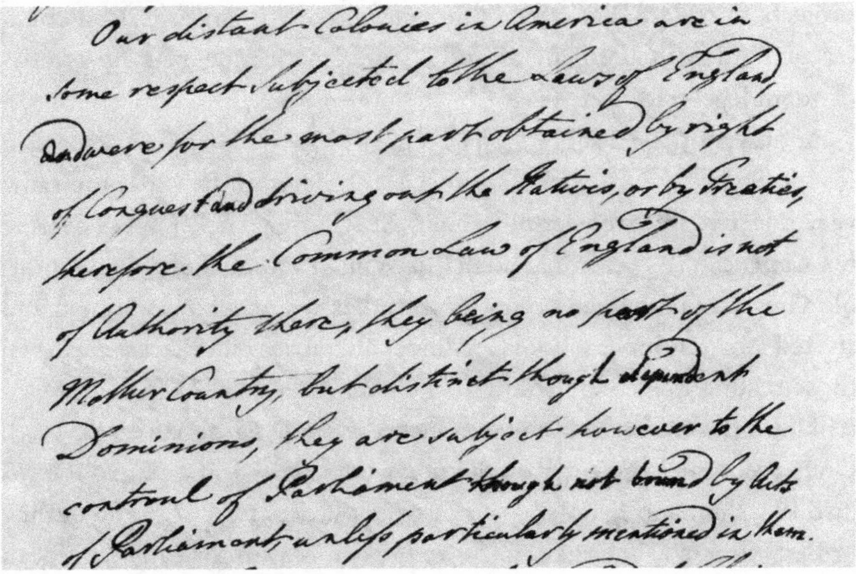

Our distant Colonies in America are in
some respect subjected to the Laws of England,
and were for the most part obtained by right
of Conquest and driving out the Natives, or by Treaties,
therefore the Common Law of England is not
of Authority there, they being no part of the
Mother Country, but distinct though dependent
Dominions, they are subject however to the
controul of Parliament though not bound by Acts
of Parliament, unless particularly mentioned in them.

Fig. 4.3 George III, "A Short Abridgment of Mr Blackstone's Commentaries on the Laws of England," RA GEO/ADD/32/1005. Royal Archives/© Her Majesty Queen Elizabeth II 2018.

America before the pirated Philadelphia edition of 1771.[45] However, the copies I examined, including those owned by the authors discussed here, suggest that most of them bought the cheaper 1771 American edition first and acquired the more accurate and expensive Oxford edition later. In 1786, twenty-three-year-old James Kent bought the 1771 Philadelphia edition when he started his fabulous legal library.[46] Even Adams's copies at the Boston Public Library indicate that for his first systematic study of the *Commentaries* he used the 1771 edition, while his incomplete and mixed set of 1768–1770 Oxford editions shows signs of a more selective, later engagement, for instance on self-defense and juries.[47] Adams, who used an

45. Daniel R. Coquillette and Neil L. York (eds.), *Portrait of a Patriot: The Major Political and Legal Papers of Josiah Quincy Junior* (6 vols., Boston 2005–2014), II.19–20 n. 37. Stourzh shows that John McKenzie in Charleston must have used the early Oxford editions. "William Blackstone: Teacher of Revolution," 190.
46. Hulsebosch, "Empire," 409.
47. 1771 Philadelphia ed.: BPL, Adams 151.19. 1768–70 Oxford ed.: BPL, Adams 93.2.

eclectic range of items as bookmarks, left a delivery order for hay in volume 4 of the Oxford set, dated March 18, 1791. This seems to support Adams's own recollection in an October 9, 1815 letter to Richard Rush: "When I began the study & indeed the practice, the name of Blackstone, had never been pronounced in America, & scarcely in England."[48]

Of course, there are counter-examples. John Dickinson's 1774 *Essay on the Constitutional Power of Great-Britain over the Colonies* cites Blackstone approvingly more often than disapprovingly. In undated and unpublished essays written by James Madison, Blackstone is cited as an authority for the equality of all people in the state of nature that survives the transition to the polity, for the consequent natural right to suffrage, and to show the risk of extending the state of nature argument to support a natural right to property, which would complicate Virginian legal reform concerning slavery and Native Americans.[49]

4.3 BOSTON AGAINST THE STAMP ACT

As mentioned, the sixty-three merchants engaged James Otis, Jr. and Oxenbridge Thacher to represent them in *Paxton's Case* in 1761, and Thacher was active in the Junto with Gridley, Otis, John Adams, and other Boston lawyers. Over fifty years later Adams described him as universally loved and respected, and not motivated by personal interests, like Otis, in his ferocious opposition to what he saw as a conspiracy by Parliament and its colonial allies such as Hutchinson and Andrew and Peter Oliver to annul all colonial charters and introduce uniform government with heavy taxes and episcopacy.[50] Adams's account is

48. Early Access document at Founders Online, http://founders.archives.gov/documents/Adams/99-02-02-6524.

49. James Madison, drafts, University of Chicago, Regenstein Library Special Collections, George Nicholas Papers, Folder 31.

50. John Adams to Hezekiah Niles, February 13, 1818. Early Access document at Founders Online, https://founders.archives.gov/documents/Adams/99-02-02-6854. Here Adams ranked Thacher after Otis, and ahead of Samuel Adams and John Hancock, in his influence on the "Revival of American Principles and Feelings" in 1760–66.

corroborated by Thacher's surviving writings, including *The Sentiments of a British American* opposing the Sugar Act, and a letter he sent in 1762 to Benjamin Prat, Chief Justice of New York, in which Thacher described Massachusetts as "in the deep sleep or stupor that Cicero describes his country to be in a year or two before the civil wars broke out."[51]

Though ideally positioned for a leading role in the Revolution, Thacher died in the summer of 1765, too soon to engage even in the Stamp Act controversy. Nevertheless, his contribution to American independence may not be limited to his better-known argument against the Sugar Act.[52] In February 1764 Thacher wrote to Robert Treat Paine, a fellow lawyer and later signer of the Declaration of Independence, that he was planning to be inoculated against smallpox. The inoculation was unsuccessful. Thacher infected his wife, who died that summer.[53] Shortly before Thacher's own death on July 9, 1765, John Adams visited and asked him if he had seen the May 29, 1765 Virginia Resolves against the Stamp Act. Thacher replied that he had and that he would also deliver a speech "as my dying testimony against this infernal tyranny, which they are bringing upon us." He flew into a frenzy, and Adams changed the subject, so as not to upset the sick man any further.[54]

It is tempting to speculate that a one-page document among Thacher's surviving and unpublished papers is an early draft of this speech. It explicitly addresses the Stamp Act. The title, if I am deciphering "BP" and "BC" correctly, is "Minutes for the Argument on whether the British Parliament have a Right to tax the Colonies according to the British Constitution." (fig. 4.4).

51. Thacher to Prat, 1762. *Proceedings of the Massachusetts Historical Society* 20 (1882–83), 46–48, at 46.
52. Thacher, *The Sentiments of a British American* (Boston, 1764). See Reid on the Sugar Act, recognized by most only in retrospect, in light of the Stamp Act, as a constitutionally debatable attempt to raise revenue in the colonies. Reid shows that the few people who immediately grasped its constitutional significance included Hutchinson on the pro-empire side, and Thacher and Edmund Burke on the opposing side. *Authority to Tax*, chap. 17.
53. Putney, "Thacher."
54. John Adams to Hezekiah Niles, February 13, 1818.

Unlike Otis, who drew on British liberties but also on natural law and the rights that survive from the state of nature, Thacher argued that the British constitution, as higher law, provided the baseline against which statutory law must be assessed. Further, Parliament could not be trusted to make such assessments of its own laws. Implied is the argument for American judicial review over matters that concern the American colonies. Another criterion for good law is that the delegation of state of nature rights must be understood as a means toward the end of political stability; therefore the delegation of the exercise of natural rights to representatives cannot exceed the aim and extent that this intention makes necessary. Insisting on this principle of proportionality in limiting state of nature rights only as far as necessary is a characteristic feature of the texts in the first, remonstrative stage of the American state of nature discourse, which emphasized protest and grievances more than the stability and independence of the natural community of American settlers.

> Constitution is the establish'd form of Government (Johnson). What is establish'd, must be something already done, a Standard to which to repair, and try all Acts of Government.—Ergo, if we have any Constitution at all, it is not alter'd, as some suppose, by every New Acts. They surely are not to be tried by themselves, but are to be measur'd by this Standard and must Square with this establish'd form of Government.

While Otis began to work out this doctrine on the basis of popular sovereignty, inspired partly by Rousseau, Thacher was led to this point by a creative reconstruction of common law constitutionalism. Agreeing on the ends and offering complementary but non-overlapping means is the pattern that best characterizes Otis and Thacher, Gridley's star pupils.[55] As Thacher certainly followed Otis's work closely, this possible draft of his

---

55. The unclear interpolation above the first line of Point 4 may show that Thacher insisted that his argument is based on the common law alone, without natural rights. The corresponding note suggests that he was planning to elaborate on this point and cite authorities. Thacher as a student of Gridley's: Coquillette and York, *Portrait*, 2:76–77, 5:878.

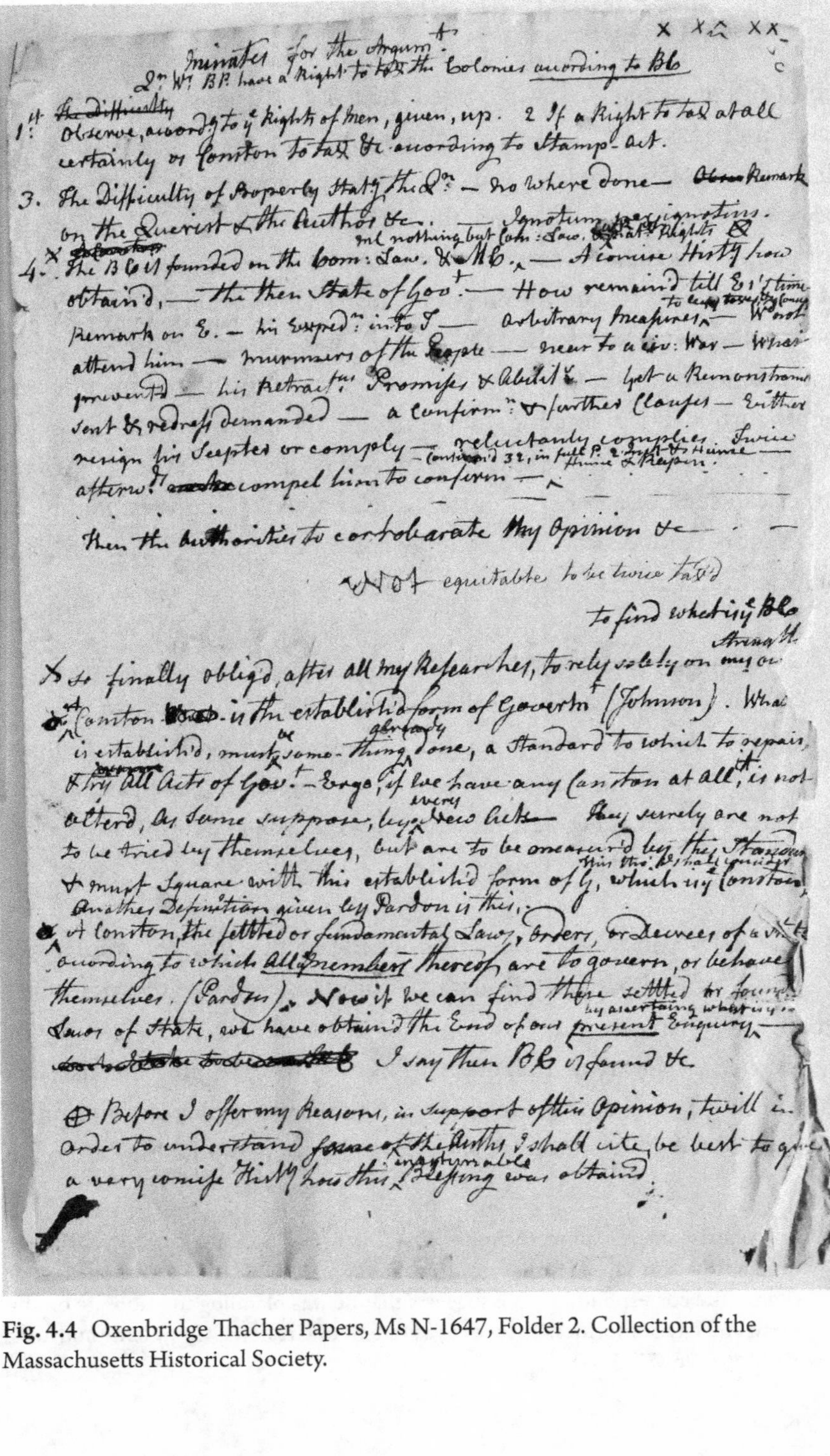

final speech would fit the pattern. At the same time, Thacher never gave the speech, Adams was unaware of it, the note was not recovered until the papers were donated to the Massachusetts Historical Society in 1882, it seems to remain unknown to historians, and Otis's arguments based on both state of nature and British rights are the ones that were picked up by Gridley, as well as in all official remonstrances that Massachusetts sent to both King and Parliament.

That said, later versions of Thacher's planned speech also survive, mostly in fragments, but including another full version under the slightly different title, "Minutes for the Argument on whether the British Parliament have a Right according to the British Constitution to tax the Colonies."[56] Also original, this version shifts in emphasis and integrates more state of nature than the first draft. The accompanying fragments show Thacher experimenting with possible building blocks of his argument. In one fragment, he cites Burlamaqui to show that the Stamp Act was void because fundamental laws are really covenants between the people and the legislature, and can only be changed by "the unanimous concurrence of all contracting Parties who have fixed the form of Government by the primitive Contract of Association." When the legislation violates the original contract, the people are not only entitled but obliged by natural and divine law "to refuse Obedience."

Thacher took notes on various scraps as he built his argument, adding distinguishing marks (manicules, double manicules, a cross in a circle, etc.) to some of them, and in some drafts noting where such citations and supporting arguments might go. Rapin, Hume, Montesquieu, and Locke were his chief sources. One scrap was intended for this final, full version (fig. 4.5). Unlike the first draft, it features not only natural rights, but also the state of nature, from chapter 9, section 123 of the *Second Treatise*. This is the passage in which Locke sets limits to the legislative, and to which therefore Blackstone objected.[57] Though other details of their reasoning differed, both Otis and Thacher adapted Locke's (and in

56. Oxenbridge Thacher Papers, Massachusetts Historical Society, Ms N-1647.
57. Blackstone, *Commentaries* I.2.52 (in the first American edition, Philadelphia, 1771).

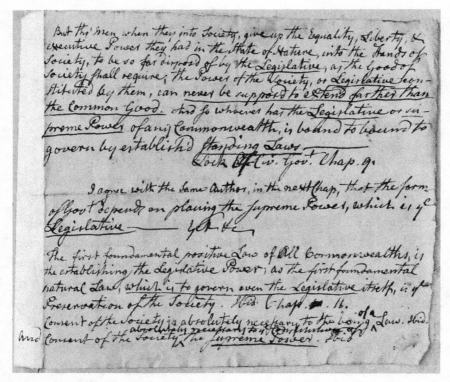

Fig. 4.5 Oxenbridge Thacher Papers, Ms. N-1647, Folder 3. Collection of the Massachusetts Historical Society.

Otis's case, Vattel's) state of nature to raise boundaries to Parliament's authority in the colonies. The addition of state of nature in Thacher's later drafts suggests that by May 1765 the state of nature was becoming an unavoidable reference point.

In drawing on Montesquieu, Otis, Adams and Thacher ignored Montesquieu's uncanny recommendation for something very much like the Stamp Act, his insistence that slavery destroys republics, and other inconvenient notions.[58] It was not without irony that Richard

58. Nugent's 1752 ed., I.301, 303, 307–308 on how per capita taxes are for slaves, but duty on goods fits liberty. Taxing paper used for private contracts, Montesquieu argues, is a particularly good idea, as such contracts are based on choice. And I.354–56 is one of several places where Montesquieu explains that slavery and republics cannot coexist.

Peters, Pennsylvania judge and legislator and delegate to the Continental Congress, wrote to Adams on June 15, 1789:

> The Sentiments of Montesquieu the Subject you mention have indeed been miserably construed. He was a great & sensible Man but has in many Passages of his Works rendered his Meaning obscure by a Habit of too much condensing his Ideas so as to avoid Prolixity. He is a Kind of Bible for Politicians & it fares with his as it does with the good Book—every one finds a Text to suit his own Purposes. If indeed the Text does not exactly fit, convenient Interpretations must do the Business.[59]

By 1765, Otis took the claims he laid out in *Rights* further and mobilized additional state of nature arguments against the Stamp Act, including those that Justices Holt and Pollexfen made during the Glorious Revolution. On December 20, 1765 Adams, Otis and Gridley argued in front of Governor Bernard in Council that the courts must be reopened despite the Stamp Act, which all three refused to recognize as binding.[60] Adams opened with the statement that the Stamp Act violated the colonists' natural and English rights. Parliament can err. When it does, it must be disobeyed.[61] He quickly moved to the broader point that Americans are not represented in Westminster, and therefore not bound by any laws passed there. This is clear from both the British Constitution and the principle of *quod omnes tangit ab omnibus approbetur* (what concerns all,

---

59. Richard Peters to John Adams, June 15, 1789. Massachusetts Historical Society, Adams-Hull Collection, Ms N-1776, Box 1, folder 37.
60. In a February 4, 1766, letter Thomas Cushing explained to John Cushing that Gridley did not think the courts could be legally opened after the Stamp Act. After some research, Gridley changed his mind. Massachusetts Historical Society, William Cushing Papers, Ms. N-1069. Given the prominent role of the state of nature in Otis's, Adams's, and Gridley's arguments at the December 20 meeting, the state of nature may have been the constitutional trope that convinced Gridley.
61. Echoed by Otis, *Quincy's Reports*, 205. Adams cited the list of limitations on Parliament's authority given in Wood's *Institute*, 9, that Evert Wendell in 1725 and Otis in 1744 also noted, as discussed above (chapter 3, footnote 101). "Notes on the Opening of the Courts, 19 December 1765."

should be considered by all). Otis took over, expressing agreement with Adams concerning the invalidity of the Stamp Act. In a Montaignesque appeal to man in the state of nature as an arbiter of justice, Otis announced that Adams's argument was "sufficient to convince the most illiterate Savage that the Parliament of England had no Regard to the very first Principles of their own Liberties."[62]

Otis next argued that when England had small baronies, as Germany does now, the common law used to allow for suspending the administration of justice in cases of war, invasion, rebellion, or insurrection. However, "War has now become so much of a Science, and gives so little Disturbance to a Nation engaged," that it cannot justify closing the courts. This line strongly recalls some arguments concerning ship money in 1637, where it was said that war alone does not justify the King's violation of the constitutional need for consent to raise money. The conditions that must exist simultaneously for the king to raise funds without consent are a state of war, the king's personal presence in the field of battle, and a state of disarray such that the courts are unable operate.[63] Some manuscript variants, different from the published version of the trials, add that in such cases the country has lapsed into a state of nature already, and not only the king, but no one is legally culpable for seizing property. The king is only allowed to raise money without consent in a condition of anarchy in which the king's own person and property enjoy no protection, either.[64]

Similarly to Hawley's characterization of Lanesborough's rejection of the Stamp Act as evidence that the residents had the English constitution written on their hearts, Otis presented colonial resistance to the Stamp Act as a replication of the rightful and revolutionary resistance to the king during the English Civil War, on the one hand, and a faithful continuation

62. *Quincy's Reports*, 203. Michel de Montaigne, "Des Cannibales," in *Essais* (Bordeaux, 1580), 185–203 ; *The Complete Works* (tr. Donald M. Frame, Everyman's, 2003), 182–93.
63. Howell's *State Trials*, vol. 3 (London, 1816), 904–5.
64. Anon., "Arguments in the case of ship money," 1637, Harvard Law School MSS HLS MS 141, 72–74.

of the order established by the Glorious Revolution, on the other hand.[65] There may be inconsistencies in *Rights*, but Otis did not necessarily contradict himself when he compared eighteenth-century colonial opposition to the Stamp Act to seventeenth-century parliamentary resistance to ship money, while simultaneously insisting that the Glorious Revolution created a clean break in constitutional authority and should be seen as the kind of moment that Machiavelli, Harrington, and others described as taking the state back to its beginnings.[66] The common element between the two constitutional crises is successful resistance; but while the link between American resistance and the English Civil War is merely a strong comparison, the Glorious Revolution is the starting point of an abiding constitutional continuity. Otis explicitly drew the analogy between Parliament's opposition to Charles I's attempts to raise ship money in the 1620s–1630s and colonial grievances against Parliament's imposition of taxes for defense in the 1760s.[67] In a move that confirms that his intention was to firmly equate the passage of the Stamp Act with the

65. Others pointed out the link between the Hanover dynasty's legitimacy and the Glorious Revolution. December 29, 1773 Proceedings of the Town of Medford: "We have a Firm affection to the Illustrious House of Hanover and heartily wish that his present Majesty might long Reign over a free and happy people and that the dignity of the British Crown and Sceptre may descend in peace & set easy on the Heads of his Royal Descendants for Ages and Generations yet to come. As the highest Evidence of this we must say we Cordially acquiesce in Revolution principles and are determined upon those principles to the utmost of our power to defend and maintain the Invaluable Liberties to which we are thereby entitled against all usurpations & Encroachments as we Suppose every real friend to the present Royal Family must do if he would act in consistence with those principles upon which the happy Revolution took place." Boston Committee of Correspondence records, NYPL MssCol 343, p. 525, image 76 in b.1.f.6. Billerica made the same point after the *Boston Port Act*. See June 5, 1774 Resolutions, Res. 2, Boston Committee of Correspondence records, NYPL MssCol 343, b.3.f.18 p. 2.

66. Ioannis Evrigenis, *Fear of Enemies and Collective Action* (Cambridge, 2008); Evrigenis, "Hobbes's Clockwork: The State of Nature and Machiavelli's Return to Beginnings of Cities," in Sharon R. Krause and M.A. McGrail (eds.), *The Arts of Rule: Essays in Honor of Harvey C. Mansfield* (Lexington, 2009), 185–99.

67. Otis, *Rights*, 89–90. A rarely discussed aspect of ship money is that the constitutional literature preceding the English Civil War connected the disputed forms of tax to grievances about royal restrictions on the commoners' trade, and to the

dethronement of James II, Otis forcefully announced: "The shutting up of the Courts is an Abdication, a total Dissolution of Government"; and when the King "shuts his Courts, he unkings himself in the most essential point." The authorities he cites include Pollexfen and Holt in 1688, as reported in Paul de Rapin's *History,* and Grotius's *De iure belli ac pacis,* I.iii.2, II.iv.9, II.vii.2 n. 2, II.xx.2, with Jean Barbeyrac's notes.[68]

Signing as John Hampden, a leading parliamentarian in the ship money controversy, Otis published an expanded version of his argument in the *Boston Gazette* on January 6, 1766. Adams included an insider's summary of it in his January 7, 1766 diary entry.[69] Arguing that not even partial tumults qualify as war, Otis made unrest in Boston compatible

abuse of royal prerogative to create commercial advantages for the king and for those who could afford to buy exemptions and monopolies. Colonial objections to the Navigation Acts and to Parliament's restrictions on American manufacturing therefore echoed not only ship money, but the whole package of linked griev-ances, which were reprinted throughout the eighteenth century. The outrage at the Tea Act was not only because it extracted revenue and upheld the principle of Parliament's right to tax the colonies, but also because the colonists understood that objections to monopoly and taxes were historically connected in the common law. See, e.g., Robert Cotton, "Extractes out of the recordes wherein it may bee collected by what means the kings of England have and maye rayse monyes," and "The manner and means how the Kings of England have supported and improved their states," in numerous manuscripts and printed collections such as *Cottoni posthuma* ... (London, 1651).

68. *Quincy's Reports,* 204–5. Russell L. Caplan, *Constitutional Brinksmanship: Amending the Constitution by National Convention* (Oxford, 1988), 6–40. Blackstone also came close to formulating conditions in which a king would unking himself and could therefore do no wrong: *Commentaries,* III.17 (1768). Interestingly, in 1764 Francis Bernard, Governor of Massachusetts, described the sovereign of the British Empire as King-in-Parliament, which "in a political sense, can do no wrong." Bernard, "Principles of Law and Polity" in Bernard, *Select Letters on the Trade and Government of America* (2nd ed., London, 1774), 71. Bernard's formulation may be an attempt to overturn conventional and new argumentative templates in which the legislative or the executive could unseat itself through unconstitutional actions or laws.

69. "At Boston. Hampden has given us in Yesterdays Gazette, a long Letter to Pym upon shutting up the Courts, in which he proves from Holts and Pollexfens Arguments at the Revolution Conference, from Grotius De Jure Belli, B. 1. C. 3. §. 2. that shut-ting up the Courts is an Abdication of the Throne, a Discharge of the Subjects from their Allegiance, and a total Dissolution of Government and Reduction of all Men

with his December 20, 1765 claim that modern warfare is conducted scientifically and does not necessarily involve the whole population; therefore shutting the courts and ceasing to administer justice under the pretext of war amounts to an abdication of legitimate government. This point, in turn, served Adams and others as the foundation for the claim, made several times between 1765 and 1774, that even if Britain and the imperial administration wished to throw Massachusetts into the state of nature by depriving it of legitimate government, the fact that—minor skirmishes notwithstanding—Massachusetts continued to function in relative social order *de facto* showed that it was not in an anarchical but in a constitutive state of nature, which corroborated its *de jure* claim to self-government.

Hampden, Pym, Cromwell and other key figures of the Civil War became guiding lights and contested forerunners in the imperial conflict. While Otis and Adams chose them as pen names, and—as we will see—Witherspoon praised them for being forced into conflict despite their profound love of peace, in his 1764 *History of . . . Massachusetts Bay* Hutchinson explained that according to his research, Haslerigg, Pym, Hampden, Cromwell, and others decided to emigrate to Massachusetts but they were forbidden to do so by the King. William Fiennes, 1st Viscount Say and Seele, and Robert Greville, 2nd Baron Brooke, also thought about moving to New England but could not decide whether they should go to Massachusetts or establish a new colony. Such members of the nobility and "principal commoners" had

> what appears at this day to be very strange, apprehensions of the relation they should stand in to Great Britain, after their removal to America. Many of the proposal were such, as imply that they thought themselves at full liberty, without any charter from the crown, to establish such sort of government as they thought proper, and to form a new state as fully to all intents and purposes as if they had been in a state of nature, and

> to a state of Nature. And he proves from Bracton that partial Tumults, &c. are not a Tempus Guerrium, (Bellorum) a Time of War."

were making their first entrance into civil society. The importance of the colonies to the nation was not fully understood and considered. Perhaps the party, which then prevailed in England, would have been content to have been rid of the heads of what was deemed a faction in the government, and to have had no further connexion with them. Be that as it may, this sentiment, in persons of such figure and distinction, will in a great measure excuse the same mistake which will appear to have been made by our first settlers, in many instances in the course of our history.[70]

Given the other state of nature texts in and shortly before 1765, it is clear that when Hutchinson wrote that his contemporaries must find "very strange" the idea, entertained by opponents of Charles I and the first colonial settlers, that moving to the colonies would bestow the rights and independence one finds in the state of nature, he was taking a stand in an ongoing debate. His reference to Hampden and Pym may be one reason why soon after Hutchinson's volume was published, Adams and Otis chose them as pseudonyms when they argued that Britain had pushed the colonies into a state of nature, where they proved remarkably stable.[71]

Jeremiah Gridley, who professionally opposed Thacher and Otis in *Paxton's Case* nearly five years earlier, now weighed in on the side of Otis and Adams on December 20, 1765, addressing the Council against the Stamp Act. Even more forcefully than Otis or Adams, Gridley asserted that the Massachusetts objections to the Stamp Act touched on the fundamental legitimacy of government. Although the Stamp Act affected private law and not criminal law proceedings, this made the situation more,

70. Hutchinson, *History of . . . Massachusetts Bay* (2nd ed., London, 1765), 41–42, passage cited on 42. Ferdinando Warner also took exception to the revolutionaries claiming the mantle of seventeenth-century figures. In a chapter in his 1767 *The History of the Rebellion and Civil-War in Ireland* on the 1643 riots against a new excise, Warner compares the ignorant rabble misusing the notion of liberty to the Americans who fail to understand that all government restrains liberty, and unless we are prepared to "recur to a State of Nature," we must accept such restraints, including excise. 273–75, cited phrase on 274.

71. The list of writers and factions that adopted these pen names in the revolutionary controversy is long. Reid, *The Authority to Tax*, 22–23, 26–27, 117–18, *passim*.

not less, critical. The state can punish an offender against contract or property, but it cannot determine the offense. Depriving individuals of remedy means effectively shutting down the courts, which is tantamount to "a Renuntiation of Government," in which case the "People must return to a State of Nature." In fact, according to Gridley, the situation was worse, because the state of nature meant living in the woods with other barbarians, but the Stamp Act dissolved a society that had already bestowed knowledge and skills on its members, thereby making them more dangerous to one another.[72] Unlike Adams's and Otis's variety, Gridley's state of nature, similarly to Hawley's in 1767, was better than the anarchy caused by the Stamp Act, but impossible to return to. The four lawyers agreed that the Stamp Act was unconstitutional and threw the colonies into a state of nature; but they had slightly different states of nature in mind.

After the December 20, 1765 confrontation with Governor Bernard, on January 28, 1766, another Harvard-graduate lawyer, Thomas Cushing, soon to become Speaker of the Massachusetts Assembly, wrote to John Cushing speculating that the courts must reopen despite the Stamp Act.

72. *Quincy's Reports*, 207–8. Years later, in an interesting echo of Gridley's argument that the closure of courts due to the Stamp Act placed Massachusetts in a condition worse than the state of nature, because civilized people suddenly deprived of government have greater skills for mutual harm than savages, Josiah Quincy, Jr. (even though he was Ebenezer Richardson's defense when Richardson shot the eleven-year-old Christopher Snider during a mob attack on Richardson's house) wrote about the judges' bias in the February 10, 1772 *Boston Gazette*: "If political views should ever actuate the Judges of the land, who have the lives, liberty and property of us all in their power, society is worse than a state of nature: because the members of it have a greater opportunity, more abilities to do mischief, less danger of detection, and a more flattering prospect of impunity." Coquillette and York, *Portrait*, 6:78. Similarly, on July 29, 1776, shortly after he signed the Declaration of Independence, William Whipple wrote from Philadelphia to Joshua Brackett about reforming New Hampshire: "I call it a great work; for, in my opinion, it is more difficult to reduce a society of men, who have drunk deep of waters of corruption, to the true principles of virtue, than to bring a society from the state of nature to the same meridian." *Proceedings of the Massachusetts Historical Society* 5 (1860–62), 1–30, at 6. Conversely, some thought that it was the Declaration of Independence that placed the colonies in a state of nature. " 'The Republican' to the Freeholders and Inhabitants of New Hampshire," January 30, 1777 (Dartmouth College, Rauner, ms 777130).

The House are resolutely bent upon having the Courts open & I doubt whether they will grant any Sallery to a Judge till they are well assured that they will be open. I hope the Judges will make no difficulty; shall the impracticability of executing a Single Act of Parliament (an Act in its own nature null & void) stop the whole Course of Justice & render all our laws of no Effect, & reduce us to a State of Nature?[73]

A fifth relevant meaning circulated at the same time. The day on or before Otis, John Adams and Gridley presented their argument against the Stamp Act, Samuel Adams wrote a letter to a certain John Smith in London, in which he introduced consent as a precondition for just dealings in private property that is preserved after the transition from the state of nature to society.[74] This sense did not appear in the Stamp Act objections in Council, perhaps because consent was subsumed under representation in those arguments. I have not been able to identify John Smith, but he may have belonged to the large and vibrant community of American merchants in London.

Stephen Sayre (1736–1818) was a colorful character in the same community. Better known as a friend of John Wilkes, and alleged instigator of a 1775 plot to kidnap George III, Sayre often appears in histories of the Revolution as a polemicist whose first work was *The Englishman Deceived*, published in 1768.[75] Numerous historians describe Sayre as a radical and cite powerful passages from this book.[76] The problem is

73. Massachusetts Historical Society, William Cushing Papers, Ms. N-1069.
74. December 19, 1765. "No Man in the State of Nature can justly take anothers Property without his Consent. It is an essential Part of the British Constitution that the Supreme Power cannot take from any Man any part of his Property without his Consent in Person or by his Representative." Several copies may exist. Adams's modern editor claims to transcribe a copy in the "Collections of the Earl of Dartmouth" (*Writings*, 39). The manuscript in Samuel Adams's hand, now at the New York Public Library, is dated December 20.
75. This is the date in Sibley and Shipton, *Biographical Sketches* (1968), 14:206, 215. John R. Alden, *Stephen Sayre: American Revolutionary Adventurer* (Louisiana State University, 1983), 27–28 also dates it to 1768.
76. John P. Reid, "In the Taught Tradition: The Meaning of Law in Massachusetts-Bay Two Hundred Years Ago," *Suffolk University Law Review* 14 (1980), 931–74,

that the passages that often capture their attention are misattributed to Sayre in 1768. They were written in 1765 by Dennys DeBerdt, colonial agent for Massachusetts, Delaware, and Connecticut, as the text of *The Englishmen Deceived* itself makes clear. Letter I, which opens the book, already appeared in the December 30, 1765, issue of the *Supplement to the Boston Evening-Post*. The patriot Esther DeBerdt, daughter of Dennys DeBerdt, sent a letter to a friend on May 20, 1768, describing Sayre composing *The Englishman Deceived* and including two of her father's letters, one from November 1765 and another from January 1768.[77] Indeed, the important state of nature text that Reid, Eacott, Bezanson and others cite, and Greene describes and attributes to "Franklin's friend Stephen Sayre" in 1768,[78] is introduced in Sayre's book as a letter "presented not long since to a noble Lord, by an old, firm, steady friend of the constitution."[79] The letter form is therefore not Sayre's stylistic device, but an accurate acknowledgment that the text that has exercised historians was written not by Sayre in 1768 but by DeBerdt in November 1765, the same month he was appointed to represent Massachusetts in London.

DeBerdt rejected the position that the American colonies should pay for their own defense. Importantly, he did not ascribe this position to misguided ministers but, suggesting a separation of peoples rather than governments, wrote that this was the "popular cry" in England. This cry was wrong because the public in Britain misunderstood how empires work; everyone pays for the defense of the whole. The defense of Scotland, or the unsuccessful fight for Hanover, created a financial burden for the empire, but Parliament did not impose new taxes on the lands that Britain fought for. New colonial taxes are not only unprecedented. They also

at 964–65 n. 142; Greene, *Constitutional Origins*, 107–8; Randall P. Bezanson, *Taxes on Knowledge in America* (Pennsylvania, 1994), 59; Jonathan Eacott, *Selling Empire: India in the Making of Britain and America, 1600–1830* (North Carolina, 2016), 195.

77. William Bradford Reed, *The Life of Esther De Berdt* (Philadelphia, 1853), 129–30.
78. Greene, *Constitutional Origins*, 107.
79. Sayre, *The Englishman Deceived* ... (London [perhaps false, in reality New York?], 1768, reprinted Salem, MA, 1768), 32–41.

make no sense, because the "infant colonies" already labor under disproportionate burdens, they have contributed to imperial defense, the damage to trade caused by the taxes will harm the metropolis, sending troops to the colonies was unnecessary as the colonists have been successfully repelling the French and the Native Americans for one hundred years, and the whole thing violates the colonists' charters that they obtained when they moved to the howling wilderness to escape Stuart oppression. According to DeBerdt, the Grenville ministry's real reason for imposing taxes and sending troops was to oppress and, frankly, to fleece the colonies. This is short-sighted, because the "mutual interest between Great Britain and her Colonies" means that injuring the colonies can only cause harm to the mother country, both in terms of trade and by losing the opportunity for further expansion. Finally, DeBerdt, who in the first two-thirds of the text focuses on policy, not law, explains that the new taxes also violate "equity."

All colonies, except Georgia and Nova Scotia, were settled by Englishmen oppressed and seeking "civil and religious liberties." When they moved to America, "they were then in a state of nature, under no civil government, but what they form'd themselves." Having established themselves, they sent agents to London not out of any obligation but "out of regard to their mother country." These agents made sacred, mutually binding deals—these are the charters, which the colonies consider their Magna Carta. Given how much Britain had spent on settling Georgia and Nova Scotia, Britain should appreciate how much it saved when the other colonies established themselves at their own expense. Together, the charters add up to a "compact" with Britain, stipulating allegiance from the colonies and confirming their privilege of taxing themselves. Violating the charters and this compact would provoke the same response as other Englishmen had to violations of Magna Carta. "An army is necessary therefore to carry such measures into execution, though not necessarily for the people's defence," DeBerdt ominously ends his argument, before a final summary of the letter.

The community of exiled and self-exiled colonists was formed and remains in the American state of nature. That is how they became independent from England, and where they set up their new polities.

Interestingly, in DeBerdt's formulation eleven of the thirteen colonies are still united, and united through the American state of nature, having the same constitutional foundations and independence. It is important that Sayre republished this text in 1768, as tensions reached new heights after the Townshend Acts, after the Massachusetts Circular Letter, after Bernard dissolved the Massachusetts Assembly, and after Lord Hillsborough, Secretary of State for the Colonies, sent four regiments to Boston. Yet when Greene describes Sayre as "one of the very few" who challenged Westminster's right to legislate in the colonies as early as 1768, it is useful to note that the text first appeared in December 1765, penned by the newly appointed colonial agent to London, in the context of the Stamp Act.[80]

4.4 THE ROAD TO REPEAL

Rockingham replaced Grenville as Prime Minister in July 1765. After intense parliamentary debate concerning the injustice and economic harm caused by the Stamp Act, a resolution to repeal was passed on February 21, 1766, and accepted by the King on March 18. According to the notes of Grey Cooper, secretary of the Treasury and MP for Rochester, when the bill for repeal was read for the second time on March 11, Hans Stanley, Lord Commissioner for the Admiralty and MP for Southampton, denounced those who in the Stamp Act debate "have reasoned as if the first Planters had recovered their State of Nature. This Doctrine mischievous to the Colonies. No British Subject can renounce his Allegiance."[81] Despite reactions in Britain, the nascent American state of nature discourse continued to thrive and evolve. Extending what they started at least as early as 1759, in January 1766 Adams and Otis continued to build powerful new state of nature arguments with a view to forensic debate and influencing public opinion under the pen names of the English Civil War parliamentarians John Hampden and John Pym (Otis) and Clarendon, Lord Chancellor to Charles II, then exile and author of a great history of

80. Also reprinted in the *Newport Mercury*, January 6, 1766.
81. Harold W. V. Temperley, "Debates on the Declaratory Act and the Repeal of the Stamp Act, 1766," *American Historical Review* 17:3 (1912), 563–86, at 566.

the civil war (Adams). After the abovementioned January 7, 1766 diary entry, which matches Quincy's account of Otis's speech in Council on December 20, 1765, Adams next considers whether they should argue that Massachusetts was in a state of nature, and whether the need for a functioning government justified ignoring the Stamp Act.

1766. Jan. 9. Clarendon to Pym

Thus all the Rules, that have been framed by Phylosophers, Civilians, and Common Lawyers, for the Interpretation of Promises, Covenants, nay Oaths, Treaties, Commissions, Instructions, Edicts and Acts of Parliament, are exactly coincident with the Maxim of Common sense, in the Conduct of private Life, that Cases of Necessity and Impossibility are always excepted. That there is a Necessity for proceeding with Business, has been proved by your old Friend Hampden, beyond all Contradiction. He has proved that Protection and Allegiance are reciprocal, that a Failure of Justice without actual Violence as in Cases of Invasion and Rebellion, is an Abdication of the Crown and Throne. So that if the Prevention of a total Dissolution of Government and an universal Reduction of all Men to a state of Nature, is a Case of Necessity, this Province is at present in that Case.

This line of reasoning, rehearsed with Otis, remained unpublished at the time. Instead of arguing that *avoiding* the state of nature was a necessity that justified expanding colonial government into the vacuum left by self-negating British rule, Adams crafted the position that Britain and the pro-British colonial administration already placed themselves in a state of nature vis-à-vis the colonies, but once there, the colonies proved self-sufficient. They created and maintained social order. They were peaceful in the state of nature of self-government, as well as in the other state of nature, namely the relationship between sovereign states.

Saturday Jany. 11th. 1766. Clarendon to Pym.

Shutting the Courts of Law strictly speaking, which is to appear and be tryed by the Records, is a partial and temporary Dissolution of the

Government, even in Cases of Invasion and Rebellion, and as I take it so far forth reduces the People to a state of Nature, and leaves every Man in every Case to do him self Justice, and to carve out his own Remedy with his Tongue, his fist or his Sword. Now, I should be very glad to know, whether it appears upon Record, that the Courts of Justice are shut. If it does, I apprehend that Record will justify me in judging in my own Cause, and becoming in all Cases where I am injured or have a Demand, my own Lawyer, Judge, Juror and sheriff. And the same Record will prove too that we are in a state of War foreign or domestic. But We are at Peace no doubt with all foreign Nations. Well then, the only Supposition that remains is that We are in a state of actual Rebellion, and that the Judges cannot sit in Judgment for fear of actual Violence. Will any Man pretend this is our Case?

A fascinating set of texts tested imperial legitimacy in the wake of successive crises against the standard established by Otis's, Adams's, Bland's, and other colonial patriots' view of American state of nature as a peaceful and relatively stable stage of transition from British rule to a pre-political sphere of specifically American sociability, capable of legitimating self-government. In the immediate aftermath of the Stamp Act crisis, in a notable address to Governor Thomas Hutchinson dated June 3, 1766, the Massachusetts House of Representatives described the failure and breakdown of imperial government, followed by a natural order from which a new polity might be formed.

> But for many months past there has been an undisturbed tranquillity in general, in this province, and for the greater part of the time, merely from a sense of good order in the people, while they have been in a great measure deprived of the public tribunals, and the administration of justice, and so far thrown into a state of nature.[82]

82. *Writings of Samuel Adams*, ed. Cushing, 1904, 1:74–83, at 78. Compare Straumann on Cicero's *Pro Milone* as a "model for Grotius' state of nature, characterized by the absence of state judicial organs, but not by lawlessness." Straumann, *Roman Law*, 171. The text with the vote to send it to Hutchinson is recorded in the *Journal of the*

Adams's and Otis's rehearsal of the constitutive American state of nature made its debut. It also became Hawley's position in *Warren's Case*. As shown in chapter 7, the constitutive state of nature played a prominent role in the public polemic surrounding the First Continental Congress. Remarkably, the constitutive meaning of the American state of nature that in 1775 John Adams pitted against the view that the revolutionaries were appealing to a chimerical state of nature—argued by Daniel Leonard, writing as Massachusettensis, and the British officer writing as the Veteran, discussed below—was already present in 1764–1766, when Otis refuted those who thought of the state of nature as dangerous legal fiction.

4.5 RICHARD BLAND, *INQUIRY* (1766)

A prominent rejoinder to Thacher's 1764 *Sentiments* and Otis's 1764 *Rights* was *The Regulations Lately Made Concerning the Colonies*, published anonymously in London in 1765.[83] Often ascribed at the time to Grenville himself, it was written by Thomas Whately, secretary to the Treasury under Grenville, later the author of pamphlets defending Grenville's financial schemes[84] and of *Observations on Modern Gardening* (which Jefferson

Honourable House of Representatives, of His Majesty's province of the Massachusetts-Bay, in New-England, begun and held at Boston, in the county of Suffolk, on Wednesday the twenty-eighth day of May, Annoque Domini, 1766, dated June 3, on 21–28, cited passage on 25. On 356 of the same journal we find the House using the same term to mean uncultivated land. Also printed in the *Connecticut/Hartford Courant* on June 23, 1766.

83. These texts were Whately's main target according to Ian R. Christie, "A Vision of Empire: Thomas Whately and the Regulations Lately Made concerning the Colonies," *English Historical Review* 113:451 (1988), 300–20, at 303–4.

84. Thomas Whately, *Remarks on The Budget; or a Candid Examination of the Facts and Arguments Offered to the Public in that Pamphlet* (London, 1765); and *Considerations on the Trade and Finances of the Kingdom and on the Measures of the Administration since the Conclusion of the Peace* (London, 1766). Sometimes attributed to Whately but probably written by William Knox: *Present State of the Nation* (1768; appendix, 1769), and *The Controversy between Great Britain and her Colonies Reviewed* (1769). Whately's authorship of *Regulations* is interesting but does not mean that he did

and John Adams carried on their tours of English gardens).[85] An influential refutation of this work was penned by Richard Bland. His *An Inquiry into the Rights of the British Colonies* has been recognized as an unusually astute argument ever since it first appeared in the week of March 7–14, 1766.[86] By then, Bland had served in the Virginia House of Burgesses for twenty-four years. As it was formally a response to Whately's counterattack, Bland restated some of the Bostonians' arguments but gave them his own twists. Moreover, he added original arguments of his own and brought new issues into the debate, further widening its scope.

Bland attacked Whately's theory of virtual representation, according to which those who did not vote for members of Parliament were still represented in Parliament, which looked after the good of the whole.[87] In refutation, Bland offered a brief history of English representation, starting with the laws of nature, which must surely be the foundation of English laws. The Saxons allowed every freeholder to participate in the "Wittinagemot."[88] Those without property were slaves or workers, any of whom could become freeholders by acquiring land. It is unclear when representation replaced direct participation, but when Henry VIII raised the property qualification, he limited the represented to a tiny group, as small as one-tenth of the population, according to Whately. If this were true, Bland pointed out, it still would not validate virtual representation. Instead, it shows "a great Defect in the present Constitution,"

not reflect Grenville's position accurately; see the citations and summaries in Reid, *Authority to Tax*, 16.

85. Thomas Whately, *Observations on Modern Gardening...* (London, 1777). Jefferson's 1783 catalog notes his copy. Adams's annotated copy is Boston Public Library, Adams 290.9, with notes on the 1786 visits.

86. Kevin J. Hayes, *The Road to Monticello: The Life and Mind of Thomas Jefferson* (Oxford, 2008), 153.

87. As we saw, Adams described a section of Otis's state of nature speech in *Paxton's Case* as also a criticism of the "phantom of virtual representation." Whately's argument that towns, corporations, and other entities were obliged and protected by English law, without being directly represented in Parliament, was echoed by Jonathan Boucher in the 1774 *A Letter from a Virginian*, 25.

88. Bland, *An Inquiry*, 7.

under which not only the colonists, but nine-tenths of England's population, are effectively disenfranchised and enslaved.[89] Once we draw the shocking inference from the absurdity of Whately's theory of representation, we must acknowledge that the English constitution has failed. If so, what can make laws binding again? Bland's system turned on his version of the state of nature.

When men leave the state of nature, according to Bland, they subject their natural rights to society, but imperfectly so. Their continued natural right to pursue happiness implies the right to withdraw from society and enter another existing one, or even to form a new one. Those who stay and enjoy protection give their tacit consent to obey the laws.[90] Parliament has treated the colonies as independent for a long time, given the long-standing provision that laws passed in Westminster do not apply to them unless they are explicitly named in the bill. Yet the actual relationship between the mother country and the colonies cannot be found in the laws, nor in historical examples, since previous imperial systems dealt with conquered provinces, while the American colonies are free. Without relevant English laws and ancient history, the only source for this relationship is the law of nature.[91]

Bland returns to the argument he primed when he first invoked the state of nature. Not only can people withdraw from a polity, in principle, and form a new one thanks to the natural rights they retained from the state of nature, but in the case of the American colonies this is actually what happened. The colonies were already founded as independent. Their independence was not created but at best further codified by charters, often defectively. In the case of Virginia this means Raleigh's original charter, transferred to a corporation, rescinded by James VI/I

89. Bland, *An Inquiry*, 11–12. See also Dickinson's 1774 *Essay*, 341–42.
90. Bland, *An Inquiry*, 9–10.
91. Bland, *An Inquiry*, 14. It is notable that Bland leaves out colonial custom as a potential source of law. Compare Montesquieu, *The Spirit of the Laws*, II.60–61 in Nugent's 1752 ed.: there is no ancient equivalent of modern colonies, which were designed to enhance imperial power not through conquest of territory, but through one-sided trade advantageous to the mother country.

in 1624, reinstated with all of Virginia's liberties as a royal charter, and further acknowledged by the Commonwealth, and later by Charles II.[92]

Bland also adapts the arguments for independence we found in other texts, including Otis's *Rights*. He declares that Virginia, the first "independent country," was "possessed by a savage People" and "settled by Englishmen at their own Expense."[93] In addition to property and self-government, Bland locates what he calls the right of resistance in a sphere of natural rights that he does not here explicitly call the state of nature,[94] but which looks and works like the source of the right to withdraw from, or enter into, polities that he earlier described as the state of nature.

> If a Man invades my Property, he becomes an Aggressor, and puts himself into a State of War with me: I have a Right to oppose this Invader; if I have not Strength to repel him, I must submit, but he acquires no Right to my Estate which he has usurped. Whenever I recover Strength I may renew my Claim, and attempt to regain my Possession; if I am never strong enough, my Son, or his Son, may, when able, recover the natural Right of his Ancestor which has been unjustly taken from him.[95]

The relationship between Parliament and the colonies is different because civil rights, as well as natural rights, already exist between them. But if Parliament ignored all grievances and requests for remedy, Bland warns, they would break principles of good imperial government toward the colonies that even Corinth and Corcyra agreed on.[96] Fighting words indeed. For good measure, Bland cites federal states that were created by revolution.

> Oppression has produced very great and unexpected Events: The *Helvetick* Confederacy, the States of the *United Netherlands*, are Instances in the

92. Bland, *An Inquiry*, 15–20.
93. Bland, *An Inquiry*, 20.
94. Bland, *An Inquiry*, 26.
95. Bland, *An Inquiry*, 25.
96. Bland, *An Inquiry*, 27.

Annals of *Europe* of the glorious Actions a petty People, in Comparison, can perform when united in the Cause of Liberty.[97]

Bland's radical criticism of the failure of virtual representation in both Britain and the American colonies was not as obvious a point as it seems now. Bland's implied republican assumption, namely that representation is essential for legitimacy, was not shared by all of his contemporaries. The idea that the House of Commons serves elite interests was actually well-established in English history. In one of the books the founding generation still cited, the 1701 *Jura populi Anglicani*, the author (probably John Somers) explains that the House of Commons does not represent the people at all. The people's representatives are those to whom they originally resigned the powers they had in the state of nature. The Commons only represents the privileged minority that still has the vote. It follows that those who make ever-expanding claims on behalf of the Commons because it is supposed to represent the people are completely mistaken (while some political rights, such as the right to petition, remain anchored in the state of nature). During the January 1766 parliamentary debate about repealing the Stamp Act, Blackstone himself pointed out that the American objection to being taxed without representation misses the point, because only the Commons is supposed to be representative in the colonists' sense of being elected. The House of Lords or the King, who are also required for passing laws, are not.[98]

Hyneman and Lutz draw attention to an untitled pamphlet by Britannus Americanus in the March 17, 1766 *Boston Gazette*.[99] According to the editors, it makes almost all the same points as Bland, and the author "deserves to be counted among the founders of our country." Both statements are debatable. It is an ambiguous text that begins with a long discussion of what would happen if Americans were in a state of nature.

97. Bland, *An Inquiry*, 29.
98. Temperley, "Debates," 568–69.
99. Reprinted in the March 17-24 issue of the *Newport Mercury*.

When the first settlers of this country had transplanted themselves here, they were to be considered, either as in the state of nature, or else as subjects of that kingdom from whence they had migrated: If they were in the state of nature, they were then entitled to all the rights of nature; no power on earth having any *just* authority, to molest them in the enjoyment of the least of these rights, unless they either had or should forfeit them by an invasion of the rights of other: If the Crown and people of England had at that time, no right, property or claim to that part of the earth, which they had fix'd upon to settle and inhabit, it follows, that in the suppos'd state of nature, neither the crown nor people of England had any *lawful* and *equitable* authority or controul over them more than the inhabitants of the moon: they had a right to erect a government upon what form they thought best . . . [100]

They could have chosen the King of England as their king, for instance, and had only the same personal union with Britain as Hanover does, with limited parliamentary authority. However, the writer continues, this is not the case. The first settlers remained English subjects, and carried all their rights with them, including the right to be represented, and not taxed without their consent.[101] Nevertheless, American representation in London is practically impossible, which is why colonial legislatures were created with the power to pass laws, subject to royal approval.

The few months between the promulgation and the repeal of the Stamp Act were a busy period. The concept spread wider, illustrated

100. Hyneman and Lutz (eds.), *American Political Writing*, 1:88–91, cited passage on 88.
101. Reid helpfully abbreviates this as the emigration theory; see e.g. *Authority to Tax*, 107. The relative insignificance of Britannus Americanus's contribution to revolutionary ideology is underscored by the anonymous article on the front page of the December 30, 1765, *Supplement to the Boston Evening-Post*, in which the author argues that the first settlers fled British oppression and "took shelter in a desert, that they might enjoy their civil and religious liberties, uncontrouled and unmolested; they were then in a state of nature, under no civil government, but what they form'd themselves." A few months before the Britannus Americanus piece, this other Bostonian endorsed the radical state of nature scenario that Britannus Americanus outlined and rejected.

by the Lanesborough residents' invocation of the state of nature and attempt to use it to frame the debate about the Stamp Act both in and out of court. The period also saw the emergence of a co-ordinated use of the state of nature, including by Boston lawyers against the Stamp Act, and a Virginian who summarized and developed the theme in his defense of Massachusetts state of nature usages. The colonial discourse was already well under way when Blackstone's *Commentaries* gave the state of nature new and influential constitutional meanings, mostly as the site of absolute personal rights. Although the state of nature was still used mainly for protest, colonists began to experiment with a more constitutive meaning in which the state of nature accommodated a natural American community.

5

CREATING AND CONTESTING THE AMERICAN STATE OF NATURE

In the midst of its semantic transformation, the meaning of the state of nature as uncultivated environment, surveyed in chapter 2, continued to play a role in the evolution of colonial rights claims. It gave colonists the raw material for theorizing a future American constitution that drew its independence from the combination of Americans' capacity for liberty and the continent's natural potential to underwrite demographic, military, and economic growth. The first settlers, this argument ran, found an inhospitable state of nature, and through sacrifice and labor they transformed it into civilization. Thereby they acquired rights, which survive intact the transition to the state. Texts built on this pattern, going back at least to the 1720s, make constitutional claims.[1] The authors usually

---

1. See the extensive state of nature arguments in Daniel Dulany, Sr., *The Right of the Inhabitants of Maryland to the Benefit of English Laws* (Annapolis, MD, 1728), as well as the remarkable community in St. John's, Newfoundland, which united on November 26, 1723, under the aegis of Locke's *Second Treatise*, chap. 8, §95. Jeff A. Webb, "Leaving the State of Nature: A Locke-Inspired Political Community in St. John's, Newfoundland, 1723," *Acadiensis* 21:1 (1991), 156–65.

spell out, and sometimes merely imply, that by virtue of their continuing battle with the state of nature and the legacy of their forefathers they hold rights to property and to a degree of self-governance independent of Britain. One example we saw is in Bland's *Inquiry*, and another is in Otis's *Rights*.

> The New-England Colonies in particular, were not only settled without the least expence to the mother country, but they have all along defended themselves against the frequent incursions of the most inhuman Savages, perhaps on the face of the whole earth, at *their own* cost: Those more than brutal *men*, spirited and directed by the most inveterate, as well as most powerful enemy of Great-Britain, have been constantly annoying our infant settlements for more than a century; spreading terror and desolation, and sometimes depopulating whole villages in a night: yet amidst the fatigues of labour, and the horrors of war and bloodshed, Heaven vouchsafed its smiles. Behold, an extensive territory, settled, defended, and secured to his Majesty, I repeat it, *without the least expence to the mother country*, till within twenty years past![2]

An example of this genre from the end of the period examined in this book is the remarkable exchange in April 1776 between Frederick Smyth, the last royal chief justice of New Jersey, and a grand jury he was instructing about the law. Smyth argued that revolution and secession were terrible ideas. British liberty emerged in a moderate and maritime climate and continues to shoot up from Britain's soil before it is extended to the colonies. Unusually, the jury wrote a reply and contradicted Smyth's explanation of the origin of law.[3] Writers who developed the American state of nature as a constitutional topos occasionally appropriated the principle Smyth cited, namely that liberty emanates from Britain's soil. Blackstone

2. *Rights*, 86–87. The same argument appears in the Assembly's memorandum to the colonial agent, Jasper Mauduit, "to be improved as he may judge proper." *Rights*, appendix, 106.
3. American Philosophical Society, Frederick Smyth Papers, Mss.B.Sm95.

cited the same, although limited to English rather than British soil, to declare that there can be no slaves in England. William Samuel Johnson, by contrast, explained that American soil is an independent font of liberty and law. Even if Britain claimed the right of government in the colonies, it cannot claim the right of soil and everything that derives from it.[4] In another instance of the extraordinary and understudied genre of revolutionary grand jury instructions, such as Smyth's, when colonial judges had to summarize and justify the law in a time of constitutional uncertainty and vacuum, Benjamin Chew, Chief Justice of the Pennsylvania Supreme Court, wrote several sets of grand jury instructions around 1776 in which he insisted that the state of nature was a real condition.[5]

American claims concerning the state of nature as a place of difficulty and war eventually sharpened to the point that in addition to emphasizing the first settlers' self-reliance, eighteenth-century colonists began to assert that England, and later Britain, never protected them from native Americans or from other European imperialist powers in the American state of nature.[6] Among other reasons, this point was important because according to Vattel's *Law of Nations*, I.xvii, a failure to protect justifies secession.

This chapter will explore the rise of a constitutive sense of American state of nature, in which the colonists formed a natural community. The expansion and consolidation of the constitutive meaning will be shown through constitutional arguments in the aftermath of the Stamp Act crisis,

4. William Samuel Johnson Papers, Connecticut Historical Society, ms 22977, Box 4, Folder 3.
5. Benjamin Chew, Historical Society of Pennsylvania, Chew Family Papers, Collection 2050, series 2, section E, Box 16.
6. E.g., *Journals of the House of Representatives of Massachusetts*, Committee's June 13, 1764 letter to agent Maudit, 41:73–74. That this was duly conveyed to London is attested in 1764–65 Privy Council, copies of papers transmitted, Huntington mss HM 2587, 9–11. The argument that in the absence of effective British protection the colonies returned into a self-sufficient state of nature, where they are free to form new governments, runs continuously after 1764. Texts have been mentioned previously; see also Anon., *The Reply of a Gentleman in a Select Society, upon the Important Contest between Great Britain and America* (London, 1775), 4–5.

in key texts on both sides of the Atlantic, such as *True Sentiments* and *British Liberties*, and in the widening of state of nature rights protected in the constitutive state of nature, matched by a growing division among the colonists that eventually hardened into Patriot-Loyalist opposition, and can be readily traced to early disagreements about valid and invalid meanings of the state of nature.

5.1 THE CONSTITUTIVE STATE OF NATURE

The negative argument for the constitutional independence of the early settlers and their descendants could only go so far. Even if they arrived in the New World without help and protection, and turned the inhospitable wilderness into civilization, what kind of community, what possible bearer of identity and rights, did they leave to their children? In 1765, John Adams published anonymous letters in the August 12, 19, September 30, and October 21 issues of the *Boston Gazette*. A sort of primer on natural rights, they were initially attributed to Jeremiah Gridley, in whose chambers Adams, Otis, and Thacher had trained. At Thomas Hollis's instigation the letters were reprinted in the *London Chronicle*.[7] Adams was identified as their author when they appeared under the collective title, the *Dissertation on the Canon and Feudal Law*, as part of the 1768 collection entitled, *The True Sentiments of America*.[8] The collection begins with the House's January 20, 1768 petition to the King. It follows a now familiar pattern. With royal and, according to the authors, therefore

---

7. November 23, 28, December 3 and 26, 1765.
8. On p. 124 of *True Sentiments*, Adams cites Rousseau. Adams made a few handwritten corrections and annotations in his own copy, now at the Stone Library (Adams 8526). In marginal notes to pp. 114 and 115, he identified William Robertson's *Charles V* as the source for his discussion of feudalism. In this work, Robertson placed independence on a continuous scale. He depicted the barbarous nations that overran Rome as developed enough to have politics, but still suffering from the centrifugal force of too much individual independence. Consequently, they approximated the pre-political state of nature. In *The Political Mirror* of 1776, "Britannicus" used the state of nature in the same sense, as the unreasonable and immature spirit of independence, in criticism of the American colonists.

national English consent, the first settlers emigrated from England "at their own great expence" to take possession of American wilderness, a land for which they also paid.

> With toil and fatigue, perhaps not to be conceived by their brethren and fellow-subjects at home, and with the constant peril of their lives, from a numerous, savage, and warlike race of men, they began their settlement, and God prospered them.
>
> They obtained a charter from King Charles the first; wherein his Majesty was pleased to grant to them and their heirs and assigns for ever, all the lands therein described, to hold of him and his royal successors in free and common soccage; which we humbly conceive is as absolute an estate as the subject can hold under the crown. And in the same character were granted to them, and their posterity, all the rights, liberties, privileges, and immunities of natural subjects, born within the realm.

This charter was unfortunately vacated in 1684, the petition continues. It was replaced with another under William and Mary, which granted essentially the same rights, especially the right not to be taxed without freely elected representatives. The colony flourished and brought the Crown great wealth and glory. The authors describe, but in this case do not name, the state of nature, and use "wilderness," "fundamental rights of nature," and other equivalents of the various meanings of the state of nature instead.[9] A major force behind this petition was John Dickinson, already famous for his 1767–1768 *Letters from a Farmer in Pennsylvania*. While the letters were being published, Dickinson corresponded with

---

9. According to John Adams, the petition was written by Otis, and polished by Samuel Adams. He describes the principles of their collaboration: "tis & the majority of the Committee derived all authority from the constitution Samuel Adams would have derived it only from the people. The People with him were everything & Constitutions nothing. Otis & Adams however might have agreed in expression for it is certain that no constitution can be made by any other power than the people." Letter to William Tudor, March 7, 1819. In this letter, Adams claimed that he wanted independence as early as 1755.

Otis from December 1767 to January 1768 and encouraged him to convince the people and legislature of Massachusetts to take the lead in a united colonial resistance to the Townshend Acts.[10] The Massachusetts petition in turn inspired New Jersey to send a letter to George III, dated May 6, 1768, which made the same case on an explicit state of nature footing.

> Nor do we apprehend, that it lies within our Power, by any Means more effectually to promote these great Purposes, than by zealously striving to preserve in perfect Vigour, those sacred Rights and Liberties, under the inspiriting Sanction of which, inconceivable Difficulties and Dangers opposing, this Colony has been rescued from the rudest State of Nature, converted into a populous, flourishing, and valuable Territory; and has contributed in a very considerable Degree, to the Welfare of Great Britain.

Like Adams's letters, the widely reprinted New Jersey petition paid lip service to the Crown, but made a powerful constitutional point by using the state of nature as both the origin and persistent locus of the colonists' rights to property and self-government. The *True Sentiments* collection is one possible source for New Jersey's petition, as it contains the Massachusetts petition, the letters to Shelburne and DeBerdt that anchor property in the state of nature (discussed next), and John Adams's primer on the state of nature; though there was no shortage of other texts in the colonies that used the concept to the same effect.

After the Massachusetts petition of January 20, 1768, the next document in *True Sentiments* is the province's letter to William Petty, 2nd Earl of Shelburne (1737–1805). Shelburne was Secretary of State for the Southern Department at the time, responsible for relations with the American colonies. The post was formally created at the Restoration in 1660. As Shelburne was considered too sympathetic to the patriots,

10. *Warren-Adams Letters*, 1. Dickinson to Otis, December 5, 1767, and January 25 and April 11, 1768.

this post's authority over the colonies was transferred to the Secretary of State for the Colonies, established on February 27, 1768, a month after Massachusetts' letter to Shelburne. The inaugural Secretary, Wills Hill, the Earl of Hillsborough (later the 1st Marquess of Downshire), was President of the Board of Trade and Plantations under Grenville, and could be counted on to hold a hard line against the colonists. In fact, Hillsborough was reappointed as President a few months after he became Secretary, thereby concentrating colonial responsibilities. The new secretarial post was specifically intended to deal with the American crisis, given the high tension and volatility after the Townshend Acts. It was abolished in March 1782 when it became clear that it had failed in its purpose (although it was reestablished in 1854–1966). The more conciliatory Shelburne became Prime Minister in July 1782, and handled the peace negotiations with the United States.

All this was yet to come when on January 15, 1768, the month before Shelburne lost responsibility for the colonies, the Massachusetts Assembly wrote him the friendly letter that comprises the second document in *True Sentiments*. It revisits the main arguments that the colonists had made so far. The first settlers carried their English rights and liberties with them when they bought and converted a wild land into civilization "without any aid from the nation" in order to propagate Christianity and "English dominion." Though Charles II vacated their charter, William and Mary gave them a new one. In a striking addition, the Assembly cites the *Plantation Act* or *Naturalization Act* of 1740 (13 Geo. 2.c.7), which empowered colonial courts to naturalize Protestants who resided in any of the British American colonies for seven years without being absent for more than two months, to show that the colonists themselves must have been "deemed natural born subjects" in the first place for their courts to receive such authority. The law of nature and nations corroborates the English, customary, and charter rights of colonists, because it is "unnatural and unreasonable" to suppose that local or other circumstances would deprive any citizen of any country of their constitutional rights. This is particularly so in the case of Great Britain, a free state with a fixed constitution, where the constitution itself is "the common right of all

British subjects." In a move reminiscent of Otis's approximation of natural and English common law, the Assembly continues,

> It is the glory of the British constitution that it has its foundation in the law of God and nature. It is essentially a natural Right, that a man shall quietly enjoy, and have the sole disposal of his own property. This Right is ingrafted into the British constitution and is familiar to the American subjects.
>
> ... The security of Right and Property is the great end of Government. Surely then such measures as tend to render Right and Property precarious, tend to destroy both Property and Government, for these must stand or fall together.—Property is admitted to have an existence in the savage state of nature. And if it is necessary for the support of savage life, it by no means becomes less so in civil society.[11]

The state of nature bears a unique weight in supporting the colonists' claims against the new taxes. Divine law, the law of nations, natural law, common law, charters, and provincial law are all marshalled in support. However, in this document the only right that negates government when it is violated is the right to property, anchored in the state of nature. Other revolutionary texts we have examined locate the freedoms of religion, expression, assembly, and other fundamental rights in the state of nature, to show that they survive the transition to civil society. Among the rights enumerated in the letter to Shelburne, only property is tied inextricably to government. It is also the only one anchored in the state of nature, which thus becomes the load-bearing component in Massachusetts's letter.

True Sentiments continues with letters by the Assembly based on permutations of the same arguments, often with the same or slightly reworded passages, calculated to better persuade the various recipients.

---

11. *True Sentiments* (London, 1768), 15. The letter to Shelburne was widely circulated in the colonies, e.g., March 21, 1768 *Boston Gazette*, March 28 *Supplement to the Boston Evening-Post*, April 4 *Supplement to the New-York Gazette, and the Weekly Mercury*, April 14 *Pennsylvania Gazette*, May 2 *South Carolina Gazette*, etc.

As already mentioned, one of these letters printed in *True Sentiments* was sent by the Assembly to Dennys DeBerdt, the province's agent in London, on January 12, 1768. With slight variations it reproduces the first half of the passage sent to Shelburne three days later, quoted previously. It also contains the second half with two noteworthy modifications: it interpolates a sentence that describes the state of nature and comes from Otis's adaptation of Rousseau to the colonists' property rights in the 1761 *Paxton's Case*, and it adds a sentence in favor of private property grounded in the state of nature, as opposed to both communism and any political system in which property rights are derived from a central authority.[12]

> Property is admitted to have an existence even in the savage state of nature. The bow, the arrow, and the tomahawk; the hunting and the fishing ground, are species of property as important to an American savage, as pearls, rubies and diamonds are to the Mogul or a Nabob in the East, or the lands, tenements, hereditaments, messuages, gold and silver of the Europeans. And if property is necessary for the support of savage life, it is by no means less so in civil society. The utopian schemes of levelling, and a community of goods, are as visionary and impracticable, as those which vest all property in the crown, are arbitrary, despotick, and in our government unconstitutional.[12]

Another item in *True Sentiments*, known as the Massachusetts Circular Letter, was the General Court's response to the Townshend Acts, drafted by Otis and Samuel Adams and dated February 11, 1768. It did not contain new arguments, but brought the ones we have reviewed into sharp focus. It was addressed to other colonies, not to London. Massachusetts thought that Parliament could not violate the fixed constitution "without destroying its own foundation." According to the Circular, the colonists have a natural right to their property, irrespective of charter rights. As they are not represented in Parliament, taxes and duties intended to raise

12. *True Sentiments*, 63.

revenue "are infringements of their natural and constitutional rights." Given the geographical distance, colonists can never be represented in Westminster, which is why only their own legislatures can deliberate about taxes. Massachusetts sent a petition to the Crown on these matters, as well as concerning the violation of equity caused by a governor and judges drawing a salary from London, or by the choice of any paymaster other than the people themselves. The Circular ends with Massachusetts assuring the other colonies that they instructed their agent to present these and other grievances and seek a royal response.

Hillsborough promptly ordered Massachusetts to revoke the Circular. When it refused, Governor Bernard dissolved the Assembly. This led to riots, and Hillsborough dispatched four regiments to Boston. They arrived in October 1768. During these months, self-defense, similarly to property earlier, began to be described as a state of nature right that could be transferred, after all. Moreover, it could also be expanded from an individual into a collective state of nature right in a way that could transfer not to the British government, but to American civil society, a legitimacy that was radically independent from any authority that the mother country may or may not have devolved on the colonies. Thus there were several ways in which Britain could have pushed the colonies into a state of nature, where they were able to rely on their natural social order and state of nature rights to reconstitute themselves into a new, federal republic. We saw texts that argue that taxation without consent created a state of nature. Others contended that the Stamp Act in particular has shut down the courts and government. Sending soldiers to suppress legitimate opposition and expressions of colonial grievances was also cited as a trigger for the state of nature.

The September 5, 1768 *Boston Gazette* published a letter by Clericus Americanus under their own heading "[Reader! Attend!]." In his own copy Harbottle Dorr, Jr. ascribed the piece to the Reverend John Cleaveland of Ipswich (1722–1799). Cleaveland (also spelled Cleveland) was educated at Yale and served as chaplain in the Essex regiment from 1776. His ingenious article is a series of nine questions that—he suggested— anyone could ask. The first wonders whether free and English people have a right to property; the second, whether they have a right to migrate; the third, whether the first settlers remained English subjects, or came under Holland's rule (in the case of the Plymouth Pilgrims); the fourth, whether the Native Americans were not "the proper Lords and Proprietors" of the lands that the first settlers purchased with their own money; and so on. The ninth and final question asks: if Bernard refuses to convene the Assembly, and "our charter is vacated and we reduced to a state of nature," would it not be advisable to convene a legislature and resume government and civil courts without London's and Bernard's approval? On the bottom of his copy Dorr added, "This Paper (Governor Bernard intimates) gave rise to the Convention."[13]

Cleaveland's questions were widely reprinted, and appear in *A Short View of the History of the Colony of Massachusetts Bay* (London, 1769), plausibly attributed to Israel Mauduit (1708–1787), former colonial agent for Massachusetts with his brother, Jasper.[14] In the introduction,

---

13. Harbottle Dorr, annotation in the September 5, 1768 *Boston Gazette*. http://www.masshist.org/dorr/volume/2/sequence/249.

14. At another peak in the controversy with Britain, the February 29, 1771 *Essex Gazette* and the March 4, 1771, *Boston Gazette* reprinted Cleaveland's 1768 text. The March 19, 1771, *Essex Gazette* carried replies to Cleaveland from a certain "Johannes in Eremo." From his reply to the first Cleaveland query, namely whether or not freemen and Englishmen have a right to property: "That all Men considered in a State of Nature (in a civil Sense) are equally free and possessed of certain personal Rights and Properties independently one of the other, I suppose all will allow." Taking another's property in the state of nature violates the positive golden rule, "all Things whatsoever ye would that Men should do to you, do ye even so to them." Civil states "are not natural Bodies, or were not created by the Almighty Bodies Politic, we must look upon them as *voluntary Bodies*, originally formed by mutual Agreement or Compact." This strange reply to Cleaveland locates property right in the state of nature "in a civil Sense," which seems to mean handling the state of nature as a constitutional fiction that is necessary for debates that can only be had in the polity. The polity itself is neither natural, nor divinely ordained. It is based on voluntary agreement, even if the state of nature and a divine formulation of the golden rule (which could have been stated in purely moral terms) are both relevant for understanding the property rights that the polity provides. I could not identify the author, but in 1774–76 Cleaveland himself published fiery denunciations of King and Parliament under the pen name, "Johannes in Eremo." E.g., John Cleaveland Papers, January 1, 1776, draft letter to Mr. Hall, Congregational Library and Archives, Correspondence, 1758–76, 116–23.

Mauduit argues that Massachusetts took the lead "in every fresh Mode of Resistance against the Laws," and other colonies followed. The reason for their arrogance is their charter, the deconstruction of which holds the key to refuting their claims. It is true, Mauduit admits, that until the Glorious Revolution, the royal prerogative in the colonies and the colonies' charter rights were unclear. The earliest charters, by James VI/I and Charles I, gave Massachusetts too much autonomy. That said, this autonomy successfully attracted settlers, and the intention and understanding of the contracting parties (both kings' and settlers') lend the charters an authority. "Though wrongly given, they are rightly established, and it would be much more unjust to take them away."[15] The first document Mauduit reprints to show the gap between the colonists' real rights and their misconstrued charter rights is Cleaveland's article. Both from Cleaveland's language, and from its interpretation by Mauduit, it is clear that in this deployment of the state of nature topos, the violation of Massachusetts's charter is understood to be sufficient to push the province into the state of nature.

While in other formulations military threat or action, attack on colonial property, abridgements of freedom of association, conscience or religion, or other reasons are given as the sole criterion for severing the link between Britain and the colonies, in this case the thin line between being a part of the empire and being in the American state of nature is the colonial charter. As Donald Lutz has shown, charters were integral to a tradition and understanding of imperial law that is best described as colonial constitutionalism.[16] This strand of constitutionalism is necessarily

15. Mauduit (?), A Short View, 3. The exact same line of reasoning appears in Richard Hussey, MP's speech in the February 3–4, 1766, Commons debate on the Declaratory Act. Temperley, "Debates," 569–70.
16. Lutz, Colonial Origins, introduction. We should add that alongside colonial constitutionalism, in the mother country Charles II's attack on London's charters in 1683 was also described as pushing Great Britain into a state of nature during the 1689 parliamentary debate about the meaning of abdication, for instance by Sir George Treby. Colonists would have read his argument in several often-cited texts, such as Rapin, The History of England (London, 1733), 2:790; or The History and Proceedings of the House of Commons of England... (London, 1742), 2:227.

localized to the place that holds the charter, creates forms of colonial self-government, and passes the laws that over time add up to a substantial legal corpus and tradition independent from King or Parliament.

Gridley's argument in Council on December 20, 1765 and Hawley's defense in *Warren's Case* were not the only applications of the state of nature to colonial criminal law, a vital part of the independent colonial legal system. An article in the August 22, 1768 issue of the *Connecticut* (now *Hartford*) *Courant* deals with the question whether theft can be punished with death. The author thinks not. People in the state of nature could not have agreed to alienate their individual right to life, and they had no right to do so, in any case. Therefore "a society or government" should not pretend to a claim on delegated rights to life. While the right to life and self-defense are inalienable, the state of nature right to punish is not. Society can punish murder with death because that was the punishment in the state of nature and remains so in natural and divine law. This is the only crime where the state, though without relevant legal authority of its own, can enact a divine and natural law. If the state's right to punish depends on the transfer of the respective individual state of nature right, and the state can act on behalf of "the community" (in the author's term), then what happens to the rights of the person being put to death, given that he or she did not alienate his or her right to life? Interestingly, the author does not agree with Hobbes that society, and the person being punished with death, are in a state of nature toward each other. Instead, capital punishment is justified by natural and divine law.[17]

Although it contains no specifics to confirm this, the reflection on the state of nature in the *Connecticut Courant* article was probably prompted by Isaac Frasier's capture, trial, and execution on September 7, 1768 in Fairfield, Connecticut. Frasier was a notorious burglar and thief,

17. A long reply appeared in the October 14, 1768 *Connecticut Journal*. Another interesting revolutionary reading of Hobbes occurs in a June 27, 1767 letter by "JH" from New York, in which JH describes the government fit for free men as one that balances the maximal preservation of state of nature rights with the prospect of "the strong Killing the weak in a State of Nature." American Philosophical Society, Sol Feinstone Collection, Mss. B.F.327, No. 1312.

according to the *Brief Account of the Life, and Abominable Thefts, of the Notorious Isaac Frasier,* which he dictated during his final captivity. He requested Noah Hobart to give a sermon at his execution. Among other things, Hobart argued that if crimes were left unpunished, everyone would be unsafe in their life and possessions, "the happiness of society is at an end, and government is in effect dissolved; for such a state is little, if at all, better than a state of nature."[18]

5.2 ENGLISH LIBERTIES (1680–1774) AND BRITISH LIBERTIES (1766–67)

We have seen that "English liberties" was a much-invoked phrase, usually denoting something inherited from the first settlers. We have also examined different types of revolutionary knowledge production, including preparations for cases, almanacs, original and creatively redacted newspaper articles, political sermons, university disputations, and arguments in court. Later we will see the role that debating societies and committees of correspondence played in discussing, developing, coordinating, and disseminating the American state of nature discourse. In addition to tracing the American reception of great state of nature theorists, such as Grotius, Hobbes, Locke, Pufendorf, Burlamaqui, Vattel, Montesquieu, Rousseau, and Blackstone, close attention to a phrase like "English liberties" isolates a relatively narrow semantic range, enabling us to focus on the contestation and development of this specific range, and thereby arrive at a better understanding of how varieties of state of nature arguments became available to participants in particular constitutional debates, such as the First Continental Congress.

18. *Excessive wickedness, the way to an untimely death. A sermon preached at Fairfield, in Connecticut, September 7th, 1768. At the execution of Isaac Frasier* (New Haven, 1768), 7. Hobart used a similarly Hobbesian notion of the state of nature in his 1750 election day sermon at Hartford, Connecticut, *Civil Government, the Foundation of Social Happiness* . . . (North London, 1751), as well as in his 1765 *An Attempt to Illustrate and Confirm the Ecclesiastical Constitution of the Consociated Churches in the Colony of Connecticut,* discussed in chapter 6, section 6.3 below.

The Americanization of British liberties took many forms. *Paxton's Case*, the remonstrances against the Stamp Act, Hawley's and Bland's work, and other cases discussed here revealed that the colonists who appropriated and often expanded common law rights, such as rights to juries and representation, frequently invoked the state of nature as part of the English constitution (as described by Locke and Montesquieu); as a prepolitical state of sociability, rights and obligations (Hutcheson, Fordyce, Blackstone); as part of natural law, as they found it in Grotius, Hobbes, and Rousseau; and as a pivotal concept in the law of nations, as they adapted it from Hobbes, Pufendorf, Burlamaqui, or Vattel. The mechanics of this appropriation are difficult to convey adequately without discussing the materials they had available for this purpose. Omitting the first chapter of Locke's *Second Treatise* from the 1773 Boston edition is a case in point; so is Ames's *Almanack*, which reached a wide audience.

A more complicated text, which illustrates the mechanics involved in the intellectual and constitutional transformation, is *English Liberties*. Notwithstanding historically questionable and contradictory interpretations, this text is one of the sources of the shared eighteenth-century language of the state of nature. *The British Liberties, or the Free-Born Subject's Inheritance* was a handbook of sources and arguments concerning rights, including state of nature rights. It has a complicated but fascinating history, illustrative of both human agency and contingency in the history of ideas. It is also the kind of handbook that is seldom analyzed in detail in histories of constitutional thought, even though it affords an insight into how state of nature arguments were transmitted, transformed, and deployed during the colonies' own transition to independence. The secondary literature on American independence often makes single, short references to this book but, to my knowledge, no historian has paid sustained attention to its history and contents. Since the Founders mention it often, some historians refer to it as one of their key sources. The facts that there were several editions with very different contents and that the publishing history of the book made some editions more relevant than others remain unnoted in every account I have come across.

Perhaps more worrying is the historically under-powered invocation of *English Liberties* in Supreme Court decisions. It is cited to this day in constitutional interpretations of the state of nature. Justice Thomas cites the 1721 edition in his dissent in the 2015 *Obergefell v. Hodges* as a source for reconstructing the original meaning of the Founders' narrow understanding of liberty as the absence of restrictions on physical motion. In *Smothers v. Gresham Transfer, Inc.* (2001), the Oregon Supreme Court argued that *English Liberties* was a major conduit in the American reception of Magna Carta and Coke's *Institutes*, and cited chapter 29 of *English Liberties* on remedy. Justice Landau cited what he described as Care's *English Liberties* in the 2006 *Liberty Northwest Insurance Corp. v. Oregon Insurance Guarantee Association* to dispute with the *Smothers* decision. Another Oregon case, the 2013 *Klutschowski v. PeaceHealth*, again turned to *English Liberties* to establish the Oregon constitution's original intent.

In 1680 a book was published in London with the title, *English Liberties, or, The Free-Born Subject's Inheritance*, without the author's name.[19] A second edition appeared in 1682, and was reprinted in 1691 and 1692. The book is commonly attributed to Henry Care. Winthrop Hudson suggests that the real author is William Penn, and the first edition may have been designed as a handbook that Dissenters could use in court.[20] The early modern owner of a much-used copy at the Virginia Historical

19. *English liberties, or, The free-born subject's inheritance containing I. Magna Charta, the petition of right, the Habeas Corpus Act, and divers other most useful statutes . . . II. The proceedings in appeals of murther the work and power of parliaments, the qualifications necessary for such as should be chosen to that great truth. Plain directions for all persons concerned in ecclesiastical courts, and how to prevent or take off the Writ de Excommunicats Capiendo. As also the oath and duty of grand and petty juries, III. All the laws against conventicles and Protestant dissenters, with notes and directions both to constables and others concern'd, thereupon: and an abstract of all the laws against Papists.* Another work with a similar trajectory is John Hawles, *The Grand-Jury-Man's Oath and Office Explained* . . . (London, 1680), which after several editions became *The Englishman's Right* . . . (Boston, 1772).
20. Winthrop S. Hudson, "William Penn's English Liberties: Tract for Several Times," *William and Mary Quarterly* 26:4 (Oct. 1969), 578–85. Hudson thinks that the real author is William Penn. Lois Schwoerer in *The Ingenious Mr. Care* (Johns Hopkins, 2002) argues for Care's authorship.

Society inscribed it, "By Daniel DeFoe."[21] The book emphasized Magna Carta, the freedom of conscience, Habeas Corpus, and the glory and operations of the jury, including the famous *Bushel's Case* of 1670.

Bushel's Case started with another lawsuit, in which William Penn and William Mead were charged with tumultuous assembly for attending and speaking at a Quaker meeting. The jury found them guilty of "speaking in the street," but not guilty of unlawful assembly. The judge tried to use strong-arm tactics to force the jury to find them guilty on both counts. Eventually he fined them for contempt of court. One of the jurors, Edward Bushel, refused to pay, and petitioned the Court of Common Pleas for a writ of *habeas corpus*. Sir John Vaughan ruled that the jury cannot be punished on account of the verdict it returns. *Bushel's Case* became a landmark in the history of jury nullification, religious toleration, and the use of *habeas corpus*, in one.[22] A triumphant account of *Bushel's Case* forms the conclusion to the 1680 *English Liberties*. The grand jury's refusal to indict the Earl of Shaftesbury in 1681 may be one reason why the book was reissued in 1682, in hope of a broader readership. The popularity of these condensed, pocket-sized compendia of English law confirms that the authors' and publishers' calculations were correct. Large legal tomes were unwieldy and unavailable to those taken to court, to local officials, and to many colonists, who often had to make do without the large and expensive legal apparatus that one found in Westminster, the Temple, and other well-supplied centers of legal practice and learning.[23]

The printer George Larkin seems to have produced the 1680 first edition for two separate publishers, Benjamin Harris and John How. The

21. *English Liberties* (London, 1680), Virginia Historical Society, JN 203 1680 C21.
22. Simon Stern, "Between Local Knowledge and National Politics: Debating Rationales for Jury Nullification after Bushell's Case," *Yale Law Journal* 111:7 (2002), 1815–59, is an excellent account, and covers the trials of Benjamin Harris, Henry Care, and others relevant to both the printing history and the content of *English Liberties*.
23. Some copies I examined contain telling signs of use. 1680 edition: Harvard Law School, Historical & Special Collections, E C271e 680 Copy 2, has manicules inscribed for emphasis on 27, 28, 30, 61, 190, 193, 194, 196, 198, 199, and the hard-to-read print carefully redrawn by hand on 30 and 103.

1682 edition gives only Larkin's name, with the note that the book is sold by most booksellers. Harris and probably also How fled England around 1686. Interestingly, after Harris published a pamphlet that advocated excluding James II from succession, he was tried and sentenced to a fine and to stand in the pillory, and the jury's reluctance to convict him in turn became part of the account of *Bushel's Case* in *The English-Mans Right* of 1680. Harris's own case is also regarded as an important part of the emergence of jury nullification.[24] After he fled, Harris set up shop in Boston, where How most likely visited him. On their return to England, the two men may have collaborated on the new 1700 London edition, which was also the basis of the 1703 version.

All titles of *English Liberties* consist of several parts. The short "English Liberties, or the Free-born Subject's Inheritance" is followed by a main list of the most important laws described, a list of less important laws, and often a fourth section of supplementary material. The changes of title do not always correspond to a change in contents, and *vice versa*. New content may be added to previous sections, while the relevant section of the title remains unchanged. Together, the title and the contents page reveal a great deal about the emphases that the publisher expected to catch the readers' attention. After the short title, the 1680 edition names Magna Carta, the Petition of Right, and the *Habeas Corpus Act* in the short list of cardinal laws. The second section promises an overview of procedures in Parliament, jury trials and ecclesiastical court, and how to overturn *excommunicatio capiendo*, legal excommunication based on a bishop's recommendation. The third section concerns laws and police procedures against Dissenters and Catholics.

The book's character changed with the 1700 edition. "Now inlarged with new and useful additions by a well-wisher to his country" was added to the title. *Excommunicatio capiendo* was omitted from the long list of laws discussed, and the third section was replaced entirely with the powers and responsibilities of justices of peace and constables. The sections on dissenting were abridged, and the summary of the common

24. Stern, "Between Local Knowledge," 1830–34.

law was expanded to become a general handbook for justices of peace, constables, coroners, and other local officials. Almost half of the book's contents changed as a result. These additions were probably made by William Nelson, named in the 1703 edition as their author. In 1704 Nelson published *The Office and Authority of a Justice of Peace*, which has much in common with the 1700 and 1703 additions to *English Liberties*.

In a remarkable turn from the pro-Penn tone of the 1680 edition, the 1700 edition was dedicated to the House of Commons.[25] Harris inserted an "Epistle Dedicatory to the Commons," complaining of the violence and lawlessness of the last few reigns. He reminded the Commons that five thousand copies of *English Liberties* were confiscated from him, and he was subjected to fines, imprisonment, and corporal punishment.[26] Harris recounts fleeing into overseas exile for eight years, in fear of his life. Some time after his return, he continues, he thought it fit

> to Reprint this Collection, having left out those Statutes relating to Dissenters, &c. for whom His Most Gracious Majesty, and both Houses of Parliament, have made such Provisions, as do render us a Happy and United People . . . Accept therefore, Great Senators, these Weak Endeavours, which in more larger Volumes are your own already; It is but an Abbreviation of the Laws, Rights and Priviledges of this Nation, which every Man and Woman become Heirs to so soon as they are Born into the World; the which (as a Rich Dowry) was so settled upon each other at first, that all the Nations under the Copes of Heaven cannot Parallel the like; who may not only Wonder and Admire the Blessed Freedom of English-men, but Condole their own Nativities, being Born under the Tyrannick Yokes of Arbitrary Princes.

The reorientation of this handbook from the practical needs of legal defense to those of law enforcement continued with the next edition in

25. The title page note of this dedication was removed from the 1703 edition, and the "Epistle Dedicatory" redacted.
26. House of Commons, hill. 31 and 32 Car. 2.

1703, when the title was changed to *English Liberties: or, the Free-Born Subject's Inheritance. Being a Help to Justices as well as a Guide to Constables.* Harris's "Epistle Dedicatory" was reprinted, but the account of his overseas exile and his note on removing legal aids for Dissenters were now omitted. Harris's 1700 and 1703 conservative version of *English Liberties*, now less an individual's legal aid in court than a survey of Parliament's and law officers' rights, no longer fulfilled the book's original purpose.

The ambition and target audience of the 1680 and 1682 versions were resumed in 1719. A new publisher produced the 1719 edition, sometimes known as the fourth edition. They significantly changed the title and further revised the contents. This edition incorporates and gives pride of place to the Charter of the Forest which, with *De tallagio non concedendo*, is added to Magna Carta and the *Habeas Corpus Act* among the headline laws. *De tallagio non concedendo* is a document from around 1297 that declares that freemen cannot be obliged without consent to pay taxes, forced loans or other forms of aid to the king. The 1628 Petition of Rights begins with affirming this document and calls it a statute. In the 1637 *King against John Hampden*, at the height of the ship money controversy, much of the debate revolved around whether or not *De tallagio* was a statute or merely an extract from the 1297 *Confirmatio Cartarum*, Edward I's confirmation of Magna Carta.[27] Hume and others in the eighteenth century regarded it as the statutory foundation of resistance to taxation without consent, whether the attempt to tax was made by Parliament or the King.[28] Though they were wrong, and *De tallagio* is not a statute but probably an imperfect extract from the *Confirmatio*, the emphasis placed on it in the 1719 *English Liberties* is indicative of its eighteenth-century interpretation as a landmark statute against taxation

27. *Complete Collection of State Trials* (5th ed., Dublin, 1793), 1:597–98, 612, 626–28, 648. *De tallagio* was discussed many more times during the trial; these are only the main passages where its status was debated. Also see H. Rothwell, "The Confirmation of the Charters, 1297," three articles in *English Historical Review* 60 (1945), 16–35, 177–91, 300–315.
28. Reid, *Authority to Tax*, 138–40.

without consent, which is what we find not only in Hume but also in the American uses.

The Petition of Rights is relegated to the third section. The Charter of the Forest is often described as the common man's companion to Magna Carta. While the latter dealt mostly with the rights of barons, the 1217 Charter of the Forest asserted free men's right to use natural resources for cooking, heating, charcoal burning, grazing and pasturing, and the like. It also rolled back the historical process whereby royal privileges laid down in so-called forest laws were extended into cultivated areas, including fields and farms. The right of access to the commons was reasserted and expanded. Blackstone's 1759 edition of Magna Carta and the Charter of the Forest is said to have renewed attention to its importance; yet we find that the 1719 edition of this practical book of law already features it prominently.[29] In any case, the emphasis continued to shift. The 1680 and 1682 editions prioritized religious self-defense in court. The 1700 and 1703 editions were meant to be used in the execution of justice and police work—a genre with a long history. The focus of the 1719 edition is political liberty.

The first American edition was based on the 1719 version. It revived features of the 1680 and 1682 editions that the 1700 and 1703 versions omitted. Such features include sections dedicated to the definition of various senses of "liberty" and "peer." Another is the incorporation of a long, free-standing text, called "A notable Discourse of the Antiquity, use and power of Parliaments, and the Qualifications of such Gentlemen as are fit to be Chosen the peoples Representatives," which was also present in the 1680 and 1682 versions, and "A Discourse of Parliaments, touching the Antiquity, Use, and Power of them, and the Qualifications of such Gentlemen as are fit to be chosen the Peoples Representatives," which is

29. Linda Colley, "Empires of Writing: Britain, America and Constitutions, 1776–1848," *Law and History Review* 32:2 (2014), 237–66, at 242–43; Nicholas A. Robinson, "The Charter of the Forest: Evolving Human Rights in Nature," in D. B. Magrow et al. (eds.), *Magna Carta and the Rule of Law* (Chicago: American Bar Association, 2014), 311–77, at 315, 320–21.

new to the 1719 edition, and appears in the 1721 and 1774 editions of *English Liberties*, as well as in the 1766 and 1767 *British Liberties*.

It is unclear what motivated these major shifts of emphasis in the 1719 edition. The bookseller, Arthur Bettesworth, seems relatively apolitical. One of the printers, Elizabeth Nutt, was known for her general opposition to the government and was arrested for selling the *London Evening-Post*.[30] On the whole, this does not tell us much about the radical innovations in the 1719 edition. One explanation might be the political context that prompted the new emphasis on *De Tallagio* and the Charter of the Forest, and a new edition of the 1680 passages, namely the 1714 *Riot Act*, which made it easier to prosecute for cases like Penn's and Mead's was in 1670 for unlawful assembly; the growing tax burden under Queen Anne, and then George II; and perhaps the expectation that the break-out of the War of the Quadruple Alliance in 1718 would lead to further schemes for public financing. Another possible explanation is that William Nelson, the scholar responsible for the additions, had a personal, partly antiquarian interest in these topics.

Importantly, the book has its own American lineage. In 1687, William Penn had *The Excellent Priviledge of Liberty and Property Being the Birth-Right of the Free-Born Subjects of England* published in Philadelphia. Hudson argues that Penn's purpose was to help the settlers protect their freedoms, that this book begins with and consists largely of excerpts from *English Liberties*, and this is evidence that Penn is the real author of the original work, perhaps with minor tasks, such as transcribing and editing laws, performed by Care. This is an intriguing suggestion, though one should add that the documents marshalled in *The Excellent Priviledge* to support Penn's own proprietary claims in America make it questionable that educating his settlers was his sole or even his main objective. Protecting his claim to Pennsylvania was at least as important, but Hudson is right that Penn's legal self-defense in 1670 had taught him how

---

30. Paula McDowell, *The Women of Grub Street: Press, Politics, and Gender in the London Literary Marketplace, 1678–1730* (Clarendon, 1998), excellent account on 70.

important it was for the non-lawyer layman to have access to a comprehensible, practical and cheap introduction to the common law.

What is known as the fifth edition of *English Liberties* also has an American connection. It was published in Boston in 1721 by James Franklin, again with revised contents. Its significance in the colonial political context is illustrated by the episode when James was thrown into jail from June 12 to July 7, 1722, for his younger brother, Benjamin, mocking the Massachusetts government under the pen name of Silence Dogood in the *New-England Courant*. On his release, further mockery, censorship, and attempts to evade censorship followed. The July 23–30, 1722 issue of the journal begins with James Franklin's note on his amazement at his countrymen's ignorance of the happy English constitution, followed by a reprint of chapter 29 from his own 1721 edition of *English Liberties*. This is a commentary on the "none shall be condemned without trial" provision from Magna Carta.

The book remained relevant in the colonies throughout the century. Benjamin Franklin re-offered copies of his brother's edition of *English Liberties* for sale in 1744.[31] In the tumultuous year of 1765, the Philadelphia Library Company ordered several new volumes.[32] Some time between 1765 and 1776, Harbottle Dorr transcribed sections of the 1721 *English Liberties* as an appendix to his extraordinary annotated newspaper collection. From annotations and provenance marks we can reconstruct the trajectory of an interesting Harvard copy. It was bought by Benjamin Ellery (b. 1669, Gloucester, MA, d. 1746, Newport, RI), probably in Boston, and taken to Rhode Island when Ellery moved. Perhaps there it found its way to Francis Dana Channing (b. 1775, Newport, RI, d. 1810 at sea), 1794 Harvard graduate, lawyer, secretary of the Boston Social Law Library and Massachusetts representative in 1808–1810, before his death at thirty-five.[33] The copy has numerous handwritten marks

---

31. *A Catalogue of Choice and Valuable Books* (Philadelphia, 1744), item 356.
32. Trevor Colbourn, *The Lamp of Experience* (North Carolina, 1965). This may have been the 1719 edition, shown in the Library Company's 1770 and 1807 catalogs.
33. Houghton *EC65 C1803 680eh. The copy was then picked up by Arthur Henry Lea, son of the Philadelphia historian Henry Charles Lea. Harvard acquired it when Arthur died in 1938.

of emphasis. The first annotation on the front flyleaf proudly speculates that Benjamin Franklin "doubtless composed in part" this edition, since he was working as his brother's apprentice. Another copy seems to have passed from student to student at Yale in the mid-1750s, suggesting that Ezra Stiles, who was a tutor at Yale from 1749 until he left for Newport, Rhode Island, in 1755 (only to return to Yale in 1778), placed it on the curriculum.[34]

In 1766 the history of the *English Liberties* took another turn when the London publishers H. S. Woodfall and W. Strahan printed *British liberties: or the free-born subject's inheritance; containing the laws that form the basis of those liberties, with observations thereon; also an introductory essay on political liberty and a comprehensive view of the Constitution of Great Britain*, with a second edition under a new title in 1767. Woodfall later published the Junius letters between 1769 and 1772 and was charged with seditious libel against the King for his trouble. Note the change from "English" to "British" in the title. Moreover, the work now contained a remarkable eighty-page introductory essay that drew on Sidney, Locke, Coke, and others seen as champions of progressive liberty.

The introductory essay, which replaced the proem on the magnificence of the English constitution that prefaced all other editions, was written or, more likely, commissioned by one or both of two radical booksellers and publishers, Edward and Charles Dilly. Like Benjamin to James Franklin, Charles Dilly (1739–1807) was bound as apprentice to his brother Edward (1732–1779), a bookseller in The Poultry. Charles visited America as a young man, with a brief appearance in Philadelphia in early 1764, where he made valuable contacts for the business and may have become acquainted with the eighteen-year-old Benjamin Rush. By the spring of 1764 we find Charles back in London, joining his brother's bookselling business as a partner. They were Dissenters and published

34. Beinecke, Franklin 391.1721c, with the inscribed names and dates of Ebenezer Garnsey, 1754; Job Wright, 1755; and John Pell, who joined the Linonian Society in 1757, together with Garnsey's note that he is studying under Stiles.

radical texts, as well as less controversial ones.[35] J. J. Caudle, author of the *Oxford Dictionary of National Biography* entry for Charles, notes their "particular specialism in dissenting and 'American' literature, reflecting the brothers' whig and patriot political sympathies." Caudle writes that although Charles was known for supporting American independence, he was more moderate than his brother. Their house was famous for its hospitality. Dr. Samuel Johnson and John Wilkes met there in 1776 and 1781. The 1776 dinner was also attended by Arthur Lee, of whom Johnson disapproved for being "not only a *patriot,* but an *American.*"[36] Benjamin Rush visited their shop, describing it as a "kind of Coffee house for authors."[37] The brothers held an interest in the *London Magazine.*

In the preface of the new, 1766 edition, the author states that his intention was to give "a comprehensive view of the British Constitution," in clear ideas, as introduction to the whole work. The whole work covers positive laws, for which they drew on the old *English Liberties.* For the rest, they relied mainly on Coke, except for the new statutes. The essay should be understood as the author's introduction to the common law as a whole.

The introduction consists of its own separate introduction, followed by "Observations on some of the most essential of the following laws."[38] The introduction's introduction is theoretical, while the observations seem to be an attempt to survey legal historians' work on the English

---

35. Sylvester H. Bingham, "Publishing in the Eighteenth Century with Special Reference to the Firm of Edward and Charles Dilly," PhD diss., Yale, 1937; Daniel W. Hollis III, "Edward and Charles Dilly," in J. K. Bracken and J. Silver (eds.), *The British Literary Book Trade, 1700–1820* (Detroit: Gale Research, 1995), 97–102; Lyman H. Butterfield, "The American Interests of the Firm E. and C. Dilly, with Their Letters to Benjamin Rush, 1770–1795," *Papers of the Bibliographical Society of America* 45 (1951), 283–332; *The Autobiography of Benjamin Rush: His "Travels through life" Together with His Commonplace Book for 1789–1813* (ed. George. W. Corner, Westport, CT, 1948); Colin Bonwick, *English Radicals and the American Revolution* (North Carolina, 1977); Edwin Wolf, *The Book Culture of a Colonial American City* (Oxford, 1988), 119.
36. Boswell, *Life of Johnson* ([1791] London, 1816), 3:69.
37. Rush, *Autobiography,* 62–63.
38. *British Liberties,* introduction: i–lxiii. Observations: lxiv–lxxix.

constitution. The conclusion refers to the two parts as a whole, suggesting they were meant to be read in conjunction. The introduction's stated aim is to combine and harmonize Montesquieu and Locke in order to explain why and how individual rights, the jury system, the separation of powers, fair and equal representation, and other features of the British constitution create and sustain political liberties. The author provides long quotations from both writers. It is not a straightforward amalgam, as the author also explains that Montesquieu and Rousseau drew heavily on Locke, and brings in other writers as well, notably Rousseau and William Temple.[39] Locke is the most prominent source in the introduction to *British Liberties*, and the author cites and comments on Locke's state of nature passages in the *Second Treatise* more than a dozen times throughout the first part.

The passages are used to support several points, such that commonwealths are in a state of nature vis-à-vis absolute princes, with other commonwealths, people outside the commonwealth, and anyone else with whom they do not share predetermined rules or an independent arbitrator;[40] that there are not only rights, but also deprivation and dangers in the state of nature, therefore the commonwealth should make sure never to become a worse proposition;[41] and that property arises in the state of nature through labor and through the emergence of the idea of a right to property thus created.[42]

It is not only state of nature themes in the 1766 new introduction that resurface in similar form in colonial texts. The author describes the 1679 Habeas Corpus Act under Charles II as "one GREAT BULWARK OF BRITISH

---

39. He cites Rousseau's *Social Contract* in French, e.g., xxvii, xl. The errata notes that almost all the typographical mistakes in the book are concentrated in these passages, as the editor originally forgot to correct them. On p. xli the writer pauses to add that if Locke, Montesquieu, and natural reason are not enough to convince his reader, the reader should consult Pufendorf, Temple, Cumberland, Burlamaqui, Plato, Cicero, Domat, and others.
40. *British Liberties*, xvi–xx, xlix–lix.
41. *British Liberties*, xlii.
42. *British Liberties*, xliv, where the author combines Rousseau's *Emile*, first published in 1762, with the relevant passages in Locke's *Second Treatise*.

LIBERTY."[43] He cites Tacitus on Germanic tribes to establish a version of the ancient constitutionalist argument that supports Parliament. However, he recommends this interpretation not through his own but through other writers, such as William Lambarde and Montesquieu who, according to the author(s), rightly understands Tacitus to describe the invention of "this beautiful system from the woods."[44] The introduction also criticizes recent parliaments heavily, for instance for changing representatives' terms from three to seven years.[45] In a long passage, it builds a wonderful argument about representation.[46] Every individual has the right to fair and equal representation in the legislative. Rotten boroughs, royal intervention, corruption in Parliament, and other dangers threaten this right. This part of the argument is conventional. However, the author proceeds to assert that whoever attempts to establish a representative body for the people who are unrepresented is not guilty of sedition or attempted secession, but a friend to government, and strives for the restoration of order—a conservative revolutionary, as it were. This is similar to Bland's rejoinder to Whately's virtual representation thesis in the *Inquiry*, also published in 1766.

The "Observations" section charts an eccentric path across works on English constitutional history.[47] It cites William Lambarde's *Archion* (1568),[48] Henry Spelman and William Dugdale extensively, William Temple's 1695 *Introduction to the History of England*, a 1744 book on the use and abuse of Parliament attributed to Algernon Sidney but probably

43. *British Liberties*, lxxvi.
44. *British Liberties*, xxxix–xl.
45. *British Liberties*, xxxiii.
46. *British Liberties*, xxiii–xxv.
47. *British Liberties*, lxiv–lxxix.
48. The author cites Lambarde's "Archion" several times, including an ancient constitutionalist defense of Parliament's antiquity based on Tacitus's famous account of deliberation in Germanic tribes. On p. lxxviii, however, the author admits that he has not read Lambarde directly, which makes one wonder whether he confused *Archaionomia* (London, 1568), Lambarde's edition and commentary on Anglo-Saxon laws, with his later *Archeion, or, A Discourse upon the High Courts of Justice in England* (1591, wide manuscript circulation, first publ. 1635).

written by Franklin's long-time friend James Ralph;[49] Blackstone's 1759 *The Great Charter and the Charter of the Forest*, and Smollett on the Glorious Revolution (presumably Smollett's 1760–1765 *Continuation of the History of England*, which extended Hume's *Complete History*). To prove the antiquity of juries, the author cites Spelman, Dugdale, Bacon, William Temple, Rapin, Anthony Ellys's *The Spiritual and Temporal Liberty of Subjects in England*, and the 1741 edition of Selden's 1616 edition, translation and wonderful notes on Fortescue's 1543 *De laudibus legum Angliae*. Ancient constitutionalism, a "country" criticism of corruption in court and Parliament, and pride in the antiquity and mechanics of the constitution, are merged here.

Though not noted in the preface, there is considerable editorial work in the main text, as well. The editor names Coke and Care as the source of most comments placed after the text of the laws. The new editors' own marginal notes start to appear early in the book. Edward I's address at the beginning of Magna Carta was not, according to the first such note, directed at archbishops and bishops; and the phrase "kings of England" was also missing from the original list of those whose souls Magna Carta was meant to save. Other changes include downplaying, even removing, passages from the Charter of the Forest.

While the first part of the introductory essay makes a political argument about British liberties and combines state of nature sources ranging from Locke and Pufendorf to Burlamaqui, Montesquieu, and Rousseau, the second, technical part complements the first by grounding more or less the same arguments in common law decisions and authorities that can be cited in court. It also contains numerous references to British statute and common law cases that one could invoke in support. It is remarkable

---

49. Though the author of the long introductory essay to *British Liberties* mentions this work explicitly only twice, he describes the work as one "which I have several times quoted" (lxxiv). Therefore unattributed passages in the essay may also draw on Ralph, who in 1744 was also working on a large *History of England*. John B. Shipley, "Franklin Attends a Book Auction," *Pennsylvania Magazine of History and Biography* 80:1 (1956), 37–45; Shipley, "James Ralph's Pamphlets, 1741–1744," *Library* s5-19 (1) (1964), 130–46.

that the introduction to the renamed *British Liberties* is a long essay with state of nature arguments in the first part, which are harmonized with the common law in the second part. The introductory essay, together with the successful fusion of an eclectic range of state of nature sources, helps to explain the text's impact in the colonies. Among other things, it makes more explicitly Otis's point in the 1765 *Considerations* that representation is an individual right anchored in the state of nature, and survives the transition to civil society.[50]

Hudson writes that this handbook "had more to do with preparing the minds of American colonists for the American Revolution than the larger but less accessible work of Coke, Sidney, and Locke." The title change from "English" to "British" may be a corroboration of Peter de Bolla's statement that the 1766 edition was produced specially for export to the colonies.[51] If so, then the introductory essay's presentation of the state of nature as a foundation of British rights dovetails with the rest of the evidence for a renewed fascination with the state of nature in the colonies. One might even speculate that some colonists, perhaps including those Charles Dilly met on his 1764 trip, suggested that a book like *British Liberties*, with the change of title, introductory essay and new, politically charged annotations, would be well-received in the colonies. John and Abigail Adams corresponded with Edward Dilly in 1774–1775, sometimes via Catharine Macaulay, and in 1780 under a pseudonym.[52] On January 15, 1775, Dilly wrote to Adams that he was "Printing the Whole Proceedings of the American Congress."[53]

---

50. A stronger version is in Granville Sharpe's *A Declaration of the People's Natural Right* (London, 1774), copies of which both Franklin and John Adams owned.
51. De Bolla, *The Architecture of Concepts* (Fordham, 2013), 152.
52. February 20, 1780, letter from John Adams to Edward and Charles Dilly in *Papers of John Adams*, vol. 8, digital edition: http://www.masshist.org/publications/apde2/view?id=ADMS-06-08-02-0221. Charles Dilly printed Adams's *A Defence of the Constitutions* ... (London, 1787-88).
53. January 13, 1775, letter from Edward Dilly to John Adams in *Papers of John Adams*, vol. 2, digital edition: http://www.masshist.org/publications/apde2/view?id=ADMS-06-02-02-0069.

However, as we saw, the 1719 version of *English Liberties* also played a crucial role, while the 1700 and 1703 editions, despite being produced by Harris and How, were conservative by comparison. This is not to say that the *British Liberties* was not influential, notably because of the introductory essay's detailed discussion of state of nature theories in Locke, Pufendorf, Burlamaqui, Montesquieu, Rousseau, and others, and its attempt to integrate them into a theoretical, partly natural law foundation for common law liberties. While a full survey of the various editions, including the number and distribution of surviving copies, early annotations and references, and their likely date of arrival in the colonies, remains to be made, it is clear that they had a considerable impact. The 1741 catalog of the Library Company of Philadelphia shows no copies, but the 1754 catalog of the Union Library and the 1757 catalog of the Library Company both record the 1719 edition of *English Liberties*, and so do subsequent catalogs.[54] The 1770 catalog and all later ones show that a copy of the 1767 edition of *British Liberties* came early into the Company's possession. Harvard had a copy of the 1766 edition of *British Liberties* by 1830 at the latest. The catalog for that year contains two entries, one for the book, another, curiously, as a cross-reference to Penn's 1670 account of his trial, prefiguring Hudson's connection between Penn's trial and the *English Liberties* series.[55] Jefferson's 1783 book catalog has an entry on Care's *English Liberties* 8vo, and *English Liberties* 12mo.[56]

What is known as the sixth edition of *English Liberties*, corrected and improved, appeared in 1774 in Providence, Rhode Island. Strangely enough, it reprints the preface to the reader praising the progress of liberties "under our august monarch" that appeared in the 1719 London

54. *Charter, Laws, and Catalogue of Books, of the Library Company of Philadelphia* (Philadelphia, 1757), 78–79, item 275; *A Catalogue of Books Belonging to the Union-Library-Company of Philadelphia* (Philadelphia, 1754), 39, item 126. The Union Library merged with the Library Company only in 1769.

55. *A Catalogue of the Library of Harvard University* (Cambridge, MA, 1830), 1:101, 471.

56. 1783 Catalog at the Massachusetts Historical Society, digital version: http://www.masshist.org/thomasjeffersonpapers/doc?id=catalog1783_1.

and 1721 Boston editions. This seems to be by choice rather than necessity or expediency in reprinting, as the 1774 edition also contains a note after the contents section indicating that this edition, with additions by William Nelson, had been adapted for American audiences. It omits content that was deemed not useful for the colonies, but "to compensate amply for those Omissions, and make the Work as truly valuable," it catered to colonial readers by adding legal forms for the use of justices of the peace, and "Extracts from several late celebrated Writers on the British Constitution, which serve to illustrate and enforce the very important Doctrines advanced by the ingenious Author."[57] The 1774 edition also introduces notes from Blackstone's *Commentaries*, for instance on high treason, the *Habeas Corpus Act*, juries, and *Bushel's Case*.[58] The identity of the presumably Tory editor is unknown. The 1774 edition was published just months after the passage of the Intolerable Acts. Colonial patriots read the discussions of Magna Carta, treason, and fundamental rights with interest. Not surprisingly, George Mason used this book while drafting Virginia's Declaration of Rights (1776).[59] There are several such handbooks that aimed to make the common law, legal procedure, and individual rights, easy to understand and use in court.

5.3 ANCIENT CONSTITUTIONALISM

Another source of right claims against the British government that was anchored in the state of nature, and one we also find in the 1766 *British Liberties*, is known as ancient constitutionalism. Ancient Celts, Germans, the Batavians, or other tribes described as fierce and independent, notably by Tacitus, were sometimes depicted in the eighteenth century as groups with certain rights and customs, and fitted into a historical

---

57. *English Liberties*, viii.
58. Treason: 78–79. Cf. same text, without note, in 1721 ed., 75. *Habeas Corpus Act*: 1774 ed. 183, cf. 1721 ed. 175. Juries: 1774 ed. 216, cf. 1721 ed. 203. *Bushel's Case*: 1774 ed. 233, cf. 1721 ed. 219. These notes are also absent from the 1766 *British Liberties*.
59. Holly Brewer, *By Birth or Consent* (North Carolina, 2005), 32–35.

continuity that led all the way to the people on whose behalf the writer made similar claims. The hoax of Ossian, a third-century blind bard invented by James Macpherson and admired by Jefferson (who unsuccessfully solicited Macpherson for the originals) is a famous example.[60] The way these historical reconstructions operated becomes particularly relevant when semi-imaginary ancestors and their ancient constitutions were placed in the state of nature; and especially when they were compared to groups contemporary with the author. The account of Celts and Native Americans in James Macpherson's 1771 *An introduction to the history of Great Britain and Ireland* is an important case. Macpherson describes the Celts as being in a state of nature, but already worshipping the one and unitary God. This conjecture is supported by reference to some Native American tribes, and has a similarly moderating effect on attempts to see and treat them as fully pagan.

Another ancient constitutionalist account of the Celts and the staying power of ancient rights situated in a state of nature comes in Paul Henri Mallet's 1755 *Introduction à L'histoire du Danemarch où l'on traite de la religion, des moeurs, des lois, et des usages des anciens Danois*, edited and translated into English in 1770 by Bishop Thomas Percy as *Northern antiquities: or, a description of the manners, customs, religion and laws of the ancient Danes*. The Swiss Mallet argues that Scandinavians and Germans emerged from the state of nature slowly and gradually, and they retain ancient rights, similarly to Native Americans.[61] Percy makes fun of these genealogies and counters that if Celts, ancient Britons, and Native Americans paint their faces and bodies, so do other groups in a state of nature. Superficial similarities of customs and laws do not prove direct

60. Gilbert Chinard, "Jefferson and Ossian," *Modern Language Notes* 38:4 (1923), 201–5. Also see William Petyt, *The Antient Right of the Commons of England Asserted*... (London, 1680), annotated and donated to Harvard by Thomas Hollis, Houghton Br 143.2*. On Petyt and his eighteenth-century influence see Pocock, *The Ancient Constitution*. In 1763 Hollis also donated a copy of the 1738 edition of Molesworth's *An Account of Denmark*, with his laudatory annotations (Houghton *EC75.H7267.Zz738m). The copy survived the 1764 library fire because it was still unpacked.

61. E.g., Mallet, *Northern Antiquities* (London, 1770), 1.183–84.

descent or historical connections that could sustain constitutional claims to ancient liberties, especially when the similarities are juxtaposed with the relatively greater diversity in manners, customs, and laws.[62] Some things (body painting, nature worship, liberties) are simply cherished everywhere.

The Celtic lineage and the Gothic connection between other texts (including Grotius's 1610 *Antiquity of the Batavian Republic*, Molesworth's 1692 *Account of Denmark*, and Andrew Fletcher of Saltoun's 1698 *Discourse of Government*) were recurring themes in a discourse of ancient constitutionalism that often crossed over into the law of nations. The general form of the claim was that specific nations were exceptionally attached to liberty, had a longer history of exercising said liberty than other nations, and were therefore better placed to resist tyranny and spread freedom. A subset of these texts placed these nations' ancient liberties in the state of nature, recoverable under threat of oppression. This is why looking at a range of such texts, including Mallet's and Macpherson's, is useful for establishing the versatility and the commonalities in this stream of the state of nature discourse.

Edward Wynne's fascinating 1768 *Eunomus, or, Dialogues Concerning the Law and Constitution of England* explains that since men in the state of nature enjoy perfect equality, a democracy or a republic is the obvious first form of government when they leave the state of nature, or after they shake off a monarchy that has abused natural liberties.[63] In his 1760–1761 *A New Estimate of Manners and Principles . . .*, John Gordon, archdeacon of Lincoln, critic of Rousseau, and probably the first to introduce the word "civilization" into English, explained the state of nature as personal maturity in any stage of civilization, and as a state of equality in *The Causes and Consequences of Evil Speaking Against Government*, his 1771 Cambridge sermon.[64]

62. Percy in Mallet, *Northern Antiquities*, Preface, 7–11.
63. Wynne, *Eunomus* (London, 1768), III.33.
64. Gordon and "civilization": Michael Sonenscher, *Sans-Culottes* (Princeton, 2008), 191. His criticism of Rousseau: Henry V. S. Ogden, "The State of Nature and the Decline of Lockian Political Theory in England, 1760–1800," *American Historical Review* 46:1 (1940), 21–44, at 25–27.

A recurring colonial and metropolitan Whig objection to the par-liamentary imposition of taxes was that taxes should be granted by the free will and consent of the taxpayer. This well-known argument actually had an ancient constitutionalist component, one that George III was fa-miliar with, as well.[65] Simply put, this strand of thought traced taxation in the common law back to the Gothic constitution, where free warriors in a state of rough equality participated in deliberation and decided to make financial and military contributions as and when they saw fit. Earlier we saw Bland's 1766 invocation of Saxon rights to participate in the Wittinagemot, but texts were not the only part of the ancient con-stitutionalist component of American revolutionary ideology. One of the prominent revolutionary practices that was reinvigorated by ancient constitutionalism is the dedication and celebration of liberty trees. Silas Downer's "A discourse at the dedication of the tree of liberty," delivered in Providence, Rhode Island in 1768, is a striking text, rightly cited by numerous historians for its notion of fundamental law.[66] It is less often placed in the contexts of the state of nature discourse and ancient con-stitutionalism. Downer, a Harvard graduate, was secretary of the Sons of Liberty in Providence and involved in the town's Committee of Correspondence.[67]

In the "Discourse," Downer rehearses the arguments we have seen before. The first settlers lawfully emigrated to America to escape op-pression. They brought their rights with them to an inhospitable, wild

65. George III, "History of Tenures," RA GEO ADDL MSS 32, 960.
66. Downer, *A Discourse, Delivered in Providence* ... (Providence, RI, 1768). Reprinted in Hyneman and Lutz, *American Writings*, 1:97–108. Anticipating the Declaration of Independence: George W. Carey, "Natural Rights, Equality, and the Declaration of Independence," *Ave Maria Law Review* 45 (2005), 45–67, 49. Downer's *Discourse* on fundamental law: Suzanna Sherry, "The Founders' Unwritten Constitution," *University of Chicago Law Review* 54:4 (1987), 1127–77, 1132 n. 22. It presents Magna Carta as the basis of the principle of no taxation without representa-tion: Harry T. Dickinson, "Magna Carta in the Age of Revolution," *Enlightenment and Dissent* 30 (2015), 1–67, 51.
67. Carl Bridenbaugh, *Silas Downer* (Providence, RI, 1974); Thomas W. Ramsbey, "The Sons of Liberty: The Early Inter-colonial Organization," *International Review of Modern Sociology* 7:2 (1987), 313–35.

country where they fought the savage natives, and built a virtuous civilization without luxury. The richness and variety of American nature make it "the promised land," "a land of milk and honey." Their descendants, the current generation, must preserve the liberty they inherited. History and a comparative view of other countries show that religion, politics, art, and industry all fail without liberty. Colonial governments have been faithful and effective custodians of liberty in America. Colonists are not, and cannot be, represented in Westminster, so the rights and responsibilities of representation belong to colonial governments, which have long been protecting natural liberty. However, as DeBerdt did in 1765, Downer lays the decisive blame not on the government, but the people of Britain. According to Downer, the common people there now claim sovereignty over the colonists, and intend to enslave them and diminish their natural right to trade and to develop their own industry and manufacturing. The British claim is based simply on being the mother country, which is an unacceptable argument. Population growth and colonization are natural. Massachusetts does not claim sovereignty over Rhode Island just because the latter's founders came from Massachusetts. One of Britain's founding generations came from France, but no British person would admit a comparable French claim. Yet they sent soldiers and warships to New England and suspended colonial government.

> Wherefore, dearly beloved, let us with unconquerable resolution maintain and defend that liberty wherewith GOD hath made us free. As the total subjection of a people arises generally from gradual encroachments, it will be our indispensible duty manfully to oppose every invasion of our rights in the beginning. Let nothing discourage us from this duty to ourselves and our posterity. Our fathers fought and found freedom in the wilderness; they cloathed themselves with the skins of wild beasts, and lodged under trees and among bushes; but in that state they were happy because they were free.[68]

---

68. Downer, *Discourse*, 1:107. Also see Dickinson's 1774 *Essay*, 359–60.

This is the condition that the liberty trees, on which famously effigies of Hutchinson, Oliver, and others were burned, stand for.[69] Alongside the American revolutionary ancient constitutionalism based on the trope of German liberty, there are also hints of a colonial strand of ancient constitutionalism that appealed to the less than two centuries of the colonies' existence as if they had the force of Saxon or mythical past.[70]

5.4 THE FREEDOMS OF CONSCIENCE, SPEECH, RELIGION, AND THE PRESS

As we saw, the 1766 *British Liberties* was probably produced for the American market, and it drew its materials from the freedom of speech lawsuits of William Penn and William Mead, Benjamin Harris, and others. The timing suggests that the decision to adapt the book to the American market may have been inspired by the controversy surrounding the Stamp Act. John Adams was one of many who regarded the Stamp Act as a violation of the freedom of conscience, and of the press. In the October 21, 1765 issue of the *Boston Gazette*, in the last of the four letters collected as the *Dissertation on the Canon and Feudal Law*, Adams took pride in colonial literacy and support for printing, and in Jonathan Mayhew's

69. John Adams was not overly keen on ancient constitutionalism. February 1, 1773, *Boston Gazette*: "I would not be understood however to lay any great stress, on the opinions of historians, and compilers of antiquities, because it must be confessed, that the Saxon constitution, is involved in much obscurity, and that the monarchical and democratical factions in England, by their opposite endeavors, to make the Saxon constitutions, swear for their respective systems, have much increased the difficulty of determining to the satisfaction of the world, what that constitution in many important particulars, was." In his 1787–88 *A Defence of the Constitutions of Government of the United States of America*, Letter 37, Adams points out that according to Tacitus, the Germans had two forms of government: monarchy and aristocracy. The latter is sometimes mistaken for a mixed constitution. On natural aristocracy in Adams see Luke Mayville, *John Adams and the Fear of American Oligarchy* (Princeton, 2016). In his 1790 manuscript notes on the *Defence*, now at the New York Society Library, James Kent is more interested in the aristocratic than the monarchical reading of Germans based on Tacitus.
70. George Chalmers, *Letter to Lord Mansfield*, John Carter Brown Library, Codex Eng=150, pp. 20–21. Hulsebosch, *Constituting Empire*, 72, 141.

May 8, 1765, Dudleian Lecture observation that in the colonies "we are all of us lawyers, divines, politicians, and philosophers." Adams praises Edes and Gill, publishers of the *Boston Gazette*, for their work, and calls on the popular resistance to the Stamp Act to be better informed, as the spirit of liberty, "without knowledge, would be little better than a brutal rage."[71] But let there be no mistake, Adams continues: unlike the Sugar Act, the Stamp Act not only extracts revenue, but also suppresses colonial thought and freedom of opinion.

> But it seems very manifest from the Stamp Act itself, that a design is formed to strip us in a great measure of the means of knowledge by loading the press, the colleges, and even an almanack and a newspaper, with restraints and duties; and to introduce the inequalities and dependencies of the feudal system.

We also saw Jonathan Sewall, writing as Philanthrop, attack Seth Warren in print in 1766.[72] Sewall continued to defend the colonial administration, including Governor Bernard, in a series of letters under the same name. John Adams was among those who took up his pen to refute Philanthrop. Another was a certain "Freeborn American," who in the March 6, 1767 *Supplement to the Boston Gazette* called on all colonists to valiantly resist Britain's, Bernard's, and Sewall's assaults on their rights. The letter begins with the contention that the key to this struggle will be the free press. "Man, in a state of nature, has undoubtedly a right to speak and act without controul." This state of nature right is curtailed after entering the polity but, in keeping with the principle of proportionality, only as far as necessary. "That society whose laws least restrain the words and actions of its members, is most free." So far this has been Britain; but vigilance and even resistance remain critical for the British imperial constitution to remain a protector of political rights. Blackstone's use of absolute, state

---

71. For Hutchinson's 1768 attempt to indict Edes and Gill for libel, see Jensen, *Founding*, 254–55.
72. See chapter 4, section 4.1.

of nature rights as a yardstick for constitutional excellence is applied here to the freedom of speech and press.

The almanacs that Adams praised in the *Dissertation* as a means of public education were among the most popular, widely owned texts in colonial America. Earlier we saw an original state of nature essay reach a wide audience in Nathaniel Ames's 1764 *Almanac,* and Marrett's notes in his copy on the waves of contradictory news reaching Boston about the Stamp Act. Nathanael Low's Boston *Almanack* for 1767 reprinted a section from Alexander Pope's 1733–1734 *Essay on Man* with a few lines above each month, and entitled the January section "The state of nature" (fig. 5.1).

The Massachusetts calendar, or An almanac for the year of our Lord 1772, composed by "Philomathes" and printed in 1771, begins with a picture and a poem about the Boston Massacre. The first text appended to the

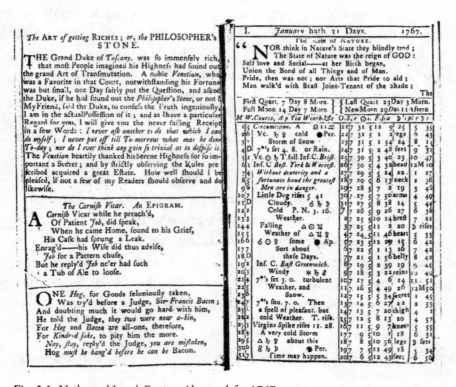

Fig. 5.1 Nathanael Low's Boston *Almanack* for 1767

almanac itself is a redacted essay from the May 8, 1735 issue of the *London Magazine*. Its author, "Old Whig," explains that on entering society, man gives up only as much natural liberty as is required to meet his purpose. The freedom of learning and opinion are among natural liberties, and not among those that should be alienated. "In a State of Nature, I had a Right to read homer, or Virgil, or Horace, in order to instruct or amuse myself; and therefore under a Government instituted to support my Life, and Property, and civil Interests, I retain my Liberty to read them still."[73] Far from primitive savagery, here is an expansive sense of the state of nature as the place where one could read the best of ancient literature. Impeding the free study and use of Scripture, Old Whig continues, is as much a violation of natural liberty, which persists after the transition to civil society, as an attack by a highwayman. A close comparison with the 1735 original shows that the American editor was actually less interested in property, and cared less about the natural rights that follow from having property in a state of nature, than about the natural right to free inquiry and the right, even duty, to practice free speech on political issues. These are the sections that she or he kept. This 1771 reorientation of a 1735 text toward a state of nature right to the freedom of opinion and press is part of an uninterrupted discussion that the Stamp Act had amplified.

The same year saw intense attacks on Hutchinson and the British government in the *Massachusetts Spy* by, among others, Joseph Greenleaf, Samuel Adams, and John Warren. Hutchinson tried to sue the paper for libel for a November 14, 1771 piece by "Mucius Scaevola," which implied that Hutchinson was a "monster" and compared him to Caesar. The ever-ready "Centinel," in letter 28 in the January 2, 1772, *Massachusetts Spy*, wondered whether such a case could be brought. Centinel begins by dismissing civil law: if culpable, Scaevola can only be tried under common law. But common law must harmonize with "natural conscience, natural

73. Also see Elisha Williams's 1744 *Essential Rights*, 61: "In a state of nature men had a right to read Milton or Lock for their instruction or amusement: and why they do not retain this liberty under a government that is instituted for the preservation of their persons and properties, is inconceivable."

Law and *every* Maxim of a *free* constitution"—it would be absurd to suppose otherwise. Centinel thus swiftly reframed the libel question as one of comparative constitutionalism and natural law.

Sparta applauded theft, Britain punishes it with death, the colonies with corporal punishment, Centinel notes. Such variety in particulars does not change the salient fact that they are all free constitutions, but their regulations and the structure of their executive powers differ. The freedom of a constitution is determined by the legislative, which was "founded and must be regulated on those primitive reasons, which induced men to leave a state of nature and enter into society." To decide whether a speech or printed text meets the barrier for libel or not, one must return to state of nature principles, "principles by which alone all the properties of government are regulated, principles which existed long before courts of record had being in the world, and principles which will remain eternal and unalterable, while the disposition of executive courts varys with the revolutions of time, and accommodate themselves to the policy of ages and the different genius of mankind."[74] By this standard, Scaevola is innocent. He exercised his "freedom of writing," and if the case comes to court, the jury should recall that "A FREE PRESS is a RIGHT."

74. The 1767 *King against Taylor*, published as case 76 in Lord John Maclaurin Dreghorn's *Arguments, and decisions, in remarkable cases, before the High Court of Justiciary, and other Supreme Courts, in Scotland* (Edinburgh, 1774), 308–66, at 326–29, goes further. Societies past the initial, most primitive stage need to develop criminal law. However, not all states are formed for the same purpose (defense of property and other natural rights, for instance). Some are formed for conquest; others for self-defense, for hunting-gathering, for agriculture; and yet others for commerce. The different aims of civil society led to different forms of government, with different criminal law systems to match. States are in a state of nature toward each other partly because they cannot recognize other states' criminal laws as binding. Here not only the legal system and the constitutions, but even the spirit of constitutions differs from one state to the next, and the state of nature is not the spirit of the constitution, but the structure of interstate relations. Nonetheless, states can develop conventions to guide relations between them in the international state of nature where, despite deep-running constitutional differences, moral obligations exist to preclude a Hobbesian state of nature.

It is possible that Centinel quickly reframed the accusation against Scaevola in state of nature terms partly because of the British and American arguments mentioned here, but also partly influenced by Cesare Beccaria's *An Essay on Crimes and Punishments*. The book first appeared in 1764 and was translated into English in 1767. In chapter 9, on honor, Beccaria posits that laws and magistrates came into being to prevent "the natural despotism of individuals." Presumably this refers to criminal law, which the 1767 opinion in the Scottish *King against Taylor* also regarded as the first step in the rise of civilization. According to Beccaria, once society gets going, "the despotism of opinion" replaces natural, physical despotism. Laws cannot regulate opinion completely and, regardless of our resources or moral qualities, we are all affected by others' opinions, which determine our reputation or honor. Honor is necessary for our existence, and we all strive to improve ours, whether we deserve it or not.[75] Honor loses meaning in the despotisms of "extreme political liberty" or tyranny. Because it can never become fully subject to law, and because it restores us to radical equality, in limited despotisms (i.e., monarchies) honor "is a momentary return to a state of nature, and original equality," acting as "revolutions in despotic states." In Centinel's terms, Scaevola's criticism of Hutchinson insulted the Governor's honor. This is a state of nature act. It cannot be fully subject to law because it is an eternal principle that predates (and will outlast) courts. Juridifying it

---

75. Finnis points out that reputation is a state of nature right in Blackstone. He argues that Blackstone is inconsistent, because "reputation and good name are inconceivable in abstraction from society." "Theoretical," 180. I think Blackstone is not inconsistent if he holds that reputation is one of the state of nature rights that arise before states and laws come into existence, and states and laws are meant to protect. Finnis next argues that Blackstone refuses to derive human laws from nature, and the concept of the common good disappears from his system, because the "only natural good is individual and presocial" (181–82). This is an individualist interpretation similar to Justice Thomas's, discussed in this book's conclusion. It ignores the fact that Blackstone's absolute rights to life, liberty, and property are relational, and explicitly located in a state of nature that gives rise to rights that survive the transition to the state. While Blackstone does not go as far as Hutcheson, his state of nature resembles society, or Locke's civil society, a pre-political but sociable and collective condition.

actually amounts to despotism, a condition in which insulting the over-reaching legislator would prompt a revolutionary return to the state of nature. Thus, when political criticism is legally deemed to be libel, and when it is not, the state of nature is the guiding principle in both scenarios—in the first case to justify criticism, and in the second to justify revolution, when the power to legislate is abused to suppress the freedom of speech.

While Centinel invoked constitutional comparisons and natural law as it applies everywhere, others brought out the materiality of the American state of nature discourse. The geography and climate of the continent were often essential to arguing American independence. Some of the texts we examined describe the first settlers arriving in a state of nature, even though they carried their English rights with them. By working American lands, they acquired state of nature rights, especially the right to property, that anchored their and their descendants' liberty in America. However, material conditions also determined other rights, including that of free speech and opinion. In his 1774 valedictorian commencement oration at Rhode-Island College (now Brown University), Barnabas Binney (1751–1787) exclaimed that America is a new model for all nations because minds here are still free, and the continent is unburdened by institutions arising from a history of powerful men generating artificial ignorance to suppress religious liberty.[76] William Livingston, governor of New Jersey, pointed out in 1788 that in the state of nature no violence can be done by simply holding an opinion.[77] In 1809, Yale held disputations in which one side argued that property must be the main qualification for voting, since property is a natural right but voting is not, because one cannot organize voting in the state of nature. Another disputation treated the state of nature as a historical fact and ingeniously pointed out that since paper did not exist there, the freedom of the press could not be a natural right.[78]

76. John Carter Brown Library, D774 B614o 1-Size. Binney was the surgeon who discovered that Deborah Samson, now the official heroine of Massachusetts, disguised herself as a man to be able to fight in the Revolutionary War.
77. Niles, *Principles*, 306.
78. Yale University Archives, Jonathan Lee Papers, ms 958, series III, Box 9, Folder 126.

While intellectual property rights and the right to free speech are very different, state of nature discussions of them overlap. The immateriality of property was often brought up, for instance in copyright cases. In the landmark *Millar v Taylor* (1769) at the King's Bench, with Lord Mansfield presiding, the court found that even when a publisher's statutory rights to a work have expired, they still hold a perpetual common-law copyright.[79] This victory for booksellers and publishers was overturned by the House of Lords in the 1774 *Donaldson v. Beckett*.[80] In *Millar v. Taylor*, Justice Willes wrote, "I have avoided a large field which exercised the ingenuity of the Bar. Metaphysical reasoning is too subtile; and arguments from the supposed modes of acquiring the property of acorns, or a vacant piece of ground in an imaginary state of nature, are too remote. Besides, the comparison does not hold between things which have a physical existence, and incorporeal rights."[81]

It was not only the enthusiastically revolutionary elements that were preparing to justify various forms of resistance to Britain by locating

79. 4 Burr. 2303, 98 Eng. Rep. 201.
80. Brown's Parl. Cases (2d ed.) 129, 1 Eng. Rep. 837; 4 Burr. 2408, 98 Eng. Rep. 257; 17 Cobbett's Parl. Hist. 953 (1813).
81. 4 Burr. 2334. Willes's point was also made in Bishop William Warburton's *An Enquiry into the Nature and Origin of Literary Property* (London, 1762), 9–10. In the American texts, the state of nature often becomes the font of both property and free speech rights. William Leggett fascinatingly extends the American tradition of property in a state of nature to intellectual copyright in "Rights of Authors," *Plaindealer*, February 11, 1837. *A Collection of the Political Writings of William Leggett* (ed. Theodore Sedgwick, Jr., New York, 1840), 2:207. In his January 20, 2015, dissent in *Teva Pharmaceuticals USA, Inc. v. Sandoz, Inc.*, 574 U.S.__ (2015), Justice Thomas described invention patents as disanalogous with contracts, but instead "describing rights that the owner holds against the world." Citing Caleb Nelson, "Adjudication in the Political Branches," *Columbia Law Review* 107:3 (2007), 559–627, Justice Thomas argued that the "Anglo-American legal tradition has long distinguished between 'core' private rights—including the traditional property rights represented by deeds—and other types of rights," with patents belonging to the latter category as rights "created purely for reasons of public policy and which ha[ve] no counterpart in the Lockean state of nature." This ignores the distinct, only partly Lockean, American state of nature tradition that informed US copyright and patent law from the start, and constitutes the proper context for judicial interpretation and construction.

inalienable or only provisionally alienated rights of freedom of conscience, speech and religion in the state of nature. Samuel Henley (1740–1815), recruited from Cambridge, England, taught moral philosophy at the College of William & Mary between 1770 and 1775. He seems to have been friends with Thomas Jefferson, who bought some of his library, and he was much liked by his students, including St. George Tucker, Madison, Monroe, Edmund Randolph, and Jefferson's younger brother, Randolph. Henley also had enemies, chief among them Robert Carter Nicholas, Sr. In 1775 Henley returned to England due to disagreements with the revolutionaries, who went too far for his taste by then. Yet on March 1, 1772 he preached "the distinct claims of government and religion" to the Honourable House of Burgesses at Williamsburg, in which he posited that several rights, including the right to freedom of conscience, remain intact due to their roots in the state of nature, a condition that persists between all individuals and God.[82]

Henley's oration is equally embedded in the English and Virginian politics of religion. It is a combative text right from its dedication to John Jebb, the Cambridge physician, divine and reformer, who supported the movement that began in 1771 to abolish the requirement that university professors and the clergy must subscribe to the Thirty-Nine Articles, effectively the credo of the Church of England since 1563. Henley praises Jebb for applying Francis Bacon's scientific principles to revelation, and compares his vicissitudes in Cambridge to Galileo's persecution by professional academics.[83] He contrasts the epistemic arrogance of established academics with the unlearned intelligence of a Native American who charted a straight easterly path just to discover where the sun rose, and naturally ended up in Virginia. In the advertisement, Henley claims to be subjected to comparable persecution for his views and invokes

82. Samuel Henley, *The Distinct Claims of Government and Religion* . . . (Cambridge, MA, 1772).

83. On the "anti-authoritarianism" resulting from the combination of "Low-Church ideals with Enlightenment rationality," specifically including natural science, see Leslee K. Gilbert, "The Altar of Liberty: Enlightened Dissent and the Dudleian Lectures, 1755–1765," *Historical Journal of Massachusetts* 31:2 (2003), 151–71.

Locke to prove that political views, especially concerning toleration, can and should be preached from the pulpit.

At the same time, Henley was also preaching against the leadership of his college and the conservative party allied with it.[84] John Camm, the hard-line Tory minister and fellow Cambridge graduate, had just become the seventh president of William & Mary in 1771. Camm led the opposition to the *Two-Penny Acts* of 1755 and 1758, which effectively cut Anglican ministers' salary at a time when a long drought depressed tobacco prices. In London, Camm lobbied intensely for George III to veto the Act, arguing that it reflected weakening colonial respect for both the Crown and the Church of England. After returning to Virginia, Camm entered a fierce polemic with the legislators Landon Carter and Richard Bland. Dismissed from his post at the College in 1758, he appealed to London. Camm was reinstated in 1763 just as Patrick Henry won his case defending Hanover County against the claim of Virginia ministers for pay lost due to the brief operation of the *Two-Penny Act*. The Reverend James Maury, who represented the ministers, now told the reinstated Camm that Henry essentially argued that George III's repeal proved him to be a tyrant. The pendulum of power continued to swing between Tories and Whigs, latitudinarians, dissenters, and those in favor of some form of established religion, a notion famously raised by Patrick Henry at the First Continental Congress. Camm's rise to prominence in 1771 as the seventh president of the College is part of the Anglo-American context for Henley's defiant address to the Virginia burgesses.

To establish where "the claims of Government and Religion are distinct from each other," Henley reverts to first principles.[85] Society is a human institution, he begins, emphatically side stepping the large literatures that derive political principles from divine or natural foundations.[86]

---

84. On this context see George T. Morrow II, *Of Heretics, Traitors and True Believers* ... (Telford, 2011).
85. Henley, *Distinct Claims*, 4.
86. As he sums up this section, "From the preceding view of Society and Government, it is evident, Religion had no part in the formation of either." Henley, *Distinct Claims*, 8, with further elaborations throughout.

Security and enjoyment of property are "the grounds of alliance between man and man," and individuals contribute to the common defense according to their ability and the protection of property they enjoy. The magistrate's duty is to direct the state's united strength to the defense of property and peace. Henley takes the line that "any crime committed in Society can be punished as a crime against Society, alone. It is only in a social capacity that man is amenable to man." Even acts that violate divine law can only be punished if they breach civil law, as well. To do otherwise would be to curtail or usurp God's right to punish.[87] People's relationship to God is individual, and precedes politics. With regard to divine law, they must follow their conscience.

> In this respect, all men yet are in their natural condition:—This "state of nature" is "the reign of God." Their right, possessive and personal, in part they might alienate. Certain portions were relinquished for advantages in return; but they were advantages of a similar kind. The rights of conscience are unlike the claims of Society, and cannot therefore be submitted to its direction. Whatever is required by the law of our nature, every individual must, in his own person, perform. For every talent, intrusted to our care, a separate account must be given. However desirous we may be of a general conformity in religious opinions, yet to make nonconformity criminal, would in any Legislature be highly impious.[88]

Soon after Henley's speech, on August 15, 1772, twenty-two-year-old James Madison, cousin of the future president of the same name, gave "An oration in commemoration of the Founders of William and Mary College." Madison dedicated the oration to Henley, whose student he probably was before his graduation in 1771, and whose colleague he became the next year, teaching philosophy and mathematics at William & Mary until 1775, when he travelled to England and was ordained an Anglican priest. After his return to Virginia, Madison resumed his duties

87. Henley, *Distinct Claims*, 5–8.
88. Henley, *Distinct Claims*, 10–11.

at the College and rallied his students into a militia at the outbreak of hostilities. He was removed from William & Mary by Camm, and became its eighth president when Camm was ousted in 1777.[89]

All this was yet to come when Madison rose to deliver his Founders' Day oration in 1772. Like Henley's, Madison's subject is civil and religious liberty, but his is the free, but violent and uncertain state of nature we know from Hobbes.[90] The mutual consent to move from the state of nature into society first led to an "early State," where a simple senate met under an oak tree to administer justice. Despite the idyllic ancient constitution that replaced it, aspects of the state of nature survive, transformed into civil liberty.

> The same Motives which induced Man to alienate those precarious Rights which a State of Nature afforded, would also prompt him to secure such as his Entrance into Society had left unimpaired. To effect this, determinate Laws must ascertain the exact Lines which should circumscribe his civil Liberty. That Part of his natural Liberty, which not only Necessity but Justice required, he therefore appropriates to the Safety and Prosperity of Society. What he thus donates becomes the Right of the Legislature; what he reserves constitutes that civil Liberty which cannot be diminished either by the Russian Hand of the self-deputed Tyrant, or by those ambitious Deeds which strike Mankind with Horror.[91]

Madison cites chapter 9, section 131 of Locke's *Second Treatise* in support. The people's will on where to draw the lines of civil liberty, and their sentiments on whether or not the rich, the restless, or the magistrate have violated them, are the only valid standards. According to Madison, the laws of nature are not abrogated but reinforced by human laws. Weaving

89. On Madison's career see Spencer W. McBride, *Pulpit and Nation: Clergymen and the Politics of Revolutionary America* (Virginia, 2017).
90. Madison, *An Oration* (Williamsburg, 1772), 5.
91. Madison, *An Oration*, 6.

in citations from Sidney and Milton, Madison presents the people's will, "tempered by Reason," as the guarantor of a civil liberty in which the creative energies of the state of nature, from sociability to intellectual vigor, are harnessed for the common good.[92]

While Blackstone thought that the Glorious Revolution made little difference to constitutional continuity, and Otis celebrated it as a radically clean break, Madison recounted how William of Orange, the College's royal founder, returned England to its original freedom and toleration. Toleration relies on understanding the proper bounds of the magistrate's authority, which encompasses only politics, not religion.[93] Although Madison closely and emphatically follows Henley here, he also points out the daily improvements of human understanding and the dangers in all forms of dogmatism. Further, Madison explicitly extends Henley's argument for the freedom of religion to the freedom of opinion.[94] He also adds that freedom of opinion and religion, and the magistrate's strict confinement to political matters, are the reasons why some states are rich, while the suppression of these freedoms makes countries poor.[95]

Madison's link between freedom and prosperity, as derived from the American state of nature, appears in other configurations, as well. As we saw, in his 1768 "Discourse at the Dedication of the Tree of Liberty," Silas Downer combined colonial right claims based on the state of nature and ancient constitutionalism when he called on all Americans to boycott British trade, rely on the natural fertility and industrial potential of their continent, and add political liberty and economic growth to launch a natural virtuous cycle that will create and sustain American independence.

92. Madison, *An Oration*, 7–8.
93. Madison, *An Oration*, 9–10.
94. "The Power, which the social Compact confers, extending no farther than to the Advancement of public Utility, the Subject cannot, in Justice, be accountable for any Opinions he may entertain, that do not effect its political Interests." Madison, *An Oration*, 11.
95. Madison, *An Oration*, 12.

5.5 LOYALIST VERSUS PATRIOT STATES OF NATURE
(1769–72)

The state of nature became an unavoidable reference point in a growing number of contentious political and constitutional topics. Within the evolving American state of nature discourse, we can discern a coherent conservative strand designed to directly answer and refute the revolutionary argument. Daniel Leonard, George Galloway, Jonathan Boucher, and other Loyalists discussed below belong to this conservative thread of the distinctly American tradition. An earlier example is Hutchinson in 1769, who emphasized the advantages and duties that stable government brings to those who leave the state of nature. Hutchinson sent a letter from Boston, dated January 20, 1769, to none other than Thomas Whately, author of *The Regulations Lately Made* of 1765.

> This is most certainly a Crisis. I really wish that there may not have been the least degree of Severity, beyond what is absolutely necessary to maintain, I think I may say to you, *the dependance* which a Colony ought to have upon the Parent State, but if no measures shall have been taken to secure this dependance or nothing more than some Declaratory Acts or Resolves, *it is all over with Us.* The Friends of Government will be utterly disheartned and the friends of Anarchy will be afraid of nothing be it ever so extravagant. . . . I never think of the measures necessary for the Peace and good Order of the Colonies without pain. There must be an Abridgment of what are called English Liberties. I relieve myself by considering that in a Remove from the State of nature to the most perfect State of Government there must be a great restraint of natural Liberty. I doubt whether it is possible to project a System of Government in which a Colony 3000 miles distant from the parent State shall enjoy all the Liberty of the parent State.[96]

96. Hutchinson et al., *The Representations of Governor Hutchinson* . . . (Boston, 1773), 16.

Later that year, after Governor Bernard's fall partly due to the scandalous publication of his leaked letters (a story we will return to below), Hutchinson became acting governor of Massachusetts in August 1769. Andrew Oliver, who was commissioned in 1765 to administer the Stamp Act in Massachusetts, took over from Hutchinson as lieutenant governor in 1771, when Hutchinson received his formal commission as governor. When Whately died in 1772, letters he received from Hutchinson and Andrew Oliver came into the possession of Whately's brother, William. Benjamin Franklin obtained about twenty letters, probably through Thomas Pownall. Franklin considered Hutchinson's reports to London dangerously misleading and sent copies to Thomas Cushing, speaker of the Massachusetts Assembly, in December 1772, requesting that they be shown only to a small group of prominent colonial politicians. Instead, the entire Assembly saw and discussed the letters and concluded that Hutchinson sought to "overthrow the Constitution of this Government, and to introduce arbitrary Power into the Province."[97] As leaking Bernard's letters had already proved effective in forcing out a governor, Hutchinson's letters were likewise promptly leaked, published in the *Boston Gazette* in June 1773, and reprinted on both sides of the Atlantic in numerous newspapers, as well as in *The Representation of Governor Hutchinson and Others* ... (1773), *The Letters of Governor Hutchinson, and Lieut. Governor Oliver* ... (1774), and other polemical publications.

An enormous scandal erupted about the letters' content and about the leak. William Whately accused John Temple of handing the confidential letters to Franklin, and challenged him to a duel. Temple wounded Whately, but both parties remained unsatisfied and planned a rematch. Partly to prevent this, Franklin came forward and admitted to acquiring and forwarding the letters. He was later accused of theft and dishonor in Privy Council for these acts. The famous dressing-down he received in Parliament is often cited as the decisive moment when he shifted his allegiance from Britain to an independent union of the

97. Thomas Cushing to Benjamin Franklin, June 25, 1773. Franklin, *Works* (ed. Jared Sparks, Philadelphia, 1840), 8:52–53.

American colonies.[98] In the meantime, Bostonians burned Hutchinson and Oliver in effigy. Oliver died of a heart attack. The furor over the letters raised tempers to such a degree that the incident can be seen as a direct precursor to the Tea Party, which in turn prompted Parliament to pass the Coercive Acts and to replace Hutchinson with General Thomas Gage as Governor of the Province of Massachusetts Bay (the last one, as it turned out), effective from May 13, 1774. Although there is extensive literature on the scandal and on the January 20, 1769 letter in particular, little or no attention has been paid to Hutchinson's use of the state of nature and how it fit into the context of the emerging American state of nature discourse.[99]

Shortly after writing to Whately, Hutchinson made a state of nature argument in public that echoed his letter to Whately, but with noteworthy differences. In his instructions to the grand jury at the start of the March 1769 term, Hutchinson tried to explain how members of the jury should think about their task. Their main function was to protect people's rights. In the state of nature, everyone has the right to do as they please. Once we join society, we must "submit to the Laws of the State." To enjoy society's protection of our person and property, "which we could not have in a State of Nature," we must give up some of our original rights. In a variation on Blackstone, Hutchinson noted that the best constitution, which happens to be the British, requires giving up the fewest natural rights. This in turn means that British laws are necessary and sufficient, and there are legal ways to seek protection and redress for grievances. Appealing to natural law or extra-legal means instead "is to bring Everything into Confusion." The jury's role is to execute the law, not to wonder "whether it is constitutional or not."[100]

98. Gordon S. Wood, *The Americanization of Benjamin Franklin* (Penguin, 2004).
99. Bernard Bailyn, *The Ordeal of Thomas Hutchinson* (Belknap, 1974). Andrew S. Walmsley, *Thomas Hutchinson and the Origins of the American Revolution* (New York University, 1998); John Alexander, *Samuel Adams* (Rowman & Littlefield, 2011).
100. *Quincy's Reports*, 306–8. 307: "Now, as the End of Society is to preserve to us that Security in our Persons and Property which we could not have in a State of Nature, we are under a Necessity of giving up some of our original Rights, in Order to a full Enjoyment of the Remainder."

The same point is made in a lighter tone in *The Controversy between Great Britain and her Colonies Reviewed*, also from 1769. Written by William Knox but also attributed to Thomas Whately, with a section by Grenville, the book surveys and refutes the colonists' various claims. Knox lived in Georgia from 1757 to 1761 and became agent for Georgia and East Florida in London. He lobbied for repealing the Stamp Act, but wrote in support of Parliament's power over the colonies so effectively that Georgia dismissed him in 1765.[101] Indeed, a refutation of the colonists that frequently appears in *The Controversy* is that they cannot claim the rights and privileges of Englishmen if they refuse to acknowledge Parliament's authority. Knox also tackles the other common theme he identifies, namely colonial claims based on natural rights. Here, like Hutchinson writing to Whately in January 1769, Knox accepts that perfect liberty exists, but only in the state of nature, and it must be limited to the act of creating a state. The rights and liberties guaranteed by "the British state" are superior to natural rights and cannot be derived from them.

Knox explains that not Massachusetts but Virginia "first waved the standard of American defiance, and the other colonies have no merit but that of humbly following what they had dictated." Against the claims of Virginia and Maryland that the first settlers carried their liberties, Knox points out that the Habeas Corpus Act and the Bill of Rights postdate Virginia's first settlement, and it is illogical to pretend that the first settlers carried rights that even those who stayed in England gained only later. Knox then turns to Pennsylvania's September 21, 1765 resolutions against the Stamp Act. According to Knox, Pennsylvania did not ground its claims on the first settlers' migration of rights, but on natural rights alone. Natural rights cannot create English rights, Knox exclaims; but while the Pennsylvania argument is silly, at least it seems benevolent, Knox writes mockingly, as it extends English rights to "the native Indians in North America, the Hottentots at the Cape of Good Hope, the Tartars, Arabs, Cafres, and Groenlanders." The conceit that Pennsylvania's constitution

101. Leland J. Bellot, *William Knox* (Texas, 1977).

"*is* or *ought* to be *perfectly free*," as the phrase from Pennsylvania's resolutions runs, is also meaningless.

> To be *perfectly free* is, I apprehend, to be in a state of nature absolutely independent of, and uncontrolable by, any other, in all cases whatever: and when applied to states, is the most complete definition of equality and independency that can be given.[102]

There are several reasons why this is an interesting passage. First, Knox adds the state of nature to interpreting Pennsylvania's resolutions, which do not contain the term. By 1769, this was the obvious orientational concept for discussing colonial appeals to natural law and the natural right to secede and form a new community.[103] Second, he criticizes the resolutions as if they were made by a province on the verge of revolution. Third, when the passage was reprinted at least in one colonial newspaper, the *Nova Scotia Gazette* of February 4, 1769, the sense of the state of nature as a relationship between independent states was redacted, and black people were added to the list of those who would gain English rights, if one accepted the colonial emphasis on the state of nature foundation for English rights. Knox's abovementioned phrase becomes "to the natural Indians in North America; the Negroes, the Hotentots, the Tartars, Arabs, Cuffrees and Greenlanders." The state of nature passage redacts a few lines from the book and now reads,

> To be perfectly free, is to be in a state of nature absolutely independent of and uncontrollable by any other in all cases whatever, therefore no act whatever of the *British* parliament, *is* or *ought* to be in force in Pennsylvania, otherways the government of that country cannot be as it *is* or *ought to be* perfectly free. . . . The colonists seem to be intoxicated with a fond conceit of their own importance, and to dream, nay even appear to listen to the alluring whispers of independency.

102. Knox, *Controversy*, 13.
103. Hamburger, "Natural Rights," 939, makes the same point about what he calls, more broadly and imprecisely, "state-of-nature or modern natural rights analysis."

Knox reduces the valid meanings of the state of nature to the same inter-state relations that we find in Galloway and other Loyalists: "Either the Colonies are a part of the community of Great Britain, or they are in a state of nature with respect to her."[104] There is no middle ground. Other moderates agreed with Knox and Galloway. The anonymous author of "A letter to the Right Honourable the Earl of Shelburne, on the motives of his political conduct" sided with Britain against the colonies, but gave American independence serious consideration. If it were to happen, she or he wrote, and the British Empire were to come to an end, let it happen by consent. That would render the undesirable dissolution legitimate, and in itself worthy of British liberties. Loyalists countered the Patriots' attempt to co-ordinate and create a revolutionary state of nature language with an equally coordinated effort to either restrict usages of the state of nature to meanings that could not support colonial independence; or, as discussed later in section 7.4 in chapter 7, to deny that the state of nature was a meaningful concept at all.

The Loyalist judiciary of Massachusetts also followed Hutchinson's and London's lead in forging a counter-revolutionary state of nature language. Andrew Oliver's younger brother, Peter, was one of three judges at the Boston Massacre Trials. The famous incident, in which British soldiers killed five men and wounded another six, took place on March 5, 1770. The trial began on November 27. John Adams defended the eight soldiers, one officer, and four civilians from the charge of murder. According to Adams's notes, in his December 5, 1770 instructions to the jury, Oliver compared the authors of vengeful newspaper articles unfavorably with "the savages of the wilderness" who, "in the untutored state of nature," avenge their own injuries.[105] Like Gridley in 1765, Oliver considered a re-turn to the state of nature impossible, and the consequences of the break-down of government worse than any state of nature. By contrast, those who called for revenge in a state of society subverted and destroyed the

104. Knox, *Controversy*, 50–51.
105. Peter Oliver's Charge to the Jury, December 5, 1770. *Founders Online*, National Archives, http://founders.archives.gov/documents/Adams/05-03-02-0001-0004-0019.

law and the mutual protection that society is based on. Hutchinson appointed Oliver to the post of Chief Justice of the Superior Court in 1772. He was impeached in 1774 for being the only judge to accept the Crown's offer to raise the justices' salary, and he fled Boston in March 1776.[106]

Samuel Adams threw himself into the newspaper polemic surrounding the soldiers' trial. In an article dated January 15 and published on January 21, 1771 in the *Boston Gazette*, Adams, signing as Vindex, reviewed the testimonies and suggested that the jury was misled and the verdict, six acquittals and two found guilty of manslaughter, was too light. Next, he addressed Philanthrop, the pen name of Jonathan Sewall, attorney general of Massachusetts from 1767 until his exile to England in 1775. In analyzing the trial, Adams disagreed with Sewall that the "happiness of the whole depends on subordination." Subordination is characteristic of the state of nature, where might is right, Adams explained. This condition still exists in the world, even under established governments, most of which are tyrannical. Men left the state of nature to enjoy the fruits of reason and sociability, which are both natural faculties, more than they could in the state of nature. Their other aim was to establish equality, which did not exist there. It follows that when measured against the features of the state of nature and the intentions for leaving it, the best constitutions are those that maximize equality. Government requires some subordination, but cannot justify slavery or tyranny.[107] Samuel Adams's maximization of natural equality is subtly but importantly different from Blackstone's and Hutchinson's preservation of individual rights as the yardstick for measuring governments' excellence against the state of nature. It is closer to Otis's view of equality as grounded in the state of nature, though without drawing conclusions concerning slavery.

106. In 1781, in his London exile, Peter Oliver wrote a book-length manuscript about the Revolution up to 1776. After a brief, two-paragraph *exordium*, his substantive explanation begins with an account of how the colonists mistook liberty in the state of nature (which never really existed) with civil liberty. Douglass Adair and John A. Schuts (eds.), *Peter Oliver's Origin & Progress of the American Rebellion: A Tory View* (Stanford, 1961, reissued 1967), 4–6.

107. Samuel Adams, *Writings*, 2:142–53, at 151–52.

In the January 28, 1771 *Boston Evening-Post,* in a Philanthrop letter dated to January 24, Sewall replied that the British mixed constitution of monarchy, aristocracy and democracy replaces "the miserable effects of unbounded *natural freedom* of action" with "*freedom* of choice," which is the real key to personal happiness, and better than "full liberty, as in a state of nature." The same "social liberty" of exercising freedom of choice in society is the reason why jury trials are fair. In accordance with "the constitutional rules of law" and in the presence of plaintiff and defendant, the jury examines evidence, and exercises its freedom of choice. According to Sewall, the right understanding of due process, and of the conditions in which the jury's freedom of choice can be correctly exercised, show that Samuel Adams cannot retry the case by presenting printed pamphlets and depositions to the public.

As the volume of the American state of nature discourse increased, some state of nature texts increasingly became fixed loci, regularly discussed formulations that none of the debating parties could avoid without risking irrelevance. The state of nature in Hobbes, Locke, and Montesquieu became such a locus early on. We also find greater complexity and experimentation with patterns of reasoning. The way Otis and Adams constructed legal arguments with state of nature components from Grotius, Pollexfen, Holt, Locke, Montesquieu and Rousseau, to all of which they added their own, is a clear case in point. The connection Otis drew between independence and abolition by justifying both from the radical equality in the state of nature, which was picked up by Benezet, Rush, and others, but made Adams and others uncomfortable, is another instance of the formalization and systematization of the state of nature discourse. Earlier we saw Thacher adapt Locke's state of nature as the first link in a chain of reasoning that ran through Burlamaqui, Montesquieu, Rapin, and Hume. Although Thacher's argument remained unfinished and probably unknown to Otis, John Adams and Gridley when they protested against the Stamp Act, it is useful to compare it to a latter chain of state of nature reasoning.

As shown by the small sample of state of nature texts discussed so far, by 1768 the colonists were equipped to make elements of their emerging ideology, including the state of nature, cohere in a number of ways. In a January 20, 1772 article in the *Boston Gazette*, Samuel Adams, writing as Candidus, disputes with the pseudonymous Chronus about Parliament's right to raise taxes without the colonists' consent. Adams lays out a train of thought, and supports its components with authorities. He cites Montesquieu on liberty being the object of the English constitution; his favorite enemy, Hutchinson, as an authority for Massachusetts being "an epitome of the British constitution"; John Dickinson to show that a free people retains control of the purse strings;[108] and Locke on the security of property as the reason for leaving the state of nature. Exiting the state of nature for the sake of the security of property is the foundation on which Samuel Adams built the argument against taxation without representation.[109]

Locke was the starting point for both Thacher and Samuel Adams. Montesquieu in Adams's article played a comparable role to Rapin and Hume in Thacher, as authorities for the view that the English constitution secured a mechanism for the progressive expansion of liberty. Adams drew on Hutchinson to particularize the argument to Massachusetts, a move for which Thacher in 1765 could only rely on the narrower point that it was the ancestors of Massachusetts settlers who bought and worked this particular land. In addition to positioning Massachusetts at the vanguard of expanding British liberty, Adams could now also plug in Dickinson on the correlation between American liberty and control of the purse. The latter was a long-standing argument with numerous earlier English formulations, including the ship money controversies of the 1620s–1630s.

The rising volume and increasing sophistication of American state of nature texts, the emergence of fixed loci, the references that colonial state of nature writers made to each other, and the layers of new meaning they added when they contested and developed others' arguments, are vital

---

108. John Dickinson, *Letters from a Farmer in Pennsylvania*, Letter 9 (Philadelphia, 1767–68).
109. Samuel Adams, *Writings*, 2:313–21, at 316.

features of the distinctly American state of nature discourse. By 1772 every side in every colonial constitutional debate, be it the right to property, representation, taxation, the independence of the judiciary, militias or standing armies, or the freedom of religion, assembly and speech, regarded the state of nature as a crucial component of the intellectual and ideological debates concerning imperial reform and the colonies' future.

THE TURN TO SELF-DEFENSE

6.1 COLONIAL INDEPENDENCE

Retrospectively, in the light of the Boston Pamphlet and its impact throughout the colonies, the so-called Abingdon Resolves seem less like an unusually radical document than the starting point of a major transformation of the American state of nature discourse. This is the beginning of stage two, in which the American state of nature was reoriented toward the right to self-defense, accompanied by an expansion of the constitutive sense of the state of nature as a sphere where the right to self-defense, hitherto seen as an essentially individual right, could be aggregated into the collective right of a natural community such as the colonies, without an explicit claim to secession and a new polity.

The exact date of the extraordinary Abingdon Resolves is unclear. They are commonly said to be a response to the Boston Massacre of March 5, 1770. Originally dated to March 10, the Resolves were printed in the April 2, 1770 issue of the *Boston Gazette* and in the 1770 *Political Register*, both of which put the first publication of the Resolves to March

19. *The Scots Magazine* dates them to August 1770.[1] However, all these sources concur that before they were printed, the Resolves were actually debated and adopted on February 21. This was the day before eleven-year-old Christopher Snider was fatally shot by Ebenezer Richardson, a minor customs officer, during a February 22 mobbing of his house. Richardson was tried in April and found guilty, but the judges refused to pronounce verdict and held Richardson in custody while they waited for a royal pardon or an opportunity to smuggle him out of Massachusetts. Samuel Adams arranged for young Snider's funeral, attended by over two thousand people. Snider is sometimes called the first victim of the Revolution. Nonetheless, section 8 of the Abingdon Resolves makes it probable that the February dates are wrong and that the Resolves were written, or at least finalized, after March 5, 1770:

> That the troops (may we not more properly say murderers?) sent to Boston by Lord Hillsborough, at the request of Governor Bernard, *to aid and protect* the comissioners of the customs, in levying the taxes imposed on us by the said acts, amount to *an open declaration of war* against the liberties of America, and are an unjust invasion thereof; and as we are refused any legal redress of these grievances, we are, in this instance, reduced to a state of nature, *whereby our natural right of opposing force with force is again devolved upon us.*

Some uncertainty clouds the authorship of the Resolves, as shown by the note that Harbottle Dorr Jr., the Boston merchant and Son of Liberty who in 1765 began to enter wonderfully informative annotations in his newspapers, made at the bottom of his *Boston Gazette* copy (fig. 6.1).

Dorr was usually meticulous, and the fact that he crossed out "supposed to be" suggests that at some point he confirmed Joseph Greenleaf's

1. *Boston Gazette*, April 2, 1770; *Political Register* 7 (1770), 37–39; *Scots Magazine* 32:417–19. The *Gentleman's Magazine* printed extracts from the Resolves in June 1770, but without dates. It also added, "It is said, however, that these Resolves were fabricated in Boston, under the inspection of a certain holy Doctor, and sent to the poor, ignorant, deluded people, to pass as a public act of the town."

Fig. 6.1 Harbottle Dorr, Jr., annotation in April 2, 1770, *Boston Gazette*. Collection of the Massachusetts Historical Society.

authorship.[2] Captain Greenleaf (1720–1810) was an extraordinary figure. He married Abigail Paine, elder sister of Robert Treat Paine, in 1749. They had seven children. They first lived in Braintree, then from around 1750 in Abingdon, and returned to Boston in 1771. Greenleaf joined the Boston Committee of Correspondence in 1772 and ran a printing office from 1773 until 1775, when his son, Thomas Greenleaf, took over the business.

The state of nature as the lawless war into which Britain pushed Massachusetts is not the only use of the concept. The Resolves begin,

1. That all nations of men that dwell upon the face of the whole earth, and each individual of them, are naturally free; and while in a state of nature, have a right to do themselves justice when natural rights are invaded.
2. That mankind, while in their foresaid natural state, always had, and now have, a right to enter into compact, and form societies, and erect such kind of government as the majority of them shall judge most for the public good.

The rights to self-defense, to contract, and to forming new associations (i.e., secede from existing ones) are all located in the state of nature. It is noteworthy that the author or authors maintain that both individuals and nations can be in the state of nature. The entity that Britain pushes

2. The name Dorr crossed out begins with "Wm," William. My best guess is that Dorr heard the rumor that the Resolves were drafted by William Cooper, Boston's town clerk from 1761 until his death in 1809. His younger brother, Rev. Samuel Cooper, might be the "holy Doctor" that the *Gentleman's Gazette* refers to as the author behind the scenes. Frederick Griffin, *Junius Discovered* (Boston, 1854), 275, speculates the same.

into the state of nature in section 8 of the Resolves, cited previously, is not the incoherent mass of colonists, but a nation that already exists and holds rights independently. Like Adams and others, Greenleaf in 1770 is already operating with a constitutive American state of nature, even as he combines several distinct meanings established in European texts.

Reid writes that the Abingdon Resolves were "condemned for radicalism in the House of Commons."[3] Although Reid is generally excellent, it is telling that he, like other scholars, misses the significance of the state of nature references. He discusses the Resolves in chapter 5, on "the second original contract." He cites section 2 as "the first paragraph," ignoring section 1; and he calls it a definition of the social contract, rather than a statement of state of nature rights to self-defense, contract, and association.

The front page of the March 4, 1771 *Boston Gazette* features two pieces. The second, responding to popular demand, is a reprint of the September 5, 1768 *Boston Gazette* letter from Rev. John Cleaveland of Ipswich, discussed above. The first is an extraordinary essay by Mutius Scaevola, who notes that he composed the letter in Bridgwater (*sic*), 8.5 miles from Abingdon, on January 28, 1771. Bailyn identifies Greenleaf as the author of a different Scaevola piece. It was published on November 14 the same year in the *Massachusetts Spy*. It enraged Hutchinson so much that he stripped Greenleaf of his post as justice of the peace and planned to sue him for libel, which he was strongly advised not to do.[4] Bailyn lists Thomas Young, Samuel Adams, and Greenleaf among the *Spy*'s core writers. Forman adds Joseph Warren to this list, suggesting that he also published as Scaevola.[5] While that is possible, based on the 1770 Abingdon Resolves, Greenleaf is not unlikely to be the March 4, 1771 Scaevola who wrote,

---

3. Reid, *The Authority to Tax*, 56.
4. Bailyn, *The Ordeal*, 198–99. Greenleaf denied authorship. In *The Treat Family* . . . (Salem Press, 1893), 242, John Harvey Treat, who was related to Greenleaf, identified him as the author without any expression of doubt.
5. Samuel A. Forman, *Dr. Joseph Warren* . . . (Pelican, 2012), 158–59.

No one will pretend that the King of Great-Britain has a right to make any alteration in the settled form of government, or to rule the people by any laws which do not *originate* with themselves. An attempt of this kind, being an infraction of the compact, reduces the subject again to a state of nature, which being a state of *war*, the party so reducing, may be said *rebellare*: For by breaking the compact, he has put himself into the original state of nature, is a rebel against the state, dissolves the allegiance of the subject, and leaves him at full liberty to resume his delegated power, and hold it himself, or again entrust it as he thinks proper.

This is both a combative American state of nature and a constitutive one. In chapter 19, sections 226 and 227 of the *Second Treatise*, Locke describes either the people or the legislature as rebels, depending on which one introduces a state of war by opposing the laws. By contrast, Scaevola justifies secession and the formation of a new state by calling the *king* a rebel who puts everyone in a state of nature, which is war. However, unlike Gridley, Scaevola did not believe that the state of nature after the dissolution of the bond with Britain was worse than the original state of nature. It is a stable condition which, once resumed, can serve as the scene for erecting a new government.[6]

A more fully constitutive meaning is offered in the June 13, 1771 *Massachusetts Spy*, in which Centinel declares in Letter 7 in the simplest terms that George III has no right to send troops to the colonies, because when the first settlers left Britain, they became independent. According to Vattel in *The Law of Nations*, I.xix, citizens have an absolute right to leave when the monarch breaks a compact or violates their freedom of conscience. Centinel continues to apply this to the settlers: "[t]he connection between them and the sovereign is broke, and consequently they fall into a state of nature which preceeded government." There the

6. The April 4, 1771 *Massachusetts Spy* gleefully reprinted No. 60 from *Cato's Letters* (1721): "So that to know the Jurisdiction of Governors, and its Limits, we must have Recourse to the Institution of Government, and ascertain those Limits by the Measure of Power, which Men in the State of Nature have over themselves and one another."

settlers created their own constitution and bought land from the Native Americans, after which they had "all those titles to an absolute sovereignty any nation can vouch." Sovereign and independent, they applied to Britain for protection. According to Centinel, Vattel explains that in such relationships between sovereign states, the one offering protection must honor the conditions under which obedience, but not sovereignty, had been offered. To this Centinel adds that this relationship is analogous between states and private individuals in a state of nature, because when the monarch fails to provide protection, his subjects relapse into a state of nature, as well.

6.2 THE BOSTON PAMPHLET

The Abingdon Resolves could have been a radical, one-off formulation of the American constitutive state of nature and the state of nature right to self-defense in the wake of the Boston Massacre. Instead, they represent a turning point. The Boston Pamphlet contains a milder version of the same formula, but the responses that Boston received both from Massachusetts and from the other colonies, especially after the Boston Port Act of March 1774, solidified the new, dominant meaning of the revolutionary state of nature as the state of nature right to self-defense and the broader constitutive state of nature where this right could be aggregated.

In addition to the connections between the arguments in these texts, there was also personal continuity between the Abingdon Resolves and the Boston Pamphlet. Soon after Greenleaf moved back to Boston with his family, he joined the Committee of Correspondence in 1772. He was one of the twenty-one men in the Committee that drew up the 1772 *The Votes and Proceedings of the Freeholders and Other Inhabitants of the Town of Boston, in Town Meeting Assembled, According to Law*, better known as part of the Boston Pamphlet.[7] And though the Boston Pamphlet did not connect rights in the state of nature with a state of nature into which

7. The Committee chose Greenleaf to answer Abingdon's letter in September 1774. Boston Committee of Correspondence Records, New York Public Library,

Britain had pushed the colonies in a constitutional sense, it located more extensive and provocative rights in the state of nature than the Abingdon Resolves did.

The Boston Pamphlet is one of the founding documents of the first committee of correspondence, effectively shadow governments in the thirteen colonies.[8] The Pamphlet begins with a short account of the meetings on October 28 and November 2, 1772, when the Committee of Correspondence was established. Samuel Adams, James Otis, Jr. and Dr. Joseph Warren were instrumental in its formation and in shaping its mission to coordinate resistance to Britain. Echoing Samuel Adams's January 20, 1772 article, which in turn drew on John Dickinson's 1768 point in *Letter IX from a Farmer in Pennsylvania* concerning the power of the purse, one of the chief grievances expressed by the Committee of Correspondence was the British measure to start paying officials directly rather than allow Massachusetts to pay them and thereby have some sort of financial check on their powers.[9] The second part of the Pamphlet is the Committee's November 20 report to the town. In this text, entitled "Rights of the Colonists: The Report of the Committee of Correspondence to the Boston Town Meeting," the state of nature again became a load-bearing feature. The Pamphlet's discussion of rights is

MssCol 343, p. 795, b.1.f.9, image 82. Richard D. Brown, *Revolutionary Politics in Massachusetts* (Harvard, 1970).

8. Committees of correspondence had existed before. However, this committee and those that were modeled on it were designed as permanent institutions. By this time, the British government had come to regard all-colony coordination as highly dangerous. See e.g. the October 1, 1765 Whitehall assessment of the June 8, 20, and 24, 1765 Massachusetts proposals to hold an all-colony meeting in New York, later known as the Stamp Act Congress. 1765 "Copies and extracts regarding the Stamp Act . . . ," Huntington, mssHM 1947, p. 24: "And as this appears to be the first Instance of any General Congress appointed by the Assemblies of the Colonies without the Authority of the Crown a Measure which we conceive of dangerous Tendency." Final version printed as report of the Lords Commissioners for Trade and Plantations in Cobbett's *Parliamentary History* (London, 1813), 16:122.

9. For the Committee's intention see *inter alia* Samuel Adams to James Warren, November 4, 1772, in *Warren-Adams Letters*, 1:11–12; Mark Puls, *Samuel Adams, Father of the American Revolution* (Palgrave, 2006).

explicitly divided into three sections: on the natural rights of colonists, on their rights as Christians, and on their rights as subjects. Clearly implied is the correspondence to natural (or international), divine, and civil (in this case, English common) law. The Boston Pamphlet ends with the Committee's address to 240 towns to join the cause in the Massachusetts Bay Colony.[10] At least 144 replied by the end of summer 1773.

On closer inspection, the tripartite division runs through not only the Report, but every part of the document, including the description of the design of the Committee and its concluding letter to other towns.[11] Many of the towns repeated the same structure in their reply.[12] The Pamphlet's opening sentence shows that the options that the state of nature is invoked to support are no longer limited to bargaining with Westminster and justifying resistance, but now include the foundation of a new state.

Among the natural Rights of the Colonists are these First, A Right to *Life*; secondly, to *Liberty*; thirdly, to *Property*; together with the Right to

10. The arrangement of the Boston Pamphlet shows an understanding of what Putnam calls a two-level game, between domestic politics and external diplomacy. Robert Putnam, "Diplomacy and Domestic Politics: The Logic of Two-Level Games," *International Organization* 42 (1988), 427–60. The Boston Pamphlet's petition section is moderate and expresses hope for reconciliation with Britain. By contrast, the letter to other towns justifies independence based on British tyranny and despotism. Evidence of reception and reaction shows that London, the colonists, and the writers all understood that the Pamphlet used the threat of independence to bargain for better terms.
11. Boston Pamphlet, iii, on design: "to state the Rights of the Colonists, and of this Province in particular, as Men, as Christians, and as Subjects; to Communicate and Publish the same to the several Towns in this Province, and to the World, as the Sense of this Town, with the Infringements and Violations thereof that have been, or from Time to Time may be made; also requesting of each Town a free Communication of their Sentiments on this Subject." The report is discussed above. In Boston's November 20 letter to other towns, see pp. 31 and 32 for recapitulations of the three-fold rights of the Colonists as men, Christians, and British subjects. Elbridge Gerry objected to invoking Christian rights. Letter to Samuel Adams, November 10, 1772, and Adams's reply from November 14, in James T. Austin, *The Life of Elbridge Gerry* (Boston, 1828), 1:18–21.
12. Boston Committee of Correspondence Records, New York Public Library, MssCol 343, b.1.ff.1–3, http://archives.nypl.org/mss/343Gerry

support and defend them in the best manner they can. These are evident Branches of, rather than Deductions from the Duty of Self Preservation, commonly called the first Law of Nature. . . . All men have a Right to remain in a State of Nature as long as they please; And in Case of intolerable Oppression, civil or religious, to leave the society they belong to, and enter into another.[13]

The radicalness of this position was not lost on the government. The parliamentary committee appointed to review the tensions in Massachusetts from 1764 until 1774 emphatically began its summary of the Boston Pamphlet with this state of nature point.[14] Samuel Adams's notes reveal that an early draft featured the state of nature even more heavily: "Every Man in the State of Nature hath a Right to Life Liberty and Property with the Right to support & defend them. The Natural Liberty of Man is to govern or defend his own Rights according to his own Ideas of the Law of Nature. When Men enter into the State of Nature Society it is with the View of promoting their own Safety by Means of Union" (fig. 6.2).[15]

In the final draft, the state of nature rights to life, liberty, and property became natural rights. The draft's second reference to the state of nature is presumably a slip of the pen, but it suggests that the concept was very much on the drafters' mind. In the final version, subsuming the rights to life, liberty and property under the broader right of self-preservation is a profound conceptual move. It recalls Otis's contention in the 1764 *Rights* that a general constitutional principle

13. Boston Committee of Correspondence Records, New York Public Library, MssCol 343, b.8.f.4, image 1, http://archives.nypl.org/mss/343#detailed.

14. *The Report of the Lords Committees appointed to Enquire into the several proceedings in the Colony of Massachusetts Bay, in opposition to the Sovereignty of his Majesty over that Province, and also what hath passed in the House of Lords, relative thereto from the first of January, 1764* (London, 1774), 27–28. Often reprinted, e.g. in *A Collection of Interesting, Authentic Papers, relative to the Dispute between Great Britain and America* . . . (London, 1777), 250.

15. Samuel Adams Papers, New York Public Library, MssCol 20, b.1.f.130, http://archives.nypl.org/mss/20#detailed.

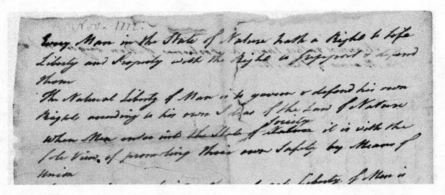

Fig. 6.2 Samuel Adams Papers, MssCol 20, b.1.f.130. Manuscripts and Archives Division, The New York Public Library, Astor, Lenox, and Tilden Foundations.

that one should derive from the maxim *salus populi suprema lex esto* is that the people's welfare depends on life, liberty, and property. In the 1772 Boston Pamphlet, the people's welfare, the responsibility for and the means to which can be alienable, has turned into "the Duty of Self Preservation."

Nor is the list of these three goods obvious. Locke and others regarded freedom of religion as more important than life, liberty or property insofar as eternal life depended on the right faith, and eternal life was a greater good than life on this earth. (Recall that in his 1762 election day sermon Williams considered the state of nature rights to self-defense and property to be alienable, but not the right to conscience, on which eternal life depends.) The draft of the Committee's report, now at the New York Public Library, shows signs of careful and meticulous revision and differs from the published version in several ways. For instance, it begins by explaining that Boston appointed a committee of twenty-one. The number is struck from the version they published. Another revision shows that the Committee originally placed the freedom of religion in the state of nature, as well (fig. 6.3).[16]

16. Boston Committee of Correspondence Records, New York Public Library, MssCol 343, b.8.f.4, image 2, http://archives.nypl.org/mss/343#detailed.

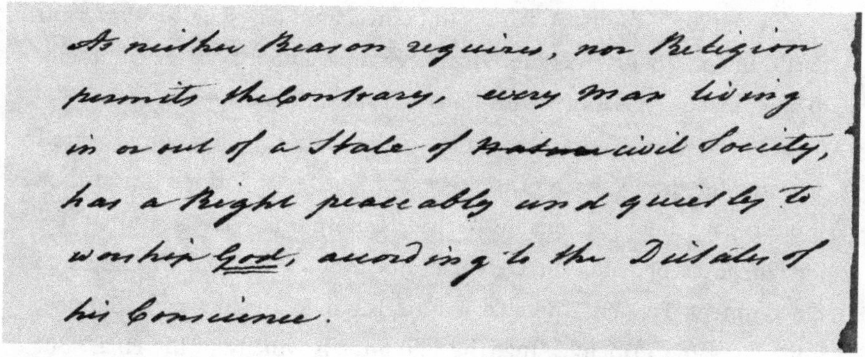

As neither Reason requires, nor Religion permits the Contrary, every man living in or out of a State of ~~Nature~~ civil Society, has a Right peaceably and quietly to worship God, according to the Dictates of his Conscience.

Fig. 6.3 Boston Committee of Correspondence records, MssCol 343, b.8.f.4. Manuscripts and Archives Division, The New York Public Library, Astor, Lenox, and Tilden Foundations.

How is this group of rights exercised? After referencing Locke's *Letter Concerning Toleration* and *Two Treatises of Government*, the Pamphlet continues.

> In the State of Nature, every man is, under *God*, Judge and sole Judge of his own Rights and of the Injuries done him. By entering into Society, he agrees to an *Arbiter* or indifferent Judge between him & his Neighbors; but he no more renounces his original Right, than by taking a Cause out of the ordinary Course of Law, & leaving the Decision to Referees or indifferent Arbitrators.[17]
>
> In the last Case he must pay the Referees for time and trouble; he also should be willing to pay his just Quota for the Support of Government, the Law and the Constitution, the End of which is to furnish indifferent and impartial Judges in all Cases that may happen, whether civil ecclesiastical marine or military.

17. George Dawson draws on Pufendorf and Grotius to make the same point in *Origo Legum* . . . (London, 1694), I.29. Dawson goes to great lengths to refute Hobbes's "Nonsensical Paradox" (31) that the state of nature is a state of war and provides an alternative set of natural laws to replace Hobbes's. The tenth law that follows from his version of the state of nature is that, given their radical equality, people in a state of nature must appoint a third-party arbiter to settle their disputes.

"The *natural* Liberty of man, is to be free from any superior Power on Earth, and not to be under the Will or legislative authority of man, but only to have the Law of Nature for his Rule." (Locke on Government)

In the State of Nature, Men may, as the *Patriarchs* did, employ hired Servants for the Defence of their Lives Liberties & Property; and they should pay them reasonable Wages. *Government* was instituted for the Purposes of common Defence; and those who hold the Reins of Government have an equitable natural Right to an honorable Support from the same Principle "that the Labourer is worthy of his Hire." But then the same Community which they serve ought to be the assessors of their Pay.[18]

The revision of "state of nature" to "civil society" on the first page of the Boston Pamphlet may help us to better understand section 3, "The Rights of the Colonists as Subjects." The second paragraph runs, "The absolute Rights of Englishmen, and all Freemen in or out of civil Society, are principally, personal Security, personal Liberty and private Property." If we substitute "state of nature" for "civil society," as it was first drafted, we get Blackstone's definition of absolute rights. As we saw, according to Blackstone only personal rights can be absolute rights, since they are the ones that exist in the state of nature "and which every man is intitled to enjoy whether out of society or in it."[19] These are the rights that civil societies and states must protect and constrain as little as possible.[20] Given

18. Boston Committee of Correspondence Records, New York Public Library, b.8.f.4, images 4–5, http://archives.nypl.org/mss/343#detailed.
19. Blackstone, *Commentaries*, I.i.119.
20. Blackstone, *Commentaries*, I.i.120–21. This is the passage that Mercy Otis Warren, sister of James Otis, Jr. and wife to James Warren, picks up on in her 1788 *Observations on the new Constitution, and on the Federal and State Conventions*, published under the pen name, "A Columbian Patriot," to argue against ratifying the US Constitution, which she thought went far beyond the standard of minimal constraint. The 1772 adaptation of Blackstone's use of absolute rights in the state of nature as a yardstick for measuring the quality of a government belonged to the earlier stage of the American state-of-nature discourse, when justifying resistance to Britain was the priority. Another contrast is offered by William Tudor's March 5, 1779 oration on the anniversary of the Boston Massacre, in which Tudor made the

the sophistication of the Boston Pamphlet, Otis's and other revolutionary lawyers' engagement with Blackstone after 1765, and the close attention the drafters evidently paid to the language of the Pamphlet, it is probable that the revision we find in the manuscript was deliberate, and the "absolute rights" in the Boston Pamphlet are patterned on Blackstone. The crucial difference is that while for both Blackstone and Boston absolute rights are in the state of nature, for the Boston Committee of Correspondence they survive the transition even to the English commonwealth. By contrast, according to Blackstone, and Hutchinson's 1769 letter to Whately, the English commonwealth protects state of nature rights as much as possible, thus justifying the cases in and degrees to which it must abridge them. This interpretation is reinforced by the other sources discussed here, from which a distinct American constitutive state of nature emerges.

Similarly, Samuel Adams's draft of the Boston Committee's March 23, 1773 letter to Hutchinson, condemning Hutchinson's letters, replaced a reference to the "Law of Nature" with the "Law of Selfpreservation."[21] Many texts offer self-preservation as one of the natural laws, but this is not the same thing. The choice to invoke self-preservation as a high-order category in the Boston Pamphlet and in the 1773 March letter, together with increasingly frequent references to an "appeal to heaven," attest to rising tensions and a deliberate decision to diminish the scope for negotiation. (In the next chapter we will see invocations of the state of nature praised and condemned during the First Continental Congress for reducing the scope for compromise with Britain.) Even in Blackstone's *Commentaries*, where self-defense is described as "the primary law of nature," it is not broad enough to encompass life, liberty and property as derivative rights, in other words simply as the means to self-preservation. When a problem is framed in natural law terms, one can bring in and debate natural laws.

same point about state of nature rights as the appropriate yardstick by referencing not Blackstone, but Hume's *History*, 2:132. Niles, *Principles*, 36–47, at 46.

21. Samuel Adams, draft of the Boston Committee's March 23, 1773 letter to Governor Hutchinson. Boston Public Library, MS G.41.23.

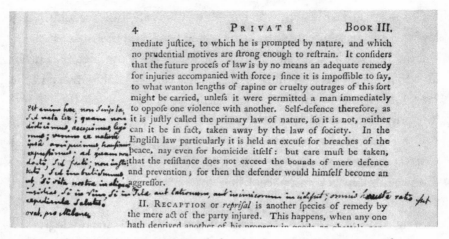

Fig. 6.4 John Adams's annotations in Blackstone, *Commentaries*, III.i.3–4, Adams 93.2. Boston Public Library.

When the matter is reduced to pure self-preservation, a half-way compromise is unlikely.

We find such deliberate radicalization and a purposeful reduction of the scope for compromise in the drafts and printed version of the 1772 Boston Pamphlet, the March 1773 letter to Hutchinson, and more subtly in one of John Adams's copies of *Commentaries*, volume 3, where Adams copied the famous passage from Cicero's *Pro Milone* 10 about self-defense as the unwritten law of nature, next to Blackstone's discussion of self-defense (fig. 6.4).[22] This is the passage Grotius used to develop his version of the state of nature.[23]

Continuing the revolutionary trend in his *Lectures on Law*, James Wilson yokes together the same two passages, from Blackstone and Cicero, to offer a self-defense doctrine even more expansive than the 1772–1773 Boston documents, reaching universal jurisdiction.

> The defence of one's self, justly called the primary law of nature, is not, nor can it be abrogated by any regulation of municipal law. This principle

22. Boston Public Library, Adams 93.2, III.i.3–4.
23. Straumann, *Roman Law*, 140.

of defence is not confined merely to the person; it extends to the liberty and the property of a man: it is not confined merely to his own person; it extends to the persons of all those, to whom he bears a peculiar relation—of his wife, of his parent, of his child, of his master, of his servant: nay, it extends to the person of every one, who is in danger; perhaps, to the liberty of every one, whose liberty is unjustly and forcibly attacked. It becomes humanity as well as justice.[24]

Not only Blackstone, but Locke was also subjected to considerable "remix" during the formulation of the revolutionary, constitutive American state of nature doctrine.[25] The only American printing of Locke's *Second Treatise* in the eighteenth century, published by Edes and Gill in 1773 in Boston, omits the first chapter, and begins with the second chapter, on the state of nature. Interestingly, Slauter suggests that Edes and Gill published their version as part of the controversy surrounding the 1772 Boston Pamphlet.[26] They advertised their Locke edition as a counter-measure to contemporary "Promoters of Arbitrary Power," corrupted by Richelieu's *Testament*, Mandeville's *Fable of the Bees*, and Hobbes's *Leviathan*, the same three works Otis railed against in 1762. Edes and Gill's advertisement for their 1773 Locke, bereft of chapter 1, proposes that it should be "early and carefully explained by every Father to his Son, by every Preceptor in our public and private Schools to his pupils, and by every Mother to her Daughter" (fig. 6.5).[27]

24. James Wilson, *Works* (Liberty Fund, 2007), 2:1082–83.
25. Lawrence Lessig, *Remix: Making Art and Commerce Thrive in the Hybrid Economy* (Penguin, 2008).
26. Eric Slauter, "Reading," 20. Slauter briefly mentions that Edes and Gill cut the first chapter but does not explain its significance. Other editions, of course, continued to circulate. For instance, Franklin's copy of the 1764 London version of the *Two Treatises*, edited by Thomas Hollis, contains manual annotations (Library Company of Philadelphia, Ii Lock Log. 1457.O (Mackenzie)), and so does Dartmouth's copy (Rauner Woodward Room, 78).
27. First item in *Boston Gazette*, March 1, 1773. Slauter notes that it was reprinted on April 12 and in the March 4 and April 1, 1773 issues of the *Massachusetts Gazette*. "Reading," 25 n. 30.

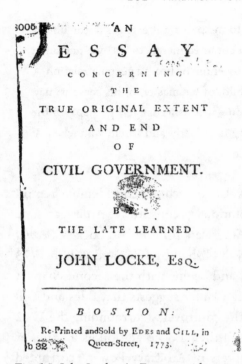

AN ESSAY

CONCERNING THE TRUE
ORIGINAL EXTENT AND END
OF CIVIL-GOVERNMENT.

Of the State of Nature.

TO understand political power right, and derive it from its original, we muſt conſider what ſtate all men are naturally in, and that is, a *ſtate of per-fect freedom* to order their actions, and diſpoſe of their poſſeſſions and perſons, as they think fit, within the bounds of the law of nature, without aſking leave, or depending upon the will of any other man.

A *ſtate alſo of equality* wherein all the power and ju-riſdiction is reciprocal, no one having more than another; there being nothing more evident, than that creatures of the ſame ſpecies and rank, promiſcuouſly born to all the ſame advantages of nature, and the uſe of the ſame fa-culties, ſhould alſo be equal one amongſt another with-out ſubordination or ſubjection, unleſs the lord and ma-ſter of them all ſhould, by any manifeſt declaration of his will, ſet one above another, and confer on him, by an evident and clear appointment, an undoubted right to dominion and ſovereignty.

This *equality* of men by nature, the judicious *Hooker* looks upon as ſo evident in itſelf, and beyond all queſtion, that he makes it the foundation of that obliga-tion to mutual love amongſt men, on which he builds the duties they owe one another, and from whence he derives the great maxims *of juſtice* and *charity*.

Fig. 6.5 John Locke, *An Essay . . .* , title page and first page of the first American edition

The Library Company of Philadelphia holds a copy of the 1773 Boston edition, heavily annotated by Nathaniel Ames, Jr., whose almanac for 1764, published in 1763, included his father's last essay on the American state of nature.[28] Ames's marginalia are wonderful and speak for them-selves (figs. 6.6, 6.7). Slauter notes that Ames, Jr. lent his copy to friends, including Abner Ellis, Dedham's deputy to the Massachusetts House of Representatives and fellow Son of Liberty, in 1774 and 1809. Slauter also shows that Ames's marginalia are more likely to date from the early nine-teenth century.

The growing emphasis on the constitutional state of nature and the *collective* state of nature right to self-defense in the early 1770s was ac-companied by an evolving redefinition of the colonial self as increasingly independent. One form of this evolution was a sharper focus on the state

28. Library Company of Philadelphia, Am 1773 Loc 67121.O.

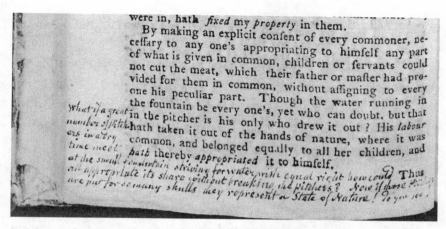

were in, hath *fixed* my *property* in them.

By making an explicit consent of every commoner, necessary to any one's appropriating to himself any part
of what is given in common, children or servants could
not cut the meat, which their father or master had provided for them in common, without assigning to every
one his peculiar part. Though the water running in
the fountain be every one's, yet who can doubt, but that
in the pitcher is his only who drew it out ? His *labour*
hath taken it out of the hands of nature, where it was
common, and belonged equally to all her children, and
hath thereby *appropriated* it to himself.

[marginalia, left:] What if a great number of those ers in a dry time meet at the small fountain striving for water, with equal right how could aal appropriate its share without breaking the pitchers? Now if those are put for so many skulls they represent a State of Nature! So you see.

Fig. 6.6 Nathaniel Ames Jr., annotations in John Locke, *An Essay...*, 16. Library Company of Philadelphia.

To conclude, The *power that every individual gave the*
society, when he entered into it, can never revert to the
individuals again, as long as the society lasts, but will
always remain in the community ; because without this
there can be no community ; no commonwealth, which is
contrary to the original agreement: so also when the society
hath placed the legislative in any assembly of men, to
continue in them and their successors, with direction and
authority for providing such successors, *the legislative can*
never revert to the people whilst that government lasts ; because having provided a legislative with power to continue
forever, they have given up their political power to the
legislative, and cannot resume it. But if they have set limits to the duration of their legislative, and made this
supreme power in any person, or assembly, only temporary ; or else, when by the miscarriages of those in authority, it is forfeited ; upon the forfeiture, or at the de-
termination of the time set, *it reverts to the society*, and
the people have a right to act as supreme, and continue
the legislative in themselves ; or erect a new form, or under
the old form place it in new hands, as they think good.

[marginalia, right:] Here are true american sentiment on government. That the body of People are the sole fountain of power whenever they find expedient to exert it and express their irresistable sovereign voice, or fiat.

F I N I S.

Fig. 6.7 Nathaniel Ames, Jr., annotations in John Locke, *An Essay...*, 129. Library Company of Philadelphia.

of nature that the first settlers found themselves in, and the state of nature rights they had to form a new constitution, which their descendants in turn had a state of nature right to defend. This move required that the centuries separating the first settlers from the revolutionary generation were reimagined as less of a period that saw the extension of the British empire, and more as a relationship between autonomous states. One way to argue this was to show that the American colonies followed the ancient Greek pattern of colonization, in which colonies grew naturally out of metropolitan overpopulation and a sense of adventure, rather than the Roman model of purposeful, top-down colonization with clearly defined metropolitan and colonial rights and obligations, and the tiered system of interdependence that could contain and accommodate the Roman colonies' increasing self-government without affecting their ties and obligations.[29] Another way of making the same point was to reinterpret the charters as not giving, not even confirming colonial rights, but as a contract between the settlers and the monarch that side stepped Parliament's authority, held the monarch accountable to the standards of an international treaty, and left the American settlers intact as an autonomous state when the monarch broke the treaty and/or Parliament made demands on the settlers without, or in excess of, the monarch's authority. A review of state of nature discussions of colonial charters as contracts between autonomous states in a state of nature shows that this shift in emphasis mirrors quite well the shift in the discussion of the state of nature to the right to self-defense.

In September 1765, the Massachusetts Assembly instructed James Otis, Thomas Cushing, and Thomas Gray to draft a response to the Stamp Act. The instructions emphasize the colonists' rights as freeborn subjects of Britain and, in language stronger than the Assembly's

---

29. Mark Somos, "Sigonius' Method: A Sixteenth-Century Italian Source of British Imperial Reform, 1751–1780," in Arthur Weststeijn and Jeremia Pelgrom (eds.), *Divergent Discourses on Roman Colonization: Sigonius, Lipsius, and the Development of Roman Colonial Studies* (Oxford, forthcoming).

1765 statements addressed to London, they declare that the Stamp Act destroyed the colony's charter. As we saw, DeBerdt in December 1765, Bland in March 1766, Cleaveland in September 1768, and John Adams in 1774, declared that the colonies were already founded as independent. Their independence is protected, but not created by royal or proprietary charters. While the January 1768 Massachusetts letter to Shelburne, published in newspapers and in *True Sentiments*, invoked natural law to confirm the province's charter rights, the Massachusetts circular letter issued in February 1768 claimed that colonists have natural rights, including to property, irrespective of the charter. We also saw Richard Hussey in the Commons in 1766, and Mauduit in 1769 in *The Short View*, posit that successive English monarchs were wrong to grant extensive charter rights, but since these charters were accepted and used by the colonists in good faith, they should be honored as far as reason of state and policy allow. By contrast, Cleaveland in 1768 and Adams in 1774 argued that what had reduced the colonies to a state of nature was nothing more and nothing less than the violation of their charter rights. From this, it was a short step to the position that the settlers entered the state of nature when they left England, formed their own constitution, and the charters codified relationships between independent American communities and the Crown. We find this view in the 1771 Centinel Letter 7, discussed previously, in the March 28, 1774, *Newport Mercury* in a front-page rejoinder by "Tertius Cato" to a Mr. Southwick's defense of Hutchinson, and in Moses Mather's 1775 sermon, discussed below. Conversely, Hutchinson in 1765 and Samuel Johnson in 1775 (also discussed below) invoked the charters as evidence that the colonists could not be in a state of nature, because even if it were the case that Britain afforded them no protection, and they gained property rights by buying the land from Native Americans and mixing their labor with it, they would still be claiming charter rights as well, which implies imperial government. In the same vein, in his 1773 *An Appeal to the Public for Religious Liberty* . . . , Isaac Backus scorned the Massachusetts General Court for forcing Baptists to pay taxes to support the Congregational minister in Ashfield.[30] Backus explained that they petitioned against the tax "as men, as christians, and subjects of a free government," echoing the tripartite structure of the 1772 Boston Pamphlet, and asserting a violation of their charter privileges. Boston, however, replied that the natural rights of Baptists were irrelevant, because civil government superseded them. Backus then reminded Boston that even if that were the case, it would not place them in a state of nature, for they would still have their charter rights and their rights as free subjects.[31]

According to the Boston Pamphlet, religious toleration (except for Catholics) and the right to criticize civil laws when they clashed with natural laws were also located in the state of nature. So was the colonists' right to create and maintain the desirable dependence of the judiciary on the people through the provincial assemblies', rather than London's, control of judges' and administrators' salaries. When the town of Sheffield, Massachusetts, formulated a reply to the Boston Pamphlet, the writers drew the same inference concerning the necessary dependence of judges on the people alone, but from a different state of nature argument. Instead of the equal right that everyone in the state of nature has to identify their own rights and injuries against them, the Sheffield Declaration (or Sheffield Resolves) placed "a right to the undisturbed enjoyment of their lives, their liberty and property" in the same radical equality grounded in the state of nature. The point of entering the polity is to make this defense more effective.

> RESOLVED, That mankind in a state of nature are equal, free, and independent of each other, and have a right to the undisturbed enjoyment of their lives, their liberty and property.
>
> Resolved, That the great end of political society is to secure in a more effectual manner those rights and privileges wherewith God and nature have made us free. Resolved, That it hath a tendency to subvert the good end for which society was instituted, to have in any part of the legislative

30. Bailyn, *Ideological Origins*, 261–70.
31. In Sandoz, *Political Sermons*, 1:331–68, at 351.

body an interest separate from and independent of the interest of the people in general.

Judges must also receive their salaries from the colonists, because that particular dependence is what makes the defense of state of nature rights more effective.

The Declaration was drafted on January 5, 1773 by a committee of eleven men, including Theodore Sedgwick, and moderated by Col. John Ashley.[32] It was approved by the town on January 12 and printed in the *Massachusetts Spy* on February 18. Eight years later, Sedgwick famously argued in *Brom and Bett v. Ashley* that the Colonel had no property right to Elizabeth Freeman, known as Mum Bett, given that Massachusetts's 1780 constitution declared that "all men are born free and equal." According to Catherine, Sedgwick's youngest daughter, Freeman decided to ask Sedgwick to help her sue for freedom after she overheard this phrase when someone read out loud the Declaration of Independence.[33] As Ashley served at the time as judge of the Berkshire Court of Common Pleas, the lawsuit was brought in Berkshire, and it was designed to test the legality of slavery in Massachusetts rather than directly charge Ashley, it has been suggested that Ashley was part of planning this landmark case.[34]

32. Sedgwick's name appears on the Boston Committee of Correspondence records at NYPL (MssCol 343), p. 202, image 24 of f.3 at http://archives.nypl.org/mss/343#detailed.

33. "It was soon after the close of the revolutionary war, that she chanced at the village 'meeting house,' in Sheffield, to hear the Declaration of Independence read. She went the next day to the office of Mr. Theodore Sedgewick, then in the beginning of his honourable political and legal career. 'Sir,' said she, 'I heard that paper read yesterday, that says, "all men are born equal, and that every man has a right to freedom." I am not a dumb *critter*; won't the law give me my freedom?' I can imagine her upright form, as she stood dilating with her fresh hope based on the declaration of an intrinsic, inalienable right. Such a resolve as hers is like God's messengers—wind, snow, and hail—irresistible." Miss Sedgewick, "Slavery in New England," *Bentley's Miscellany* 34 (1853), 417–24, at 421.

34. Arthur Zilversmit, *First Emancipation: The Abolition of Slavery in the North* (Chicago, 1967), 616–17, cited at http://www.mass.gov/courts/court-info/sjc/edu-res-center/abolition/abolition-7-gen.html.

On December 21, 1772, the inhabitants of Marlborough gathered to listen to the Boston Pamphlet. They agreed to set up a committee to draft a reply, and to debate it on January 21. That day they passed resolves that begin by effectively copying the Abingdon Resolves and invoking one of the most powerful rights in the state of nature, that of self-defense. While in Hobbesian and, as we shall see, Loyalist formulations this is one of the key rights that must be surrendered for a state to become viable, Marlborough builds from it a constitutive American argument, in which the continued presence of the state of nature is all-important.

> Resolve 1st. That the Inhabitants of this Earth are naturally free, & while in a State of Nature, have a Right to do themselves Justice when their Rights are Invaded.
>
> Resolve 2ndly. That Mankind have a Right & Power to form themselves into Society, make Compacts, Covenants, & just Laws, so as to form a good & equitable rule of Government.
>
> Resolve 3.dly That it is the opinion of this Town that the British Nation have Enjoy'd, perhaps, as complete a System of Government as any Nation whatever, agreeable to, & by which the King was as much bound as the people, & had no Longer Right by the Constitution & his Coronation-Oath to the Throne... During the time of ruling according to the same.[35]

When the monarch violates the constitution, "then that free-born people are not Requir'd by the religion of Jesus-Christ to submit themselves as Slaves to such Irreligious Tyranny, but may make Use of Such Power as God has given them, to preserve & defend themselves, & Recover & Support their Laws & Liberties Civil & Religious, & this must be admitted by all who approve that happy Revolution bro't about by the hand of divine Providence in 1688."

Though Marlborough decided to copy the first two Abingdon resolves concerning the state of nature, unlike Abingdon, they continued not by elaborating the right to free association, but by praising the British

---

35. Boston Committee of Correspondence Records, NYPL MssColl 343, b.4.f.39.

constitution as the most equitable. Confirmed by Christian resistance theory, they argued that a violation of this constitution activates the state of nature right to resist. Unlike in some Hobbesian and Loyalist formulations, state of nature rights are never fully transferred. Among these rights, Abingdon emphasized free association (with the right of secession implied), while Marlborough came back to resistance.

Ten days after Marlborough's meeting, on the last day of 1772, the town of Littleton also chose a committee to respond to the Boston Pamphlet. On February 2, 1773, the town listened to the committee's draft. The moderator was the Harvard graduate and lawyer "Dummer Rogers," the same "Jeremiah Dummer Rogers, of Littleton" who was evacuated by British troops from Boston in March 1776 and appears in the list of Loyalists deprived of property and privileges in the 1778 Massachusetts Banishment Act.[36] In 1772, according to Marlborough's letter to the Boston Committee of Correspondence, some Littleton residents demanded an (unspecified) amendment. The amendment was debated and accepted on March 2, and the reply was sent to Boston. The amended and accepted draft begins,

> The British Constitution appears to us to be the best calculated to answer the ends which mankind proposed to themselves in forsaking their natural state of Independence and entring [sic] into Society then perhaps any form of Government under Heaven; as here we find a more happy Union of the three great qualities of Government than could be expected in any other form.[37]

The rest of the argument is familiar. The first settlers brought with them "the Liberties and Immunities of Englishmen" and "the privileges of the British Constitution." Parliament's attempt to render judges dependent

36. Rogers became a commissary to the British army in Charlestown and died in Halifax, Nova Scotia in 1784.
37. Boston Committee of Correspondence Records, NYPL MssColl 343, p. 281. B.1.f.4, image 17, http://archives.nypl.org/mss/343#detailed. The whole Littleton letter is pp. 279–83, images 15–19.

on the Crown, the extension of the powers of the Court of Admiralty
and the Board of Commissioners, and posting soldiers are all violations
of charter rights and of English rights that best answer the purposes for
which people left the state of nature.

The town of Wrentham passed resolutions in support of Boston on
January 11, 1773. John Messinger, the town clerk, sent them to Boston
in February 1773, with a cover letter assuring Boston of their solidarity.
Further correspondence followed. In May, Wrentham appointed what
appears to be a standing revolutionary committee.[38] As part of this correspondence, on June 3, 1774 Wrentham listened to and voted favorably
on another response to Boston, drafted by their committee. Jabez Fisher
was chosen to represent the committee during the discussion with the
residents. The committee included Dr. Thomas Man, Lemuel Kollock
and John Smith. It may have also considered the views of Major William
Thomson, who served on the Committee of Precinct Correspondence
created on December 28, 1772, and of Dr. Ebenezer Daggett, who was a
member of Wrentham's Committee of Correspondence set up on August
29, 1774. He was the brother of Naphtali Daggett, President of Yale at
the time.

Fisher was well versed in revolutionary arguments. He was Wrentham's
delegate to the 1768 Massachusetts Convention of Towns, probably a
broad-based radical response to rising tension with Britain.[39] He also
attended the October 7, 1774 assembly in Salem, which resolved itself
into a provincial congress and moved to Concord, as well as the second
and third provincial congresses in February and May–July 1775, respectively. Fisher was elected to the Massachusetts Council, effectively the
state's executive power, from 1775 to 1780. He represented the new
town of Franklin, previously the West Precinct of Wrentham, at the
Massachusetts convention convened "for the sole purpose of framing a

---

38. Boston Committee of Correspondence Records, NYPL MssColl 343, images 5–6,
   http://archives.nypl.org/mss/343#detailed.

39. Richard D. Brown, "The Massachusetts Convention of Towns, 1768," *William and
   Mary Quarterly* 26:1 (1969), 94–104. Provincial congresses: *American Archives*,
   3:271, list of representatives at the July 19, 1775, Watertown session.

new Constitution of Government" in 1779, as well as at the 1788 convention, where he voted to ratify the constitution.[40] Whether Fisher, Daggett, or another member of Wrentham's committee added the state of nature to Wrentham's June 3, 1774 response to Boston's circular letter, the authors thought that the Boston Port Act triggered Hobbes's version of the state of nature.

> The late acts and resolutions of the British parliament to tax the Colonies in all cases whatsoever is founded on such principles that in its Consequence will involve the fall of the Nation, and the late attempts to carry such acts and resolutions into Execution evinces the truth of the foregoing proposition and carries us back from a state of society to that of nature, and from a State of peace to that of war. [A]nd when that is the case of any Society or Common wealth the case becomes truly alarming, and must be felt to its very Center.[41]

I have not been able to find the Resolves of Dartmouth, a coastal town forty miles south of Abington, but the letter that its clerk, the formidable Benjamin Akin (1715–1806) sent to Samuel Adams on July 29, 1774, survives.

> I trust we shall not have one man in Dartmouth will take any office under the new Regulation of Parliament. It appears to me, if there is any force in the Late acts of Parliament, they have sett us, a float that is, have thrown us into a State of Nature. We Now have fair Opportunity Choosing what form of Government we think proper, and Contract, with any Nation, we pleas, for a King to Rule over us.[42]

---

40. *Journal of the Convention for Framing a Constitution of Government for the State of Massachusetts Bay* ... (Boston, 1832). Fisher's name is on p. 9.
41. Boston Committee of Correspondence Records, NYPL MssColl 343, b.6.f.51, image 7, http://archives.nypl.org/mss/343#detailed.
42. Boston Committee of Correspondence Records, NYPL MssColl 343, b.3.f.42, http://archives.nypl.org/mss/343#detailed.

Although Akin seems to suggest that the colonies re-enact the Glorious Revolution and invite a monarch, his point about the colonies staying afloat in the state of nature that Britain has pushed them into is the same as the other constitutive state of nature arguments, including the Massachusetts Assembly's June 3, 1766 address to Hutchinson, and John Adams's letter and *Novanglus* piece in early 1775.

Not only did the Boston Port Act intensify resistance, it also changed some towns' allegiance. On January 11, 1773, Chelmsford instructed Simeon Spaulding to explain the virtues of loyalty and patience and the dangers of rashness and imprudence to the Massachusetts General Court in response to Boston's call for colonial coordination. By contrast, on May 30, 1774 the incensed freeholders of Chelmsford informed the Boston Committee of Correspondence of their ire at "the arbitrary, lawless, tyrannical" government that threatened them with "absolute slavery" and destruction, which they vowed to oppose with "those Powers given us by the god of nature." They were particularly enraged by the Boston Port Act, which they described as "the Bird of noah, Sent over the Waters: if it find footing here, every other Evil will certainly follow."[43]

In his seminal *Constitutional History of the American Revolution*, Reid draws attention to the October 4, 1774 instructions that Worcester gave their newly elected delegate to the House of Representatives. Worcester believed that the Coercive Acts, under which Gage dissolved the colonial assembly, had destroyed the colonial charter. They instructed their representative "to consider the people of this province as absolved, on their part from the obligation therein contained, and to all intents and purposes reduced to a state of nature." Raphael describes this as "America's first recorded declaration of independence."[44] Reid comments that the "state of nature was a drastic argument, indicative that many colonists, not just the people in Worcester, realized that they had reached the constitutional

---

43. Chelmsford, *General Records and Assessments*, Book I (1770–79), 147–48, 222–26, https://archive.org/details/generalrecordsas1770chel.

44. Ray Raphael, *The Founders: The People Who Brought You a Nation* (New Press, 2009), 151.

exigency of their epoch" as a consequence of the Coercive Acts.[45] Reid is right about this, though his assessment is not unproblematic. First, the instructions were not given to Worcester's newly elected representative to the House of Representatives, Joshua Bigelow, as Reid has it, but to the famous soldier Timothy Bigelow, whom Worcester chose on the same day as delegate to the Provincial Congress.

There were doubts about the viability of the meeting of the assembly, scheduled to begin on October 5 in Salem. Indeed, Governor Gage had already declared that the House of Representatives should not convene. Its members regrouped in Concord and resolved into the Provincial Congress on October 7. Foreseeing this possibility, on October 4, Worcester sent Joshua to Salem with instructions to do what he could there, and to join the Provincial Congress in Concord if the House assembled in Salem was unviable. On the same day, Worcester sent Timothy directly to Concord. The instructions Reid attributes to Joshua were given to Timothy.[46] This may seem like a minor error, but the Provincial Congress was, strictly speaking, an extralegal assembly, acting as the provisional revolutionary government of Massachusetts from October 7, 1774 until the constitutional convention of 1780. The drastic instructions to consider Massachusetts to be in a state of nature were given to the person sent straight to Concord, the leading Worcester Patriot, Timothy.

A second problem with Reid's assessment is that it treats this crucial state of nature reference as unusual. This is a very rare case of due attention to the state of nature. As such, it is misunderstood as an exception rather than the norm, its context is absent, and its significance is misinterpreted. As mentioned, Reid considers the Abingdon Resolves, which begin with two resolves on the state of nature, to be primarily

45. Reid, *The Authority of Law*, 28–29.
46. John Davis, *An Address Delivered at the Dedication of the Town Hall, in Worcester . . .* (Worcester, 1825), 29–31; William Lincoln, *History of Worcester, Massachusetts: From Its Earliest Settlement* (Worcester, 1837), 100–101. Reid's mistake comes from his source, Richard L. Bushman, *King and People in Provincial Massachusetts* (North Carolina, 1985; 1992 paperback), 189.

about the colonial contract, and misidentifies the second resolve as the first. Third, despite their drastic effect the Worcester Resolves were not exceptional. They make more sense in the context of the other texts discussed in this book, as one of several state of nature statements about the importance of colonial charters. As we saw, DeBerdt in December 1765, Bland in March 1766, Cleaveland in September 1768, John Adams in 1774, and Moses Mather in 1775 agreed with Worcester that what put the American colonies into a state of nature was Britain's violation of colonial charter rights. This position was based on the notion (often spelled out in these texts) that the colonies had a considerable degree of independence from the start, whether because the first settlers were escaping persecution, bought and worked the land, created civilization without British protection, or because of the collective autonomy they built up gradually over the years, capitalizing on colonial charters and accumulating a body of colonial law independent from King, Parliament, and courts in Britain. The texts that argued that the colonies entered the state of nature after Britain violated the charters drew in equal measure on several senses of the state of nature: as a condition without a strong government, as the relationship between states, and as the idyllic state of a natural community. Reid is correct, and unlike most historians he recognizes the importance of this state of nature text; but his treatment of the Worcester instructions exemplifies the disadvantages of neglecting the state of nature discourse in constitutional histories of the Revolution.

Variations in the formulation of the state of nature used in response to the Boston Pamphlet can be telling. Greenleaf was the moderator who oversaw the drafting of the famously radical Abingdon Resolves, which explained that Britain pushed Massachusetts into a state of nature, where they regained their rights to enter contracts and form new associations, with the implied right to leave the existing association with Britain. Greenleaf also served on the committee that wrote the Boston Pamphlet, which asserted that the colonists could leave Britain and form a new polity in a state of nature that is not created by war or special circumstances, but always exists, either in the absence of government or in parallel with it. When people in the state of nature set up government and the judiciary, they do not surrender these state of nature rights, but pay judges and officials for governmental services that do not diminish these rights in any way. Marlborough recalled that the right to punish was in the state of nature, praised the Glorious Revolution for creating a constitution that best protected state of nature rights, and faulted Parliament for eroding this constitution, for instance by sending troops to America and seizing control of Castle William. The Sheffield Declaration posited that the state of nature rights to life, liberty, and property remained similarly unaffected by the establishment of the judiciary and the government, the sole purpose of which was to protect these rights better. According to the Dartmouth Resolves, Britain pushed the colonies into the state of nature by making legitimate government impossible; but in this condition, the colonies were stable and free to form a new government. The meanings of the state of nature in these documents are partly similar, partly different, but always expansive and serve to constitute a unified American public with distinct rights. By contrast, the disputed Littleton Resolves, drafted under the moderation of Rogers, who declared himself a Loyalist three years later, responded to the Boston Pamphlet with a state of nature that people must abandon to enter the polity, and especially to enjoy the British constitution, which best remedies the losses incurred upon exiting the anarchical state of nature.[47]

47. The committee of the district of New Salem, whose draft reply to the Boston Pamphlet was accepted by the district on February 5, 1773, also used the negative sense of the state of nature, but less emphatically than Rogers. "We would beg leave to observe in the first place that since by the most perfect Wisdom of the Governor of the Universe the Humane Race is greatly multiplied & become numerous on many parts of this Globe. Experience (no doubt) hath long since taught Men that it was not so happy living in a State of Nature as under some form of Goverment [sic]; man being by Nature a sencible Creature is from a principle of self preservation naturally led to be in love with Society and Goverment." Boston Committee of Correspondence records, NYPL MssCol 343, p. 597, b.1.f.7, image 56, http://archives.nypl.org/mss/343#detailed. In addition to examples already mentioned, see Jacob Green's *Observations on the Reconciliation of Great-Britain, and the Colonies* . . . (Philadelphia, 1776), 9–15. Green, an influential Harvard-educated New Jersey preacher and politician, argued that the state of nature right of self-defense had to be surrendered to the state, but not irrevocably. When Britain

State of nature language was brought to bear on the role of judges in several contexts. The last paragraph of the Boston Pamphlet cited previously, on the people employing "hired servants" as their government, captures the view that the best government is noninvasive, administrative, and "dependent on the people alone."[48] Alexander Pope's "For Forms of Government let fools contest; / Whatever is best administered is best," was among the most cited passages in the eighteenth century and appears in John Adams's 1776 *Thoughts on Government* (where Adams disputes it), Hamilton's *Federalist* No. 68, and Kant's 1795 *Perpetual Peace*.[49] The Boston Pamphlet expands the moral and political content of the state of nature into a condition in which people are a cohesive enough community to hire servants to be their government, and their rights and deliberative processes endure the transition into the polity in so practical and detailed a manner that even setting their servants' specific wages remains legitimized by the state of nature.

In Locke and Francis Hutcheson, the state of nature is home to a real community with rights and functions that survive the transition to the polity. However, even though their constitutive formulation contrasts with the view of Hobbes, Montesquieu, Rousseau, Burlamaqui and others who hold that all or most rights and collective functions in the state of nature disappear with this transition, the American expansive notion goes far beyond even Locke, Hutcheson and Vattel. In the Boston

---

failed to protect the colonies, and when Britain attacked, this state of nature right reverted to America.

48. James Madison, *Federalist Papers* No. 52, February 8, 1788. Wood cites the distinction between the people as masters, and the government as servants, in the 1776 instructions of Orange and Mecklenburg, North Carolina to their representatives, as a radical position that challenged even the Whig theory of representation. *Creation*, 364–65. The 1772 Boston Pamphlet deployed the same language to justify keeping judges dependent on the people for their livelihood.

49. Though a detailed discussion is beyond this book's scope, changes in Kant's notion of the state of nature owe more to the American Revolution than the current secondary literature recognizes. Ioannis Evrigenis and Mark Somos, "The State of Nature," in Aaron Garrett and James Schmidt (eds.), *The Oxford Handbook of the Enlightenment* (Oxford, forthcoming).

Pamphlet, the community in the state of nature survives and retains rights and functions that extend not only to deciding when their rights might have been violated, but even to the specifics of determining the government's wages. It expands the colonists' rights in the state of nature and diminishes the moral and political content of British and Tory government in Massachusetts. The Boston Pamphlet fits the pattern we noticed in other texts that formulate an American state of nature that functions independently from and despite British misgovernment, and comes to serve as the foundation of a new, American state. Most importantly, texts surrounding the Boston Pamphlet, from the Abingdon Resolves to responses that arrived only after the Boston Port Act, signify a shift to self-defense as a defining part of the American state of nature, alongside internal concord. Be it the constitutional bedrock of individual and collective self-defense, independence, or the matter of the power of the purse, this central document in the history of American independence, and the dozens of responses by the towns it successfully mobilized, make extensive use of this key concept.[50]

50. The United States also aggregates, without obviously abrogating, the individual citizens' state of nature right to self-defense vis-à-vis pirates. It is the state, not individuals, that acts on this collective right of self-defense, which nevertheless remains a state of nature right, not a political one. James Wilson, "A Charge Delivered to the Grand Jury in the Circuit Court of the United States, for the District of Virginia, in May, 1791," *Collected Works*, 331–32. The state of nature right to self-defense remains relevant in constitutional interpretations today. For instance, the Supreme Court found in *District of Columbia v. Heller* (2008) that self-defense was such a fundamental right that DC's handgun ban violated the Second Amendment. After this ruling, several suits were filed in Illinois to challenge gun bans. In the landmark *McDonald v. City of Chicago*, 561 U.S. 742 (2010), the Court found that the Fourteenth Amendment makes the natural right to keep and bear arms for self-defense applicable to the states. In his last dissent before his retirement, Justice John Paul Stevens argued that recognizing individuals' right to hold deadly weapons is irreconcilable with the sovereign state's monopoly on legitimate violence. As Locke noted in section 129 of the *Second Treatise*, the state of nature right to self-defense is surrendered, to a large extent, on entering the state. At another point of his dissent (n. 32), citing state of nature passages from Blackstone's *Commentaries* and section 128 of Locke's *Second Treatise*, Stevens also challenged the Court's competence to establish the natural right to self-defense, even if it

The Boston Pamphlet's repeated tripartite classification of the rights of colonists as men, Christians, and British subjects is probably the result of collective authorship. The reference to Locke to explain what leaving the state of nature is like, and the references to Magna Carta, Coke, Blackstone's *Commentaries*, Locke, Vattel, the Bill of Rights and the Act of Settlement could be Otis's work. The second section, on the colonists' rights as Christians, invokes Locke's *Letters on Toleration* and agrees with Locke that toleration should not extend to Catholics. This is unlikely to come from Otis, but could have come from Samuel Adams, especially if we consider John Adams's detailed account of how closely they collaborated on the 1768 petition.[51] The tripartite structure itself may owe something to John Adams, whose first essay, pretending to be written by Governor Winthrop to Governor Bradford, published in the January 26, 1767 *Boston Gazette* against Jonathan Sewall's defense of Governor Bernard, begins with the same structure.[52] A closer analysis of all members of the Committee may help identify the most likely author.

But whoever suggested that the rights of the colonists as Christians should form the second part of the Committee's argument, inserted between their rights as men and their rights as subjects, he was tapping into a specific strand of a vigorous and distinct New England state of nature discourse. That political sermons played a part in Boston's move toward independence is well known. In a famous August 15, 1765 letter that Governor Bernard sent to Westminster to complain about Boston, and Franklin published to the outrage of Parliament, Bernard described an Anglican minister inciting popular resentment against the Stamp Act.[53] Harbottle Dorr noted that Bernard attributed colonial

survived the transition to the state; and noted that there is no reason why the states cannot "place substantial restrictions on its exercise" when they see fit.

51. John Adams to William Tudor, March 7, 1819, http://founders.archives.gov/documents/Adams/99-02-02-7094.
52. John Adams, *Papers*, vol. 1, *September 1755–October 1773* (ed. Robert J. Taylor, Harvard, 1977), 191–93.
53. 1765 *Copies and extracts regarding the Stamp Act* . . . Huntington, HM 1947.

self-organization to Cleaveland's September 5, 1768 letter in the *Boston Gazette* as Clericus Americanus. Three points to bear in mind here are that these political sermons often relied on the state of nature to make their case; that the state of nature theme in revolutionary Christian arguments was not only powerful but also covered a wide array of notions; and that unlike centuries of Christian state of nature references, a set of American Revolution-era political sermons presented the state of nature not as a condition of sin but as God's community, united and ruled by divine laws that protect its civil operation even when human government has failed. To understand how the idea of the state of nature shaped the American Revolution, it is as useful to understand the Christian version as it is to recognize the spectrum and variety of the Christian state of nature theme.

6.3 CHRISTIAN RESISTANCE

The relationship between religion and the American Revolution is a rewarding but immense topic. Even surveying American religious texts that refer to the state of nature between 1761 and 1775 would be casting our net too wide, as not all of them are directly relevant to the constitutional concerns of the Revolution. Instead, this section begins with a brief survey of some Christian senses of the state of nature, followed by a few American cases that directly engaged constitutional issues in state of nature terms. One of the most common eighteenth-century meanings of the state of nature was the condition opposed to the state of grace. This meaning has existed for centuries before the American Revolution and seems equally prevalent among Anglican, Baptist, Catholic, and other denominations. To appreciate the range of this consensus, consider that the state of nature is used in this sense by John Brown (1610?–1679), a Scottish minister jailed and banished after the Restoration who ended up leading a church of exiles in Rotterdam; by the prolific Anglican divine, writer and translator Thomas Broughton (1704–1774); and by Samuel Buell (1716–1798), the Yale graduate turned influential revivalist preacher based in East Hampton, Long

Island.[54] So common was this meaning that in sermons and hymns it was often taken as a given and formed the basis of explaining ills, predicting damnation, and offering ways around them.

At other times, the preacher or moralizing essayist drew a more specific contrast between the state of nature and that of grace. In a sermon in York Cathedral, Cuthbert Allanson (1727–1780), Chaplain to the House of Commons, presented the state of nature as a consequence of the Fall. By contrast, the author of *The Ground and Nature of Christian Redemption* from 1768 used the state of nature to denote the condition that preceded the Fall, when man was evil and corrupt by nature but, like other animals, unthinking and unaware. The Scottish schoolmaster and minister Thomas Boston (1676–1732) and the Baptist pastor John Gill (1697–1771) explained it as a state of sin (where God nevertheless nourished the elect), while the universalist, radical preacher and pamphleteer Richard Coppin (fl. 1646–59) with elegant simplicity equated the state of nature with the Kingdom of Satan.[55] Bezaleel Woodward's 1772 valedictory oration at Dartmouth named human ignorance in the state of nature as one of Satan's strongholds.[56]

A slightly more encouraging theological formulation saw the state of nature as a condition that, once they understood it, people leave for Christianity. This version also covered a range of meanings. Thomas Sherlock (1678–1761), an Anglican bishop and patron of Broughton

54. John Brown, *An Exposition of the Epistle of Paul the Apostle to the Romans* . . . (Edinburgh, 1766); Thomas Broughton, *A Defence of the Commonly-Received Doctrine of the Human Soul* (Bristol, 1766); Samuel Buell, *Narrative of the Remarkable Revival of Religion* . . . (Aberdeen, 1773).

55. Anon., *The Ground and Nature of Christian Redemption* (Philadelphia, 1768), 6–7. Thomas Boston, *Human Nature in Its Fourfold State of Primitive Integrity* . . . (Edinburgh, 1720, with editions in 1730, 1735, 1744, 1753, 1756, 1759, 1761, 1763, 1767, 1760, 1770, 1771, 1772, New York in 1811, etc.); John Gill, e.g. in *The Doctrines of God's Everlasting Love to His Elect* . . . (3rd ed., London, 1770), 43–46, and in several of his *Sermons on Important Subjects* (London, 1790); Richard Coppin, *A Blow at the Serpent* . . . (London, 1656).

56. Bezaleel Woodward, Valedictory Oration, April 19, 1772, Dartmouth, Rauner, MS 772269.

known for his attacks on Deists, described the state of nature as the former general state of mankind, still persisting among some people, in which individuals could rely only on observations of nature to gain spiritual insight. The religion of nature is appropriate for those who are in the state of nature; but not for those who have access to a knowledge of revelation.[57] In his *A Treatise on God's Love to the World* . . . , James Sloss (1698–1772) posits a similar stadial history of mankind's epistemic and moral trajectory, but unlike Sherlock, Sloss depicts humans in the pre-Christian state of nature as remarkably modern, riven by civilized, materialistic anxieties about property and success.[58]

Contrary to the view of the state of nature as the postlapsarian condition, a state of sin, or the Kingdom of Satan, some described Christians as those who have finally arrived in the state of nature. We find this position stated and debated several times in Connecticut around 1765 and, in an interestingly evolved form, in and around revolutionary Boston, as part of a discussion whether by virtue of their religion Christian colonists had specific rights or obligations that inflected their relationship with Britain and the colonies.

The Hobbesian sense of the state of nature guides Noah Hobart's argument that without the Saybrook Platform – a fifteen-article constitution for Connecticut congregations in force since 1708 – local congregations "would be very much in the Condition of a Number of unconnected Individuals in a State of Nature; and they would soon verify the observation, 'That a State of Nature is a State of War.'"[59] The specific form and

57. Thomas Sherlock, *Several discourses preached at the Temple Church* (London, 1754, reprinted into the 1770s in London and Edinburgh, in at least six distinct editions).

58. James Sloss, *A Treatise on God's Love to the World* . . . (London, 1770), 60. "The Man who is in a State of Nature, is afraid of Poverty, lest he should not have enough wherewithal to eat, and to drink, and to be cloathed; he fears lest his Trade be diminished, and the Profits of it sink and fail; lest by some Turn of Providence his Riches should not encrease, and his Wealth should waste; but all this is owing to his carnal, covetous Heart."

59. Noah Hobart, *An Attempt to Illustrate and Confirm the Ecclesiastical Constitution of the Consociated Churches in the Colony of Connecticut* (New Haven, 1765), 10. Also see James B. Bell, *A War of Religion* (New York, 2008), chapter 5.

practice of right religion also underpinned civil government in Edward Dorr's May 9, 1765 election day sermon, "The duty of civil rulers to be nursing fathers to the church of Christ: a sermon preached before the General Assembly of the colony of Connecticut, at Hartford." While government was instituted to bring people out of the Hobbesian state of nature, which has no common judge or law enforcement, their right temper depends on religion.

Unlike in these Connecticut texts from 1765, the rightly constituted Christian community is not ancillary to government but stands on its own, according to a set of Boston-based texts written and preached a few years later. In 1773, less than a year after the Boston Pamphlet's declaration of the state of nature rights that the colonists have as Christians, the radical preacher Simeon Howard (1733–1804) anchored strongly in the state of nature the right to bear arms, the unconstitutionality of a standing army, and the right to collective resistance against a government whose unjust laws violate the laws of nature. The unconstitutionality of the standing army was noted in similar terms in *An Appeal to the World* from 1769, probably by Samuel Adams.[60] The right to resist for either political or religious reasons appears in numerous texts. Typical is Braintree's March 1773 letter to Boston in response to the Boston Pamphlet: "That by the divine constitution of things, there is such a connection between civil, & religious liberty, that in whatever Nation or Government the one is crushed the other seldom if ever survives long after of this. History furnishes abundant evidence."[61] In their letter from March 1774, reporting resolutions made on February 24, the authors of the Braintree letter write that "the Doctrine of Passive obedience, and non resistance, is not

---

60. Simeon Howard, *A Sermon Preached to the Ancient and Honorable Artillery Company in Boston* . . . (Boston, 1773); Bailyn, *Ideological Origins*, 62–63; Don B. Kates and Clayton E. Cramer, "Second Amendment Limitations and Criminological Considerations," *Hastings Law Journal* 60:6 (2009), 1339–69; David B. Kopel, "The Religious Roots of the American Revolution and the Right to Keep and Bear Arms," *Journal of Firearms and Public Policy* 17 (2005), 167–84; Samuel Adams[?] in *An appeal to the world or a vindication of the town of Boston* . . . (Boston, 1769), 27.

61. Boston Committee of Correspondence records, NYPL MssCol 343, p. 3, image 2.

less mischeivous [*sic*] in Politiks, than religion," and "we know of no instance wherin a People have been deprived of their civil rights, but they have lost their religious Rights also; and in the nature of things they must stand, or fall together."[62]

In 1774 the Reverend Nathaniel Whitaker (1732–1795) published an attack on two, much earlier tracts by John Wise (1652–1725), *The Churches Quarrel Exposed . . .* (1710) and the famous *A Vindication of the Government of New England's Churches* (1717), both of them reprinted in a single volume in two separate editions in 1772, with John Adams among the subscribers. Wise is best known for leading his congregation in 1687–1688 in protests against taxes and Edmund Andros, governor of the short-lived Dominion of New England. Wise's two tracts that Whitaker chose to dispute six decades later drew on Whig political theory in order to reject Increase Mather's 1705 proposal for a presbyterian church government. Going beyond Hobart's and Dorr's point that the right religion underpins good government, Whitaker contended that Wise was wrong to consider Christians as being in a state of nature: surely they have a common ruler in Christ. Contrary to Hobart and Dorr, Whitaker's Christians could not lapse into the violent state of nature even if politics failed.[63] On a similar note, Gad Hitchcock delivered his 1774 election day sermon in front of General Thomas Gage, the recently appointed Governor, and his newly arrived British troops. Hitchcock chose to speak on Proverbs 29:2, "When the righteous are in authority, the people rejoice: but when the wicked beareth rule, the people mourn." He argued that the radical equality in the state of nature becomes a political standard, according to which only good rulers are just. People in the state

62. Boston Committee of Correspondence records, NYPL MssCol 343, p. 1 of letter, image 5, p. 2, image 6, b.3.f.23, http://archives.nypl.org/mss/343#detailed.

63. Nathaniel Whitaker, *A confutation of two tracts . . .* (Boston, 1774). The polemic continued with Samuel Gatchel, *A contrast to the Reverend Nathaniel Whitaker . . .* (Danvers, 1778). Heimert emphasizes Whitaker's wariness that the rich and influential could adversely influence and corrupt an overly democratic church. Alan Heimert, *Religion and the American Mind: From the Great Awakening to the Revolution* (Harvard, 1966), 501–2; James B. Bell, *A War of Religion: Dissenters, Anglicans, and the American Revolution* (Palgrave Macmillan, 2008), chapter 5.

of nature still have one authority in common, namely the law of God, written on their hearts. Apparently some of Hitchcock's British audience walked out mid-sermon.[64]

We find the same point two years later in an election day sermon delivered by Samuel West (1730–1807), "On the Right to Rebel against Governors," a few months before the Declaration of Independence, noting that the state of nature is not a state of licentiousness but of law, with God as "our supreme magistrate."[65] Locke's state of nature is a good principle to return to, West explained, if one wishes to understand the origin and nature of government; but people also needed guidance and unity of purpose. Locke's state of nature was too individualistic and not sufficiently constitutive of a collective identity. West went on to serve as member of the convention that adopted the Constitution of Massachusetts, as well as of the 1788 convention that ratified the Constitution of the United States. One possible explanation for this reading of the state of nature in mid-1770s' Massachusetts is that Whitaker was a Presbyterian, and West was addressing the House of Representatives of the Colony of Massachusetts-Bay. It was probably Wise's insistence on the radical egalitarianism and omnipresence of the state of nature that Whitaker and West, who both combined ecclesiastical and political representative offices in their person, found disagreeable.[66]

64. Gad Hitchcock, *A Sermon Preached Before His Excellency Thomas Gage, Esq., Governor...* (Boston, 1774), also in Hyneman and Lutz (eds.), *American Political Writing*, 1:281–304, at 288. On the importance of election day sermons see Arthur W. Plumstead, introduction to *The Wall and the Garden: Selected Massachusetts Election Sermons, 1670–1775* (Minnesota, 1968). This is the strand of religious thought described by Oliver Goldsmith's 1771 *History of England*, 3:216: "Since the times of Elizabeth, a new religious sect had been gaining ground in England; which, from the supposed greater purity of their manners, were called *Puritans*. Of all other sects, this was the most dangerous to monarchy; and the tenets of it more calculated to support that imagined equality which obtains in a state of nature."
65. Samuel West, *A sermon preached before the Honorable Council, and the Honorable House of Representatives, of the colony of the Massachusetts-Bay* (Boston, 1776), 10–11. While drawing on Locke's *Second Treatise*, section 6, West goes beyond Locke, who only claims that the laws of nature limit licentiousness in the state of nature, and the responsibility to God, our maker; not that God is the "supreme magistrate."
66. On Samuel West's politics see Heimert, *Religion*, 411, 443–45.

The same year that Samuel West gave his sermon in Boston, the remarkable Richard Watson (1737–1816) gave one in Cambridge, England, on May 29, entitled *The Principles of the Revolution Vindicated*. Watson was a professor of chemistry and an anatomist before he succeeded to Thomas Rutherforth's chair of divinity in 1771.[67] He was an unusual professorial appointee as he had no degree in theology, and he made no bones about his lack of relevant training before his appointment.

Like the clergyman and natural philosopher Rutherforth, whose 1754–56 *Institutes of Natural Law* became an influential conduit of Anglicized Grotianism in the colonies, Watson had a polymathic view of the state of nature. He used the concept and term in chemistry, theology, and agriculture with equal ease, sometimes in overlapping senses. In addition to his scholarly work in chemistry and theology, Watson took a strong stance on several political issues of the day. He often signed his political pamphlets as "a Christian Whig" and distributed them among members of the House of Commons. After retiring from Cambridge, he bought land in Westmoreland, where he made extensive agricultural improvements and published papers on the subject. Watson was much liked in the colonies. In 1788 he was elected Foreign Honorary Member of the American Academy of Arts and Sciences, and in 1807 to the Massachusetts Historical Society. His most widely read work was *Apology for the Bible . . .* , published in 1796 against Paine's 1795 *Age of Reason, Second Part*. The *Apology* was very well received in the United States, and printed in Albany, New York, Boston, New Brunswick, and Philadelphia in 1796 alone.

In the 1776 sermon, Watson called the English Civil War a state of nature and drew a parallel between the 1688 Glorious Revolution and the American colonists' right to rebel. He also compared the equality of people with the equality of other creatures within their own class. The sermon caused great offense at court. Watson suspected that his career suffered setbacks as a result. John Dunning, later Lord Ashburton, was

67. Bill Palmer, "Richard Watson, Bishop of Llandaff (1737–1816): A Chemist of the Chemical Revolution," *Australian Journal of Education in Chemistry* 68 (2007), 33–38.

quoted as saying that Watson's sermon "contained just such treason as ought to be preached once a month at St James's." Watson's exposition in this sermon of the state of nature, and radical equality and the essential right of independence grounded in it, was singled out for applause in Richard Price's *Additional Observations on the Nature and Value of Civil Liberty and Free Government* (1777). Fox praised it eloquently in Parliament as late as 1795.

Watson's 1776 sermon also provoked several reactions, including visceral ones, such as the 1776 "Remarks on a pamphlet, entitled The Principles of the Revolution vindicated," which stated—without giving good reasons—that Watson was terribly wrong. One criticism worth mentioning here is William Stevens's 1776 *Strictures on a Sermon, entitled, The Principles of the Revolution Vindicated*... Stevens, who published a *Discourse on the English Constitution* the same year, argues that Watson was wrong because the state of nature is a condition not of independence, but of dependence.

Its Christian connotations were one of the reasons why the state of nature was often understood as a foundational principle that, once invoked, left little room for compromise. At the same time, the Christian state of nature texts produced in Boston by Howard (1773), Whitaker (1774), and West (1776) illustrate the variety and intensity of this discourse in eighteenth-century New England. They also explain Joseph Porter's joke that James Sullivan recounted for John Adams, who reported it to his wife Abigail in his July 5, 1774 letter. The joke is based on the interplay between the meanings of the state of nature as sin and as lack of government. In spring 1774 Sullivan, later Massachusetts' attorney general, then governor, represented Biddeford at the General Court meeting in Salem. The Boston Port Act came into effect on June 1, and Sullivan was one of the most vocal proponents of a plan to organize a pan-colonial congress to take place in 1775. He visited Adams at Falmouth on July 5 and told him the following story.

Another Story was of a Piece of Wit of Brother Porter of Salem. He came upon the Floor and asked a Member "What State are you in now?" The

Member answered "in a State of Nature."—Ay says Porter, "and you will be d———d before you will get into a State of Grace."

Samuel Sherwood's famous *Scriptural Instructions to Civil Rulers, and All Free-Born Subjects* . . . , delivered in Fairfield, Connecticut in August 1774 (and published with a sermon by Ebenezer Baldwin, whose Yale student notes on the state of nature were discussed earlier), was aimed against the Coercive or Intolerable Acts passed after the Boston Tea Party. Sherwood's first point is that while God's government is fixed, all men have imperfections, and none can claim to rule *de iure divino* or to be otherwise God's delegate on earth. All people are equally free agents, "and considered as in a state of nature." Sovereigns, Sherwood explains, can dissolve society by acting contrary to the intention that guided the establishment and design of their office. In this case, men return to a state of nature, regain their original liberties, and re-form society "on what terms they please." The sermon is too sophisticated to fully summarize here, but the appearance of our theme at these two key points makes it an excellent example of how legal, political, and biblical justifications of resistance and revolution were combined and reconciled in the Christian strand of the American state of nature discourse.

A new wave of political sermons featuring the state of nature followed the opening of the First Continental Congress. Moses Mather's 1775 *America's Appeal to the Impartial World*, published in Hartford, Connecticut, begins with a pattern that recalls Otis and Warren, not Sherwood: the first English settlers fled an oppressive government and enjoyed none of the protections of England in America. They bought or conquered their lands from the natives and built the government they wanted.[68]

When our ancestors left the kingdom of England, they were subjects of that kingdom, and entitled to equal privileges with the rest of its

---

68. Cf. Montesquieu on commercial disadvantages to colonies, justifiable only in return for the mother country's protection: *Spirit of the Laws*, IV.21, p. 391.

subjects; when they came into America, where no civil constitutions were existing, they joined themselves to none: the lands which they entered and possessed, they acquired by purchase, or by conquest of the natives: they came over of themselves, viz. were not colonies sent out, to make settlements by government; not to mention the intolerable oppressions, by which they were driven out, crossed the Atlantick, and availed themselves of possessions, at their own risque and expence, and by their own sword and prowess. Now, in America, they were still subjects of the kingdom of England, or they were not; if the former, then they were entitled to enjoy, in America, the same or equal privileges, with those enjoyed by the subjects residing in England—if the latter, then that kingdom had no right of jurisdiction over them, and they were in a state of nature, at liberty to erect such a constitution of civil government as they should chuse.

Mather then offers a remarkably coherent explanation of the colonial charters. Even if the settlers, already independent from Britain, chose to enter such contractual agreements with the Crown, it would still give Parliament no authority over them.

Should France offer the king of Great-Britain the crown of that kingdom, and he accept it; could not France be subject to the king, without being subject to the kingdom of Great-Britain, and subordinate to the power of parliament? Upon these principles, should the king of England be elected emperor of Germany, the British parliament, would legislate for the whole Germanic body. And the case would not be otherwise, with a people in a state of nature, that should make choice of the king of Great-Britain for their king, and he accept thereof, they would not thereby, elect the kingdom for their masters nor be subjected to its parliament.

There are two American senses of the state of nature in play here. One came into existence when the mother country ceased to be able to protect the first settlers. The other is the state of nature that their descendants inherited, which supports their right to choose their own sovereign irrespective of Parliament.[69] Another exemplary political sermon is *The Dominion of Providence Over the Passions of Men*, preached at Princeton by John Witherspoon (1723–1794) and printed in Philadelphia in May 1776. Witherspoon, a Scottish Presbyterian, was encouraged by Benjamin Rush and Richard Stockton to take up the post of sixth President of the College of New Jersey, one of the nine colonial colleges, now Princeton University. Witherspoon's twenty-six-year presidency transformed Princeton's mission from training ministers to forming a new generation of American leaders. Witherspoon joined the Committee of Correspondence in early 1774, signed the Declaration of Independence, and was a major force in Congress from 1776 until 1782.

The Dominion is among Witherspoon's earliest political engagements, although the first half barely refers to politics.[70] Slowly, Witherspoon introduces the theme of persecution and divine intervention on behalf of the persecuted. Discussions of early Christians, the English under attack from the Spanish Armada, and the peace-loving Hampden and Cromwell, by providence made victorious, prepare the ground for Witherspoon's most relevant case, that of the New England settlers. After

---

69. Compare Charles Yorke's *Considerations on the Law of Forfeitures for High Treason*, first published in 1745 to justify sentences against Scottish Jacobites. Yorke argues that the state of nature right to property is limited to bare subsistence; thus the right of inheritance cannot be a state of nature right but must derive from civil law (16–20), which makes sense because it is only in the polity, not in the state of nature, that children are a public concern (27–28). The book was cited often in lawsuits and parliamentary debates. Chalmers notes that the corrected and enlarged fourth edition appeared in 1775, "at the eve of another revolt." George Chalmers, *Opinions of Eminent Lawyers* . . . (London, 1814), preface, 1:xliv. Blackstone's view is slightly different. When someone deserves forfeiture, for instance by not taking an oath to the government, the property that may be forfeited is "placed as it were in a state of nature, accessible by all the king's subjects," who may inform on the person, and sue for a reward out of the forfeiture. *Commentaries* (1766), II.29.438. He also allows for the state of nature right of donation *causa mortis*, disposing of property on one's death bed. *Commentaries*, II.32.514.

70. Hamburger argues that Witherspoon's lectures on moral philosophy, including lecture X on the state of nature, were composed in 1768, the year he left Scotland to become President of the College of New Jersey (now Princeton). "Natural Rights," 915 n. 25.

a short detour into the history of divine interventions, Witherspoon delves back into doctrine and religious exhortation. He particularly encourages his listeners to deepen their faith and leave the state of nature that is incomplete grace.

> Unless you are united to him by a lively faith, not the resentment of a haughty monarch, but the sword of divine justice hangs over you, and the fulness of divine vengeance shall speedily overtake you. I do not speak this only to the heaven daring profligate, or grovelling sensualist, but to every insensible secure sinner; to all those, however decent and orderly in their civil deportment, who live to themselves and have their part and portion in this life; in fine to all who are yet in a state of nature, for "except a man be born again, he cannot see the kingdom of God."

Witherspoon folds a new political significance into the conventional meaning of the state of nature as sin. Leaving the state of nature and returning to God is Witherspoon's recipe for establishing a commitment to the new, true, and independent state, and securing God's future interventions on its behalf. William Whipple, Jr., another signatory to the Declaration, in the same summer of 1776 described the work of the First Continental Congress in a vocabulary of corruption and state of nature that seems similar to Witherspoon's, but probably refers to the established political theme of corruption and not to anything biblical.[71]

> Perhaps it may take some time to do this great work. I call it a great work; for, in my opinion, it is more difficult to reduce a society of men, who have drunk deep of waters of corruption, to the true principles of virtue, than to bring a society from the state of nature to the same meridian.

Witherspoon's 1776 sermon restates a point Gridley made in December 1765 against the Stamp Act, Hawley in 1767 in *Warren's Case*, and Quincy,

---

71. William Whipple, Jr. letter to Joshua Brackett, July 29, 1776. *Proceedings of the Massachusetts Historical Society* 5 (1862), 6.

Jr. in 1772 in Richardson's case: Parliament had thrust the colonies and the whole British Empire into a condition that was more dangerous and corrupt than the state of nature. While these Christian state of nature arguments formed an important part of the revolutionary state of nature discourse, some uses also served the purpose of sidestepping the issue of Christianity in the initial waves of American constitutional theory, partly to minimize disagreement among the religious groups involved.[72]

6.4 THE BOSTON TEA PARTY AND THE POLITICAL ECONOMY OF THE STATE OF NATURE

The importance of Christian rights in the Boston Pamphlet gave us a chance to briefly survey the Christian strand of the American state of nature discourse. Similarly, the Boston Tea Party, the next well-known event before the First Continental Congress, and one generally regarded as an expression of colonial economic frustration and self-confidence, is a great opportunity to see whether the state of nature was relevant to revolutionary economic thought.

Many of the state of nature texts we examined so far had something to say about political economy. Propagandists for empire began to shape the image and expectations of America before the continent was fully mapped. In chapter 2 we saw early advertisements aimed to attract settlers that described the British colonies in America as fertile enough to become self-sufficient and wildly profitable when cultivated by diligent and upright settlers. The colonists adopted the same thought and imagery to describe the land they inherited and continued to cultivate. The belief in a potential economic advantage over Europe due to the natural resources of the American colonies was the main calculation behind the boycotts of the early 1770s and the declaration of independence. The sources revealed a variety of positions concerning the ubiquitous connection between views on the state of nature and the stadial theory of economic

72. Pauline Maier, *American Scripture: Making the Declaration of Independence* (New York, 1997), 135–36.

progress, the material benefits of the freedom of speech, the political economy of controlled westward expansion as an optimal path between the Scylla of continued dependence on British manufactures and the Charybdis of corruption and social disruption caused by overly rapid technological and commercial catch-up, and the economics of slavery, all tied to the constitutional trope of the state of nature. As mentioned in chapter 5, *The True Sentiments of America* described the state of nature as not warlike, but already containing property and the rights thereunto, which survive intact the transition to civil society. This is a sentiment and register similar to New Jersey's May 1768 petition discussed above, in which property was acquired with great difficulty and sacrifice in the American state of nature, and remains anchored there, protected from British encroachment. From start to finish, the American state of nature discourse was always relevant to political economy. The matter of property and other economic relations in the state of nature is central to understanding the way in which this notion was used to work out and justify American independence, and then design the country's institutions anew. The questions were not limited to whether property exists in the state of nature, whether it transfers into the polity, and if it does, how (for instance, do rights to inherited property function the same way as rights acquired by adding one's own labor?). The political economy of the early revolutionary ideology was far more rich than a narrow focus on Locke's influence on the Founders would suggest.

The December 1773 Boston Tea Party is one of the best-known episodes of the American Revolution. The Tea Act, passed in May 1773, gave the East India Company a monopoly over tea sales in the American colonies. It angered most colonists, who had long complained about Britain's restrictions on colonial trade. Reid points out that the Act actually lowered the cost of tea; but it also sought to establish an undisputed precedent for Parliament's right to tax the colonies, which the colonists found unacceptable.[73] One of the popular pamphlets that objected to the Tea Act was a series known as "The Alarm," published in late 1773 in the

---

73. Reid, *Authority to Tax*, 224–29.

New-York Journal, under the pseudonym of Hampden, perhaps written by Alexander McDougall, a former privateer. In the October 14, 1773 issue Hampden conceded that those who invented something new or took a risk and opened up a new trade should be rewarded with commercial privileges; but maintained that the East India Company's monopoly was unwarranted and disproportionate. The standard by which the author measured the injustice of this particular monopoly, granted by the polity, is the state of nature, in which people can acquire property and exchange with each other whatever they wish. What they cannot obtain in this rich sphere of collective economic activity, and leave the state of nature for, is guaranteed security for their property. The responsibilities of the state follow from this expansive definition of political economy in the state of nature. If the state cannot guarantee the security of property, people might as well stay in the state of nature, where they have the right to take their enemy's property, if they think it contributes to their own security.[74] In exchange for surrendering this right and supporting the state, they should be compensated with a fair share of collective gains. Anything that violates the principle of fair share makes it counterproductive to exit the state of nature for the state, and therefore destroys not only the state's economic life, but its very constitution.

A provocative response in defense of the tea tax was offered by Poplicola (probably John Vardill) in the December 2, 1773 *Rivington's New-York Gazetteer.* Poplicola argued that divine laws apply in the state of nature, therefore the freedom of exchange is limited by the common good. The political analogue of this is the limit that the common good, as determined by the government, imposes on the fair share that, according

---

74. A similar argument is made in "A few reflections and hints concerning American affairs" in the August 22, 1774 *Newport Mercury,* with the addition that a government that regulates property without consent reduces people to a condition worse than the state of nature, because only consent can guarantee the fair management and redistribution of property. Britain's failure to secure American consent means that Britain threw the colonies into a state of nature, where they regain "a right to defend themselves by every means in their power." Fortunately, "America wants only union, military disciplining, and the introduction of a few manufactures, to render her independent of the whole world."

to Alarm I, belongs to those who left the state of nature to support and benefit from the state. The limits that divine laws set on individual state of nature rights excuse much of the burden that civil laws impose.[75]

Warren's Case in 1765–1766 exemplified the widespread understanding of the state of nature and how popular revolutionary action was based on it. The case began with a refusal to pay a debt not because the debtor did not wish to pay, but because residents believed that the Stamp Act had effectively shut down the courts, Massachusetts was in a state of nature, and neither creditor nor debtor could legally transact business. The same property-based dualism, between being able to legally settle debts or being in a state of nature, appeared in Maryland in June 1774 with regard to debts owed by Americans to Britain. When news of the Boston Port Act reached Maryland in May 1774, many agreed that Boston was suffering for the sake of all colonies. Maryland was one of the colonies that signed up to the trade boycott and agreed to neither import from nor export to Britain.[76] It was proposed that lawyers should refuse to sue for recovery of debts that Marylanders owed to British subjects. In the package of retaliatory proposals, this was the only one that Marylanders did not agree to on the first attempt. On June 4, however, Annapolis and Arundel County passed this resolution, too.[77] Shortly thereafter, on June 13, 1774, "Candour" published her or his objections, starting with the point that the boycott would instantly deprive "artificers and labourers of every denomination" of their livelihood. Their "natural and inextinguishable right of self-preservation" allowed them to "appeal to heaven and a strong arm" when the legal protection of property ceases, and "every thing relapses into a state of nature." Here it is colonial revolutionaries who upset the economic order of things, including trade and

75. Poplicola was in turn promptly accused by "A Mechanic" of trying to reduce the colonists to a state of nature in "To the Worthy Inhabitants of New York..." (1773).
76. Jane W. McWilliams, *Annapolis, City of the Severn: A History* (Johns Hopkins, 2011), 87–88.
77. June 4, 1774 Anne Arundel County Resolutions, in Niles, *Principles*, 259–60, Res. IV on 260.

the settlement of debts, and thereby reduce the community to a state of nature that triggered the natural right to armed resistance.[78]

By contrast, an anonymous defender of the colonists, who thought the Boston Tea Party was not unjustifiable, "only impolitic and foolish," argued in the April 7, 1774 *London Gazetteer* that Britain's attempt to tax the colonists without their consent would destroy the foundation of their property and place them "in a worse condition than the state of nature, wherein they had liberty to defend their right against the injuries of others." This is an unacknowledged citation from the *Second Treatise*, section 137, where Locke describes not an attack on property but "absolute arbitrary power" "without settled standing laws," a condition that no one would leave the state of nature for. The more relevant section seems to be 138, which explains why not even supreme political power can take anyone's property without their consent. The anonymous author probably conflated the two, as this text seems to neither give nor imply a logical or rhetorical reason why taxation without consent would be the equivalent of the lack of standing laws.

In "A few political reflections . . . ," published in the June 20, 1774 *Pennsylvania Packet*, the moderate Quaker merchant Richard Wells recommended political and commercial reconciliation with Britain. A colonial regimen of non-importation would make Britain see the errors of its ways, and the mutually beneficial exchange of British manufactures and American agricultural production would be restored.[79] The East India Company's tea monopoly was wrong, but everyone who suffered damages from the Boston Tea Party should be recompensed.[80] Despite the pragmatic and conciliatory tone, Wells is clear about the line that the

78. These objections may have been submitted during the debate as well. Some editions print the resolutions and Candour's objections together. At least *American Archives*, published by Peter Force by the order of Congress, thought it official enough to print them together in the Fourth Series (Washington, DC, 1837), 1:384–85.
79. Reprinted in the June 27 *New-York Gazette*.
80. The Pennsylvania committee that met in July 1774, a month after Wells's article, and encouraged Dickinson to publish his *Essay*, made the same recommendation. Dickinson, *Essay*, 317, 323.

colonists must hold. If Britain is not ready to meet the colonists half-way, America is reduced "near to a state of nature, and have all to begin anew." The colonists have always worked for the glory of Britain, and their love and understanding of liberty captures the best of British traditions. If there is no reconciliation, and the colonial assemblies are ineffective, then there must be a directly elected continental congress to enable the people "to raise from the ruins, a new fabrick somewhat resembling the old . . . A new Phoenix." Again, American nature was unique and able to underwrite a unique proposition for independence.

In the same vein, on February 7, 1774, Silas Deane wrote an extraordinary letter to William Samuel Johnson about westward expansion. He described the colonies as caught between the state of nature and the commercial stage of progress. Deane urged Johnson that the colonies must expand, and occupy American nature. His insight was that nature could not be forced, and it would be unwise to try to jump too many stages of development at once. It is only after the lands had been occupied, and used as well as their natural qualities allow, that the colonies should develop manufacturing. Then their economies will be more sustainable and independent than any "Commercial System in Europe," because they will be self-sufficient, supported by the "internal commerce among a People, of the Same Language, and Manners, inhabiting in one continued Chain all the Climates on Earth." All European states, and even China, were susceptible to external shocks, because there population followed trade. America would be the first empire where trade would organically follow population growth.[81]

The political economy of the state of nature was a prominent theme in discussions of the American Revolution.[82] At first, Richard Price's 1776 "Observations on the Nature of Civil Liberty, the Principles of Government, and the Justice and Policy of the War with America" may not seem like a particularly rich state of nature text. It mentions the state

81. William Samuel Johnson Papers, Connecticut Historical Society, ms 22977, Box 6, Folder 13.
82. Hont, *Jealousy of Trade*.

of nature once, in passing, as the consequence of defaulting on the public debt due to one of the many risks posed by paper money. Price does not explain what the state of nature is, whether it is good or bad, what rights or constructs it may contain, and so on. But many writers chose to amplify the state of nature language in their response to Price, because it had become an integral part of discussing many of the issues that Price raised. In fact, the 1776 *Civil liberty asserted, and the rights of the subject defended, against the anarchial principles of the Reverend Dr. Price*, by "Friend to the Rights of the Constitution," brings almost every single issue back to the state of nature. "A letter to the Rev. Dr. Price. By the author of The defence of the American Congress, in reply to Taxation no tyranny," published the same year, grounded equality in the state of nature, from which the author deduced that hereditary princes and parliamentary representatives are wrong. The power delegated by those who are equal in a state of nature belongs to the office, not to the men who occupy it.[83]

> A Tribe of Savages, unrestrained by Laws, human or divine, may live in some Harmony, and endure for Ages, because in the State of Nature, there are at the most but two or three Subjects, to contend about.[84]

By contrast, in the post-state of nature society new facts, interests, and disagreements "in Trade, in Politics, and Religion" arise "by Thousands every Hour; no Constitution can subsist a Moment, without a constant Resignation of private Judgment, to the Judgment of the Publick," that is, Parliament.[85] In his August 1774 contribution to the burgeoning literature on American expectations for the First Continental Congress, James Wilson described the state of nature as a condition of individual self-sufficiency and independence, left through consent for the sake of

83. "A letter to the Rev. Dr. Price" (London, 1776), 4–5.
84. "A letter to the Rev. Dr. Price," 13. No. 119 of *The Adventurer*, a 1752–54 London biweekly paper, makes the same point (4th ed., London, 1762), 4:114–15.
85. The rest of the pamphlet is an impassioned attack on proposals of non-importation and non-exportation, and a final long flourish on the benefits of continued allegiance to Britain.

social happiness. For Jefferson, it was a regrettable fact of lawlessness into which Britain pushed the colonies through illegitimate, self-negating government. For Jonathan Boucher (1738–1804), it was both a fundamental notion that confused colonists invoked to explain liberty, and a happy, sustainable condition as long as needs and wants remained restricted to a few simple things.

The last meaning of the state of nature as one of economic simplicity recalls Priestley's application of the term to America. In his influential 1771 *Essay on the First Principles of Government* . . . , the natural philosopher, clergyman, Rational Dissenter, and overall polymath Joseph Priestley (1733–1804) argued that the greatest inconveniences in the state of nature were caused by an absence of the division of labor, which is a providential arrangement to strengthen sociability. According to Priestley, Greenland and America have no division of labor, which is why they remain in a state of nature. By contrast, when Pownall asked Adam Smith whether value came from labor alone, or from the combination of labor and its object, Pownall posited a "state of nature, somewhat advanced in the division of labour and community."[86]

6.5 RIVAL EPISTEMOLOGIES

Controversies concerning whether or not the state of nature was a real or imagined condition, and whether it was useful in constitutional debates, appear in many of the texts we examined. Hutcheson believed that the state of nature was sociable but preferred to call it a state of natural liberty. In *A Treatise of Human Nature*, Hume explained that the state of nature is pure fiction and could never be historical reality; but it is useful fiction, if one were to understand morality.[87] Burlamaqui found it useful, whether or not he thought it survives the transition to the polity. Vattel (based on Christian Wolff) thought that the state of nature between

86. "A letter from Governor Pownall to Adam Smith" (London, 1776), 9.
87. Hume, *Treatise of Human Nature* (1739–40) in *Philosophical Works* (Edinburgh, 1826), II.ii.263–65.

individuals is analogous with the state of nature among nations, and useful in both cases, especially to refute Hobbes and others who do not think that natural and moral laws apply among individuals and states in the state of nature. In 1754 Fordyce wrote that Hobbes's state of nature is a chimera, but the real state of nature, which is social, is useful and important. In 1763 the satirist John Shebbeare published *Select Letters on the English Nation*. Under the invented persona of the Jesuit Batista Angeloni, Shebbeare pointed that if the state of nature ever existed, it only applied to the first generation of humans. It certainly would not exist now; even Native Americans were not in a state of independence. In an interesting 1768 sermon, the Reverend Robert Thorp praised the great British constitution and its basis in feudal laws and natural rights, not on a foolish invention like the state of nature.[88] In his *History of the Colony of Massachuset's Bay*, Thomas Hutchinson jeered at those colonists who thought that their charter was no longer valid and they held their rights by virtue of some kind of polity that the first settlers created in the American state of nature. In the 1776 *Experience Preferable to Theory*, Hutchinson's contribution to the pamphlet war surrounding Richard Price's paper, Hutchinson ridiculed the whole notion of a state of nature, even though he used it to formulate his views on the Native Americans in *The History*.

Though most of the time all sides in the debate agreed that the state of nature was a useful concept, defending its intellectual validity from accusations of over-theorizing sometimes became part of constructing the more narrow American state of nature theme. In 1764 Otis condemned those who regarded the original compact, which he located in the state of nature, as "a piece of metaphysical jargon and systematical nonsense." In the March 26, 1771, *Essex Gazette* "Johannes in Eremo" wrote that the state of nature was a necessary constitutional fiction, useful to understand and debate the right to property and the duty to obey. Echoing Otis and Johannes, an essay by Observator in the April 30, 1771 *Connecticut*

88. Robert Thorp, *A Sermon Preached at the Assizes, at Newcastle upon Tyne, Aug. 2, 1768* (Newcastle, 1768).

Courant described the state of nature as "the first regulation and form of government, which ever had, and forever will have its rise from necessity." Thomas Dawes's 1781 oration celebrating the new Massachusetts constitution has the same structure. Around 1776 Benjamin Chew, Chief Justice of the Pennsylvania Supreme Court, composed and delivered several sets of instructions to grand juries, insisting that the state of nature is a real condition and should provide the starting point to understanding and enforcing the law even in a time of revolutionary war.[89]

In his 1765 *History*, Hutchinson presented Native Americans as not in a state of nature, but as close to it as possible. This is exactly how Fordyce, White and Rush used the state of nature as a standard for public health practices in 1773–1774.[90] In his March 1767 instructions to the grand jury, Hutchinson found the concept useful to explain the adverse consequences of passing laws without making sure they are executed. He also found it useful in his January 1769 letter to Whately, and his March 1769 instructions to the jury, arguing that some state of nature rights must be surrendered. By contrast, in 1772 the encyclopedist John Mills described the state of nature as a "phantom of the brain" that only multiplies errors.[91] As discussed below, in 1775 Daniel Leonard admitted that he first thought that the state of nature was a chimera, but instead of buying into the revolutionary notion of a constitutive state of nature, the prospect of a revolution alerted him to the possible reality of Hobbes's state of nature. In 1776 the Reverend John Brand commented on Thomas Gilbert's poor law bill that the state of nature is not a chimera, but an attainable

89. Benjamin Chew, instructions to the grand jury, Historical Society of Pennsylvania, Chew Family Papers, Collection 2050, series 2, section E, Box 16.
90. William Fordyce, *A New Inquiry Into the Causes, Symptoms, and Cure, of Putrid and Inflammatory Fevers* . . . (London, 1774); Charles White, *A Treatise on the Management of Pregnant and Lying-in Women* . . . (London, 1773); Benjamin Rush, *An oration, delivered February 4, 1774, before the American Philosophical Society, held at Philadelphia Containing, an enquiry into the natural history of medicine among the Indians in North-America, and a comparative view of their disease and remedies, with those of civilized nations* . . . (Philadelphia, 1774).
91. John Mills, *Essays Moral, Philosophical, and Political* (London, 1772), 118, in the essay "Of Love and Jealousy."

end-point of progress, "that ultimate point to which nature originally destined human society to attain and rest in."[92]

The anonymous 1774 *A Letter from a Veteran, to the Officers of the Army Encamped at Boston* offers a trenchant criticism of political theory, and of the American revolutionaries' application of it to real life. The author, sometimes identified as Robert Prescott, praised Harrington, Locke, and other theorists with good intentions, but warns against mistaking their utopias and thought experiments for real politics, and especially against those who misapply the seductive power of their theories to manipulate the common man. Even Locke's fine theory, according to Veteran, is "fit only for the Cabinets of the Curious."[93]

The Veteran pointed to political theory constructs, such as the divine right of kings, Harrington's republic, and the social contract, as examples of theory's mischief. Harrington proposed his utopia to save England from anarchy, but Montesquieu was right to mock his impracticable idealism. The Veteran replaced Blackstone's eulogy of the 1688 judges for averting a constitutional catastrophe with a praise of the English people. Fortunately, "the irresistible and salutary Force of Habit and Opinion" of the people revived the British constitution despite the "splendid and promising Theories" on offer during the Civil War.[94] In a curious echo of Otis's 1764 *Rights*, the Veteran argued that the social contract, if it ever existed, must have been made at the Glorious Revolution, between a patriot Prince and a patriot People. Unlike Otis, the Veteran doubted that it lasted very long. Even if that moment qualified as an actualization of the theory, the social contract would have been immediately broken, and "Men were at Liberty, to return if they pleased, to the State of Nature from whence they originally came."[95] Fortunately the people ignored Locke, just as they ignored Harrington. Only the colonial elite, especially in New England, pretended to be absolved from allegiances and sought

92. John Brand, *Observations on Some Probable Effects of Mr. Gilbert's Bill . . .* (London, 1776), 44–46.
93. Robert Prescott[?], *Letter from a Veteran . . .* (New York, 1774), 10.
94. Prescott[?], *Letter from a Veteran*, 7.
95. Prescott[?], *Letter from a Veteran*, 10.

to incite the people to advance their own interests. Although the state of nature is the only political theory construct that the Veteran did not explicitly criticize, it is safe to infer that he considered revolutionary usages of the term, especially when they drew on Locke, as part of the deliberate and self-serving abuse of political theory.

John Adams came to the defense of English revolutionary theory and its colonial use in his January 23, 1775, first Novanglus letter. Though mostly aimed at Leonard's Massachusettensis letters, it also takes on the Veteran. Widening the canon that the Veteran ascribed to the colonists, Adams added Aristotle, Plato, Livy, Cicero and Sidney to Harrington and Locke as authors of the "revolution-principles," which are as effective and real as the laws of science, and on which British imperial government stands.

> Yet we find that these principles stand in the way of Massachusettensis, and all the writers of his class. The Veteran, in his letter to the officers of the army, allows them to be noble, and true, but says the application of them to particular cases is wild and Utopian. How they can be in general true, and not applicable to particular cases, I cannot comprehend. I thought their being true in general was because, they were applicable to most particular cases.
>
> Gravity is a principle in nature. Why? because all particular bodies are found to gravitate. How would it sound to say, that bodies in general are heavy; yet to apply this to particular bodies and say, that a guinea, or a ball is heavy, is wild, &c? "Adopted in private life," says the honest amiable Veteran, "they would introduce perpetual discord." This I deny, and I think it plain, that there never was an happy private family where they were not adopted.[96]

This summary shows that whether or not a writer considered the state of nature to be real, theoretical, useful, or dangerous, tells us little about the writer's political views and allegiances. However, defenders

---

96. Adams also discusses the Veteran's letters in Novanglus III and V.

of colonial rights tended to emphasize a constitutive state of nature, in which Americans could collectively claim, hold, and protect various rights. At best, the fictionality of the state of nature is a weak indicator. At least in the 1761–1776 period, Patriots seldom, if ever, denied its utility in constitutional debate, and often vocally defended it from those who regarded it as an unjustifiable and dangerous abstraction.

7

THE FIRST CONTINENTAL CONGRESS

The Consolidation of an American Constitutional Trope

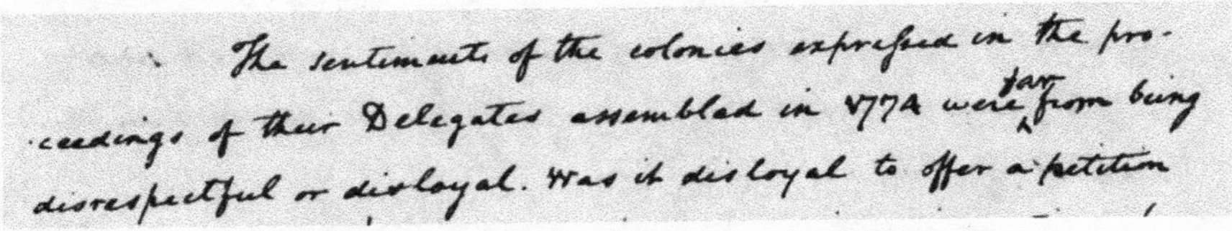
The sentiments of the colonies expressed in the pro-
ceedings of their Delegates assembled in 1774 were far from being
disrespectful or disloyal. Was it disloyal to offer a petition

Fig. 7.1 "The sentiments of the colonies expressed in the proceedings of their Delegates assembled in 1774 were from being disrespectful or disloyal." Madison's record of James Wilson's February 13, 1776, draft of Congress's address to American citizens. Madison later inserted the word "far." Library of Congress, Manuscript Division, James Madison Papers.

We have examined numerous discussions of the state of nature that were directly relevant to revolutionary constitutional theory. Otis on taxation and judicial review, John Adams on the stable American state of nature and the right dependence on the judiciary on the people alone, Hawley on the operation of courts, Bland on representation, DeBerdt on the independence of the early settlers, Centinel, Henley and Madison on the freedom of opinion and the press, Hutchinson, Knox and Sewall on the trade-off between natural and political rights, and Whitaker, Mather, Sherwood and Witherspoon on Christianity, as well as Loyalist responses to these speeches and texts, have all explicitly connected their version of the state of nature with constitutional issues affecting the American colonies.

It was through these evolving and overlapping usages that the American state of nature discourse emerged, with set loci that participants shared an understanding of, even while they contested their implications for the colonies' affairs. The records of the Boston Committee of Correspondence attest to a remarkable continuity between the Boston Pamphlet and the meeting of delegates from twelve of the thirteen colonies in Philadelphia in September and October 1774. The continuity is both organizational and substantive. Many of the committees of correspondence, and the towns, counties and provinces they reported to, were increasingly excited about the prospect of a colonial congress. Every topic mentioned before appears in the intense exchange among the towns and between the colonies. Most letters discuss the first settlers carrying the rights of Englishmen and conquering the wilderness without protection from Britain, drawing their right not to be taxed without representation from the laws of God, nature, and the colonial constitution.[1] Even modeling themselves on seventeenth-century parliamentary resistance to royal taxation appears, for instance in the June 5, 1774 resolutions that Billerica sent to Boston, particularly provoked by the Boston Port Act.

> That a Right, in the British Parliament, to Tax his Majesty's American
> Subjects, & to make Laws binding upon them, in all Cases, without their

---

1. An aspect of this recurring formula that requires further research is the possibility that colonists sometimes emphasized the barrenness of the land the first settlers found in order to make *Dutton v. Howell* relevant. Counsel in this 1693 case stated that when "Subjects of England, by Consent of their Prince, go and possess an uninhabited desert Country; the Common Law must be supposed their Rule, as 'twas

Consent by Representatives, wou'd effectually deprive them of those Rights & Privileges, which as Men, & as British Subjects, they have a just Claim to; & wou'd have no better Foundation in Reason & Equity, than the unlimited Prerogative contended for, by those arbitrary & misguided Princes, *Charles* the First & *James* the Second, for which the One lost his Life, & the Other his Kingdom.[2]

According to a letter sent to the Boston Committee of Correspondence, a group of five hundred armed men elected Col. Israel Putnam, Aaron Cleveland, Hezekiah Bissell, Daniel Tyler Jr., Jedediah Waterman, and Nathaniel Cary as a committee to respond to the incident known as the Powder Alarm. On September 1, 1774 General Gage tried to secretly move the King's gunpowder from Somerville, and two field pieces from Cambridge, to Castle William. The maneuvers were discovered and started widespread rumors of an impending war and bombardment of Boston. Thousands of men from New England gathered to save Boston, before the rumors proved unfounded and the crowds dispersed. According to the September 4 letter, five hundred armed men gathered in Putnam's house in Pomfret, Connecticut. The letter reports "news" of cannonade in Boston, "all the Powder Houses being robbed of their contents from Cambridge up as far as Framingham." The letter exclaims that forty thousand men instantly rose to arms, three million "bold, undaunted & desperate Freeman" were ready to die—except Putnam's troops soon found out that "we had been falsely alarmed!" Nonetheless, they welcomed the episode, as it made it clear to "our Enemies" that the

---

their Birthright, and as 'tis the best, as so to be presumed their Choice." Bartholomew Shower, *Cases in Parliament* (London, 1698), 32. Cited in Reid, *Authority of Rights*, 120, and Yirush, *Settlers*, 42. According to *Cobbett's State Trials*, vol. 20 (1814), the case was in currency, and cited e.g. in the 1773 *Fabrigas v. Mostyn*. In other words, the line of inquiry would be whether some colonists tried to show that America was an inhospitable environment in order to establish that the first settlers carried the common law with them.

2. Boston Committee of Correspondence records, NYPL MssCol 343, b.3.f.18 p. 1, http://archives.nypl.org/mss/343#detailed.

colonists were ready for action. They requested that Boston inform them if armed support were ever needed.

> We must recommend to you, to make diligent Search for all those dastardly Villains, who have had a Hand in perpetrating that wicked Act of Robbing your Powder Houses. And as you are in a State of Nature, the Punishment is easy & quick; and we much desire you to keep a strict Guard over the Remainder of your Powder; for that must be the great Means under God, of the Salvation of our Country.[3]

In response to the Boston Pamphlet, in January 1773 Marlborough also invoked the state of nature right to punish. Unlike in the September 1774 letter from Pomfret, in Marlborough's version this right belonged only to individuals. Conversely, while Marlborough derived collective colonial rights from the state of nature, their formulation of American state of nature rights did not include punishment. The Pomfret letter, sent in a more bellicose situation, which nonetheless came about in direct continuity from rising tension (marked by incidents like the March 1770 Boston Massacre or the June 1772 burning of the customs schooner HMS *Gaspee*) uses the state of nature right to punish to justify expansive American self-government, with marks of sovereignty such as the summary punishment of traitors.

James Wilson and Thomas Jefferson, though temperamentally and politically aligned at the time, deployed very different senses of the term. Wilson wrote the first draft of the *Considerations on the Nature and Extent of the Legislative Authority of the British Parliament* in 1768, three years after he left his native Scotland for the colonies. After a brief stay in New York, he moved to Philadelphia in 1766. Wilson started teaching at the Academy and College of Philadelphia in 1766, then switched to reading law at John Dickinson's office. He was called to the bar and set up his own practice in 1767. The *Considerations*, occasionally attributed to

---

3. Boston Committee of Correspondence records, NYPL MssCol 343, b.7.f.10, image 6, http://archives.nypl.org/mss/343#detailed.

Witherspoon, was not published until 1774, dated to August 17.[4] A well-known section runs,

> All men are, by nature, equal and free: no one has a right to any authority over another without his consent: all lawful government is founded on the consent of those who are subject to it: such consent was given with a view to ensure and to increase the happiness of the governed, above what they could enjoy in an independent and unconnected state of nature. The consequence is, that the happiness of the society is the *first* law of every government.

Next, Wilson argues that Parliament, consisting of fallible humans, can err. Higher levels of happiness, not order, is the primary good to gain from exiting the state of nature. Wilson was born and educated in Scotland. We saw in the section on colonial pre-revolutionary education (chapter 2, section 2.4) that the College of Philadelphia, where Wilson's colonial career began, was a stronghold of Scottish philosophy. His focus on happiness fits the influential principle that the best action causes the greatest happiness to the greatest numbers, which Hutcheson formulated as early as 1726.[5] It is rooted in the idea that humans are so

4. Whether or not Wilson wrote an earlier version is important but does not substantially affect my point about the range of state of nature meanings right before the First Continental Congress. In the absence of a surviving earlier draft, one could speculate that if Wilson wrote one, he could have used in it a meaning of the state of nature that he thought appropriate to the situation in 1768, and left it unchanged in 1774. Yet this triple supposition is less likely than the scenario that Wilson chose to publish a state of nature argument in 1774 that he considered to be relevant to the occasion. Moreover, the reception of his text is at least as important as his intention, and Wilson's readers saw his state of nature argument in 1774.

5. "In comparing the moral Qualitys of Actions, in order to regulate our Election among various Actions propos'd, or to find which of them has the greatest moral Excellency, we are led by our moral Sense of Virtue to judge thus; that in equal Degrees of Happiness, expected to proceed from the Action, the Virtue is in proportion to the Number of Persons to whom the Happiness shall extend; (and here the Dignity, or moral Importance of Persons, may compensate Numbers) and in equal Numbers, the Virtue is as the Quantity of the Happiness, or natural Good; or that the Virtue is in a compound Ratio of the Quantity of Good, and Number of

fundamentally sociable and social that they cannot maximize happiness outside society.[6] By reorienting exit from the state of nature toward happiness without asserting that life in the state of nature is untenable, Wilson avoids contradicting those, such as John Adams, who wrote in 1774–1775 that the American state of nature was a viable though suboptimal condition, better than Locke's state of nature but not as good as an independent republic. While the *Considerations* established Wilson as a major political figure, Jefferson's reputation similarly sky-rocketed with the tract he published the same month, *A Summary View of the Rights of British America*. Jefferson refers briefly to the state of nature as the condition to which Parliament reduced the colonies. This is essentially the same text he gave as instructions to Virginia's delegates to the Continental Congress.[7]

The Boston Tea Party of December 1773 was followed by punitive laws from Westminster, passed between March and June 1774 and known collectively as the Coercive Acts in Britain, or the Intolerable Acts among revolutionaries. Fifty-six representatives gathered in Philadelphia at the First Continental Congress between September 1774 and May 1775 to consider the options. Congress opened on September 5 with a

---

Enjoyers. In the same manner, the moral Evil, or Vice, is as the Degree of Misery, and Number of Sufferers; so that, that Action is best, which procures the greatest Happiness for the greatest Numbers; and that, worst, which, in like manner, occasions Misery." *An Inquiry into the Original of Our Ideas of Beauty and Virtue: In Two Treatises* (London, 1726), 177–78.

6. This remains Wilson's view, for instance in chapter 6 of his 1790–92 Philadelphia *Lectures on Law*, where he criticizes Hobbes, "the celebrated sage of Malmesbury." The modern editors misidentify this as a reference to William of Malmesbury. *Collected Works*, 622–23. Holland shows how Wilson argued in *Considerations* that Blackstone misappropriated Pufendorf's thesis concerning the supremacy of municipal law, omitting the Pufendorfian foundation of a pre-political community that delegates state of nature rights to the legislative power in return for effective protection, and replacing Pufendorf's comparative formulation of sovereignty with a superlative one. Ben Holland, *The Moral Person of the State: Pufendorf, Sovereignty and Composite Polities* (Cambridge, 2017), 159–60.

7. *The Papers of Thomas Jefferson*, vol. 1, 1760–1776 (ed. Julian P. Boyd, Princeton, 1950), 121–37.

discussion of procedure. The first record of substantive debate we have of this nation-making event is John Adams's and James Duane's notes on the September 6 session. Their accounts agree: the First Continental Congress began with Patrick Henry announcing that government is dissolved, the colonies have reverted to a state of nature, and a new state and government must be formed.[8] In this extraordinary opening salvo, Henry used the state of nature theme to show that a radical, fundamental departure from the status quo was taking place. Curiously, the dramatic opening statement of Congress was not unexpected. On September 5, 1774 (at 7 a.m.), Col. Gurdon Saltonstall wrote a letter to Silas Deane, his son-in-law, predicting that the Congress, where Deane, Roger Sherman and Eliphalet Dyer represented Connecticut, would begin with an announcement that the colonies were now in a state of nature. On September 19 Deane wrote to his wife that he wished he could convey to her the music of Henry's voice.[9]

The following day Congress appointed its first committee, charged with formulating the rights of the colonies, formulating grievances, and identifying means of redress. On September 8, Adams and Duane wrote notes on the committee's first day. In Adams's account, Richard Henry Lee, delegate from Virginia, suggested placing colonial rights on four foundations: nature, the British constitution, charters, and immemorial usage. As we saw, the first three already appeared in Otis's 1761 speech. John Jay agreed that it "is necessary to recur to the Law of Nature," but warned that the British constitution does not encompass some of the colonies' charter rights. Citizens have a right to emigrate. If the mother country fails to extend protection, their allegiance ceases, and they are free to erect any government they please. John Rutledge,

8. Adams's notes: Diary 22A, September–October 1774. *Adams Family Papers: An Electronic Archive*, Massachusetts Historical Society, http://www.masshist.org/digitaladams/archive/doc?id=D22A. James Duane's notes for the same day confirm Adams's notes, which are undated. Silas Deane's diary shows that Henry held to this firm line, drawn from the state of nature, throughout the Congress.

9. Both letters are in Connecticut Historical Society, Silas Deane Papers, ms Deans1789, Box 1, Folder 9.

from South Carolina, objected that subjects cannot unilaterally renege on allegiance. Lee repeated that it would be best to "lay our Rights upon the broadest Bottom, the Ground of Nature. Our Ancestors found here no Government." Rutledge restated that the British constitution is a better foundation than the law of nature. Jay interjected: the constitution derives its authority from compact, therefore it can be dissolved. Duane thought the British constitution, the common law, and charters were good foundations, but it would be misguided to rely on natural law. Lee now rephrased his point about nature as the best foundation, clarifying that he meant that the first settlers arrived in a land without government. Rutledge countered: "The first Emigrants could not be considered as in State of Nature—they had no Right to elect a new King." Galloway agreed, but for different reasons. He gave a long speech about finding colonial rights not in the state of nature but in the English constitution, which thereby links property and representation.[10] Galloway did not, however, think that any English laws that had been passed since the first settlers emigrated to America could apply to them and their descendants.

Like Boucher's, Galloway's case is remarkable because it shows how clearly participants understood the radical, foundational importance and implications of the state of nature. Adams, as we saw, thought that Otis's state of nature speech sowed the seeds of American independence. But colonial legislators such as Daniel Leonard in Massachusetts, Galloway in Pennsylvania, and Robert Carter Nicholas, Sr. in Virginia also came close to endorsing independence. At the September 8 session Galloway argued that colonial rights must be derived from the rights of landholders and from the invalidity of all parliamentary acts passed since the first settlers emigrated, and not from the state of nature. He concluded, "I am well aware that my Arguments tend to an Independency of the Colonies." This speech bears comparison with a pamphlet Galloway had printed

10. In his *Candid Examination* (New York, 1775), Galloway asserted that the colonies had always acted as parts of Britain until 1765 (p. 19). The recent "declaration of American rights" in Congress shows that the laws of nature are one of the sources of the newly invented claim for independence.

before the first session, *Arguments on Both Sides in the Dispute between Great Britain and Her Colonies.*[11] The point here is that both advocates and opponents of the state of nature foundation of colonial rights were driven by the same insight: the state of nature is such a radical principle that, once invoked, it reduces room for compromise and negotiation. In 1774 Robert Carter Nicholas, Sr., asserted that the state of nature is often used to bring a debate to a head by making opposing positions more extreme. "If, in attempting to reason on these Principles, I am drawn back to the State of Nature, where, according to the old Vulgarisms, *Might* was sure to overcome *Right*, and, where the *weakest* always *went to the Wall*, I must drop my Pen, and go in Quest of a new Topick."[12]

Some of the disagreement concerning the state of nature and the advisability of bringing it into negotiations with Britain is, of course, due to the different interests and perspectives of the participating colonies, and divisions among the delegates. While attending and shaping this Congress, John Adams continued to work with the Boston Committee of Correspondence. The position that he and Otis experimented with in early 1766 in the immediate aftermath of the Stamp Act, namely that the relative stability of Massachusetts in the state of nature that Britain thrust the province into proved that the Massachusetts state of nature was a legitimate foundation for independence, was revived and deployed during the First Continental Congress. Towns' replies to the Boston Pamphlet, such as Dartmouth's July 1774 letter, attest that the notion of an American constitutive state of nature was in broad circulation. As we saw, Adams developed his 1766 idea further in a published letter to a friend written in January 1775, and in his February 6, 1775 Novanglus retort to Leonard. In these texts, the constitutive American state of nature argument consists of two parts: the fact of Boston or Massachusetts remaining in a state of order and cohesion despite vitiated government;

11. Galloway, *Arguments* (Philadelphia, 1774), reprinted in *Archives of the State of New Jersey*, 1st ser., 10 (1886): 1480–81.
12. Nicholas, *Considerations on the Present State of Virginia Examined* (Williamsburg, 1774).

and the inference that they have autonomy, even independence, due to Britain's injustice and the proven stability of colonial communities in the state of nature.[13] That Adams formulated the same state of nature argument for Massachusetts as Henry did for all colonies on September 6 is clear from William Tudor's September 3, 1774 letter to John Adams, in which he echoed John Cleaveland's widely read September 5, 1768 *Boston Gazette* article arguing that violating its charter is enough to reduce Massachusetts to a state of nature.

> The present State of this Province will lead to the Discussion of a most important Question, and which may not be unsuitable for the Contemplation of the Congress. On the one hand, the Execution of the Acts of Parliament

---

13. The earliest formulations of the American idea of the constitutive state of nature, including Adams's in 1766, seem closest to Vattel's Prelim, 4. "Nations being composed of men naturally free and independent, and who, before the establishment of civil societies, lived together in the state of nature,—*Nations*, or sovereign states, are to be considered as so many free persons living together in the state of nature." This makes it possible to legally consider colonies, or all the American colonists together, as a nation. The revolutionaries quickly moved beyond Vattel, who argued that natural rights must be delegated or given up entirely; but the initial idea of a non-individualistic, collective entity in a state of nature probably came from both Hutcheson and Vattel. The same connection between collective identity and the state of nature, unthinkable in Hobbes and barely possible in Locke, featured in *The Cherokee Nation v. The State of Georgia*, 30 US 1 (1831) case, when the Supreme Court refused to rule on the Cherokee appeal for an injunction against Georgia's laws depriving the Cherokee of their rights, because they deemed the Cherokee as less than a nation: either savages (in Justice William Johnson's view), or a "domestic dependent nation" similar to a ward with the United States as their "guardian." In his dissent, joined by Justice Joseph Story, Justice Smith Thompson invoked this Vattel passage to show that the Cherokee are an autonomous nation, "competent to make a treaty or contract," even if they share characteristics with those who are in a state of nature. The next year, the Supreme Court ruled that the Cherokee were a sovereign nation in *Worcester v. Georgia*, 31 US 515.

    Interestingly, the view that by 1774 the colonists were in a constitutive state of nature persisted. In an undated essay, Silas Deane described 1774 as the year when British government in America was dissolved, followed by a two-year period of ungoverned, non-anarchic idyll, until the Declaration of Independence ushered in an age of American corruption. Connecticut Historical Society, Silas Deane Papers, Ms Deans1789, Box 7, Folder 36.

never will be suffered; on the other, this Refusal, which involves in it an intire Stoppage of every Court of Law and a Dismission of all executive public Officers, may plunge Us in Anarchy and Confusion. The People are eager to have Recourse to the first Charter, or adopt some new Mode of Government. Our last Charter is vacated and the Province reduced to a State of Nature. Can there ever be a more favourable Opportunity than the present for claiming, resuming and maintaining the Rights of Mankind, for a thorough Discussion, Definition and Confirmation of them. Great Britain, by her despotic Edicts, has forced Us to the Alternative of either becoming Slaves, or recurring to the Principles of Nature for Protection.[14]

Among Adams's papers we find a letter addressed to the Boston Committee of Correspondence, probably also from September 1774, that makes the first point about constitutional rupture, but not the second about Massachusetts' relative stability. Interestingly, here Adams holds George III, not Parliament, responsible.

As I am of the Opinion, that the Subjects of the Massachusetts Bay are without a King, Governor, civil or military Officers; so the People are again left in a State of Nature. For if it be Fact that the King has broke his Coronation Oath, by clipping our Charter &c.; it must be Fact, that we are at Liberty to choose what way of Government we like best. So have sent the worthy Committee, an imperfect Sketch of a Method for America to come into when all other milder Means shall fail; of securing our selves and Libertys &c.[15]

In the constitutional design that follows, Adams suggests playing European powers off against each other to maximize their military support, and creating a representative federation modeled closely on the United Provinces, with a high degree of local autonomy and Benjamin Franklin as its Stadtholder. The Patriot James Warren (who was married to Mercy Otis

14. *Adams Papers*, 2:138–41.
15. *Adams Papers*, 2:178–85. The editors believe it may have been written by Samuel Swift, another Massachusetts lawyer.

Warren, sister of James Otis, Jr.) wrote to John Adams on October 16, 1774 with a formula for an American state of nature that encompassed both a rupture with Britain and relative stability without government.

> It can be no longer A question whether any People ever subsisted in A State of Nature. We have been and still remain in that Situation, with this Additional Misfortune, that we dare not Attempt to Form A Civil Constitution or redress our Inconveniencies, least our Attempts should be disapproved of at Philadelphia and that perhaps made A Pretence to Justice our being left to the Mercy of our Enemies.[16]

Adams's notes from Congress, and the papers of the Boston Committee of Correspondence, show that the decision whether or not to anchor claims and rights in a state of nature was both the starting point and the *leitmotif* of the early sessions, frequently revived throughout the First Continental Congress. Moreover, although the ubiquity and volume of state of nature references are evident from the primary sources, they may have actually been downplayed in retrospect. In his diary, Adams recorded that there were two cardinal issues.

> Whether We should recur to the Law of Nature, as well as to the British Constitution and our American Charters and Grants. Mr. Galloway and Mr. Duane were for excluding the Law of Nature. I was very strenuous for retaining and insisting on it, as a Resource to which We might be driven, by Parliament much sooner than We were aware. The other great question was what Authority We should conceed to Parliament.[17]

Even though Henry, Rutledge, Lee, Adams, Galloway, and others referred to the state of nature, Adams's diary entry describes the debate as pertaining to natural law. Yet the relationship between the state of nature and natural law was far from obvious. In some texts, the state of nature

16. *Adams Papers*, 2:190–92.
17. Adams, *Works* (ed. Charles F. Adams, Boston, 1850), 2:374.

served as both the source of natural law and the sphere in which natural law continued to operate, since the state of nature survives the transition to the state. In other texts, such as Hawley's defense of Warren, state of nature rights applied in the polity in ways in which natural rights did not. In some cases, as we saw with the right to freedom of religion according to Williams, and the emphasis on self-defense in several towns' resolutions after the Boston Port Act, rights that had to be surrendered to allow the polity to function were called natural rights, while inalienable natural rights were described as rights grounded in the state of nature. Another difference between natural and state of nature rights was that the latter also invited an engagement with meanings that ranged from a pristine condition without corruption, through the physical environment, to a state of Christian perfection. The reason for Adams's uncharacteristic elision between natural law and the state of nature in this single diary entry may have been his political sensitivity to disagreements among delegates, who evidently disputed the meaning and scope of the state of nature. Adams's unusually cavalier notes on this occasion suggest that under the guise of the less controversial natural law he was trying to establish the Massachusetts sense of the state of nature as a historical record for all colonies. In any case, the discrepancy between Adams's and others' notes raises the possibility that some state of nature speeches were recorded as speeches on natural law.

More strikingly, Duane's account of his own speech differs from Adams's version insofar as Duane redacted his rejection of either natural law or the state of nature. In his own notes, Duane recounts the Stamp Act and its repeal, and how Townshend found a way around it to tax the colonies unjustly. More fundamental principles needed to be found to establish the source of colonial rights. What were they? Duane suggested the common law and charters. He set the latter aside to examine the former, starting from the principles that England had a limited monarchy and a free constitution, and common laws and statutes that predated the colonists' emigration remained integral parts of colonial constitutions. The colonists cannot give up, nor be deprived of, their inherited privileges. That is Duane's whole summary.

The omission of Duane's discussion of the state of nature in Congress from his own notes cannot be accidental. It was a point of cardinal importance, as we see from the debate and from Adams's notes. The likely explanation is that Duane was reluctant to record that he was on the losing side of the argument.[18] That he was worried and aware of this risk is shown not only by his initial support for Galloway's failed plan for imperial reform and reconciliation with Britain, but also by the fact that, according to Galloway, Duane and Galloway gave each other a secret certificate to show that they were trying to figure out a compromise with Britain which, as we saw, delegates even on opposing sides agreed would not be possible once the fundamental principle of the state of nature was invoked.[19]

We know surprisingly little about the committee's second meeting the next day, September 9, other than that it "[a]greed to found our rights upon the laws of Nature, the principles of the English Constitution, and charters and compacts; ordered a Sub-Committee to draw up a Statement of Rights."[20] We are not even certain who formed the subcommittee, which sat from the 10th to the 14th. John Adams, John Rutledge, Samuel Ward, and some North Carolina delegates were among its members. According to Ward's diary entry for September 12, the North Carolinians were probably Joseph Hewes and William Hooper, who arrived that day and did not take part in the discussions on the 10th and the 11th.[21] Uncharacteristically, Adams gives no details of their sessions. His usually detailed diary entries and letters contain nothing about the debate in the subcommittee. Although this is the subcommittee that formulated the rights of the colonies (the first item of business at the First Continental Congress), in all the sources we usually rely on to reconstruct the early

18. For Madison's manipulation of his record of the 1787 Constitutional Convention see Mary Sarah Bilder, *Madison's Hand: Revising the Constitutional Convention* (Harvard, 2015).
19. *The Examination of Joseph Galloway* ... (London, 1779), 57–58.
20. Adams, *Diary and Autobiography* (ed. Butterfield et al.), 2:131.
21. Samuel Ward, Diary, September 12, 1774. In Edmund C. Burnett (ed.), *Letters of Members of the Continental Congress* (Washington, DC, 1921), 12–13.

sessions we have at most a few terse statements by Adams and Ward that they spent the entire day in this subcommittee. The dearth of records is probably not an accident but, similarly to the arrangements made at the Stamp Act Congress, due to an agreement between committee members not to take notes and allow instead an open discussion without fear of repercussions.[22]

What is clear is that this founding debate revolved around the state of nature. Of the four possible foundations for colonial rights, this was the one that aroused the most discussion. As we saw, the others, namely the British constitution, colonial charters, and immemorial usage, were often debated in terms of their relationship to the state of nature. A subcommittee had to be appointed because the full, twenty-four-member committee was unable to agree about the state of nature, which was deemed too radical a principle by Rutledge, Duane, Galloway and others to leave any room for negotiation with Britain. Whatever happened in the subcommittee, in retrospect it is clear that Adams's side won. Its recommendation to the grand committee included adding the state of nature as one of the foundations of colonial rights.

7.1 GALLOWAY'S PLAN AND THE STATE OF NATURE

Repeating his September 8 declaration of commitment to colonial rights, Galloway emphasized his revolutionary *bona fides* at the beginning of his September 28 speech in Congress. He proposed reconciliation with Britain, a part of what is known as Galloway's Plan: "I am as much a friend of Liberty [as] exists—and No Man shall go further, in Point of Fortune, or in Point of Blood, than the Man who now addresses you." Even Adams's notes do not give the impression that Galloway advocated unconditional reconciliation. Rather, he eschewed the state of nature

---

22. See, e.g., Silas Deane's September 8, 1774, letter to his wife about the delegates' decision to keep proceedings secret, immediately justified by unseemly partisan bickering about choosing Carpenter Hall over the State House for the meetings. Silas Deane Papers, Connecticut Historical Society, Ms Deans1789, Box 1, Folder 9.

foundation of colonial rights in favor of extending British liberties into a distinct set of rights that were specific to the colonists.[23]

Galloway's constitutional proposal consisted of a President General appointed by the King, and a Grand or General Council chosen by colonial representatives once every three years. The Council would meet at least once a year, or at an earlier date determined at the last session's adjournment, or as convened by the President General. The Council would elect its own Speaker and generally operate like Parliament. The President General would hold his office at the King's pleasure, and have responsibility for exercising all legislative rights, for policing the colonies, for civil, criminal, and commercial matters for all colonies, and in cases involving more than one colony. The President and the Council would be "an inferior distinct branch of the British Legislature, united and incorporated with it." In a considerable show of ambition for autonomy, Galloway proposed that Parliament and the Council must approve each other's laws and regulations before they come into force in the colonies. One exception is the Council's and the President's bills for granting colonial aid to the Crown in times of war, which become law without the assent of Parliament. Congress rejected Galloway's plan in a vote of six to five and went to the extraordinary length of having the proposal struck from its records. The delegates adopted the Suffolk Resolves instead, denying Parliament's power to tax the colonies and called for a boycott of British goods.

Several versions of Galloway's plan exist, including three published by Galloway or with his consent. Galloway published the two-page proposal with a sixty-page account of events and exposé of his thinking

23. In *A True and Impartial State of the Province of Pennsylvania* (Philadelphia, 1759), 171–72, Galloway invokes the law of nature only once, briefly, and then in support of the English Constitution. To connect Galloway's loyalism to the conflict Adams and others generated by insisting on using the state of nature trope is not to propose that Galloway would have otherwise become a revolutionary; his allegiance to the British government ran deep. See e.g. Richard Peters's November 26, 1765 letter to Jasper Yeates about a masonic lodge meeting, where only Galloway thought that the Stamp Act was perfectly legal. Historical Society of Pennsylvania, Jasper Yeates Papers, Collection 0740, Box 7, Folder 2.

as *A Candid Examination of the Mutual Claims of Great-Britain and the Colonies.*[24] In 1779, Galloway read out his plan to the parliamentary committee that conducted an inquiry into General Howe's conduct and competence, at Howe's and his brother Richard's own request. His testimony was printed as the "Examination of Galloway."[25] The texts of the plan are substantially the same, with minor variations, such as the accompanying one-paragraph resolution placed after the plan in Chandler's version and missing from the "Examination," and Galloway using italics in the "Examination" to emphasize that he meant the American government to be "an inferior distinct branch of the British Legislature, united and incorporated with it."

Galloway's own explanations of his plan in 1775 for the American public, and in 1779 to the parliamentary committee, are different enough to suggest that focusing on the two-page text of the plan proper is insufficient to understand it and its reception. Galloway's three printed versions, Adams's notes on Galloway's actual September 28, 1774 proposal in Congress, and Dickinson's and Thomson's criticism of Galloway's *Candid Examination,* in fact offer considerably different interpretations of the events. In Galloway's commentaries, and in his debate with other members of Congress, the state of nature is invoked explicitly, because it is a fundamental principle behind the actual constitutional provisions of the plan.

According to Adams's notes, on September 28, 1774 Galloway, echoing Jonathan Boucher, opened his speech by criticizing the proposed trade embargo with Britain as counterproductive. He then introduced the preamble to his own plan. Unfortunately Adams summarized this only as "Burlamaqui, Grotius, Puffendorf, Hooker.—There must be an Union of Wills and Strength. Distinction between a State and a Multitude." Based on all printed versions of the plan, as well as on these writers' account of the state of nature, it is safe to assume that Galloway's preamble referred

24. New York, 1775. Galloway's plan also appeared in 1775 as an appendix to Thomas Chandler's *What Think Ye of Congress Now?*
25. *Examination of Joseph Galloway,* 46–48, with Galloway's note running to p. 50.

to the exit from the state of nature. Galloway continued with the declaration that the American colonies were independent from Britain as well as from each other, but they should continue negotiations with Britain partly because of their shared history, and partly in the hope of British military protection.[26] He then proposed his plan, seconded by Duane and supported by Jay and Edward Rutledge.

In the 1775 *Candid Examination*, Galloway begins with the point that all states must have a supreme legislative authority. In support, he cites Cicero, Locke, "the judicious Burlamaqui," and Acherley. Had members of Congress recognized the indivisibility of the necessary supreme legislative power,

> it would have shewn that there can be no alternative; either the colonies must be considered as complete members of the state, or so many distinct communities, in a state of nature, as independent of it, as Hanover, France, or Spain.[27]

As we saw, in Congress Galloway came close to advocating precisely for this independence, invoking Burlamaqui, Grotius, Pufendorf, and Hooker. The reference to Hanover either muddles Galloway's point or compresses it beyond comprehensibility, given the personal union between Hanover and Britain via George III. Was he pointing out that this personal union still left Britain and Hanover in a state of nature with respect to one another? Or was Galloway's thought similar to his reply to Dickinson and Thomson later that year, namely that the King had no legislative but only executive authority, and as Parliament was the supreme

26. In June 1787 Luther Martin also argued in Congress that the colonies were in a state of nature in relation to each other, which Hamilton denied. James Madison, *The Writings of James Madison, comprising his Public Papers and his Private Correspondence, including his numerous letters and documents now for the first time printed*, vol. 3, *The Journal of the Constitutional Convention I* (ed. Gaillard Hunt, New York: G.P. Putnam's Sons, 1902), 223–25, 297–98.
27. Galloway, *Candid Examination*, 6.

legislative authority, it could not legislate for Hanover, any more than it could for the American colonies or, for that matter, for France?

Echoing Sewall's January 28, 1771 Philanthrop letter, Galloway's next point in this text, however, is that Britain's constitution is unique because it is mixed, as the King, Lords, and Commons jointly hold supreme legislative power. Therefore the colonists are wrong to believe that they can pledge allegiance to the King but not Parliament. Even if supreme power "does not always exist," for instance when Parliament is not in session, and the King represents the nation by virtue of his executive power, his power is still subordinate to the legislative.[28] That said, colonial obedience to the King is important because while the King may be subordinate to the complete legislative power, of which he is only one part, in his capacity as "the supreme executive representative" it is he who grants charters, appointed chief colonial officials, and otherwise embodied continuous authority, something that the intermittently extant legislative cannot do.[29]

Galloway's reply to his own question is surprising and illuminating. Contrary to Adams's notes that Galloway agreed with Henry that the colonies were in a state of nature toward Britain, Galloway ended up arguing that the colonies were "members of the British government."[30] There are two notable features of the train of thought that leads here. First, consistently with other uses surveyed above, Galloway posed the fundamental question of the colonies' relationship with Britain in state of nature terms.[31] Second, he denied that the colonists ever were in a state of nature. The lands where the first settlers arrived were either discovered or conquered. In either case, the mother country owned them. Galloway did not consider these lands to be, or to have ever been, in a state of nature for any of the reasons his contemporaries gave, namely

28. Galloway, *Candid Examination*, 7.
29. Galloway, *Candid Examination*, 16.
30. Galloway, *Candid Examination*, 11.
31. "Let us next enquire whether the colonies of right are members of that state, or so many independent communities in a state of nature, with respect to it." Galloway, *Candid Examination*, 10.

because they were a wilderness, or the settlers invested money and labor to turn them into cultivated land, or because Britain afforded the settlers no protection, or because the settlers entered the state of nature when they emigrated to escape Stuart oppression. According to Galloway, starting with Henry VII's commission to Cabot, every colonial project was based on the mandate to expand the sphere of British influence and dominion. This was confirmed, according to Galloway, by the colonists' recent remonstrances and grievances, which invariably invoked the rights carried over from Britain—rights that, as Locke also pointed out, only made sense if corresponding duties were acknowledged.[32] That the colonists had never been in a state of nature vis-à-vis Britain meant that all legal matters, from grievances to punishments, must be settled in accordance with the supreme British legislative authority, with no room for claims to anything external to it, such as the state of nature.[33]

Furthermore, Galloway hinted that there were peculiarly British reasons to discard the state of nature as a source of rights. On entering society in search of protection, people surrender their natural rights. This surrender is proportional to the perfection of security that is offered. Partly due to its mixed form, the English constitution is uniquely excellent and offers unrivalled protection. The clear inference is that British subjects must give up their natural rights even more than subjects of other, less perfect states.[34] This is the third, subtly different yardstick for measuring the excellence of constitutions that we have come across. For Blackstone and Hutchinson, the English constitution was exceptional because it required the surrender of fewer state of nature rights than other constitutions. For Samuel Adams, the excellence of the

32. Galloway, *Candid Examination*, 13–15.
33. Galloway, *Candid Examination*, 25–26.
34. Galloway, *Candid Examination*, 34–35. Bailyn astutely points out that praising the excellence of Britain as a mixed constitution posed problems for arguments in favor of remaining in the British empire, because it was difficult to indisputably identify the aristocratic element in colonial governments. *Ideological Origins*, 274–75.

English constitution depended on its ability to preserve and maximize the equality one found in the state of nature. For Galloway, the ultimate criterion was protection.[35]

To support the joint points that Englishmen's liberties were unique and based in landed property, Galloway offered a Whig historical survey of broadening franchise and ever-lower property qualifications as *the* defining story of the progress of the English constitution and common law toward "a perfect idea of civil liberty, and free government."[36] That raises the question: what about American lands? Since colonial lands are British property, Americans retain the right to representation, but somehow lost the enjoyment of this right. According to Galloway, the right to representation did not matter much until recently. The first settlers needed protection and worked hard to survive and expand Britain's dominion. By the hitherto unimportant loss of the enjoyment of the right to representation, Galloway presumably meant that the early settlers were too busy with survival to realize or protest that they were practically unable to hold imperial elections and send representatives to Westminster. Now, however, the colonies are established and rich enough to start exercising this right. They still need British protection, unless they wish to lapse into a state of nature, "to desert all your present blessings, & retreat from superior force into a wilderness inhabited by wild beasts and savages, destitute of the necessaries of life, and incapable of obtaining them."[37]

35. To these accounts of the state of nature as the standard of constitutional excellence, one could add the letter that a certain "JH" sent to unnamed acquaintances from New York on June 27, 1767, continuing an exchange about the Norman Conquest being far less oppressive than the current British government toward the colonies. JH adds that it is the ability of the British constitution to represent citizens that makes it exceptionally successful in providing justice and rights comparable with the liberty and rights available in the ungoverned state of nature. One would even put up with "a little Corruption now & then" in order not to have to "look at the strong killing the weak in a state of nature." American Philosophical Society, Sol Feinstone Collection, Mss.B.F.327, #1312.
36. Galloway, *Candid Examination*, 35–40.
37. Galloway, *Candid Examination*, 62.

It was in the interest of both Britain and the colonies to form a union based on English liberties, Galloway argued, or the colonies would secede. Touching a raw nerve at the First Continental Congress, where representatives held a wide spectrum of mandates and opinions concerning the desirable degree and nature of new inter-colonial and federal powers, Galloway portrayed the relationship between the discontented colonies as a Hobbesian state of nature. Britain must be the linchpin that holds the colonies together, as otherwise they are "in respect to each other, so many perfect and independent societies, are very different in natural circumstances, economy, and government." [38] Galloway concluded that French and Spanish ambition, the cost of rivalry among the colonies, and the risk that the colonies would incur by provoking any European power into an armed conflict that they were bound to lose, together with their current liberties, all pointed to the desirability of a reformed and strengthened union.[39]

John Dickinson and Charles Thomson, secretary of the Continental Congress, were the likely authors of *To the Author of a Pamphlet, entitled "A Candid Examination of the Mutual Claims of GREAT BRITAIN and her COLONIES, &c.,"* dated March 8, 1775, Philadelphia. They went straight for the jugular, charging that Galloway "ignorantly misunderstood or wilfully misapplied" his sources on government. They took issue with Galloway's use of authorities to argue that people who left the state of nature must be in a state of society, which means submitting to a power that can "make laws obligatory to all." So far Dickinson and Thomson reluctantly agreed. Next, they set out to use Galloway's own quoted sources to show that the legislative powers constituted by the transition from the state of nature to society were the *American* colonial legislatures, not the British. Despite their claim to refute Galloway from his own sources, Dickinson and Thomson used quotations only from Locke, merely referred to Acherley, and omitted Cicero and

38. Galloway, *Candid Examination*, 43–44.
39. Galloway, *Candid Examination*, 44–48.

Burlamaqui from Galloway's list. In the contest for Locke's mantle, similarly to Otis's 1765 description of Martin Howard as "Filmerian," Dickinson and Thomson told Galloway, "you and your attempts will only be remembered to show posterity that even in these days of liberty, *America* had some degenerate sons—a *Jefferies* and a *Filmer*."[40] They also accused Galloway of a confused understanding of the English constitution. Pennsylvanians could owe allegiance to the King of Britain as the executive power for Pennsylvania, without owing allegiance to Parliament as the legislative.[41] They could also swear allegiance to the King as the executive of the common laws and statutes that continue to remain in force since the time before the settlers left England. The oath of allegiance does not, in sum, entail an acknowledgment of Parliament's authority in the American colonies. Dickinson and Thomson also denounced Galloway for misrepresenting his own plan. According to Dickinson and Thomson, what Galloway proposed in Congress, based on the same authorities and even the same passages from Locke and Acherley, was that since land was the basis of political representation and American lands were not represented in Westminster, Parliament had no authority over the colonies, not even to regulate trade.

Notwithstanding the transformations of Galloway's meaning of the state of nature as he moved from Congress into exile, the enduring importance of the concept for his constitutional theory is clear from his *Reply to an Address*. He portrayed Dickinson and Thomson as agreeing that an exit from the state of nature means entering society, where someone must have the power to make and enforce laws. Echoing his opponents, who claimed to destroy the foundations of his argument, Galloway then set up a counterattack that he believed would decisively demolish his opponents' whole "group of assertions." It is that

40. In his 1680 *Patriarcha, or the Natural Power of Kings*, Robert Filmer defended absolute monarchy and denied that the state of nature ever existed.
41. For an interesting rejoinder to this point by Galloway on what makes the king representative, see his 1775 *Reply to an Address* ... (New York, 1775), 19–22, 32–33.

Pennsylvanians did not "from a state of nature enter into a state of society"; but some of them were originally members of the British State, who emigrated from one part of its territory to another, with intent to populate that territory, and to extend the commerce and interests of the nation, of which they still remained a part; and the others came from other established societies, which they relinquished, in order to become members of the British government.[42]

Galloway rejected the revolutionaries' historical construction that the settlers had ever been in a state of nature. At the same time, he used the legal fiction of the state of nature extensively, most importantly in the sense of the relationship between sovereign states, in order to contest and crowd out the revolutionary sense of a constitutive American state of nature.

In the 1780 *Historical and Political Reflections on the Rise and Progress of the American Rebellion*, his later account of the proposal, debate, rejection and afterlife of his plan, Galloway claimed to reconstruct his September 1774 speech to Congress. He emphasized that he was using his original notes. In this reconstruction he claimed that in his original speech he seized on the use of the term "state of nature" by Henry, Lee, Adams, and others, and presciently gave it a threatening twist in order to awaken the colonists to the dangers they were likely to face while in an actual state of nature, lacking a common arbiter.

> In regard to the political state of the Colonies, you must know that they are so many inferior societies, disunited and unconnected in a polity. That while they deny the authority of Parliament, they are, in respect to each other, in a perfect state of nature, destitute of any supreme direction or decision whatever, and incompetent to the grant of national aids, or any other general measure whatever, even to the settlement of differences among themselves. This they have repeatedly acknowledged, and

42. Galloway, *Reply to an Address*, 11–12.

particularly by their delegates in Congress in the beginning of the last war; and the aids granted by them since that period, for their own protection, are a proof of the truth of that acknowledgment.[43]

Several features of the American state of nature discourse come to the fore in Galloway's references. His refusal at the First Continental Congress to endorse the radical sense, that of a natural American community, matches the reluctance of Church, Leonard, and many others discussed here to cross the line from colonial Whig criticisms of the British government to a politics of independence. As part of this refusal, Galloway systematically tried to replace revolutionary uses with the meaning of the state of nature as interstate and intercolonial relations. As he became a Loyalist, Galloway's references to the state of nature, and his retrospective reinterpretation of his own earlier uses, became increasingly emphatic about the non-revolutionary meanings. Finally, his polemic with Patriots clearly brings out the significance that all sides attached to the state of nature. The same type of polemic also occurred in contexts that were not directly related to the First Continental Congress, and they tend to reinforce the same pattern that we saw in Galloway's case.

7.2 LOYALIST VERSUS PATRIOT STATES OF NATURE (1773–76)

We saw how Otis in 1761–1765, the New Jersey petition of 1768, and the 1772 Boston Pamphlet used old and new ideas to craft a constitutive American state of nature. Due precisely to its foundational character, the state of nature discourse can serve another useful historiographical function as a rough ideological index for tracking how and why colonists with grievances against Britain left the revolutionary

---

43. Galloway, *Historical and Political Reflections* (London, 1780), 77. This is the version of the speech that was printed in the retrospectively compiled Worthington Chauncey Ford et al. (eds.), *Journals of the Continental Congress* for 1774 (Washington, DC, 1904), but it is uncertain that Galloway, writing in 1780 in London, reported it accurately.

cause when it became too radical. If the negative version was used, in which the state of nature is antithetical to an American community, the author was likely to become a Loyalist. Tracing the shift in their views of the state of nature is probably the best way to start reconstructing why Adams, Hawley and others became radicalized, while Jeremiah Dummer Rogers, Daniel Leonard, Joseph Galloway, Samuel Henley, Benjamin Church, Benjamin Franklin's son William, and others turned Loyalist when the high principle of the state of nature was pressed into service to eliminate any middle ground and scope for a compromise or settlement with Britain.

In 1774 Benjamin Church (1734–1778) was elected to the Massachusetts Provincial Congress and later to the Committee of Safety. In July 1775, Church sent a coded letter to Major Cane in the British army, reporting on American forces outside Boston. The letter was intercepted and deciphered in September. Church was tried and arrested, and expelled from Boston by the 1778 Massachusetts Banishment Act, together with Bernard, Hutchinson, Leonard, and Sewall. He seems to have been dissembling Patriot sentiments at least since 1772. Nagy cites Hutchinson writing in January 1772 that "the Doctor Church is now a writer on the side of Government," anonymously publishing Tory arguments.[44] Still publicly seen as a Patriot, Church gave an oration on March 5, 1773, on the third anniversary of the Boston Massacre. He began with an account of man in the state of nature, savagely independent but weak, driven to violence and treachery to ensure his survival. Recognizing his limits, he entered society at the cost of "the sacrifice of that *liberty* and that *natural equality* of which we are all conscious." As we saw, the revolutionary formulation of the state of nature insisted that liberty and natural equality in the state of nature survived the transition to the state; and if the state, or the British empire, threatened either, then the solution was to re-enter the state of nature and form a new state instead. By contrast, in 1773, already a covert Tory but still two years before he was caught,

44. John A. Nagy, *Dr. Benjamin Church, Spy: A Case of Espionage on the Eve of the American Revolution* (Yardley, PA: Westholme, 2013).

Church called this surrender "a glorious inspiration of reason, by whose influence, notwithstanding the inclination we have for independence, we accept controul."[45]

Daniel Leonard (1740–1829), King's Attorney and wealthy member of the Massachusetts House of Representatives and of the Boston Committee of Correspondence, is usually labeled a Loyalist. He was not, at first. In "To All Nations of Men," published in November 1773, Leonard adopted from Hobbes the state of nature as a viable and sustainable framework for relations between sovereign entities.

> Separate states (all self-governing communities) stand in the same relation to one another as individuals do when out of society; or to use the more common phrase, in a state of nature. And it is necessary says the same learned author that there should be *some law* among nations to serve as a *rule of mutual commerce*. This law can be no other than the law of nature, which is distinguished by the name of the law of nations. Mr. Hobbes says "natural law is divided into natural law of man, and natural law of states." The latter is what we call the law of nations.[46]

From this follows the protection of property, and the injustice of extracting taxes and "making our extreme magistrate a mere dependent on the minister of Great Britain." Conversely, the agents of the corrupt British government break the law of nature that underpins civil laws and thereby finalize the rift between Britain and the colonies as two "self-governing communities."[47] Leonard's nine-step summary of his argument relies on the state of nature to make several key points. Together,

45. Church, *An Oration, Delivered March Fifth, 1773* ... (Boston, 1773), 6. Several editions were published in 1773 alone.
46. Daniel Leonard ("Massachusettensis"), "To All Nations of Men," in the November 18, 1773 *Massachusetts Spy*, repr. in Hyneman and Lutz, *American Political Writing*, 1:209–16. Blackstone makes this point in *Commentaries*, I.43.
47. "These usurpers, or *foreign emissaries*, being screened from the power of the laws, by a corruption of both legislative and executive courts, have returned to a state of nature again with respect to this people, and may as justly be slain as wolves, tygers, or the private robbers and murderers above considered; and Jurors on their oaths

they amount to a state of nature strategy that could have been written by Hawley in 1767 about *Warren's Case.*

I. That men naturally have a right to life, liberty, and the possession and disposal of their property, in such wise as to injure none other.

II. That the same is true in society, with this difference that whereas in a state of nature each judged for himself, what was just or injurious, in society he submits to indifferent arbiters.

III. That all demands upon us for any part of our substance not warranted by our own consent or the judgment of our peers are robbery with murderous intention.

IV. That on these principles, the administration of Great-Britain are justly chargeable with this complicated crime.

V. That it is fit, and perfectly consistent with the principle of all laws human and divine, to resist robbers, murderers, and subverters of the constitution of our country.

VI. That both legislative and executive powers in this province being corrupted, the partizans of our oppressive plunderers and murderers are screened from public justice.

VII. That this corruption of public justice with regard to these internal enemies, and the deprivation of the people from the application of it for their own safety, naturally throws us back into a state of nature, with respect to them, whereby our natural right of self defence, and revenge returns.[48]

It has been argued that when in May 1774 Parliament passed one of the aforementioned Intolerable Acts, the Massachusetts Government Act, which abrogated the colonial charter of the Province of Massachusetts Bay and abolished elections for the Governor's Council, Hutchinson converted Leonard to the Loyalist cause by offering him a place on

---

are as much obliged to acquit the slayers in the one case as in the other." Hyneman and Lutz, *American Political Writing,* 1:214.

48. Hyneman and Lutz, *American Political Writing,* 1:214–15.

the Council. Leonard certainly had a sudden change of heart. Between December 1774 and April 1775 he published seventeen letters signed Massachusettensis. They were collected and published as a volume several times after 1775. A year after his revolutionary "To All Nations of Men," Leonard's Letter IX as Massachusettensis, published on February 6, 1775 in the *Massachusetts Gazette*, begins,

> Rebellion is the most atrocious offence that can be perpetrated by man, save those which are committed more immediately against the supreme Governor of the universe, who is the avenger of his own cause. It dissolves the social band, annihilates the security resulting from law and government, introduces fraud, violence, rapine, murder, sacrilege, and the long train of evils that riot uncontrouled in a state of nature. Allegiance and protection are reciprocal. The subject is bound by the compact to yield obedience to government, and in return is entitled to protection from it. Thus the poor are protected against the rich, the weak against the strong, the individual against the many; and this protection is guaranteed to each member, by the whole community: but when government is laid prostrate, a state of war of all against all commences; might overcomes right; innocence itself has no security, unless the individual sequesters himself from his fellowmen, inhabits his own cave, and seeks his own prey. This is what is called *a state of nature.* I once thought it chimerical.

Here Leonard deployed the worst popularized version of Hobbes's state of nature. Branded a Tory, Leonard joined the British army, moved to London in 1776, and served as Chief Justice of Bermuda from 1782 until 1806. Interestingly, Leonard relied heavily on state of nature models in both his Independent and Loyalist phases. The state of nature arguments he favored changed as he switched political allegiance. Leonard himself drew attention to this shift. His letters comprise good evidence for the importance of the state of nature in the history of American independence, for its deliberate uses for particular arguments (rather than as a mere vague foundation), and for the importance that the actors themselves attached to it. Leonard's shift was so dramatic that in Novanglus III, John Adams called him to task not only for his opposition to independence but also, even at this time of high-running passions and polemics, for a sensationalism that in itself threatened public safety at a dangerous time—namely when the people reverted to the state nature.[49]

Leonard changed his mind about the state of nature when he turned Loyalist. Galloway disagreed with Adams, Henry, Lee, and others, in invoking the state of nature in support of colonial rights. The separation of these Loyalists from the revolutionaries, foreshadowed by this disagreement, was often dramatic. As we saw in the case of Duane's and Jay's change of mind and other less dramatic disagreements about the state of nature, participants in the discourse had to either part ways with the revolutionaries or realign their stance on the state of nature toward the increasingly, though never fully, harmonized position adopted during the First Continental Congress. Other polemical exchanges concerning Congress also revolved around the state of nature. Some of them disputed what the state of nature was; others denied it existed and warned about the dangers of unrealistic, abstract theorizing.

Nine years after Adams's January 1766 diary entries on Boston being in a surprisingly peaceful state of nature after the Stamp Act shut down the courts and government, all sides were expecting the imminent outbreak of war. Adams wrote to a friend in London in January 1775 with the same image.

49. Adams's introduction to the 1819 Boston edition of the Massachusettensis and Novanglus letters shows that he thought that not Daniel Leonard, but Jonathan Sewall was Massachusettensis. This edition also includes Adams's letters to Tudor on Otis's 1761 speech. The William Cushing Family Papers at the Massachusetts Historical Society (Ms. N-67) seem to contain an unpublished Novanglus letter by Adams. According to Muldoon, Leonard thought of the British Empire as "an institution in a continual process of development" that reached a stage where invoking the early charters to object to imperial constitutional reform violated the spirit of progress. James Muldoon, *John Adams and the Constitutional History of the Medieval British Empire* (Palgrave, 2018). One could add that in this interpretation, Leonard's acceptance of the Massachusetts Government Act would be more in accordance with the principle of progress embedded in the common law itself than Adams's objection.

The state of this province is a great curiosity: I wish the pen of some able historian may transmit it to posterity. Four hundred thousand people are in a state of nature, and yet as still and peaceable at present as ever they were when government was in full vigour. We have neither legislators nor magistrates, nor executive officers. We have no officers but military ones. Of these we have a multitude chosen by the people, and exercising them with more authority and spirit than ever any did who had commissions from a Governor.[50]

Adams repeated the theme of a constitutive American state of nature in Novanglus III, his response to Daniel Leonard, in the February 6, 1775 issue of the *Boston Gazette*.

But this is not the first time, that writers have taken advantage of the times. Massachusettensis knows the critical situation of this province. The danger it is in, without government or law—The army in Boston—The people irritated and exasperated, in such a manner as was never before borne by any people under heaven. Much depends upon their patience at this critical time, and such an example of patience and order, this people have exhibited in a state of nature, under such cruel insults, distresses and provocations, as the history of mankind cannot parallel.

The same day a "gentleman in Boston," apparently with a view to publication, wrote to a friend in Philadelphia that Tories in Boston

are perpetually holding up to view all the terrifick consequences of treason and rebellion, wilfully mistaking, or stupidly imagining the inhabitants of this Province deeply involved in both; not considering that a state, the fundamentals of whose Constitution are subverted, which is indisputably the case with the *Massachusetts*, is reduced to a state of

50. John Adams, January 21, 1775, to a friend in London. Benjamin Akin's July 29, 1774 letter to Boston on behalf of Dartmouth is an earlier clear formulation of the constitutive American state of nature.

nature, and therefore cannot be guilty of crimes peculiar only to a regular constitutional form of Government.—But they bellow to the winds— their scheme is seen through, and they detested. So generally are the principles of liberty disseminated, and so deeply fixed, that nothing but Arms, that supreme lex of tyrants, will be able to suppress the generous ardour which now stimulates our countrymen to defend, at all hazards, the freedom handed down to them from their ancestors; nor will they be slaves without the most obstinate and bloody contest.[51]

The writer echoed Col. Israel Putnam's September 4, 1774 letter from Pomfret, Connecticut, in which Putnam and the five hundred armed men at his house who elected him to speak for them suggested that the Boston Committee of Correspondence was free to summarily deal with traitors, using the community's extralegal authority for collective self-defense in the state of nature that was created by (in this case) a military emergency.

Probably in August 1774, the same month as Wilson's *Considerations* and Jefferson's *Summary View*, appeared the anonymous *A Letter from a Virginian, to the Members of the Congress to be Held at Philadelphia, on the First of September, 1774*. The author is often identified as Jonathan Boucher, a prominent English-born preacher and teacher active in Maryland and Virginia. Boucher sought to impress upon the delegates the importance of their task. Britain and the colonies had long existed in mutually beneficial peace, which was now threatened with irreversible destruction. While the Philadelphia Congress was not perfectly representative, as perfect representation was unattainable, it was a close enough approximation in this free country where anyone might examine and pass judgement on his peers', social superiors', and political representatives' conduct. Unfortunately, people

are govern'd more by their Temper than their Judgment; they have little Leisure and still less Inclination, to inform themselves exactly of the necessary constitutional Powers of the supreme Magistrate, or of their

51. *American Archives*, 4th series, vol. 1 (Washington DC, 1837), 1216–17.

own legal Rights; they have been often told that Liberty is a very great Blessing; they talk incessantly of it, they find something inchanting in the very Sound of the Word; ask them the Meaning of it, they think you design to affront them; push them to a Definition, they give you at once a Description of the State of Nature.[52]

Boucher recognized the state of nature as a fundamental and widely shared concept, despite its multiple and contested meanings. He warns against "crafty designing Knaves, turbulent Demagogues, Quacks in Politics, and Impostors in Patriotism" who proffer their self-serving doctrines "under the Name of constitutional Principles."[53] The ignorance of the people and the opportunism of scoundrels and elites led to the unfortunate "ineffectual Resolves, Petitions, and Remonstrances" of the previous few years.[54] Boucher pits the notion of government in a complex society against the argument that Otis, Adams, and others made concerning Parliament's susceptibility to error and injustice, and the consequent necessity of judicial review. According to Boucher, Parliament "pretends not to Infallibility," but has the right to demand and enforce obedience. Its fallibility, as well as its rights, arise from complexity.

> A Tribe of Savages, unrestrained by Laws, human or divine, may live in some Harmony, and endure for Ages, because in the State of Nature, there are at the most but two or three Subjects, to contend about.

By contrast, in post-state of nature society new facts, interests, and disagreements "in Trade, in Politics, and Religion" arise "by Thousands every Hour; no Constitution can subsist a Moment, without a constant Resignation of private Judgment, to the Judgment of the Publick," that

---

52. Boucher(?), A Letter from a Virginian (Boston, 1774), 6. As noted above, Robert Carter Nicholas, Sr. made a similar point in his 1774 Considerations on the Present State of Virginia.
53. Boucher (?), A Letter from a Virginian, 7.
54. Boucher (?), A Letter from a Virginian, 12.

THE FIRST CONTINENTAL CONGRESS • 307

is, Parliament.[55] In his August 1774 contribution to American expectations for the First Continental Congress, Wilson described the state of
nature as a condition of individual self-sufficiency and independence,
left through consent for the sake of social happiness. For Jefferson, it was
a regrettable fact of lawlessness into which Britain pushed the colonies
through illegitimate, self-negating government.

Boucher's meaning became far more sinister in a sermon he gave
when Congress was already under way. His use of the state of nature between his 1774 *Letter* and 1775 sermon underwent a transformation as
drastic as Leonard's from 1774 to 1775. In the *Letter*, the state of nature
is a ubiquitous but confused term that colonists use as the final answer
when they cannot explain what they mean by liberty and rights; as well
as a viable condition among savages with very few needs. Mirroring
Leonard's change of mind about the state of nature, by the time he gave
his 1775 sermon in Philadelphia, "On Civil Liberty, Passive Obedience,
and Nonresistance," Boucher came to believe that the state of nature was
not only useless and confusing, but chimerical and positively dangerous.

It is indeed impossible to carry into effect any government which, even
by compact, might be framed with this reserved right of resistance.
Accordingly there is no record that any such government ever was so
formed. If there had, it must have carried the seeds of its decay in its very
constitution. For, as those men who make a government (certain that
they have the power) can have no hesitation to vote that they also have
the right to unmake it, and as the people, in all circumstances, but more
especially when trained to make and unmake governments, are at least as
well disposed to do the latter as the former, it is morally impossible that
there should be anything like permanency or stability in a government
so formed. Such a system, therefore, can produce only perpetual dissen-
sions and contests and bring back mankind to a supposed state of nature,

55. Boucher (?), *A Letter from a Virginian*, 13. The rest of the pamphlet is an impas-
    sioned attack on proposals of non-importation and non-exportation, and a final
    long flourish on the benefits of continued allegiance to Britain.

arming every man's hand, like Ishmael's, against every man, and rendering the world an *aceldama*, or field of blood.

Anthony Bacon (1716–1786), a transatlantic entrepreneur and MP, is the supposed author of the forty-page *A Short Address to the Government, the Merchants, Manufacturers, and the Colonists in America* from 1775.[56] After Bacon established Parliament's right to legislate for the colonies, he pointed out that the colonists' claim to natural rights "have no meaning: for men are born members of society, and consequently can have no rights, but such as are given by the laws of that society to which they belong. To suppose any thing else, is to suppose them out of society, in a state of nature."[57] The similarity to Boucher's rejection of the state of nature in the same year may not be accidental: the Bodleian copy of Bacon's pamphlet seems to be inscribed by Bacon to Jonathan Boucher, suggesting a personal relationship.[58]

Of course, not only American and transatlantic Tories, but many metropolitan writers also disputed the legal sense of the state of nature. Like Galloway, British opinion leaders were quick to point out the tension between most colonists' combination of claims based on rights grounded in the state of nature, claims based on British liberty, and those based on colonial charters and self-government. Samuel Johnson's 1775 *Taxation No Tyranny* mocked the colonists for their self-contradictory use of the state of nature. Johnson argued that the colonists could claim state of nature rights, or the rights of Englishmen—but not both.

The Americans have this resemblance to Europeans, that they do not always know when they are well. They soon quit the fortress, that could neither have been mined by sophistry, nor battered by declamation. Their next resolution declares, that "Their ancestors, who first settled the

56. Also cited in Reid, *Authority of Rights*, 90.
57. Bacon, *A Short Address*, 5.
58. Bodleian Library, http://solo.bodleian.ox.ac.uk/OXVU1:LSCOP_OX:oxfaleph-013526220.

colonies, were, at the time of their emigration from the mother-country, entitled to all the rights, liberties, and immunities of free and natural-born subjects within the realm of England." This, likewise, is true; but when this is granted, their boast of original rights is at an end; they are no longer in a state of nature. These lords of themselves, these kings of ME, these demigods of independence sink down to colonists, governed by a charter.

As contemporaries already noted, this argument, and passages, were plagiarized by John Wesley in his 1775 *A Calm Address to our American Colonies*. A large group of texts surrounds this argument by Wesley and Johnson. The author who signed the 1775(?) *A Full and Impartial Examination of the Rev. Mr. John Wesley's Address to the Americans* as "Friend to the people and their liberties" believed that the state of nature that underpins their own reasoning in fact favors the American cause. *A Cool Reply to A Calm Address Lately Published by Mr. John Wesley* by "T.S.," also from 1775, with a second edition published the same year, countered Johnson's and Wesley's accusation of American self-contradiction by arguing that the colonists could in fact claim rights in a state of nature, and rights as Englishmen. According to T.S., Johnson's and Wesley's sleight of hand suggests a contradiction between natural and civil laws, which is inadmissible.

The anonymous *Taxation, Tyranny* of 1775 tackled the same point. The author agreed with Johnson and Wesley that the colonists were wrong to believe that they were in a state of nature, but criticized them for inferring from this mistaken belief that the colonists could not claim English rights. Even those who are not in the state of nature hold state of nature rights, which are inalienable and inherent to them as humans, inherited from their ancestors, used as a standard of liberty to assess the English constitution, or survive the transition to the polity in some other form. "WY" replied to Wesley in similar terms in the 1775 *A Serious Answer to Mr. Wesley's Calm Address to Our American Colonies*: whether or not Wesley was right about the colonists' self-contradiction in claiming both state of nature and English rights, surely the latter are as good as, or better than, the former.

The March 12, 1776, issue of *The Crisis* (no. 61), a 1775–1776 London weekly supporting American protests, offers another defense. Wesley argued that the Americans' claim that they cannot be taxed without consent is as absurd as if they asserted that they could not be punished without their consent. *The Crisis* objects: "In a State of Nature every Individual is his own Avenger, his own Judge and Executioner." On entering society he has to give up these rights to deal with future offenses; but the natural right to future property cannot be analogous. The state of nature right to punish is not like the natural right to property: delegating the former is essential to the polity, the latter is not.[59]

While many British writers were sympathetic to American state of nature claims, some colonists preferred the English formulations. Between November 1774 and January 1775, Samuel Seabury (1729–1796), the first American Episcopal bishop, wrote four letters criticizing Congress under the pen name of "the Farmer" or "Westchester Farmer."[60] Alexander Hamilton, at the time a student at King's College, New York, published his first work, *A Full Vindication of the Measures of Congress...*, in response to Seabury's first letter. In his third letter, *A View of the Controversy between Great Britain and Her Colonies*, dated December 24, 1774, Seabury, who had not used the state of nature concept before, called out the young Hamilton.

> I wish you had explicitly declared to the public your ideas of the natural rights of mankind. Man in a state of nature may be considered as perfectly free from all restraints of law and government: And then the weak must submit to the strong. From such a state, I confess, I have a violent aversion. I think the form of government we lately enjoyed a much more eligible state to live in: And cannot help regretting our having lost it, by the equity, wisdom, and authority of the Congress, who have introduced in the room of it, confusion and violence; where all must submit to the power of a mob.

59. Ed. William Moore, *The Crisis* (London, 1775-76), 392–93.
60. On Seabury's career see McBride, *Pulpit and Nation*.

In February 1775 Hamilton countered with *The Farmer Refuted* . . . . After the customary exchange of *ad hominem* abuses, his first substantial point picked up on Seabury's question. Hamilton rejected Seabury's Hobbesian definition of the state of nature and presented an alternative in which the state of nature is almost the same thing as the sphere in which divine and natural law continue to operate, delimiting both national and civil law.

The first thing that presents itself is a wish, that "I had, explicitly, declared to the public my ideas of the *natural rights* of mankind. Man, in a state of nature (you say) may be considered, as perfectly free from all restraints of *law* and *government*, and, then, the weak must submit to the strong."

I shall, henceforth, begin to make some allowance for that enmity, you have discovered to the *natural rights* of mankind. For, though ignorance of them in this enlightened age cannot be admitted, as a sufficient excuse for you; yet, it ought, in some measure, to extenuate your guilt. If you will follow my advice, there still may be hopes of your reformation. Apply yourself, without delay, to the study of the law of nature. I would recommend to your perusal, Grotius, Puffendorf, Locke, Montesquieu, and Burlemaqui. I might mention other excellent writers on this subject; but if you attend, diligently, to these, you will not require any others.

There is so strong a similitude between your political principles and those maintained by Mr. Hobbs, that, in judging from them, a person might very easily *mistake* you for a disciple of his. His opinion was, exactly, coincident with yours, relative to man in a state of nature. He held, as you do, that he was, then, perfectly free from all restraint of *law* and *government*. Moral obligation, according to him, is derived from the introduction of civil society; and there is no virtue, but what is purely artificial, the mere contrivance of politicians, for the maintenance of social intercourse. But the reason he run into this absurd and impious doctrine, was, that he disbelieved the existence of an intelligent superintending principle, who is the governor, and will be the final judge of the universe. . . . Hence, in a state of nature, no man had any *moral* power to deprive another of his life, limbs, property or liberty; nor the least authority to command, or exact obedience from him; except that which arose from the ties of consanguinity.[61]

Hamilton was seventeen when he wrote this defense of the First Continental Congress, based not on a negative, antipolitical and hostile, but a morally and politically constitutive, version of the state of nature. Perhaps not an innovative contribution to the American state of nature discourse, Hamilton's first publication shows how far revolutionaries had come between 1761 and 1775 in synthesizing and transforming European state of nature traditions into something original and powerful. The distinctiveness, originality, and American specificities are also apparent in the state of nature themes that Joseph Warren presented shortly after Hamilton's defense.

Dr. Joseph Warren (1741–1775), co-founder of the Committee of Correspondence, gave an oration on March 6, 1775, the fifth anniversary of the Boston Massacre. Warren acknowledged that the Englishmen who first settled in Massachusetts in 1620 obtained a grant from King James, but doubted that they took it seriously. James might as well have granted them Jupiter, Warren exclaimed, as the king was as powerless over that planet as he was over America. The settlers entered into valid contracts with Native Americans, and bought their land. They mixed their labor with the soil. Britain remained uninterested in their plight until they began to flourish, and eventually became ripe for exploitation and taxation. In an echo of the June 3, 1766 address of the Massachusetts House of Representatives to Hutchinson and of Adams's January 21, 1775 letter to a friend in London concerning order in Boston despite the collapse of British government, Warren built his case on an opening statement that ranked anarchy above tyranny. While risk-taking and heroes are

---

61. Alexander Hamilton, *The Farmer Refuted: or, A More Impartial and Comprehensive View of the Dispute between Great-Britain and the Colonies . . .* (New York, 1775).

needed to overcome the cursed imposition of tyranny, the simple state of nature affords men the liberty to pursue their interests, and prompts them to create good government—a new one, in America's case, though not without a cost.[62] Three months after his remembrance of the Boston Massacre, Warren died in the Battle of Bunker Hill.

62. "Even Anarchy itself, that bugbear held up by the tools of power, (though truly to be deprecated,) is infinitely less dangerous to mankind than arbitrary Government. Anarchy can be but of short duration; for when men are at liberty to pursue that course which is most conducive to their own happiness, they will soon come into it; and, from the rudest state of nature, order and good government must soon arise. But tyranny, when once established, entails its curse on a Nation to the latest period of time, unless some daring genius, inspired by Heaven, shall, unappalled by danger, bravely form and execute the arduous design of restoring liberty and life to his enslaved, murdered Country."

ON SLAVERY AND RACE

8.1 CHATTEL SLAVERY

The state of nature came to dominate American discussions of slavery and race in the 1780s, particularly with the reception and afterlife of Jefferson's *Notes on the State of Virginia* (written and circulated 1781–84, first published 1785). Nevertheless, there is considerable evidence that the state of nature was becoming an increasingly important conceptual referent for race and slavery long before the 1780s. Moreover, state of nature discussions of slavery before 1776 were not isolated, but closely tied to issues, such as liberty and property, that played a dominant role in constitutional debates surrounding independence from the start. We saw that John Adams regretted that Otis placed abolition on the same state of nature footing on which he argued for the radical, natural, and inalienable rights of the colonists in the 1761 *Paxton's Case*, as it precluded "gradual abolitions."[1] In 1762 the Quaker Anthony Benezet, based in

---

1. Adams's 1761 concerns are echoed in the late 1780s' to early 1790s' notes of George Nicholas, friend of Madison and Jefferson and supporter of the Federal Constitution in 1788. In pondering slavery in Virginia and Kentucky, Nicholas (perhaps with the guidance of Madison) concludes that grounding this debate in the state of nature

Philadelphia, published *A short account of that part of Africa. . . .* Exactly like Otis in 1761, Benezet relied on the formulation of the state of nature as a condition of radical equality to argue that the slave trade was wrong, and must be stopped.

> To trade in Blacks, then, is to trade in Men; the black-skin'd and the white-skin'd being all of the same Species, all of the human Race, are by Nature upon an Equality; one Man in a State of Nature, as we are with Respect to the Inhabitants of Guiney, and they with Respect to us, is not superior to another Man, nor has any Authority or Dominion over him, or any Right to lay his Commands upon him: He that made us, made them, and all of the same Clay: We are all the Workmanship of his Hands, and he hath assigned this Globe to the human Race, to dwell upon: He hath given this Earth, in common, to the Children of Men.[2]

One of Blackstone's evocative accounts of property comes in *Commentaries*, II.1 (1766), where he describes light, air, water, and un-tamable animals as things any man can seize and use, as long as he has the intention and ability. If they escape from him, or he abandons them, they become common property again. Wild animals defined as game, unused land, shipwrecks, and other properties would be fought over, had the law not vested ownership of them in the sovereign or his repre-sentatives, "being usually the lords of manors."[3] Throughout this discus-sion, Blackstone notes the cases in which the common, civil, and natural laws agree.

would go too far, as it would inevitably bring natural equality into the debate and lead to impractical but compelling arguments in favor of emancipation, integra-tion, and giving land even to Native Americans. University of Chicago, Regenstein Library, Reuben T. Durrett Collection of George Nicholas Papers, Folder 16.

2. J. Philmore, *Two Dialogues on the Man-Trade* (London, 1760), 7, reprinted in Benezet, *A Short Account.*

3. Blackstone, *Commentaries*, II.14–15. Only the king has the prerogative to acquire property in these *ferae naturae: Commentaries*, II.27.419.

Blackstone explains that animals are divided into *domitae* and *ferae* not only by common law, but also by the law of nature. People can have absolute property in tame and tamable animals, but not in wild ones. In wild animals, man can acquire qualified property by taming them despite their nature, or by capturing and constraining them. When they escape, property instantly ceases—unless the animals showed *animum revertendi*, a natural inclination to return to their owner (such as trained hawks), or the owner puts a collar or other mark on the animal, and the animal has not disappeared for too long (in which case anyone may take it). A second way someone can gain qualified property in *ferae naturae* is from the animals' own inability, for instance by removing their young from a nest they built on a tree owned by someone. When their young learn to fly, that title ceases. The third and final way is to acquire a privilege pertaining to hunting a certain animal.[4] Similarly, humans can have no absolute property in air, water, and other fugitive substances, the way they can in land.[5] While someone enjoys a view, or uses water running through his property, the law protects him from injury caused by blocking his view or diverting his water. As soon as they are out of his use, qualified possession also ceases.[6] These ways of acquiring qualified property in *ferae naturae* are, significantly, extensions of the state of nature right that everyone had to all natural resources unclaimed by someone else.[7] Henry St. George Tucker inserted these passages into his *Commentaries on the Laws of Virginia*, a powerful instrument

4. Coke has the first two, but not the third. 1592, *The Case of Swans*. In *Selected Writings of Sir Edward Coke* (Liberty Fund, 2003), 1:232–40. With less nuance, in 1775 John Paul argued that all wild animals in a state of nature belonged to the Crown in common law. John Paul, *A Digest of the Laws Relating to the Game of This Kingdom* (London, 1775), iii.

5. An influential text on this theme, including some classical loci, is Grotius's *Mare liberum*, opposed by Selden's *Mare clausum*. Mark Somos, "Selden's *Mare Clausum*: The Secularisation of International Law and the Rise of Soft Imperialism," *Journal of the History of International Law* 14:2 (2012), 287–330.

6. Blackstone, *Commentaries*, II.25.390–95.

7. Blackstone, *Commentaries*, II.26.403.

of American legal education.[8] Since then, the doctrines of *ferae naturae* have prominently featured and continue to feature in the legal histories of American fisheries and wildlife exploitation, Native American land claims, the mineral, oil and gas industries, and intellectual property, perhaps without sufficient regard to the distinctive American sense of the state of nature.

This doctrine also played a role in colonization and slavery. In Francis Bacon's unfinished *An Advertisement Touching an Holy Warre*,[9] we find the *dramatis personae* arguing about the degree to which Native Americans are savage. What they do not dispute is that savages, like *ferae naturae*, are the property of those who hold them. The issue came to the fore again in 1765 when Jonathan Strong, a young slave from Barbados, was badly beaten by his master, David Lisle, discarded as useless or dying, saved by Granville Sharp (1735–1813) and his brother William, only to be kidnapped and sold by Lisle to a planter named James Kerr. Strong challenged Lisle and Kerr in court, and eventually won.

In 1769 Grenville Sharp published *A Representation of the Injustice and Dangerous Tendency of Tolerating Slavery . . .* , probably the first tract that attacked black slavery in England. One of Sharp's arguments was that black people are of a more noble nature than animals; but even if they were considered as wild animals, they would be free when not owned, since no one can claim absolute property in them, and they have no *animum revertendi*.[10] This was a weak argument, admitting that Lisle, and later Kerr, owned Strong legally in the first place. Nonetheless, Sharp's work impressed Francis Hargrave. When the fugitive slave James Somersett, encouraged by Strong's case, asked Sharp for help in 1772 and Sharp

---

8. He already made this connection in his 1801 handwritten annotations on Blackstone's *Commentaries*. HLS Rare Treatises B, IV.13.175.

9. Lampert argues that it may not be unfinished, but Bacon gave it an unfinished sense on purpose. Bacon, *An Advertisement Touching a Holy War* (Waveland, 2000), introduction, 5.

10. 14–16, *passim*. Steven M. Wise, *Though the Heavens May Fall: The Landmark Trial That Led to the End of Human Slavery* (Da Capo, 2005), 52–57, on Strong's case, and Sharp's use of Blackstone on *ferae naturae*. Andrew Lyall, *Granville Sharp's Cases on Slavery* (Hart, 2017).

turned to Hargrave, the latter agreed to serve as the most prominent of the five advocates on his behalf in the landmark *Somersett v Steuart*, a.k.a. *Somersett's Case*, which ruled that chattel slavery was illegal in England and Wales.[11] Benjamin Rush cited Granville Sharp at length in his 1773 *An Address to the Inhabitants of the British Settlements* and recommended that while the slave trade and slavery itself must be brought to an end, the law should provide for gradual abolition, as sudden mass emancipation might lead to grave social disorder. However, the benefits of trial by jury could be extended to non-white people immediately.

Advocates of slavery offered versions of the state of nature to refute arguments for abolition based on both radical equality and *ferae naturae*. Edward Long (1734–1813) was a prominent colonial administrator and historian of Jamaica. He returned to England in 1769 after twelve years of service. A polygenist, Long thought that black and white people had different origins. Both in his *Candid Reflections upon the Judgement Lately Awarded by the Court of King's Bench in Westminster-Hall . . .* (1772), which he published against *Somersett's Case*, and in the better-known *The History of Jamaica . . .* (1774), Long described black people as existing in a state of nature and incurably lazy, and mingling with them as a threat to white purity.[12] Citing Benezet, Theodore Parsons in *A Forensic Dispute on the Legality of Enslaving the Africans*, a 1773 Harvard thesis defense, countered that black people were not actually in a state of nature.[13] By contrast, the 1774 *A Supplement to Mr. Wesley's Pamphlet Entitled Thoughts*

---

11. Rush, *An address to the inhabitants of the British settlements*, 20–25.
12. Bryan Edwards (1743–1800), merchant, landowner, and MP from 1796, who lived in Jamaica for fifteen years, wrote a set of critical comments on *The History*, among other things offering detailed evidence against Long's account of the laziness and lack of skills among the black slaves of Jamaica. John Carter Brown Library, Codex Eng. 87.
13. The manuscript (Harvard, Houghton GEN MS Am 1423) differs from the published version. The variations do not affect the state of nature passages. Theodore's father, Moses Parsons, gave an election day sermon on May 27, 1772 in Cambridge, in front of Hutchinson and Andrew Oliver, arguing that the state of nature is terrible, but tyrannical government is worse. Parsons, *A Sermon . . .* (Boston, 1772), 13–14.

upon Slavery argues that black people did live in the state of nature, and were unconnected with the rest of mankind just as Long had argued— but contrary to Long's view, this state of nature was benign, and therefore chattel slavery was wrong.

Alongside the rule of capture and natural inequality, perhaps the most common and conventional justification of slavery was capture in war. By trying to take the victors' lives, the argument ran, the defeated have lost their own right to life and freedom. Historically, a large proportion of African slaves were not defeated in battle by Europeans, but taken prisoner by other Africans and sold to slave traders and Europeans already as property. In the December 17, 1773 instalment of a long article in the *Connecticut Journal*, the anonymous author refuted this justification of slavery by examining the property right to the vanquished in two types of the state of nature: between individuals, and between states. In the first case, if I suppose that a person has given all signs of an intention to kill me, and has even tried, that still does not pre-empt the possibility that I can win the fight and either be offered restitution or simply take it, together with a guarantee that no future attacks will occur. As long as these possibilities exist, I cannot claim a right to the attacker's life. In the state of nature I can kill the attacker only in the course of actual self-defense. Something similar applies to nations, which are always in a state of nature in relation to each other. Even if a nation unjustly attacked another, and every member of that nation consented to perform the unjust attack, that still would not exclude the possibility of restitution and a guarantee of no further attack. If it is illegal even in the state of nature to kill or claim a right to the life of a hypothetical, extremely unjust aggressor nation, it is equally illegal to kill or claim a right to the life of the members of this nation; therefore it is illegal to enslave or claim property rights to anyone under either of these titles.

8.2. NATIVE AMERICANS

The status of Native Americans in colonial society was also debated with frequent recourse to the state of nature. As mentioned previously, one of the selling points that George Johnstone attributed to West Florida to attract settlers in 1764–1765 was an uncorrupted sense of justice among the Native Americans in Florida's state of nature. Their right to land was often acknowledged as based on preoccupancy in the state of nature, and co-opted into claims for American independence. One template for such co-optation was to strengthen Native American property rights by anchoring them in the state of nature, only to argue that it is their state of nature titles that the colonists have bought at fair prices.

The long-held British claims to American lands were based on a version of the state of nature in which Native Americans were unable to hold full dominion in land because they were primitive and/or pagan, or because the Crown held and managed it for them in trust. As the colonists sought to establish property rights independently from Britain, paradoxically (at first glance) colonial lawyers began to oppose such justifications with a richer view of the state of nature, one in which Native Americans could hold full property rights in land.[14] Another colonial strategy was to appropriate the Crown's claim to hold lands for Native Americans in trust, employing a stadial theory in which Native Americans were in, or close to, the state of nature. The third strategy was to argue that not Native Americans, but the first settlers arrived in a state of nature, and acquired the right by preoccupancy. These state of nature-based strategies were occasionally combined.

---

14. Counsellor Dagge's 1755 opinion to this effect was cited at a meeting at German Flats, New York, between the Six Nations and Sir William Johnson in July 1770, where Johnson acknowledged the Native Americans' state of nature right to the land either by preoccupancy and conquest, and invoked the Crown's purchase of their title in 1768. Samuel Wharton, with Edward Bancroft(?), *View of the Title to Indiana* . . . ([Philadelphia?], 1775), 22. Also see the May 18, 1830 debate in Congress on the "Removal of Indians," *Gales & Seaton's Register of Debates in Congress* (Washington DC, 1830), 6:11. During the debate Henry R. Storrs, who strongly opposed Andrew Jackson's proposal to violate the treaty with Native Americans, emphasized that neither the Crown nor Congress ever claimed that Native Americans could not hold property rights because they were in a state of nature. *Debates in Congress*, May 15 session, 1007. Also see chapter 7, footnote 13 above.

A salient landmark case is *Mohegan Indians v. Connecticut*, running from 1705 to 1773, now known as "the first major legal test of indigenous tenure."[15] In 1659 the Mohegan transferred some of their land to John Mason and his heirs "as their Protector and Guardian In Trust for the whole Moheagan Tribe." Mason conveyed the trust to the colonial government the next year, but both the Mohegan and Mason's heirs have argued that this transfer was invalid. Connecticut received a royal charter in 1662, with the disputed lands inside its boundaries. In a 1681 treaty, Connecticut acknowledged Mohegan interest in the land, but started granting parcels to settlers in 1687. The Masons petitioned the Crown in 1704 on behalf of the Mohegan. The Crown referred the dispute to Governor Joseph Dudley and the Council of Massachusetts for decision, reserving the right to appeal to the Privy Council. Connecticut did not acknowledge their authority, and Dudley decided in favor of the Mohegan in 1705.

Connecticut appealed to the Privy Council. The appeal seems to have been ignored in 1706. In 1737 the Commission of Review, composed of politicians from Rhode Island and New York, provisionally sided with Connecticut, but the New York members accused Rhode Island of bias and withdrew. The Commission collapsed. On the third appeal, a 1743 commission determined that the colonists' deeds to Mohegan lands, granted by Connecticut, were valid. Now the Mohegan appealed to the Privy Council. The formal process began in 1770. The Privy Council found for Connecticut in 1772 without a written opinion, and the decision was upheld by the Crown in 1773. John Marshall cited the case in the 1832 landmark *Johnson v. M'Intosh* decision, which laid the foundation for the inalienable aboriginal title and the discovery doctrines. It was relitigated in 1979–1981, going all the way to the Supreme Court and eventually leading to the federal recognition of the Mohegan Tribe in 1994 and the *Mohegan Nation (Connecticut) Land Claim Settlement*

---

15. James Youngblood Henderson, "The doctrine of aboriginal rights in Western legal tradition," in Menno Boldt and J. Anthony Long (eds.), *The Quest for Justice: Aboriginal Peoples and Aboriginal Rights* (Toronto, 1985), 185–220, at 194.

Act, which extinguished all Mohegan aboriginal titles in exchange for the remaining eight hundred acres and the approval of Mohegan gaming operations.

The person representing Connecticut when the 1705–1773 case was concluded was William Samuel Johnson (1727–1819). Johnson is usually portrayed as a moderate, but his arguments in the Mohegan case reveal a more radical Patriot allegiance. Johnson served in the Connecticut legislature in 1761–1766 and 1771–1775, and represented Connecticut at the 1765 Stamp Act Congress. From 1767 to 1771 he was the colony's agent in London, where he made many friends, including Dr. Samuel Johnson. He sat on the colony's supreme court from 1772 to 1774 and in 1774 he was elected to, but refused to attend, the First Continental Congress. At Lexington and Concord he tried to negotiate an end to hostilities with General Gage, and he was arrested by the Patriots. Considered too moderate, he fell out of political favor, only to spectacularly return after 1783. He served in the 1785–1787 Confederation Congress, at the 1787 Constitutional Convention, became the first Senator of Connecticut, and President of Columbia from 1787 until 1800. His unpublished notes for the Mohegan case are at the Connecticut Historical Society.

The Mohegan case is complex, but Johnson's notes suggest that despite his supposed moderation, he started thinking about the colonies' independence early on—not as early as John Adams, who claimed to have decided to fight for independence in 1755, but long before 1776, the year some historians believe is the first time that independence was considered. To reconstruct Johnson's sympathies, we need to consider his working process as a lawyer. He had been thinking about the Mohegan claims for a long time, probably since before he was elected to the Assembly in 1761. In his diary for November 21, 1766–February 27, 1767, Johnson records a certain Mr. Brown's observation that the Native Americans believe that they acquired a right to the lands by first occupation and through the consent of their neighbors; and that this is the same combination that conveyed the rights to the Connecticut settlers, whether because of their own first occupation, or because they purchased this right from Native Americans to some of the plots. In February 1767, already in London, Johnson went to Westminster Hall to listen to arguments at the King's Bench and Chancery about the Mohegan case, then to the House of Commons to hear Grenville, Burke, Blackstone and others.[16]

To win against the Mohegan's appeal to the Privy Council, Johnson could have prioritized the 1659 Mohegan transfer of property in trust, the 1662 royal charter's acknowledgment of Connecticut's ownership of the disputed lands, or the decision in favor of Connecticut at the end of the last two rounds of appeal. The first would have given Connecticut conditional claim to the land, and the last three would have made Connecticut's ownership depend on royal approval. Instead, Johnson focused on the 1681 Connecticut-Mohegan treaty. Johnson argued that the Mohegan could certainly hold and dispose of property.[17] Moreover, the 1681 treaty established the principle that the Mohegan could sell the land without London's approval, because they enjoyed the same protections and rights as the Connecticut colonists. In fact, Johnson argued in London in the 1770s, it is the Crown's claim to represent the Mohegan that would deprive them of their rights. What the colonists have, and the King does not, is an inalienable right of pre-emption on buying land from Native Americans. Johnson emphasized that in exceptional circumstances law can become subordinate to politics, and the King can exercise flexible privilege when "Reason of State" warrants—however, if this is admitted, one must also admit that the settlers' body politic has its own reason of state, distinct from Britain's.[18] Johnson put the Mohegan

16. Connecticut Historical Society, William Samuel Johnson Papers, ms 22977, Box 11, Folder 3.
17. "To say the Native Inhabitants, tho Barbarians have no Right or Property in Lands more than the wild Beasts of Wilderness, either because they are Heathens, or because they do not improve by Culture, Pasturage & c Lands as most civilized Nations do, is to deny them the essential Rights of men as neither Property nor Dominion, are founded in Grace." Connecticut Historical Society, William Samuel Johnson Papers, ms 22977, Box 4, Folder 5. Compare Vitoria, De Indis (delivered in 1539), in Vitoria, Political Writings (ed. Anthony Pagden and Jeremy Lawrance, Cambridge, 1991), 239–40.
18. Connecticut Historical Society, William Samuel Johnson Papers, ms 22977, Box 4, Folder 3.

on stronger grounds at the Crown's expense, only to argue that since the colonists bought the land from the Mohegan, Connecticut's title has always been independent of the Crown. Even if Britain claimed a right to govern the colonies, it could not claim a right to the soil.

The thesis that the historiographical portrait of William Samuel Johnson should be adjusted, from non-revolutionary moderate to consistent but thoughtful revolutionary, is confirmed by letters he sent from London describing his disgust at the corruption of British politics. In a January 23, 1768 letter to Jedediah Elderkin, Johnson outlined a strategy to pledge allegiance to the King, distance the colonies from Parliament, renounce the King when the situation improves for the colonists, and "thereby become independent."[19] In addition to inviting a historiographical revision of his allegiance, Johnson's work in *Mohegan Indians v. Connecticut* also adds nuance to a persistent but simplistic dichotomy in critical law scholarship, according to which most colonists used the law to justify depriving aborigines of their rights, while a few champions of righteousness, typified by Bartolomé de Las Casas, defended them the best they could. William Samuel Johnson defended Mohegan rights in his covert revolutionary phase in order to construct a legal foundation not necessarily for recognizing native titles, but for strengthening colonists' rights against Britain's with a new chain of title anchored in Native Americans' state of nature rights to property.

Not only property rights, but also the manners and character of Native Americans were discussed in state of nature terms. In the 1765 second edition of *The History of the Colony of Massachuset's Bay*, Thomas Hutchinson writes,

> The life of hunters and fishermen is said to be averse to human society, except among the members of single families. The accounts which have been transmitted of the natives, at the first arrival of the Europeans, represent them to have been as near to a state of nature as any people upon

19. NYPL, Thomas Addis Emmet collection, MssCol 927, EM187, http://archives. nypl.org/mss/927#detailed.

the globe and destitute of most of the improvements which are the usual effects of civil society.[20]

Hutchinson adds a footnote on how Sallust's account of indigenous Italians fits "our natives": "Genus hominum agreste, sine legibus, sine imperio, liberum atque solutum," "a wild race of men, without laws, without central authority, unbridled and dispersed." In Sallust, the phrase "our natives" refers to the Trojans. Although Hutchinson proceeds to describe the uncivilized state of Native Americans, most of his readers would have known that Sallust's next sentences were, "After these men came together under one fortified location, men who differed in race, speaking different languages, living with different customs, it is incredible to recount how easily they coalesced. So in a brief period of time a varied and roaming multitude became a State living in harmony."

The same implication of the Native Americans' natural nobility and valor is made explicit in *An Historical Account of the Expedition Against the Ohio Indians, in the Year 1764* ... (Philadelphia, 1765), which chronicled Bouquet's expedition. The Swiss Henry Louis Bouquet's service in the British army is infamous for several episodes, such as his willingness to infect Native Americans with gifts of blankets from Fort Pitt's smallpox hospital, and the expedition into the Ohio Country that ended with peace treaties with the Shawnees, Senecas, and Delawares, and the return of over two hundred "white Indians," many of whom were abducted as children. The book became a bestseller overnight, with numerous reprints, extracts in magazines and a French translation in 1768, though its authorship remains debated. Some scholars think that it was written by Thomas Hutchins. It is also often attributed to William Smith, whom we met in chapter 2 as the first Provost of the College of Philadelphia, and who used the state of nature in his 1759 *Discourses on Several Public Occasions during the War in America* to characterize ancient Britons, civil society, and despotism.

20. Hutchinson, *The History of the Colony of Massachusetts Bay* ... , 461.

In Richard Slotkin's reconstruction, Smith wrote the book ostensibly to help fight Native Americans, but proposing at the same time that "the Indian's patriotism, independence, and love of liberty make him the model of the ideal American."[21] The section on Native Americans in the state of nature was, according to Slotkin, written by Thomas Hutchins, who later became chief geographer of the United States. That said, the description "of the temper and genius of the Indians" could have easily come from the Aberdeen-trained Smith.

> The love of liberty is innate in the savage; and seems the ruling passion of the state of nature. His desires and wants being few are easily gratified, and leave him much time to spare, which he would spend in idleness, if hunger did not force him to hunt. That exercise makes him strong, active and bold, raises his courage, and fits him for war, in which he uses the same stratagems and cruelty as against the wild beasts; making no scruple to employ treachery and perfidy to vanquish his enemy. Jealous of his independency and of his property, he will not suffer the least encroachment on either; and upon the slightest suspicion, fired with resentment, he becomes an implacable enemy, and flies to arm to vindicate his right, or revenge an injury. The advantages of these savages over civilized nations are both natural and acquired. They are tall and well limbed, remarkable for their activity, and have a piercing eye and quick ear, which are of great service to them in the woods.[22]

Slotkin compares the continued praise of Native Americans' "natural and acquired skills and endurance" to the Puritans' self-image. Hutchins

21. Richard Slotkin, *Regeneration through Violence: The Mythology of the American Frontier, 1600–1860* (Wesleyan, 1973), 231–34, citation from 231.
22. 1765 ed., 38. The same passage is in the extract printed as "An account of the temper and genius of the American Indians; with such observations and remarks as may enable European forces to engage them with advantage. From the historical account of the expedition against the Ohio Indians," *Scots Magazine* 28 (May 1766), 230–33, and in *The Gentleman's Magazine* for March 1766, 109–12, where it follows "A Summary of the Arguments against the Stamp Act."

portrayed Native Americans as "Rousseauistic patriots" whom both a new corps of rangers that he proposed, and Americans in general, ought to imitate. According to Slotkin, Hutchins believed that marrying the colonists' intellect and sentiment with Native American values would produce a "prototypal Euro-Indian American hero." Slotkin's interpretation is convincing, even though he does not discuss the state of nature that Native Americans are in, according to this passage, nor the innate "love of liberty" that is their "ruling passion."

Earlier we saw Otis adapting Rousseau's noble savage to American colonists in texts produced between 1761 and 1768; Johnstone's 1765 emphasis on Native Americans' sense of justice, which should encourage immigration from Europe; Henley's 1772 account of Native American intelligence, as opposed to the sophistry and bitterness of white academics; and Hutchinson's 1765 description of a wild race with the implied valor of Trojans. The meaning that these authors chose for the state of nature depended closely on their political view of the relationship between Britain and the American colonies. As Slotkin and others point out, colonists described themselves, and were described as, similar to Native Americans in their devotion to liberty, and in their ability to thrive in an uncultivated environment. European critics and colonial self-critics argued that these similarities made them crude and primitive, licentious or unreasonably attached to a chimerical sense of liberty. Others relished the analogy but drew further distinctions to limit its scope, such as Hutchins's or Smith's emphasis on the colonists' allegedly superior intellect and sentiment. This back-and-forth, and the evolution and contestation of settlers' and revolutionaries' image and self-image when drawn in relation to Native Americans, are part and parcel of the American state of nature discourse.[23]

Native Americans did not leave the state of nature when they left America. The anonymous 1776 *Omiah's Farewell; Inscribed to the Ladies of London* relates the visit of Mai, the second Pacific Islander to visit Europe, introduced to English society in 1774 by the great naturalist Sir

23. On normative inversion see Assmann, *Moses the Egyptian*.

Joseph Banks. Mai (known in England as Omai) stayed for two years. He became immensely popular with the English elites and public, who talked and published profusely about his charm, good looks, friendliness, innocence, simplicity and moral purity, popularized by the anecdote of Mai greeting George III with an informal, "How do, King Tosh!" Mai returned to Tahiti with Cook's third voyage in 1776 as a translator. The pamphlet, published soon after he left England, condemned the hosts' conduct and mused that instead of parading "this poor Indian, in the state of nature," the English should have been kind to him and taught him to help his people. "When we consider the injustice done to these innocent mortals in a simple state of nature, by introducing some dreadful diseases among them, our attention should have led us to have instructed him to be a service to them."[24] The author did not deny Mai's sociable nature or use of languages, but still placed him in the state of nature and wished he were protected from civilization's ails. Mai's multilingualism and other characteristics did not bring him out of the state of nature. Similarly, Pennant's *Tour of Scotland*, also published in 1776 and discussed above, attributed the ability to make complex canoes to Native Americans while they were in a state of nature. In these 1776 texts, Native Americans are in the state of nature because they are innocent and skilful.

In other texts, Native Americans, like black people, were placed in a damnatory version of the state of nature. *Concise Natural History of East and West Florida* . . . (1775) by Bernard Romans (1740?–1784) described Native Americans in terms as extreme as Long used for black people in 1772 and 1774. Romans was Dutch, born in Delft. During the Seven Years' War he emigrated first to Britain, then to the American colonies. Romans claimed to have entered the King's service in 1761 as commodore, leading expeditions on land and sea. He had exceptional cartographical skills, and he was appointed deputy surveyor of Georgia in 1766. In 1768 he became principal deputy surveyor of the Southern District, roughly present-day Virginia, North Carolina, South Carolina, Georgia, and East and West Florida. He surveyed parts of the Floridas

24. *Omiah's Farewell*, preface, ii.

in the middle of ongoing wars among Native Americans there, including the Choctaws and the Creeks. Romans collected botanical specimens in the Floridas and planned to create a botanical garden and publish his findings, even after some of his papers and specimens were lost at sea. In 1774 he became a member of the American Philosophical Society, publishing an account of his improved mariner's compass. Romans continued to work on his book, raising subscriptions and engaging Paul Revere to engrave the plates. During the Revolution, Romans fought on the Patriot side, chiefly as a military engineer.

After he resigned his commission in 1778, his main occupation became the composition of a two-volume history of British oppression in the Netherlands. Already in the 1775 *Concise Natural History*, where he described Native Americans as savages worse than anything in the state of nature, Romans cited Tacitus, Grotius, Blackstone, and other state of nature sources. He explained that the purity of morals in the Germanic tribes' state of nature was nothing like the bestial cunning of the American savage, who was incapable of being civilized.[25] This is a particularly interesting case of the state of nature theme carrying over from the Dutch to the American resistance against Britain; of finding a common denominator in the state of nature of Germanic tribes that Dutch, British, and American ancient constitutionalists claimed to descend from; and then applying it separately to the American landscape and the Native American tribes.

25. Romans, *Concise Natural History*, 39–40.

9

CONCLUSION

And therefore I think it is that some of the best because the truest history books are those which are professedly fragmentary, those which by their every page impress upon the reader that he has only got before him a small part of the whole tale. That is the reason why, though history may be an art, it is falling out of the list of fine arts and will not be restored thereto for a long time to come. It must aim at producing not aesthetic satisfaction but intellectual hunger.

—F. W. Maitland, "The Body Politic"

This book aimed to establish the state of nature as one of the defining discourses of the American Revolution. As an orienting and transformative constitutional concept, the state of nature ranks with property and liberty. The American revolutionary meaning of the state of nature was worked out during and through political conflict, between colonists and the British government, among Loyalist, moderate, and Patriot colonists, and among proponents of instant, gradual, or no abolition. The state of nature provided the conceptual space and tools for the colonists to articulate their disagreements and grievances, justify resistance and eventual secession and independence, and find the source of collective rights and identity that made them distinctive, united, and free. Like other discourses, such as representation, the American state of nature underwent several stages, from protest and revolution, through constitution-making, to consolidation and containment of the new state's critics, many of whom preserved or expanded the revolutionary senses and usages of the state of nature in reaction to centralizing proposals for the new state.[1]

A secondary ambition of the book was to offer a viable framework to model the evolution of the American state of nature discourse. The first stage of protest, with an emphasis on state of nature rights to property and freedom of conscience, speech, religion, and the press, was followed by revolution, with an emphasis on self-defense and the process whereby aggregating this and other state of nature rights created a new, pre-political, but cohesive community or nation. In the third stage, by the 1780s, the revolutionary extension of the state of nature discourse backfired insofar as from justifying the revolution against Britain, it turned into a persistent source of natural, pre- and extra-political constitutionalism, which undermined the new federal and state governments at every turn. At the same time, the Founders began to prioritize the meaning of the state of nature as the condition between sovereign states.

The final stage saw a coordinated program of rolling out political, constitutional, cultural and economic projects based on the notion of a distinct American state of nature. The prevailing meaning and function of the state of nature defines each of these artificial, historiographically useful stages, even though none of them were monolithic. The meaning of the state of nature was contested in each stage, and it is the processes of dissemination, adaptation, and evolution of the term's guiding semantic range, which never narrowed to a single and ubiquitous technical definition, that defines the discourse. We reconstructed these processes from published and unpublished texts, constitutional arguments with Britain and among the colonies, popular sources including a practical legal handbook, almanacs, newspapers, broadsides and pamphlets, criminal cases, political sermons, records of provincial assemblies, official correspondence, instructions to grand juries, and private letters and marginalia.

1. See the role of radical populism in turning revolutionary ideologies against the revolutionaries in Wood, *Creation*, chap. IX, and the three stages (to 1776, 1776–80, and 1780–early 1790s) that in *Ideological Origins* Bailyn finds emerging from the texts, and mutually enlightening events and the evolution of revolutionary ideology.

Multiple meanings of the "state of nature" co-existed and interacted in the eighteenth century. The term could refer to a state of sin, its opposite, a state of grace, a non-theological kind of innocence, uncultivated land, a place of rights, the relationship between sovereign states, and so on. Without exhausting the topic, the book showed how these meanings co-existed, competed, and interacted. The Christian meaning of the state of nature as a state of sin was inverted and became a state under God's rule in the sermons and books that used the revolutionary moment of 1773–1774 to offer a religious source of constitutional rights to freedom of conscience, religion, expression, and association. The peaceful and stable state of nature that Patriots claimed in support of independence was countered by Rutledge, Galloway and others who framed the prospect of colonies without Britain as a condition of disconnected and warring sovereign states; and by Hutchinson, Leonard, Nicholas, Boucher, and others who dismissed the revolutionary state of nature as an unfounded and dangerous abstraction.

In addition to developing state of nature claims as well-known *loci*, configured in increasingly complex arguments while also leaving room for variety and further development, in the evolution of the American state of nature discourse we also find particularly intense periods of contestation when the acceptable range of meanings was narrowed, redirected, or otherwise altered to serve the colonists' political objectives. The immediate aftermath of the Stamp Act is one such period. The colonies figuring out how to collectively respond to the Coercive Acts is another. The First Continental Congress is yet another. In these contexts, focused on short-term crises, the state of nature served to exclude compromises and the middle ground, and solidified the revolutionaries' position.

In terms of the history of constitutional thought, the American state of nature performed a role similar to what history did in justifying and operationalizing the philosophy of common law. It served as an evolving, contestable, but usable constitutional baseline.[2] The power and potential

---

2. I discuss custom as a font of colonial rights only rarely in this book, because the primary sources do not suggest a strong relationship between appeals to custom

of American nature nurtured American independence and identity in interlocking ways, from grounding independent rights claims in the first settlers' transformation of wild into civilized nature, all the way to giving revolutionaries hope of viable practical autonomy by first boycotting British trade, then creating a more co-ordinated federal economy that would outcompete the Old World largely thanks to American nature's untapped potential, released through the well-directed energies of a newly formed American republic. In this sense, one could argue that variegated and overlapping usages notwithstanding, in European invocations the state of nature often shared the same epistemic status as the concept of utopia, whereas in the distinct American state of nature discourse it was more likely to refer to something that the colonists did or could actually experience.

The rights championed by the American Revolution are those that the revolutionaries derived from the state of nature. These sometimes overlap but they are far from being identical with natural rights, because in many formulations state of nature rights survive the transition to the state, or are even perfected by it. In other cases, the state of nature is different and greater than the sphere of natural rights and natural law. It is the source of natural laws and rights; the historical and analytical condition where they can be found; a sphere where not only natural laws but divine laws and

and the state of nature. It is worth noting that custom tended to support the colonists' claim insofar as the first settlers reset the clock on the immemoriality needed for custom's authority. Reid, *Authority to Tax*, 189. While the duration required for custom to become binding in England continued to be debated, for Americans it was sometimes enough to trace it back to their foundation. In this strange and, as far as I know, hitherto unnoticed way, the common law was biased toward American independence. Another reason for custom's bias toward colonial independence was mentioned by George Chalmers around 1780 in his *Letter to Lord Mansfield*. The first settlers carried English rights with them, but American circumstances were so different that not only new black-letter and customary laws were created, but also parts of the common law came to be nullified. "And thus, the jurisprudence of England became that of the plantations, as far as it was suitable to new situations; because much of the common law being only common practice, that which is most practised, since it is no more convenient, soon falls into disuse." John Carter Brown Library, Codex=Eng 150, pp. 31–32.

the laws of civil society also apply; a baseline for specifically American freedoms, public health and way of life; and so forth. When natural law and natural rights were invoked to override British claims to authority over the colonies, they were often not nature-wide natural law and rights, but natural law and rights made specific to American nature. Once established, the state could join American nature as a separate agent that shapes American nature, both human and environmental.[3] Reid explains that American lawyers easily adapted seventeenth-century English arguments for property rights to the American revolutionary controversy, because for "them law has a timeless dimension, and physical, chronological, and geographical circumstances do not change legal principles."[4] He is correct; but alongside applying unchanging legal principles, the story of the American state of nature shows that these lawyers also invented one, and this one they tied to geographical, human, and other physical circumstances specific to the North American continent. Contrary to the historiographical view that the essence of American revolutionary ideology can be captured by a mostly Lockean theory of natural rights, especially the right to property, and through the function of such rights as the building blocks of a social contract, the actual primary sources show that the Founders posited a natural American community that aggregated individual state of nature rights, proved to be stable without British government, and offered colonists more security and prosperity than Britain thanks partly to the immense natural potential of the North American continent.

Though the evidence in this book is insufficient to draw a historical arc that is long and continuous enough to adumbrate traditions of state of nature use in constitutional interpretation, it is enough to illustrate the specific American meaning of the state of nature and its

3. The recovered role of the state of nature in the origins of the American Founding shows the historical accuracy of the intricate and close constitutional connection between the current practice and future potential of American democracy and environmentalism. See Jedediah Purdy, "The Politics of Nature: Climate Change, Environmental Law, and Democracy," Yale Law Journal 119:6 (2010), 1122–209.
4. Reid, Authority of Rights, 107.

importance. A historical exploration could continue to chart meanings as they developed up to relevant environmental laws, copyright, the rights of parents, and so on. A few examples may be useful, especially because the confusion that is evident in recent court cases demonstrates the usefulness of getting the American state of nature discourse right. Knowing the history of the American state of nature discourse is valuable regardless of where one stands on spectrums of originalism, living constitutionalism, or other interpretative methods and allegiances. Whether the historical meaning guides or informs interpretation and juridical application, or even when it knowingly decides to go against the historical meaning, clarity on the American state of nature is always useful.[5]

The success of the proposed framework of four stages in the evolution of the American state of nature discourse, and the idea that a history of this discourse can help dispel the confusion in current constitutional interpretation, should not interfere with the simple and main point of this book, namely that the primary sources show that the state of nature was a key revolutionary discourse, and that it is unduly neglected in our current understanding. This book adumbrates the first two stages of development. The American state of nature discourse became richer and louder after 1775. The wave of the states' constitution-making in the 1780s, the debate over the federal government and judiciary, the reaction against European charges of American nature's degenerative power, and the important European reception of the constitutive American state of nature, tested and proved by the successful Revolution, all invite future study. This book focused on 1761–1775 to explore the origins of the American Revolution, to see if we should take seriously John Adams's claim that the Revolution began in 1761, to problematize 1763 as the starting point of the process that led to the Revolution, and to challenge the idea that Blackstone's *Commentaries* played a defining role in American revolutionary ideology.

---

5. See appendix 2 for such cases.

In addition to the texts we examined in *Paxton's Case, Warren's Case,* state of nature responses to the Stamp Act, the 1768 wave of petitions, and the reaction against the Coercive Acts, thousands of further documents attest to direct continuities in the American state of nature discourse from 1761 through the First and Second Continental Congresses, and beyond. While drawing on European authorities, the state of nature discourse in the American colonies coalesced into a distinct tradition that complemented and, to an extent, undergirded the discourses on liberty and property that are more familiar from the secondary literature. The recognition of such a discourse on the state of nature from the early 1760s should put pressure on conventional chronologies of the American Revolution, as well as on accounts of its conceptual basis. Many historians have suggested that despite resistance to Parliament, colonial loyalty to the Crown and British identity remained unwavering in the 1760s, and that it is ahistorical teleology to see any group of colonists contemplating independence before 1773, or even 1776.[6] The evidence

---

6. E.g. Pincus, *Heart,* 22, 158 n. 23. This historiographical view persists despite explicit primary sources to the contrary. An August 3, 1770 draft of the Massachusetts Assembly's reply to Governor Hutchinson, explicitly denied that King-in-Parliament "has any Constitutional Authority to decide such Questions, or any other Controversy whatever that arises in this Province," and claimed that the Assembly "has the same inherent Rights in this Province, as the House of Commons has in Great Britain." Boston Public Library, MS G.41.22. They never sent it—but the thought occurred, and they wrote it down. The New York Public Library holds a letter, dated January 23, 1768, in which William Samuel Johnson outlined a strategy to start pledging allegiance to the King and start distancing the colonies from Parliament, and "thereby become *independent.*" Letter to Jedediah Elderkin, Thomas Addis Emmet collection, MssCol 927, EM187. In a March 10, 1768 letter to Secretary at War William Barrington, General Thomas Gage described the same plan that we find in Johnson's January letters (in Clarence Edwin Carter [ed.], *The Correspondence of General Gage,* New Haven, 1931–33, 2:450). Otis in 1764, and Oxenbridge Thacher in 1765, claimed that colonial assemblies could review any act of Parliament that affected them. They did not deny Parliament's omnipotence; but they adapted the old idea that the office of the king can do no wrong, because when the person of a king does wrong, he unkings himself, to the British Parliament—which they held more powerful than the king. The same was clear to London. McCulloh noted in his 1765 manuscript *General Thoughts . . .* that if the colonies figured out a way to raise money for joint purposes, "they would become *independent*

presented in this book suggests a strikingly different account: by 1761, we can locate early arguments for colonial self-government grounded in a distinctively American state of nature discourse. This discourse has been largely overlooked by later historians, but its import may go beyond providing the intellectual scaffolding for later revolutionary action to influencing the details of the constitutional settlement that followed.

The genealogy of the American state of nature discourse also holds an enlightening mirror to the debates surrounding the European state system. When the American writers' depiction of the New World's potential became vindicated in the global court of opinion between the 1777 Battles of Saratoga and the 1783 Treaty of Paris, their influence on Europe's receptiveness to the newly triumphant, evolutionary, and biologically optimistic state of nature models came to outweigh anti-American loci.[7] The American Revolution became a model for both successful and frustrated British, European, and Latin American revolutionaries. The English Radical endorsement of the American state of nature discourse, Jefferson's hand in drafting the 1789 Declaration of the Rights of Man and of the Citizen, Paine's speech against the execution of Louis XVI, Joel Barlow's 1792 *Letter to the National Convention of France*, and Sieyès's pamphlet on the Third Estate, are examples of its direct constitutional influence.[8]

of their Mother Country." Huntington Library, HM 1480. In his letter to William Tudor on March 7, 1819, John Adams wrote that he wanted independence as early as 1755.

7. Philippe Roger, *L'Ennemi américain. Généalogie de l'antiaméricanisme français* (2002, tr. as *The American Enemy: The History of French Anti-Americanism*, Chicago, 2005).
8. Sieyès's description of the Third Estate recalls the texts cited above on the constitutive character of the American state of nature. For instance, members of the Third Estate's proposed constitutional convention "are not limited to the powers and scope of ordinary representatives; they have the 'independence from all constitutional forms' that characterizes the whole nation, as the nation never leaves the state of nature." Emmanuel Joseph Sieyès, "What is the Third Estate?" (1789) in M. Sonenscher (ed.), *Political Writings*, 138–39 (Hackett, 2003). In 1800 John Wheelock, President of Dartmouth, proposed to write *A Philosophical History of the Advancement of Nations*, hailed by Joseph Nancrede, the prospective publisher, as the first book from the United States that would conclusively refute European

Unlike some intellectual genealogies of the American Revolution and founding, this book prioritized close textual analysis over retrospective analytical categories. Natural law, social contract, sovereignty, and individualism are important and relevant concepts. Although they prominently feature in the secondary literature, the primary sources between 1761 and 1775 mention them explicitly far less frequently than they mention the state of nature. State of nature rights, self-defense, and a standard of individual and collective freedom that sets and keeps progress in motion by being both binding and unattainable, are among the historiographical categories that emerge in this book directly from the primary sources. By recognizing the difference between the American state of nature discourse and natural law, natural rights, the social contract, and other associated but distinct tropes, we unlock interpretations of revolutionary and founding texts that are more faithful to the original documents, and more accurate in detail and nuance. This book aimed to show that despite the dearth of recognition in current literature, the state of nature was an essential part of the American pre-revolutionary constitutional discussion. In the course of this discussion, from the plurality of meanings a distinctive American revolutionary state of nature discourse emerged, with at least as much coherence as comparable eighteenth-century discourses are thought to have had. The final thought is simple. The state of nature ranks with property and liberty as a fundamental, orientational, and transformative American concept. No constitutional history of the American Revolution can be written without it.

deprecations of American civilization. The published book outline and call for sub-scriptions shows that Wheelock planned to write about the state of nature, though the project failed when reviewers deemed Wheelock's work derivative and inexcusably ignorant of Goguet. Nancrede, letters to Wheelock, 1800–1802, Dartmouth, Rauner 800378. Around 1805–6, Joel Barlow planned to write a book on political science. Chapter 6 was dedicated to the state of nature. Barlow also planned to posit a natural progression toward ever-larger states, and that the American union should be strengthened gradually to harness natural growth. Yale, Beinecke, Joel Barlow collection, YCAL MSS 568, Box 4, Folders 35, 36. For indirect influences see Doll, "American History"; Dippel, *Germany*; Axel Körner, *America in Italy: The United States in the Political Thought and Imagination of the Risorgimento, 1763–1865* (Princeton, 2017); and Evrigenis and Somos, "The State of Nature."

APPENDIX 1

A Manuscript Source for John Adams's Lost Abstract of James Otis Jr.'s Speech in the 1761 *Paxton's Case*

EXCERPT FROM AMERICAN PHILOSOPHICAL SOCIETY, SOL
FEINSTONE COLLECTION #1045 MSS. B. F327, PP. 6–14

May it please your Honours . . . I was desired by one of the court to look into the Books & consider the question now before the court concern[ing] Writs of assistance: I have accordingly considered it & I now appear not only in obedience to the order of court, but in behalf of the inhabitants of this town, who have presented another petition. & out of a regard to the liberties of the subject. And I take this oppertunity to declare that whether under a Fee or not, (for in such a cause as this I despise a fee) I will to my dying day oppose with all the faculties & influence that God has given me, all such instruments of slavery on one hand & villainy on the other as this write of assistance is.

It appears to me to be the worst instrument of arbitrary power, the most destructive of English liberty & the fundamental principles of law that ever was found in an English Lawbook. I must therefore beg your Honours' patience & attention to the whole range of an argument that may perhaps appear uncommon as to many things that are common &

well known, as well as to points of learning that are more remote & unusual that the tendency of the whole to my design & conclusion may be the better discern'd, & the force of it the better felt.

I shall not think much of any pains in this cause, as I engaged in it from principle. I was sollicited to engage on the other side of this question. I was sollicited to argue this cause as advocate general, & because I wou'd not, I have been charged with the desertion of that office. To this charge I can give (whenever I shall be called to it) a very satisfactory answer. I renounced that office, & I argue this cause from the same principle. & I argue it with the greatest pleasure as it is in favour of British liberty, at a time when we hear the greatest Monarch upon earth, declaring from his throne that "he glories in the name of Briton" & that "the privileges of his people are dearer to him than the most valuable prerogatives of his crown": & as it is in opposition to a kind of power, the exercise of which, in former periods of the English history, as we had it from your Hon. this very term, cost one king of England his head & another his throne. I have taken more pains in this cause than I ever will take for any fee whatever; altho my engaging in this & another popular cause, has raised much resentment if not malice against me,—I have been represented as a seditious person: a stirrer of uneasiness & rebellion. But I think I can sincerely declare, that I submit myself to everyone ordinance of man for conscience sake, & I most sincerely despise all those whose Guilt, or Malice, or Folly has endeavoured to represent me otherwise.—Let the consequences be what they will I am determined to proceed: For the only principles of public conduct that are worth any thing are these to sacrifice our ease, health, praise, estate & even life itself to the public good. These sentiments in private life make the good citizen, in public life the patriot & the hero: & all other principles of public conduct will be found fallible & deceitful: I do not say that when bro't to the Test I shou'd be invincible or more than others. I pray God I may never be bro't to the melancholy trial: But if it ever shou'd it will be then known, how far I can reduce to practise principles that I know to be founded in truth.

The sentiments upon patriotism & heroism are like those in the choice of Hercules.

Or wouldst thou gain thy countries loud applause
Lov'd as her father, as her God ador'd
Be thou the bold asserter of her cause,
Her voice in council, in the fight her sword
In peace, in war, pursue thy countries Good
For her bare thy bold breast, & pour thy gen'rous blood

Tully says "Nam nisi multorum praeceptis multisque literis mihi ab adolescentia suasissem, nihil esse, in vita magnopere expetendum nisi laudem atque honestatem, in ea autem persequenda omnes cruciatus corporis, omnia pericula mortis et exsilii parvi esse ducenda nunquam me pro salute vestra, in tot ac tantas dimicationes, atque in hos profligatorum hominum quotidianos impetus objecissem.["]

In the meantime I will proceed to the subject of the writ. In the first place, May it please your honours, I will admit that writs of assistance of one kind may be legal, that is special writs of assistance directed specially to particular officers, to search certain houses, warehouses, cellars & c. specially set forth in the writ itself, may be granted by the court of Exchequer at home, upon oath made before the Barons, or the Lord Treasurer by the person that asks the writ, that he suspects such goods to be conceal'd in those very places which he desires to search. It is enacted by 14 Car. 2. "that it shall be lawful for any person or persons, *authorised by writs of assistants under the seal of his majesty's Court of Exchequer*["] & c. (vid. ante p. 3') this certainly proves what I have admitted: & in this light the writ appears like a warrant granted by a justice to search for stolen goods. Your honours will find in the old Books, concerning the office of a justice, precedents of general warrants to search all suspected houses. But in the more modern Books you will find only special warrants, to search such & such houses specially named in the warrant, in which the complainant has before sworn he suspects his goods are concealed. And you will find it adjudged that special warrants only are legal & that general warrants are illegal, because they trust too much to the discretion of every common officer. Abr.t Hawk. P.C. V.2 [?]13 page 83. sect 8. There seems to be much more reason to subject a constable to an action for executing a general warrant to search for felons or stolen goods, because so large a warrant leaving it to a common person's discretion to arrest what persons & search what houses he thinks fit, seems illegal in the face of it. In the same manner I rely upon it, that the writ of assistance prayed for in this petition being general is illegal: it is an universal & perpetual Edict that places the Liberty & Privileges of every man in this province in the mercy of every petty common officer: for these Gent. of the Customs will allow that some of them are common officers, if most of them are uncommon officers.

I say I admit that special writs of assistance, to search certain places may be granted to certain persons upon oath before the Lord Treasurer & c. but I deny that the writ now prayed for can be granted, for I beg leave to make some observations upon the writ itself & the authority brought to support it, before I consider the other acts of Parliament. In the first place the writ is universal being directed to "all & singular Justices, Sheriffs, Constables & all other officers & subjects,["] so that in England this writ would be directed to every subject with all the King's dominions, as universal as any act of parliament can be, & more so than most. & here it is directed to every subject within this province. In short an officer or any body else with this writ, this commission in his pockett, is or may be a tyrant, if it is legal he may command & control every one of his fellow subjects as he will.

In the next place it is perpetual. There is no return; the possessor is not commanded to return it: he is accountable to no mortal for his doings by virtue of it. It is a perpetual Edict, a devolution of the whole power of this court, upon not only every common officer, but upon every man, & every man may keep it forever. In the third place, they are commanded to permit, the person who has the commission to enter all houses, shops, cellars & in the day time at his will.

And fourthly we are commanded to permit the same person & his deputies & servants, & afterwards we are commanded to be aiding & assisting to the said person & his deputies & servants, so that not only their known deputies, their legal representatives, but their private domestic menials are to lord it over us.

Now one of the most essential branches of English Liberty is the privilege of house. A man's house is said to be his castle & while he is quiet & peaceable he is as secure, & well guarded against all his fellow subjects, against all civil demands & even against the King, except in criminal cases, as a Prince or Monarch is in his castle. But

This writ if it shou'd be declared legal, wou'd amount to an entire annihilation of that privilege, Custom house officers it is contended may enter our houses when they please: we are commanded to permit their Entry: their deputies & menials & servants may enter: may break Locks & bars & bolts in case of resistance. And every British subject is commanded to assist them: And after all whether they enter & break thro' malice or prejudice, or revenge, or thro' mere humour & wantoness, no man, no court can enquire, for they are not to return their doings; & their bare suspicions without any oath or any probable grounds of suspicion it is said is a sufficient justification. And this suggestion of a wanton exercise of this plenitude of power is no chimerical suggestion. It is taken from fact: I will mention some instances. Mr. P, had one of these writs, & when Mr. Ware succeeded him, he indorsed his writ over to him (Mr. Ware): so that these writs are made negotiable from one officer to another, as Bills of Exchange are from one merchant to another. And thus your honours have no oppertunity to judge of the discretion of the person to whom this vast authority is delegated. Another instance is this. Mr. Justice Wally had called this same Mr. Ware before him by a constable to answer either for a breach of one of the sabbath day acts, or of the act against prophane swearing: And as soon as the justice had done, Mr. Ware asked him if he had done? the justice answered yes. Well then says Ware "now I will shew you a little of my power," I command you (whether it was by virtue of his indors'd writ of assistance or another I can't tell) to permit me to search your house for prohibited & uncustomed goods. And he went on first to search the house of the justice from the garret to the cellar: & then went & searched the constable's house in the same manner!

But to shew another absurdity & another instance in which the liberty of house will be totally destroyed by this writ, if it shou'd be established. I insist upon it that every private person by the 14 Car. 2 has as good a right to ask & receive writs of assistance as Custom-house officers have. The words of the act are, "it shall be lawful for *any* person or persons authorized & c." now what a scene does this open even supposing your Honours have a discretionary power to grant them to anybody that asks. And then every man that is prompted by revenge, ill humour, spite, curiosity, or even wantoness to examine the inside of his neighbours house will ask for a writ of assistance. Others must soon ask the same favour, out of self defence. And after a while we shall have every subject with a commission in his pockett, to search the house of every other subject; & authority to command the Aid of sheriffs, constables & all other subjects. One arbitrary application of such power will give a provocation to another till the whole society will be involved in tumult & in blood. This suggest to me another observation that must disgust these Gent. themselves. By this statute every private person, has as good a right to a writ of assistance, & to break & enter & seize as the Custom-house officers themselves. And if this writ shou'd be once established, private persons may hanker after the sweets of such power & such seizures, & taste them too as well as Custom house officers; an event that they will not rejoice at I believe. However this is only an argument *ad hominem* & they may take it as they please.

Another absurdity is the writ is without return. Now there is no such thing known in our Law as irreturnable writs. Writs are in their nature temporary things, not perpetual Edicts; They are issued for certain purposes & when these purposes are answered they exist no more. And there is no point more settled than this, if an officer will justify under a writ he must return it. 12th Mod. 396 cited from Viner. Now suppose a custom house officer with a writ in his pocket should command a sheriff to assist him in breaking a house. The owner of the house brings an action of Trespass against the sheriff. How can he justify? can he justify by virtue of a writ in the custom house officer's pocket, which he never saw perhaps which he certainly never returned.

Thus I think that reason & the British constitution are both against this writ. I shall now inquire what authority there is for it.

No more than one precedent can be found in the whole body of Law Books of such a writ, and that was published in the very zenith of arbitrary power in the reign of Charles 2d. when Star Chamber powers & all other but lawful & useful powers were pushed to extremity, by some ignorant clerk of the Exchequer. It has an Imprimatur it is true, but what authority is that? Your Honours know, that the Imprimatur of one Judge may be obtained & often has been obtained to very scurrilous performances, & has been given perhaps without reading any more of the Book than one or two of his own favourite resolutions.

But had the writ been in any Book whatever, it wou'd have been illegal. No Precedents, no authority whatever could justify your Honours in granting this writ. All precedents are under the control of the principles of Law. And if any rule or form has by inadvertancy or by the inadvertancy or corruption of Princes or Judges or Parliaments crept in, that is repugnant to the known maxims & Principles of Law, it is void & must be renounced as soon as possible. Ld. Talbot says "it is better to observe the known principles of Law, than any one precedent, tho' in the house of Lords, which is the last & highest resort of the subject.["]

The acts of Parliament that have been cited are so far from authorizing your Honours to grant it, that no act of parliament could establish such a writ. If an act of Parliament should be made in the very words of this petition, that Tho. Lechmere & oth.s should be furnished with a writ of assistance, in the words of this writ, it wou'd be void, & this court, the executive courts must pass all such acts into disuse. An act against the constitution is void. 8 Rep. 118. from Viner. an act against natural equity is void & c.

And with all due regard to precedents, authorities, parliaments & positive institutions of every kind, one good reason is a better foundation for any court or private person to build on, than all the learning of that kind that ever was wrote.

The parliament of England has treated her plantations with more rigour than was perhaps needful. The restrictions laid upon us have been vastly severe—so severe that a Noble Lord who it seems *had* some

feeling for us, was heard to say, of the rigid prohibitions of iron manufactures here, that he wondered they did not by an act of parliament oblige
us to send our horses across the atlantic to be shorn. They seem to have
considered us as a kind of cattle, not intitled to the common privileges of
humanity, or at least as savages with neither the understanding nor the
feeling of civilized nations:—They have bound us with acts of trade that
are every one of them inconsistent with common right & that nothing
but absolute necessity can justify. And they send over unto us officers to
inspect our trade & collect the customs, who seem to consider us in the
same light as a people without sense or resentment. They assume important airs & pretend to high powers & vast authority. They are the representatives of royal majesty. The management of the sacred, important
revenue is in their hands. They are to be feared & reverenced. We to be
dispised & trampled on, tamely suffering the worst of insolence. As if a
birth or a year's residence in England had given them all knowledge &
all power: & as if a birth & education in this country, had deprived us of
human senses. But it is high time that they in England & their emissaries
here, know that we have at least the sense of feeling: That we know a little
both of natural justice & common law. We have the same Books & the
same order of Ideas, excepting the common differences between man &
man, in New England as they have in old. And for my own part who know
of no title to respect in any man but what his understanding & goodness
give him, I never will regard an old Englishman—no nor a custom house
officer, without either of those titles to respect, at all the more, for the
place of his birth, or the office he sustains.

The other acts of parliament prove no more than what I have once
& again conceded—that special writs may be granted upon oath made
& probable suspicion. That of the 7th & 8th Wm. 3rd "That the officers
of the revenue in the plantations shall have the same powers with those
in England & the like assistance," I suppose intended that whenever any
officer suspected uncustomed or prohibited goods to be concealed in any
house, or warehouse, or cellar, or any other particular place he should
repair to a court, or some magistrate & make oath & shew his grounds
of suspicion; & that if such magistrate shou'd think those grounds

probable, he shou'd grant a writ or warrant to the sheriff or constable inhabiting near the suspected place to search that place. And that of the 6th of Anne which continues all legal processes, & writs of assistants among the rest—can prove no more. And it is happy they do not: For the power that is peti[ti]oned for wou'd at this day be very dangerous to use. Liberty is dear to Englishmen. They had rather you shou'd take their lives. And if any officer (whether without or with a writ of assistants shou'd break & enter the house of an innocent person, or a fair trader it wou'd be odds if violence shou'd not be repelled by violence, for it is in vain to think of enslaving Englishmen at the present day. This power of entering houses has been at all times odious to Britons, and an attempt to enable Excisemasters to enter (as this writ wou'd enable custom house officers to enter) in order to find uncustomed tobacco, begun & pushed with some zeal by a late great personage, gave occasion to the odium that at last wrought his ruin.

APPENDIX 2

Recent and Ongoing Supreme Court Cases That Would Benefit from an Accurate Historical Reconstruction of the American State of Nature Discourse

On June 26, 2015 the Supreme Court of the United States issued its decision in *Obergefell v Hodges* concerning same-sex marriage. The plaintiffs argued that the refusal of state agencies in Ohio, Michigan, Kentucky, and Tennessee to recognize same-sex marriage violated the Equal Protection Clause and the Due Process Clause of the Fourteenth Amendment. One group of plaintiffs brought claims under the Civil Rights Act as well. The Supreme Court ruled in favor of the plaintiffs with a five-to-four majority, with Chief Justice Roberts and Justices Scalia, Thomas, and Alito dissenting. Roberts argued that the matter was beyond the Court's purview and that the plaintiffs' case depended on an overly expansive reading of the Due Process and Equal Protection Clauses. Scalia wrote that the majority opinion usurped legislative powers to the Court and that same-sex marriage should be left to the state legislatures and federally to the democratic process. Similarly, Alito noted that the issue should be left to the states and that the majority opinion expanded the Court's power at the detriment of the democratic process, because the Constitution does not address same-sex marriage. Thomas made the same points and added a historical analysis to show that the "liberty" in the Fifth and Fourteenth Amendments refers not to rights to government-provided entitlements, but to the rights to the means available to individuals to protect themselves from physical restraint and government intervention. Scalia joined in this dissent.

Justice Thomas's dissent in *Obergefell v Hodges* is one of many cases that could serve as a useful starting point to survey recent references to the state of nature, because it turns on an ill-framed dichotomy between individual liberty in the state of nature and government-provided rights. Justice Thomas's thesis is that "in the American legal tradition, liberty has long been understood as individual freedom *from* governmental action, not as a right *to* a particular governmental entitlement." In support, Thomas cites Bailyn's argument in *The Ideological Origins* that Locke had a tremendous influence on early revolutionary ideology. Next, Thomas cites section 4 of Locke's *Second Treatise*, on the state of nature. This is not in Bailyn; it is Thomas who adds the state of nature to Bailyn's point about Locke's impact. His next move is to show that Locke's state of nature is the chief foundation of the American view of liberty and "permeated the 18th-century political scene in America." For this, Thomas cites a May 10, 1756 *Boston Gazette* editorial on everyone giving up a small share of natural liberty to the public only in order to enjoy the rest of their natural liberty in peace.

Clarence Thomas is sometimes presented as the most conservative justice in decades and more originalist than Scalia was.[1] Nonetheless, his dissent captures a currently typical view, prominent among conservatives as well as liberals, namely that the American notion of liberty revolves around the individual. The first English settlers were self-sufficient and self-legitimizing individuals who left England because they were denied

---

1. E.g., Jan Crawford Greenburg, *Supreme Conflict: The Inside Story of the Struggle for Control of the United States Supreme Court* (Penguin, 2008); Jeffrey Toobin, "Clarence Thomas Has His Own Constitution," *New Yorker,* June 30, 2016.

1083 to defend the state's expansion of the scope of the burglary law. In the 2009 *US v. Rivera-Oros*, 590 F. 3d 1123, the Tenth Circuit Court of Appeals used the Blackstone passage on the state of nature right to residence, and the consequent weight of burglary in common law, to distinguish between the modern, more extensive meaning of burglary, and burglary of a dwelling, which "causes psychological harm that cannot be measured solely in terms of the value of lost property."

The American constitutional tradition on parenthood tends to quote Locke's *Second Treatise*, section 71, according to which parents, even if members of the polity, retain as much right to their children's obedience as if they were still all in a state of nature. In the 2011 *In re JE*, 711 SE 2d 5, the Georgia Court of Appeals traced this "fundamental constitutional right to familial relations with their natural-born children" from Locke and Blackstone, through James Kent and St. George Tucker, to several US Supreme Court decisions, before it affirmed a juvenile court's decision to terminate a mother's parental rights. It did so again in a 2015 custody dispute, *Brawner v. Miller*, 778 SE 2d 839. New scholarly literature on the state of nature rights of parents should continue to enrich these judicial applications. For instance, Henry Stebbing's 1754 *Enquiry into the Force and Operation of the Annulling Clause* argued that parents have a state of nature right to disinherit children who marry against the parents' will and that civil laws should support this right. At the same time, the children have a state of nature right to marry whom they wish—and civil laws should support this right as well.[3]

The series of contradictory rulings between 2001 and 2016 by the Oregon Supreme Court concerning the cap on remedy for injury illustrates particularly well the need for a clarification of what the founding

---

3. Stebbing, *Enquiry*, 11. An excellent discussion of the political context and responses to Stebbing, which delved deeper into the state of nature, can be found in Brewer, *By Birth or Consent*, 316–22, in a context relevant to American constitutional interpretation. Also see Henry Dagge's popular *Considerations on Criminal Law* (London, 1772), Book I, chapter 7, section 2. Dagge surveys the intellectual history of the state of nature from Grotius and Hobbes through Locke and Pufendorf to Montesquieu (22–25), before developing his own system throughout the book.

generation meant by the "state of nature" and how they used it to develop constitutional arguments for independence, statehood, and new federal and state authority. Recognizing this aspect of the American state of nature discourse suggests that the Oregon Supreme Court was wrong in the May 2016 *Horton v. OHSU* to overturn the voidance of financial caps on remedy. To do this, the *Horton* court had to overturn several verdicts, starting with *Smothers v. Gresham Transfer*, 332 Or. 83 (2001). Terry Smothers, a technician for a trucking company, suffered lung damage from chemical fumes and mist. When his compensation claim was denied, Smothers invoked the remedy clause of the Oregon Constitution.

The Oregon Supreme Court agreed. In interpreting the remedy clause in section 10 of Oregon's Bill of Rights, which is Article I of the Oregon Constitution, the court sought to reconstruct the meaning of "remedy" by going back to Magna Carta, Coke's *Institutes*, and the early modern revival of natural law as the source of judicial review based on the principle that statute law may not be contrary to natural law. Further, the court argued that *English Liberties*, discussed in section 5.2 of chapter 5, was a major conduit in the American reception of Magna Carta and Coke's *Institutes*, and cited chapter 29 of *English Liberties* on remedy. Blackstone's distinction between absolute rights in the state of nature and relative rights in society is another such conduit and influence. Remedy is the legal method for redressing violations of rights, and civil or common laws are meaningless without remedial provisions. According to the *Smothers* court, when they developed an independent American legal system, John Adams and other Founders relied on common law as much as on natural law and adopted the notion of absolute rights, "including those respecting person, property, reputation, and liberty." The remedy clauses of state constitutions, including Oregon's, are based on this lineage.

A considerable portion of Oregon remedy disputes are decided in relation to *Smothers*. In the 2005 *Lawson v. Hoke*, 119 P. 3d 210, decision, Justice De Muniz dissented from the Oregon Supreme Court's decision because it was not as historically thorough as *Smothers* and failed to adequately construe the absolute rights that the plaintiff, an uninsured motorist injured in an accident, would have had in the state of nature. Interestingly, in the 2006 case of *Liberty Northwest Insurance Corp. v. Oregon Insurance Guarantee Association*, the Oregon Court of Appeals, with Landau presiding, Liberty invoked the *Smothers* decision to argue that the right of subrogation can be traced back to Magna Carta. The court doubted that the Oregon Supreme Court in *Smothers* was right to establish the Oregon Constitution's original intent based on Magna Carta, Henry Care (the supposed author of *English Liberties*), and Blackstone; but in any case, since only natural persons can have rights in the state of nature, *Smothers* would not help Liberty, the corporate plaintiff.

In 2013, *Klutschowski v. PeaceHealth* came before the Oregon Supreme Court, concerning a cap on non-economic damages in a case for personal injuries that a child sustained during birth. Again, the case hinged on the correct interpretation of the 1857 Constitution. The Supreme Court overturned the Court of Appeals' reversal of the trial court that removed the cap, partly because the baby's head had been already delivered at the time of injury, and it was impossible to say whether he was "part of his mother" or sufficiently separated to allow both mother and child to sue for damages, in effect doubling the cap. In a concurrent opinion, Justice Landau agreed with removing the cap. He also systematically deconstructed the textualist interpretation and method used by the Oregon Supreme Court. He characterized the "hyper-originalism" in *Smothers* as "untenable," partly because "there is little evidence that the framers of the Oregon Constitution intended that their intentions or understandings would be forever controlling." Moreover, Landau added a long section disputing the *Smothers* interpretation of Blackstone. According to Landau, Blackstone's absolute rights apply only in the state of nature and could be curtailed or otherwise regulated by Parliament. Landau misread Blackstone here. Relative, not absolute, rights cannot be curtailed by Parliament. Put differently, when absolute rights are curtailed, they are already relative. Moreover, in a section Landau ignores, Blackstone explains that absolute rights in the state of nature set the standard of personal liberty that the state should aim to approximate.

In a dramatic twist, the 2016 *Horton* court adopted Landau's retort to *Smothers* and applied it to the opposite effect of Landau's concurrence, namely to undo the Oregon Supreme Courts' several decisions removing the cap on remedy.

> To the extent that *Smothers* found in the word "absolute" the idea that Blackstone viewed absolute rights as immune from alteration, *Smothers* appears to have misperceived what Blackstone said. Blackstone used the phrase "absolute rights" to refer to a person's rights in a state of nature. Blackstone, 1 *Commentaries* at 121. He explained, however, that absolute rights are not absolute. Rather, "every man, when he enters into society, gives up a part of his natural liberty, as the price of so valuable a purchase; and, in consideration of receiving the advantages of mutual commerce, obliges himself to conform to those laws, which the community has thought proper to establish."

The *Smothers* interpretation of Blackstone is historically more accurate, but the Court's interpretation in both 2001 and 2016 overestimated Blackstone's impact. The Revolution overturned the common law insofar as it refused to recognize the source, authority, and institutions of the common law. When the body of the common law continued to be used, the states revised it as and when they thought fit, and looked to texts such as Blackstone's for guidance rather than for authority. Moreover, as shown in this book, reactions against Blackstone were at least as important in the American reception as adaptations. Finally, Blackstone's doctrine that the best state is the one that best protects absolute rights, which one finds in the state of nature, served to create a rights tradition during the American Founding that was unlike the English tradition, as shown by texts including the Boston Pamphlet, in which absolute rights survive the transition to the polity and cannot be as easily abrogated as the *Horton* court suggests.

BIBLIOGRAPHY

MANUSCRIPTS

John Adams, annotations in his copy of Montesquieu, *The Spirit of Laws* (London, 1752), Massachusetts Historical Society, Special Collections, John Adams Annotated Books.

John Adams, annotations in his copy of John James Rousseau [*sic*], *A Discourse upon the Origin and Foundation of the Inequality among Mankind* (London, 1761), Boston Public Library.

John Adams, annotations in *True Sentiments of America* (1768), Stone Library, Adams 8526.

John Adams, unpublished Novanglus essay, c. 1775, William Cushing Family Papers, Massachusetts Historical Society Ms. N-67.

John Adams, annotations in his copy of Thomas Whately, *Observations on Modern Gardening, Illustrated by Descriptions* (London, 1777), Boston Public Library, Adams 290.9.

John Adams, copies and objects in his copies of Blackstone, *Commentaries*. 1771 Philadelphia edition: Boston Public Library, Adams 151.19. 1768–70 Oxford edition: Boston Public Library, Adams 93.2.

John Quincy Adams, *The Jubilee of the Constitution: A Discourse Delivered at the Request of the New York Historical Society, in the City of New York, on Tuesday, the 30th of April, 1839; Being the Fiftieth Anniversary of the Inauguration of George Washington as President of the United States, on Thursday, the 30th of April, 1789* (New York, 1839).

Samuel Adams Papers, New York Public Library, MssCol 20, http://archives.nypl.org/mss/20#detailed.

Samuel Adams, draft of the Boston Committee's March 23, 1773, letter to Governor Hutchinson. Boston Public Library, MS G.41.23.

Nathaniel Ames, Jr., annotations in John Locke, *An Essay . . .* (Boston, 1773), Library Company of Philadelphia, Am 1773 Loc 67121.O.

John Andrew and James Allen, Student lecture notes, 1756. Archives of the University of Pennsylvania, UPA 3, Box 23, Folder 1642.

Anon., annotations in [Henry Care?], *English Liberties* (London, 1680), Harvard Law School, Historical & Special Collections, E C271e 680 Copy 2.

Anon., annotations in [Henry Care?], *English Liberties* (London, 1680), Virginia Historical Society, JN 203 1680 C21.

Anon., annotations in John Locke, *Two Treatises* (London, 1764), Dartmouth College, Rauner Woodward Room, 78.

Anon., "Arguments in the case of ship money" (1637), Harvard Law School MSS HLS MS 141.

Anthony Bacon, handwritten dedication to [Jonathan Boucher?] in Bacon, *A Short Address to the Government* . . . (London, 1775), Bodleian Library, http://solo.bodleian.ox.ac.uk/OXVU1:LSCOP_OX:oxfaleph013526220.

Ebenezer Baldwin, Student notes, Yale University Archives, Baldwin Family Papers, MS 55. Box 63, Folder 818.

Barnabas Binney, Valedictorian oration at Rhode-Island College, 1774. John Carter Brown Library, D774 B614o 1-Size.

Abijah Bisco, Student papers, 1795–1798, Dartmouth College, Rauner Library, MS 003125.

Boston Committee of Correspondence records, NYPL MssCol 343.

George Chalmers, Letter to Lord Mansfield, John Carter Brown Library, Codex Eng=150.

[Francis Dana Channing?], annotations in *English Liberties* (Philadelphia, 1721), Houghton *EC65 C1803 680eh.

Chelmsford, *General Records and Assessments*, Book I (1770–79), https://archive.org/details/generalrecordsas1770chel.

Benjamin Chew, legal notes, Historical Society of Pennsylvania, Chew Family Papers, Collection 2050, series 2, section E, Box 16.

John Cleaveland Papers, January 1, 1776, draft letter to Mr. Hall, signed Johannes in Eremo. Congregational Library and Archives, Correspondence, 1758–76, 116–23.

Commencement Collection, Archives of the University of Pennsylvania, UPA 3, Box 30.

Commencement parts records, Dartmouth College Archives, Rauner Library, DA-43.

Commencement Theses, Quaestiones, and Orders of Exercises, 1642–1818. Harvard University Archives, HUC 6642.

Copies and Extracts of all Such Papers and Letters Transmitted to the Council Office as Relate to Riots in America in Opposition to the Putting in Execution the Stamp Act . . . Likewise Copies of all Orders and Issued from the Council, Huntington Library, mssHM 1947.

Thomas Cushing, Letters to John Cushing. January 28, 1766, and February 4, 1766. Massachusetts Historical Society, William Cushing Papers, Ms. N-1069.

Dana Family Papers, Ms. N-1088, Box 34, Massachusetts Historical Society.

Silas Deane, February 7, 1774, Letter to William Samuel Johnson. Connecticut Historical Society, William Samuel Johnson Papers, Series 2, Subseries 1, Box 6, Folder 13.

Silas Deane Papers, Connecticut Historical Society, Ms Deans1789, Box 7, Folder 36.

Harbottle Dorr Jr. annotations in newspapers, 1765–1776. Massachusetts Historical Society, http://www.masshist.org/dorr/.

Solomon Drowne, Diaries, John Hay Library, Ms. Drowne Papers 1767–1792, Box 24.

Early Yale Documents, Beinecke Rare Book & Manuscript Library, GEN MSS 856.

Bryan Edwards, *Notes on Long's Jamaica*, after 1774. John Carter Brown Library, Codex Eng 87.

Charles J. Faulkner, annotations in Henry St. George Tucker, *Commentaries on Blackstone's Commentaries, for the Use of Students* (Winchester, 1826), Virginia Historical Society, K 50 B57 T79 1826.

Timothy Field, 1797 English Oration. Yale, Manuscripts and Archives, College Commencement Orations and Poems, RU 140, Box 4, Folder 35.

Benjamin Franklin, annotations in John Locke, *Two Treatises* . . . (London, 1764), Library Company of Philadelphia, Ii Lock Log. 1457.O (Mackenzie).

Ebenezer Garnsey, Job Wright, and John Pell, annotations in *English Liberties* (Philadelphia, 1721), Yale, Beinecke, Franklin 391.1721c.

General Assembly of the Province of the Massachusetts Bay, Letter to Dennys DeBerdt, March 16, 1767. Houghton, Arthur Lee Papers, bMS Am 811, 33–35.

General Assembly of the Province of the Massachusetts Bay, August 3, 1770, Draft Reply to Governor Hutchinson, Boston Public Library, MS G.41.22.

George III, "History of Tenures," Royal Collection Trust, RA GEO ADDL MSS 32, 960.

George III, "Of Laws Relative to Government in General." Royal Collection Trust, RA GEO ADDL MSS 32, 1072.

George III, "A Short Abridgment of Mr Blackstone's Commentaries on the Laws of England," Royal Collection Trust, RA GEO/32.

Great Britain, Privy Council, 1764–65 Copies of Papers Transmitted. Huntington, HM 2587.

Simon Greenleaf, *Lawyer's Commonplace Book*, Harvard Law School, Rare HLS MS 4440.

Joseph Hawley Papers, New York Public Library, MssCol 1360.

Thomas Hollis, annotations in William Petyt, *The Antient Right of the Commons of England Asserted* . . . (London, 1680), Houghton Br 143.2*.

Thomas Hollis, annotations in Robert Molesworth, *An Account of Denmark* . . . ([1694] London, 1738), Houghton *EC75.H7267.Zz738m.

Thomas Hollis, annotations in John Locke, *Two Treatises of Government* (London, 1764), Houghton *EC75.H7267.Zz764l Lobby IV.2.2.

Thomas Hollis, annotations in *The True Sentiments of America: Contained in a Collection of Letters Sent from the House of Representatives of the Province of Massachusetts Bay to Several Persons of High Rank in this Kingdom: Together with Certain Papers relating to a Supposed Libel on the Governor of that Province, and a Dissertation on the Canon and the Feudal Law* (London, 1768), Houghton AC7.M382G.768t (B).

"JH" from New York, June 27, 1767, Letter. American Philosophical Society, Sol Feinstone Collection, Mss. B.F.327, No. 1312.

William Samuel Johnson, January 23, 1768, letter to Jedediah Elderkin. NYPL, Thomas Addis Emmet collection, MssCol 927, EM187, http://archives.nypl.org/mss/927#detailed.

William Samuel Johnson Papers, Connecticut Historical Society, ms 22977.

Samuel Jones, *Book of Metaphysics, 1760.* Archives of the University of Pennsylvania, UPA 3, Box 25, Folder 1645.

Samuel Jones, *Chart of the Divisions of Moral Philosophy into Law, Rights, Property and Contracts, 1761.* Archives of the University of Pennsylvania, UPA 3, Box 25, Folder 1646.

William Kempe, [1754?] Letter, Massachusetts Historical Society, Sedgwick Family Papers, Ms. N-851, series XII, section D, Box 115.

James Kent, [1790?], Manuscript Notes on John Adams, *A Defence of the Constitutions,* New York Society Library.

William Kinnersley, *Lectures on Moral Philosophy, 1759.* Archives of the University of Pennsylvania, UPA 3, Box 26, Folder 1647.

James Madison, Drafts, University of Chicago, Regenstein Library Special Collections, George Nicholas Papers, Folder 31.

James Madison, Record of James Wilson's February 13, 1776 Draft of Congress' Address to American Citizens, in Library of Congress, *James Madison Papers: Series 7, Addenda, 1744–1845; 1979 to 1985 Addition; Part B, copies and abstracts; Photocopies; Notes on confederation and federal governments.* Manuscript/Mixed Material, www.loc.gov/item/mss31021a014/.

Edward Marrett, Diary, 1753, 1764–73. Houghton Library, MS Am 1171.

Henry McCulloh, *General Thoughts, Endeavoring to Demonstrate that the Legislature here . . . Have a Right to Tax the British Colonies.* Huntington Library, mssHM 1480.

Joseph Nancrede, Letters to John Wheelock, 1800–1802, Dartmouth College, Rauner 800378.

George Nicholas Papers, University of Chicago, Regenstein Library, Reuben T. Durrett Collection of George Nicholas Papers.

James Otis, Jr., annotations in Thomas Wood, *An Institute of the Laws of England* (London, 1734), Harvard Law School MSS Small Manuscript Collection.

Theodore Parsons and Eliphalet Pearson, *Forensic Dispute between Theodore Parsons & Eliphalet Pearson: Manuscript, 1773.* Houghton GEN MS Am 1423.

Richard Peters to John Adams, June 15, 1789. Massachusetts Historical Society, Adams-Hull Collection, Ms N-1776, Box 1, Folder 37.

Richard Peters to Jasper Yeates, November 26, 1765. Historical Society of Pennsylvania, Jasper Yeates Papers, Collection 0740, Box 7, Folder 2.

Thomas Pownall, Dedication in Pownall, *Principles of Polity* (London, 1752), Houghton, *EC75.P8758.752.p(A).

" 'The Republican' to the Freeholders and Inhabitants of New Hampshire," January 30, 1777. Dartmouth College, Rauner, MS 777130.

Benjamin Rush, Lectures, University of Chicago, Regenstein Library, Crerar Ms 277.

Jonathan Sayward, *Diaries,* American Antiquarian Society, Mss. Octavo Vols. S.

Frederick Smyth Papers, American Philosophical Society, Mss.B.Sm95.

Student Declamations, Yale University Archives, RU 145.

Oxenbridge Thacher, Papers, Massachusetts Historical Society, Ms N-1647.

Elisha Thayer, Legal Manuscript. American Philosophical Society, Sol Feinstone Collection #1045 Mss. B. F327.

George Ticknor, 1816–17 Student Notebooks from Göttingen. Dartmouth College, Rauner, MS 983, esp. Box 5, Folder 4: *Spirit of the Times,* and Box 5, Folder 7: *Progress of Politicks or History of the Theory of Constitutions.*

Edmund Trowbridge, October 15, 1771, Letter to William Bollan, Massachusetts Historical Society, Ms. S-813.

Henry St. George Tucker, Sr., annotations in William Blackstone, *Commentaries on the Laws of England* (London, 1791), Harvard Law School, Rare Treatises, B.

St. George Tucker, June 30, 1797, Letter to Prof. Christoph Daniel Ebeling, via William Bentley, Houghton GEN MS Am 1855.

Evert Wendell, annotations in Thomas Wood, *An Institute of the Laws of England* (London, 1724), author's copy.

Bezaleel Woodward, Valedictory Discourse, April 19, 1772, Rauner, Dartmouth College Archives, MS 772269.

Yale Student Disputations from 1809, Yale University Archives, Jonathan Lee Papers, ms 958, Series III, Box 9, Folder 126.

Yale Theses, Connecticut Historical Society, Yale Ephemera, Oversize.

Jasper Yeates, "A Brief Compendium of the Law of Nature, with Politicks & Oeconomicks" (1760), University of Pennsylvania, Kislak Library Special Collections, Ms Coll. 600.

PRINTED WORKS

Abingdon Resolves, April 2, 1770, *Boston Gazette. Political Register* 7 (1770), 37–39.

John Adams, "Notes on the Opening of the Courts, 19 December 1765," *Founders Online*, http://founders.archives.gov/documents/Adams/06-01-02-0059.

John Adams, *Dissertation on the Canon and Feudal Law* (orig. 1765, first published under this title in *The True Sentiments of America*, London, 1768).

John Adams, in the February 1, 1773, *Boston Gazette*.

John Adams, Novanglus III, February 6, 1773, *Boston Gazette*.

John Adams, "Charles Phelps' State of His Case, March–May 1774," *Founders Online*, National Archives, last modified March 30, 2017, http://founders.archives.gov/documents/Adams/06-02-02-0007-0002.

John Adams, *Thoughts on Government, Applicable to the Present State of the American Colonies. In a Letter from a Gentleman to His Friend* (Philadelphia, 1776).

John Adams, *A Defence of the Constitutions of Government of the United States of America* (London, 1787–88).

John Adams and Daniel Leonard, *Novanglus, and Massachusettensis: Or, Political Essays, Published in the Years 1774 and 1775, on the Principal Points of Controversy, Between Great Britain and Her Colonies. The former by John Adams, later President of the United States. The latter by Jonathan Sewall, then King's Attorney General of the Province of Massachusetts Bay. To which are added a number of letters, lately written by President Adams to the Honourable William Tudor; some of which were never before published* (Boston, 1819).

John Adams, *Works*, vols. 1–10, ed. Charles Francis Adams (Boston, 1850–56).

John Adams, Samuel Adams, and James Warren, *Warren-Adams Letters. Being Chiefly a Correspondence among John Adams, Samuel Adams, and James Warren* (Boston, 1917–25).

John Adams, *Diary and Autobiography*, ed. L. H. Butterfield, Leonard C. Faber and Wendell D. Garrett, vol. 1 (Belknap, 1961).

John Adams, *Papers*, vol. 1, *September 1755–October 1773*, ed. Robert J. Taylor (Harvard, 1977).

John Adams, Adams Papers, Digital Collection, Massachusetts Historical Society, http://www.masshist.org/publications/adams-papers/.

John Adams, *The Revolutionary Writings*, ed. C. Bradley Thompson (Liberty Fund, 2000).

Samuel Adams, *An Address to the Inhabitants of the Province of Massachusetts Bay* (Boston, 1747).

[Samuel Adams?], *An Appeal to the World; or A Vindication of the Town of Boston, from Many False and Malicious Aspersions Contain'd in Certain Letters and Memorials, Written by Governor Bernard, General Gage, Commodore Hood, the Commissioners of the American Board of Customs, and Others, and by Them Respectively Transmitted to the British Ministry* (Boston, 1769).

Samuel Adams (Vindex), article in January 21, 1771, *Boston Gazette*.

Samuel Adams (Candidus), article in January 20, 1772, *Boston Gazette*.

Samuel Adams, *Writings*, ed. Harry A. Cushing (New York, 1904–8).

John R. Alden, *Stephen Sayre: American Revolutionary Adventurer* (Louisiana State University, 1983).

John K. Alexander, *Samuel Adams: The Life of an American Revolutionary* (Rowman & Littlefield, 2011).

Johannes Althusius, *Politica, Methodice Digesta et Exemplis Ssacris et Profanis Illustrata: cui in Fine Adjuncta est Oratio Panegyrica de Utilitate, Necessitate & Antiquitate Scholarum* (Herborn, 1603). Abridged and translated by Frederick S. Carney (1964, Liberty Fund, 1995).

Nathaniel Ames, Sr., *An Astronomical Diary: or, Almanack for the Year of our Lord Christ, 1764. . . . Calculated for the Meridian of Boston, New-England* (Boston, 1763).

Anon., "Touching the Fundamentall Lawes, or Politique Constitution of this Kingdome . . ." (London, 1643), in Joyce Lee Malcolm, ed., *The Struggle for Sovereignty: Seventeenth-Century English Political Tracts* (Liberty, 1999), 1:261–79.

Anon., March 2, 1765, *Providence Gazette* article against Otis.

Anon., December 30, 1765, *Supplement to the Boston Evening-Post*.

Anon., August 22, 1768, *Connecticut Courant* article against capital punishment. Anon. reply, October 14, 1768, *Connecticut Journal*.

Anon, December 17, 1773, article in the *Connecticut Journal* on slavery.

Anon., article in the April 7, 1774, *London Gazetteer*.

Anon., "A Few Reflections and Hints Concerning American Affairs," August 22, 1774, *Newport Mercury*.

Anon., March 12, 1776, no. LXI issue of *The Crisis*.

Anon., ed., *A Collection of Interesting, Authentic Papers, Relative to the Dispute between Great Britain and America: Shewing the Course and Progress of that Misunderstanding, from 1764–1775* (London, 1777).

Anon., *The Ground and Nature of Christian Redemption* (Philadelphia, 1768).

Anon. [Israel Mauduit?], *A Short View of the History of the Colony of Massachusetts Bay* (London, 1769).

Anon., *A Supplement to Mr. Wesley's Pamphlet Entitled Thoughts upon Slavery* (London, 1774).

Anon., *Taxation, Tyranny. Addressed to Samuel Johnson, L.L.D.* (London, 1775).

Anon., *The Reply of a Gentleman in a Select Society, upon the Important Contest between Great Britain and America* (London, 1775).

Anon., *Omiah's Farewell; Inscribed to the Ladies of London* (London, 1776).

Anon., *The Political Mirror. By a Student of the Inner Temple* (London, 1776), in William Moore, ed., *The Crisis* (London, 1775–76).

Thomas Aquinas, *Summa Theologiae* [1265–74], excerpts in Aquinas, *On Law, Morality, and Politics*, ed. William P. Baumgarth and Richard J. Regan (Hackett, 1988).

Anthony Ascham, *Of the Confusions and Revolutions of Government . . .* (London, 1648).

Jan Assmann, *Moses the Egyptian: The Memory of Egypt in Western Monotheism* (Harvard, 1997).

Isaac Backus, *An Appeal to the Public for Religious Liberty, Against the Oppressions of the Present Day* (Boston, 1773).

Anthony Bacon, *A Short Address to the Government, the Merchants, Manufacturers, and the Colonists in America, and the Sugar Islands, on the Present State of Affairs. By a Member of Parliament* (London, 1775).

Francis Bacon, *An Advertisement Touching an Holy Warre*, in Bacon, *Certaine Miscellany Works*, ed. William Rawley (London, 1629), 77–184. New ed. and introduction by Laurence Lampert, in Francis Bacon, *An Advertisement Touching a Holy War* (Waveland, 2000).

Bernard Bailyn, *The Ideological Origins of the American Revolution* (Belknap, 1967; enlarged edition 1992).

Bernard Bailyn, *The Ordeal of Thomas Hutchinson* (Belknap, 1974).

Jack M. Balkin and Sanford Levinson, "The Dangerous Thirteenth Amendment," *Columbia Law Review* 112 (2012), 1459–99.

Jean Barbeyrac, notes in Hugo Grotius, *De jure belli ac pacis libri tres, in quibus jus naturæ & gentium, item juris publici præcipua explicantur. Cum annotatis auctoris, ejusdemque dissertatione De mari libero; ac libello singular De æquitate, indulgentia, & facilitate* (Amsterdam, 1720).

Jean Barbeyrac, notes in Hugo Grotius, *Le Droit de la Guerre, et de la Paix* (tr. Barbeyrac, Amsterdam, 1724).

Joel Barlow, *A Letter to the National Convention of France, on the Defects in the Constitution of 1791, and the Extent of the Amendments Which Ought to be Applied. To which is added The Conspiracy of Kings, a poem* (New York, 1793).

Cesare Beccaria, *Dei Delitti e Delle Pene* (Livorno, 1764, tr. as *An Essay on Crimes and Punishments*, London, 1767).

Carl L. Becker, *The Declaration of Independence* (New York, 1922).

James B. Bell, *A War of Religion: Dissenters, Anglicans and the American Revolution* (New York, 2008).

Leland J. Bellot, *William Knox. The Life and Thought of an Eighteenth-Century Imperialist* (University of Texas, 1977).

Anthony Benezet, *A Short Account of That Part of Africa, Inhabited by the Negroes: With Respect to the Fertility of the Country; The Good Disposition of Many of the Natives, and the Manner by Which the Slave Trade Is Carried On. Extracted from divers authors, in order to shew the iniquity of that trade, and the falsity of the arguments usually advanced in its vindication. With quotations from the Writings of several persons of note, viz. George Wallis, Francis Hutcheson, and James Foster, and a large extract from a pamphlet, lately published in London, on the subject of the slave trade* (Philadelphia, 1762).

Francis Bernard, *Select Letters on the Trade and Government of America* (London, 2nd ed., 1774).

Randall P. Bezanson, *Taxes on Knowledge in America* (University of Pennsylvania, 1994).

Mary Sarah Bilder, *Madison's Hand: Revising the Constitutional Convention* (Harvard, 2015).

Sylvester H. Bingham, "Publishing in the Eighteenth Century with Special Reference to the Firm of Edward and Charles Dilly," PhD diss., Yale, 1937.

William Blackstone, *An Analysis of the Laws of England* (Oxford, 1756).

William Blackstone, *Law Tracts, in Two Volumes* (Oxford, 1762).

William Blackstone, *Commentaries on the Laws of England* (Oxford, 1765–69).

Richard Bland, *An Inquiry into the Rights of the British Colonies* (Williamsburg, 1766).

Samuel Bochart, *Hierozoicon, sive bipertitum opus du animalibus Sacrae Scripturae* (London, 1663).

Peter de Bolla, *The Architecture of Concepts: The Historical Formation of Human Rights* (Fordham, 2013).

Colin Bonwick, *English Radicals and the American Revolution* (University of North Carolina, 1977).

Thomas Boston, *Human Nature in Its Fourfold State of Primitive Integrity, Entire Depravity, Begun Recovery, and Consummate Happiness or Misery; Subsisting in the Parents of Mankind in Paradise, the Unregenerate, the Regenerate, All Mankind in the Future State; in Several Practical Discourses* (Edinburgh, 1720, with editions in 1730, 1735, 1744, 1753, 1756, 1759, 1761, 1763, 1767, 1760, 1770, 1771, 1772, New York in 1811, etc.).

"Boston Pamphlet." *The Votes and Proceedings of the Freeholders and Other Inhabitants of the Town of Boston, in Town Meeting Assembled, According to Law: To which is Prefixed, as Introductory, an Attested Copy of a Vote of the Town at a Preceding Meeting* (Boston, 1772).

James Boswell, *The Life of Samuel Johnson, LL.D . . .*, vol. III ([1791] 8th ed., London, 1816).

Jonathan Boucher, *A Letter from a Virginian, to the Members of the Congress to be Held at Philadelphia, on the First of September, 1774* (Boston, 1774).

Louis Antoine de Bougainville, *Voyage Autour du Monde* (Paris, 1771).

William Boutcher, *A Treatise on Forest-Trees: Containing not only the Best Methods of their Culture hitherto Practised, but a Variety of New and Useful Discoveries, the Result of Many Repeated Experiment . . .* (Dublin, 1776).

James E. Bradley, *Religion, Revolution and English Radicalism: Non-Conformity in Eighteenth-Century Politics and Society* (Cambridge, 1990).

John Brand, *Observations on Some Probable Effects of Mr. Gilbert's Bill; to which are added remarks deduced from Dr. Price's Account of the national debt* (London, 1776).

Holly Brewer, *By Birth or Consent: Children, Law, and the Anglo-American Revolution in Authority* (University of North Carolina, 2005).

Carl Bridenbaugh, *Silas Downer, Forgotten Patriot: His Life and Writings* (Providence, RI, 1974).

Britannus Americanus in the March 17, 1766, *Boston Gazette*. Reprinted in Hyneman and Lutz, *American Political Writing*, I:88–91.

John Broughton, *A Defence of the Commonly-Received Doctrine of the Human Soul, as an Immaterial and Naturally-Immortal Principle in Man, against the Objections of Some Modern Writers: Including the True Scripture-Doctrine of Death, Life and Immortality, and of the Necessity and Extent of the Christian Redemption* (Bristol, 1766).

Ernest Francis Brown, *Joseph Hawley, Colonial Radical* (New York, 1931).

John Brown, *An Exposition of the Epistle of Paul the Apostle to the Romans: With Large Practical Observations* (Edinburgh, 1766).

Josiah Brown, *Reports of Cases, Upon Appeals and Writs of Error, in the High Court of Parliament; from the year 1701, to the year 1779* (London, 1779–83).

Richard D. Brown, "The Massachusetts Convention of Towns, 1768," *William and Mary Quarterly* 26:1 (1969), 94–104.

Richard D. Brown, *Revolutionary Politics in Massachusetts* (Harvard, 1970).

Jacob Bryant, *A New System, or, an Analysis of Ancient Mythology* (London, 1774–76).

Samuel Buell, *Narrative of the Remarkable Revival of Religion, in the Congregation of East-Hampton, on Long-Island, Part of the South Division of the Province of New-York: In the Year of our Lord 1764. With some Remarks* (Aberdeen, 1773).

John Bulkley, preface to Roger Wolcott, *Poetical Meditations, Being the Improvement of Some Vacant Hours* (New London, CT, 1765).

Glenn Burgess, *Absolute Monarchy and the Stuart Constitution* (Yale, 1996).

Alexander M. Burill, *A New Law Dictionary and Glossary: Containing Full Definitions of the Principal Terms of the Common and Civil Law: Together with Translations and Explanations of the Various Technical Phrases in Different Languages, Occurring in the Ancient and Modern Reports, and Standard Treatises, Embracing Also All the Principal Common and Civil Law Maxims: Compiled on the Basis of Spelman's Glossary, and Adapted to the Jurisprudence of the United States: with Copious Illustrations, Critical and Historical* (New York, 1850–51).

Edmund Burke, *Mr. Burke's Speech, on the 1st December 1783, upon the Question for the Speaker's Leaving the Chair, in Order for the House to Resolve itself into a Committee on Mr. Fox's East India Bill* (London, 1784).

Jean-Jacques Burlamaqui, *Principes du Droit Naturel* (Geneva, 1747).

Jean-Jacques Burlamaqui, *Principes du Droit Politique* (Amsterdam, 1751).

Jean-Jacques Burlamaqui, *The Principles of Natural and Politic Law* (tr. Thomas Nugent, London, 1763).

Jean-Jacques Burlamaqui, *The Principles of Natural and Politic Law* (tr. Thomas Nugent, ed. Peter Korkman, Indianapolis, IN: Liberty Fund, 2006).

James Burr, *Reports of Cases Adjudged in the Court of King's Bench since the Death of Lord Raymond* (London, 1766).

Richard L. Bushman, *King and People in Provincial Massachusetts* (University of North Carolina, 1985; 1992 paperback).

Lyman H. Butterfield, "The American Interests of the Firm E. and C. Dilly, with their Letters to Benjamin Rush, 1770–1795," *Papers of the Bibliographical Society of America*, 45 (1951), 283–332.

John Campbell, *A Political Survey of Britain: Being a Series of Reflections on the Situation, Lands, Inhabitants, Revenues, Colonies, and Commerce of this Island* (London, 1774).

Russell L. Caplan, *Constitutional Brinksmanship: Amending the Constitution by National Convention* (Oxford, 1988).

[Henry Care?], *English liberties, or, The free-born subject's inheritance: containing I. Magna Charta, the petition of right, the Habeas Corpus Act, and divers other most useful statutes ... II. The proceedings in appeals of murther the work and power of parliaments, the qualifications necessary for such as should be chosen to that great truth. Plain directions for all persons concerned in ecclesiastical courts, and how to prevent or take off the Writ de Excommunicats Capiendo. As also the oath and duty of grand and petty juries, III. All the laws against conventicles and Protestant dissenters, with notes and directions both to constables and others concern'd, thereupon: and an abstract of all the laws against Papists* (London, 1680).

[Henry Care?], *English liberties, or, The free-born subject's inheritance: containing, I. Magna Charta, the Habeas Corpus Act, and divers other most useful statutes: with large comments upon each of them. II. The proceedings in appeals of murther, the work and power of parliaments; the qualifications necessary for such as should be chosen to that great trust. Plain directions for all persons concerned in ecclesiastical courts; and how to prevent or take off the writ De Excommunicato Capiendo. As also the oath and duty of grand and petty juries, III. All the laws against conventicles and Protestant dissenters with notes, and directions both to constables and others concern'd, thereupon; and an abstract of all the laws against papists* (London, 1682).

[Henry Care?], *English liberties, or, The free-born subject's inheritance: I. Magna Charta, the petition of right, the habeas corpus act, &c. With comments upon each of them. The proceedings in appeals of murder; the work and power of parliaments, the qualifications necessary for such as should be chosen to that great trust. ... –II. Of justices of the peace; their oath, office, and power, in many respects; with several law-cases alphebetically digested for ease and brevity, ... – III. The coroner and constable's duty, relating to dead bodies, murder, man-slaughter, and felo-de-fe; arrests, escapes, and conservation of the peace. And lastly, the church-warden, overseer, and scavenger's duty at large, in the most necessary particulars. Now inlarged with new and useful additions by a well-wisher to his country* (London, 1700).

[Henry Care?], *English Liberties: or, the Free-Born Subject's Inheritance. Being a help to justices as well as a guide to constables. Containing, I. Magna Charta, the petition of right, The Habeas Corpus Act, &c. With Comments upon each of them. The Proceedings in Appeals of Murder; The Work and Power of Parliaments, the Qualifications necessary for such as should be Chosen to that great Trust. The Advantage Englishmen enjoy by Trials by Juries That they are Judges of Law as well as Fact; and are not Fineable, nor to be Punish'd, for going contrary to the Judges Directions. II. Of justices of the peace; their Oath, Office, and Power, in many Respects; With several Law-Cases Alphabetically Digested for Ease and brevity, and Warrants proper thereto. concluding with Directions for Drovers, Badgers, Butchers, Toll-Keepers, and Clerks of the Market, &c III. The coroner and constable's duty, Relating to Dead Bodies, Murder, Man-Slaughter, and Felo-de-se; Arreste, Escapes, and Conservation of the Peace, The Church Warden, Over Seer, and Scavenger's Duty at Large, in the most necessary Particulars. And Lastly, An Abstract of* the act now in force against Popery and Papists First compiled by Henry Care, and now inlarged with new and useful additions, by a wellwisher to his country. Dedicated to the Honourable House of Commons (London, 1703).

[Henry Care?], English liberties,: or the free-born subject's inheritance; containing Magna Charta, Charta de Foresta, the statute De Tallagio non concedendo, the Habea Corpus act, and several other statutes; with comments on each of them. Likewise. The Proceedings in Appeals of Murder: Of Ship-Money; Of Tonnage and Poundage. Of Parliaments, and the Qualification and Choice of Members: Of the Three Estates, and of the Settlement of the Crown by Parliament. Together with a Short History of the Succession, not by any Hereditary Right: Also a Declaration of the Liberties of the Subject: And of the Oath of Allegiance and Supremacy. The Petition of Right; with a short but impartial Relation of the Difference between Charles I. and the Long Parliament, concerning the Prerogative of the King, the Liberties of the Subject, and the Rise of the Civil Wars. Of Trials by Juries, and of the Qualifications of Jurors; their Punishment for Misbehaviour, and of Challenges to them. Lastly, Of Justices of the Peace, Coroners, Constables. Church-Wardens, Overseers of the Poor, Surveyors of the Highways, &c. With many Law-Cases throughout the Whole. Compiled first by Henry Care, and now continued, with large additions, by W. N. of the Middle-Temple, Esq. (London, 1719).

[Henry Care?], English liberties,: or The free-born subject's inheritance containing Magna Charta, Charta de Foresta, The Statute de Tallagio non concedendo, the Habeas Corpus Act, and several other Statutes; with comments on each of them. Likewise the proceedings in appeals of murder: of ship-money; of tonnage and poundage. Of Parliaments, and the qualification and choice of members: of the three estates, and of the settlement of the crown by the Parliament. Together with a short history of the succession, not by any hereditary right: also a declaration of the liberties of the subject: And of the Oath of Allegiance and Supremacy. The Petition of Right; with a short but impartial relation of the difference between K. Charles I. and the rise of the civil wars. Of trials by juries, and of the qualifications of jurors; their punishment for misbehaviour, and of challanges to them. Lastly, of justices of the peace, coroners, constables, churchwardens, overseers of the poor, surveyors of the high-ways, &c. With many law-cases throughout the whole. / Compiled first by Henry Care, and continued with large additions, by W. N. of the Middle-Temple, esq. (Philadelphia, PA, 1721).

[Henry Care?], English liberties, or The free-born subject's inheritance: containing Magna Charta, Charta de Foresta, the statute De Tallagio non Concedendo, the Habeas Corpus Act, and several other statutes, with comments on each of them: likewise of ship-money; of tonnage and poundage: of parliaments, and the qualification and choice of members, of the three estates and of the settlement of the crown by Parliament: together with a short history of the succession, not by any hereditary right, also a declaration of the liberties of the subject: and of the oath of allegiance and supremacy, the petition of right with a short but impartial relation of the difference between King Charles I. and the Long Parliament, concerning the prerogative of the king, the liberties of the subject, and the rise of the civil wars, of trials by juries, and of the qualifications of jurors ; their punishment for misbehaviour, and of challenges to them: lastly, of justices of the peace, and coroners with many law-cases throughout the whole (Providence, RI, 1774).

[Henry Care?], *British liberties: or the free-born subject's inheritance; containing the laws that form the basis of those liberties, with observations thereon; also an introductory essay on political liberty and a comprehensive view of the Constitution of Great Britain* (London, 1766).

[Henry Care?], *British liberties, or the free-born subject's inheritance: Containing the laws that form the basis of those liberties, with observations thereon; among others are Magna Charta, and other statutes in confirmation of the liberties of the subject, with comments. Laws relating to treason. The declaration of right and liberties, and the confirmation thereof. The law of appeals of Parliaments. The privilege and qualifications of members, &c. The petition of right and habeas corpus act, with comments. The laws relative to papists and Protestant dissenters. A treatise on juries; their power, duty, office, &c. highly necessary for every one to be acquainted with. Also an introductory essay on political liberty; and a comprehensive view of the constitution of Great Britain* (London, 1767).

George W. Carey, "Natural Rights, Equality, and the Declaration of Independence," *Ave Maria Law Review* 45 (2005), 45–67.

Catalogue of All the Books belonging to the Providence Library (Providence, RI, 1768).

A Catalogue of Books in the Library of The College of New-Jersey (Woodbridge, NJ, 1760).

A Catalogue of the Library of Harvard University (Cambridge, MA, 1830).

Catalogue. President Jefferson's library. A catalogue of the extensive and valuable library of the late President Jefferson (copied from the original ms., in his hand-writing, as arranged by himself,) to be sold at auction, at the Long room Pennsylvania avenue, Washington city, by Nathaniel P. Poor, on the 27th February, 1829 (Washington, DC, 1829).

J. J. Caudle, "Dilly, Charles," *Oxford Dictionary of National Biography* (online ed.), doi:10.1093/ref:odnb/7671.

"Centinel," Letter VII in June 13, 1771, *Massachusetts Spy.*

"Centinel," Letter XXVIII in January 2, 1772, *Massachusetts Spy.*

George Chalmers, *Opinions of Eminent Lawyers, on Various Points of English Jurisprudence, Chiefly Concerning the Colonies, Fisheries, and Commerce, of Great Britain: Collected, and Digested, from the Originals, in the Board of Trade, and Other Depositories* (London, 1814).

Thomas B. Chandler, Myles Cooper, and Joseph Galloway, *What Think Ye of the Congress Now? or, An Inquiry, How Far Americans are Bound to Abide by and Execute the Decisions of, the Late Congress?* (New York, 1775).

Joyce Chaplin, *Subject Matter: Technology, the Body, and Science on the Anglo-American Frontier, 1500–1676* (Harvard, 2003).

Gilbert Chinard, "Jefferson and Ossian," *Modern Language Notes* 38:4 (1923), 201–5.

Ian R. Christie, "A Vision of Empire: Thomas Whately and the Regulations Lately Made Concerning the Colonies," *English Historical Review* 113:451 (1988), 300–320.

Benjamin Church, *An Oration, Delivered March fifth, 1773. At the Request of the Inhabitants of the Town of Boston; to Commemorate the Bloody Tragedy of the Fifth of March, 1770* (Boston, 1773).

Marcus Tullius Cicero, *On Duties* (tr. Walter Miller, Harvard, 1913, repr. 1997).

William A. Clebsch, "William Smith on Education: Religion, 'The Soul of the Whole,'" *Historical Magazine of the Protestant Episcopal Church* 52:4 (1983), 369–90.

Clericus Americanus [Rev. John Cleaveland of Ipswich?], untitled, in the September 5, 1768, *Boston Gazette*, repr. March 4, 1771, *Boston Gazette*.

William Cobbett, *The Parliamentary History of England, from the Earliest Period to the Year 1803. From Which Last-Mentioned Epoch it is Continued Downwards in the Work Entitled "Hansard's Parliamentary debates"* (London, 1806–20).

Edward Coke (from books first published ca. 1600–1634), *Selected Writings of Sir Edward Coke* (Indianapolis, IN: Liberty Fund, 2003).

Trevor Colbourn, *The Lamp of Experience: Whig History and the Intellectual Origins of the American Revolution* (University of North Carolina, 1965).

Linda Colley, "Empires of Writing: Britain, America and Constitutions, 1776–1848," *Law and History Review* 32:2 (2014), 237–66.

A Complete collection of state trials, and proceedings for high treason, and other crimes and misdemeanours; commencing with the eleventh year of the reign of King Richard II. and ending with the sixteenth year of the reign of King George III. with two alphabetical tables to the whole.: To which is prefixed a new preface, By Francis Hargrave, Esquire (5th ed., Dublin, 1793, based on 1719 1st ed.).

John Cook, *Monarchy No Creature of Gods Making* (Waterford, 1652).

Richard Coppin, *A Blow at the Serpent: Or a Gentle Answer from Maidstone Prison to Appease Wrath, Advancing Itself Against Truth and Peace at Rochester…* (London, 1656).

Daniel R. Coquillette, "Justinian in Braintree: John Adams, Civilian Learning, and Legal Elitism, 1758–1775," in Coquillette, ed., *Law in Colonial Massachusetts, 1630–1800* (Boston, 1984), 359–418.

Daniel R. Coquillette, "The Legal Education of a Patriot: Josiah Quincy Jr.'s Law Commonplace (1763)," Boston College Law School Legal Studies Research Paper Series, Research Paper 114 (2006).

Daniel R. Coquillette and Neil L. York, eds., *Portrait of a Patriot: The Major Political and Legal Papers of Josiah Quincy Junior* (6 vols., Boston, 2005–14).

Robert Coram, *Political Inquiries: to which is Added, a Plan for the General Establishment of Schools throughout the United States* (Wilmington, 1791).

Robert Cotton, *Cottoni Posthuma: Divers Choice Pieces of that Renowned Antiquary Sir Robert Cotton, Knight and Baronet, Attribution Preserved from the Injury of Time, and Expos'd to Public Light, for the Benefit of Posterity* (London, 1651).

Franklin E. Court, *The Scottish Connection: The Rise of English Literary Study in Early America* (Syracuse, 2001).

J. Hector St. John de Crèvecœur, *Letters from an American Farmer* (London, 1782).

Matthew Crow, "Jefferson, Pocock, and the Temporality of Law in a Republic," *Republics of Letters* 2:1 (2010), 55–81.

Matthew Crow, *Thomas Jefferson, Legal History, and the Art of Recollection* (Cambridge, 2017).

William J. Cuddihy, *The Fourth Amendment: Origins and Original Meaning, 602–1791* (Oxford, 2009).

Henry Dagge, *Considerations on Criminal Law* (London, 1772).

John Dalrymple, *Memoirs of Great Britain and Ireland from the Dissolution of the last Parliament of Charles II until the Sea-Battle off La Hogue* (Edinburgh and London, 1771–73).

Lorraine Daston and Katherine Park, *Wonders and the Order of Nature* (MIT, 1998).

Lorraine Daston, "Nature's Custom versus Nature's Laws," Tanner Lectures on Human Values, II, delivered at Harvard, November 6, 2002.

Lorraine Daston and Fernando Vidal, eds., *The Moral Authority of Nature* (Chicago, 2003).

Lorraine Daston and Michael Stolleis, eds., *Natural Law and Laws of Nature in Early Modern Europe: Jurisprudence, Theology, Moral and Natural Philosophy* (Ashgate, 2008).

John Davis, *An Address Delivered at the Dedication of the Town Hall, in Worcester, Mass., on the Second Day of May, 1825* (Worcester, 1825).

Thomas Dawes, *An Oration Delivered March 5th 1781 at the Request of the Inhabitants of the Town of Boston, to Commemorate the Bloody Tragedy of the Fifth of March 1770* (Boston, 1781).

George Dawson, *Origo Legum: Or a Treatise of the Origin of Laws, and Their Obliging Power: as Also of Their Great Variety: and why Some Laws are Immutable, and Some Not; But May Suffer Change, Or Cease to Be, Or be Suspended, Or Abrogated* (London, 1694).

Dennys DeBerdt, letter in the December 30, 1765, *Supplement to the Boston Evening-Post*.

David J. Depew, "The Ethics of Aristotle's *Politics*," in Ryan K. Balot, ed., *A Companion to Greek and Roman Political Thought* (Wiley-Blackwell, 2009), 399–418.

Harry T. Dickinson, "Magna Carta in the Age of Revolution," *Enlightenment and Dissent* 30 (2015), 1–67.

John Dickinson, *Letters from a Farmer in Pennsylvania* (Philadelphia, 1767–68).

John Dickinson, *An Essay on the Constitutional Power of Great-Britain over the Colonies* (Philadelphia, 1774).

John Dickinson and Charles Thomson, *To the Author of a Pamphlet, entitled "A Candid Examination of the Mutual Claims of GREAT BRITAIN and her COLONIES, &c."* (Philadelphia, 1775).

Denis Diderot, *Supplément au voyage de Bougainville, ou dialogue entre A et B sur l'inconvénient d'attacher des idées morales à certaines actions physiques qui n'en comportent pas*, in *Correspondance Littéraire*, ed. Friedrich-Melchior Grimm, issues of September 1773, October 1773, March 1774, April 1774.

Horst Dippel, "Blackstone's *Commentaries* and the Origins of Modern Constitutionalism," in *Re-interpreting Blackstone's Commentaries: A Seminal Text in National and International Contexts*, ed. Wilfrid Prest (Hart, 2014), 199–214.

Horst Dippel, *Deutschland und die amerikanische Revolution: sozialgeschichtliche Untersuchung zum politischen Bewusstsein im ausgehenden 18. Jahrhundert* (Cologne, 1972, tr. as *Germany and the American Revolution, 1770–1800: A Sociohistorical Investigation of Late Eighteenth-Century Political Thinking*, University of North Carolina, 1977).

Robert Dodsley, ed., *The Preceptor* (London, 1748).

Eugene Doll, "American History as Interpreted by German Historians from 1770 to 1815," *Transactions of the American Philosophical Society*, n.s. 38, part 5 (1948), 421–534.

Silas Downer, *A discourse, delivered in Providence, in the colony of Rhode-Island, upon the 25th. day of July, 1768. At the dedication of the Tree of Liberty, from the summer house in the tree* (Providence, RI, 1768). Reprinted in Hyneman and Lutz, *American Political Writing*, 1:97–108.

Lee A. Dugatkin, *Mr. Jefferson and the Giant Moose: Natural History in Early America* (Chicago, IL, 2009).

Daniel Dulany Sr., *The Right of the Inhabitants of Maryland to the Benefit of English Laws* (Annapolis, MD, 1728).

William Duncan, *The Elements of Logick, in Four Books* (London, 1748).

Justin DuRivage and Claire Priest, "The Stamp Act and the Political Origins of American Legal and Economic Institutions," *Southern California Law Review* 88:4 (2015), 875–905.

Jonathan Eacott, *Selling Empire: India in the Making of Britain and America, 1600–1830* (University of North Carolina, 2016).

Benjamin Edes and John Gill, advertisement for John Locke, *An Essay* . . . (Boston, 1773), in the March 1, 1773, *Boston Gazette*.

Andrew Eliot to Thomas Hollis, October 17, 1768, in *Collections of the Massachusetts Historical Society*, 4th series 4 (1858), 434.

Joseph Ellis, *American Sphinx: The Character of Thomas Jefferson* (Knopf, 1997).

Joseph Ellis, *Founding Brothers: The Revolutionary Generation* (Knopf Doubleday, 2000).

Encyclopædia Britannica, or, A dictionary of arts and sciences, compiled upon a new plan; in which the different sciences and arts are digested into distinct treatises or systems, and the various technical terms, etc. are explained as they occur in the order of the alphabet, ed. Colin Macfarquhar and Andrew Bell, written mostly by William Smellie (Edinburgh, 1768–71)..

Caleb Evans, *British Constitutional Liberty: A Sermon Preached in Broad-Mead, Bristol, November 5, 1775* (Bristol and London, 1775).

Ioannis Evrigenis, *Fear of Enemies and Collective Action* (Cambridge, 2008).

Ioannis Evrigenis, "Hobbes's Clockwork: The State of Nature and Machiavelli's Return to Beginnings of Cities," in Sharon R. Krause and M. A. McGrail, eds, *The Arts of Rule: Essays in Honor of Harvey C. Mansfield* (Lexington, 2009), 185–99.

Ioannis Evrigenis, "Freeing Man from Sin: Rousseau on the Natural Condition of Mankind" in Christie McDonald and Stanley Hoffmann, eds, *Rousseau and Freedom* (Cambridge, 2010).

Ioannis Evrigenis, *Images of Anarchy: The Rhetoric and Science in Hobbes's State of Nature* (Cambridge, 2014).

Ioannis Evrigenis, "The State of Nature," in A. P. Martinich and Kinch Hoekstra, eds., *The Oxford Handbook of Hobbes* (Oxford, 2016), 221–41.

Ioannis Evrigenis, "Sovereignty, Rebellion, and Golden Age: Hesiod's Legacy," in David Matthew Carter, Rachel Foxley, and Liz Sawyer, eds., *The Brill Companion to the Legacy of Greek Political Thought* (Brill, forthcoming).

Ioannis Evrigenis and Mark Somos, "The State of Nature," in Aaron Garrett and James Schmidt, eds., *The Oxford Handbook of the Enlightenment* (Oxford, forthcoming).

The Examination of Joseph Galloway, esq.; Late Speaker of the House of Assembly of Pennsylvania. Before the House of Commons, in a Committee on the American Papers. With Explanatory Notes (London, 1779).

Robin F. A. Fabel, "Johnstone, George," *Oxford Dictionary of National Biography* online.

James M. Farrell, "The Child Independence is Born: James Otis and Writs of Assistance," in Stephen E. Lucas, ed., *A Rhetorical History of the United States*, vol. 2 (forthcoming).

Stephen M. Feldman, *American Legal Thought from Premodernism to Postmodernism: An Intellectual Voyage* (Oxford, 2000).

John Ferling, *John Adams: A Life* (University of Tennessee, 1992, repr. Oxford, 2010).

Robert Filmer, *Patriarcha, or, The natural power of Kings by the learned Sir Robert Filmer* (London, 1680).

John M. Finnis, "Blackstone's Theoretical Intentions," *Natural Law Forum* 13 (1967), 163–83.

Samuel Fleischacker, "Adam Smith's Reception among the American Founders, 1776–1790," *William and Mary Quarterly* LIX:4 (2002), 897–924.

Andrew Fletcher of Saltoun, *A Discourse of Government with Relation to Militias* (Edinburgh, 1698).

David Fordyce, *Dialogues concerning Education* (London, 1745).

David Fordyce, *The Elements of Moral Philosophy* (London, 1754).

William Fordyce, *A New Inquiry Into the Causes, Symptoms, and Cure, of Putrid and Inflammatory Fevers: With an Appendix on the Hectic Fever, and on the Ulcerated and Malignant Sore Throat* (London, 1774).

Samuel A. Forman, *Dr. Joseph Warren: The Boston Tea Party, Bunker Hill, and the Birth of American Liberty* (Pelican, 2011).

Nathaniel Forster, *An Enquiry into the Causes of the Present High Price of Provisions . . .* (London, 1767).

Mark Fortier, *The Culture of Equity in Early Modern England* (Ashgate, 2005).

Benjamin Franklin, *A Catalogue of Choice and Valuable Books* (Philadelphia, 1744).

Benjamin Franklin, *The Works of Benjamin Franklin, containing several political and historical tracts not included in any former edition, and many letters official and private not hitherto published, with notes and a life of the author*, ed. Jared Sparks (Philadelphia, 1840).

Benjamin Franklin, *Papers*, vol. 9, ed. Leonard W. Labaree, Helen C. Boatfield, Helene H. Fineman, and James H. Hutson (Yale, 1966).

Benjamin Franklin, *Papers*, vol. 18, ed. William B. Willcox, Dorothy W. Bridgwater, Mary L. Hart, Claude A. Lopez, C. A. Myrans, Catherine M. Prelinger, and G. B. Warden (Yale, 1974).

James Franklin, editorial in July 23–30, 1722, issue of the *New-England Courant*.

Isaac Frasier, *A Brief Account of the Life, and Abominable Thefts, of the Notorious Isaac Frasier, Who Was Executed at Fairfield, Sept. 7th, 1768* (New Haven, 1768).

John Freebairn, *A Caution against False Teachers: a Sermon, Preached before The Society in Scotland for Propagating Christian Knowledge, At their Anniversary Meeting, In the High Church of Edinburgh, On Friday, June 7, 1771* (Edinburgh, 1771).

Freeborn American, in the March 6, 1767, *Supplement to the Boston Gazette*.

Samuel Freeman, "Constitutional Democracy and the Legitimacy of Judicial Review," *Law and Philosophy* 9:4 (1990–91), 327–70.

"Friend to the People and their Liberties," *A full and impartial examination of the Rev. Mr. John Wesley's address to the Americans: in which That Gentleman's Inconsistencies are remarked; His Assertions proved groundless; and his Principles in general demonstrated* to be subversive of the British Constitution. The whole interspersed with Remarks upon American Affairs (London, 1775).

Lon L. Fuller, "The Case of the Speluncean Explorers," Harvard Law Review 62:4 (1949), 616–45.

Thomas Gage, The Correspondence of General Gage, ed. Clarence Edwin Carter (New Haven, 1931–33).

Gales & Seaton's Register of Debates in Congress (Washington DC, 1830).

Joseph Galloway, A True and Impartial State of the Province of Pennsylvania (Philadelphia, 1759).

Joseph Galloway, Arguments on Both Sides in the Dispute between Great Britain and Her Colonies (Philadelphia, 1774), repr. in Archives of the State of New Jersey 10 (1886): 1480–81.

Joseph Galloway, A Candid Examination of the Mutual Claims of Great-Britain, and the Colonies: With a Plan of Accommodation On Constitutional Principles (New York, 1775).

Joseph Galloway, A Reply to an Address to the Author of a Pamphlet entitled "A Candid Examination of the Mutual Claims of Great Britain and her Colonies, &c." (New York, 1775).

Joseph Galloway, Historical and Political Reflections on the Rise and Progress of the American Rebellion, in which the causes of that rebellion are pointed out, and the policy and necessity of offering to the Americans a system of government founded in the principles of the British constitution are clearly demonstrated. By the author of Letters to a nobleman, on the conduct of the American war (London, 1780).

Samuel Gatchel, A contrast to the Reverend Nathaniel Whitaker, D.D: His confutation of the Reverend John Wise, A.M. Vindication of the New-England churches; and the churches quarrel espoused (Danvers, 1778).

"A Gentleman in Boston," letter to a friend in Philadelphia, February 6, 1775, American Archives: 4th series, vol. 1 (Washington DC, 1837), 1216–17.

Antonello Gerbi, La disputa del Nuovo mondo: storia di una polemica, 1750–1900 (Ricciardi, 1955; 2nd ed. 1983, tr. as The Dispute of the New World: The History of a Polemic, 1750–1900, Pittsburgh, 2010).

Elbridge Gerry, letters in James T. Austin, The Life of Elbridge Gerry, (Boston, 1828).

Jonathan Gienapp, "Historicism and Holism: Failures of Originalist Interpretation," Fordham Law Review 84:3 (2015), 935–56.

Leslee K. Gilbert, "The Altar of Liberty: Enlightened Dissent and the Dudleian Lectures, 1755–1765," Historical Journal of Massachusetts 31:2 (2003), 151–71.

John Gill, The Doctrines of God's Everlasting Love to His Elect, and Their Eternal Union with Christ: Together with some other truths, stated and defended (3rd ed., London, 1770).

John Gill, Sermons on Important Subjects (London, 1790).

Oliver Goldsmith, The History of England, from the Earliest Times to the Death of George II (London, 1771).

Jan Golinski, "American Climate and the Civilization of Nature," in J. Delbourgo and N. Dew, eds., Science and Empire in the Atlantic World (Routledge, 2007), 153–74.

John Gordon, *A New Estimate of Manners and Principles: Being a Comparison Between Ancient and Modern Times, in the Three Great Articles of Knowledge, Happiness, and Virtue; Both With Respect to Mankind at Large, and to This Kingdom in Particular* (London, 1760–61).

John Gordon, *The Causes and Consequences of Evil Speaking Against Government, Considered in a Sermon Preached before the University of Cambridge, at Gt. Mary's Church, on the King's Accession, Oct. 25, 1771* (Cambridge, 1771).

John Gray, *A Comparative View of the Public Burdens of Great Britain and Ireland; with Aproposal* [sic] *for Putting Both Islands on an Equality in regard to the Freedom of Foreign Trade* (London, 1772).

Jacob Green, *Observations on the Reconciliation of Great-Britain, and the Colonies; in which are Exhibited, Arguments for, and against, that Measure* (Philadelphia, 1776).

Jan Crawford Greenburg, *Supreme Conflict: The Inside Story of the Struggle for Control of the United States Supreme Court* (Penguin, 2008).

Jack P. Greene, "Empire and Identity from the Glorious Revolution to the American Revolution," in P.J. Marshall, ed., *The Eighteenth Century* (Oxford, 1998, repr. 2006), 208–30.

Jack P. Greene, *The Constitutional Origins of the American Revolution* (Cambridge, 2011).

Jack P. Greene, *Evaluating Empire and Confronting Colonialism in Eighteenth-Century Britain* (Cambridge, 2013).

Frederick Griffin, *Junius Discovered* (Boston, 1854).

Michael Grossberg and Christopher Tomlins, eds., *The Cambridge History of Law in America*, vol. 1, *Early America (1580–1815)* (Cambridge, 2008).

Hugo Grotius, *Liber de antiquitate reipublicae Batavicae* (Leiden, 1610, ed. and tr. Jan Waszink et al. as *The Antiquity of the Batavian Republic*, with Notes by Petrus Scriverius, Assen, 2000).

Hugo Grotius, *De iure belli ac pacis* (Paris, 1625).

Richard Grove, *Green Imperialism: Colonial Expansion, Tropical Island Edens, and the Origins of Environmentalism, 1600–1860* (Cambridge, 1995).

Knud Haakonssen, "From Natural Law to the Rights of Man: a European Perspective on American Debates," in Michael James Lacey and Knud Haakonssen, eds., *A Culture of Rights: The Bill of Rights in Philosophy, Politics and Law 1791 and 1991* (Cambridge, 1992), 19–61.

Sally E. Hadden and Alfred L. Brophy, eds., *A Companion to American Legal History* (Wiley-Blackwell, 2013).

Philip A. Hamburger, "Natural Rights, Natural Law, and American Constitutions," *Yale Law Journal* 102:907 (1993), 907–60.

Philip A. Hamburger, *Law and Judicial Duty* (Harvard, 2008).

Alexander Hamilton, *A full vindication of the measures of the Congress, from the calumnies of their enemies: in answer to a letter, under the signature of A.W. Farmer. Whereby his sophistry is exposed, his cavils confuted, his artifices detected, and his wit ridiculed; in a general address to the inhabitants of America, and a particular address to the farmers of the province of New-York* (New York, 1774).

Alexander Hamilton, *The farmer refuted: or, A more impartial and comprehensive view of the dispute between Great-Britain and the colonies,: intended as a further vindication*

of the Congress: in answer to a letter from A.W. Farmer, intitled A view of the controversy between Great-Britain and her colonies: including a mode of determining the present
disputes finally and effectually, &c. (New York, 1775).

Alexander Hamilton, Federalist Papers No. 68, March 12, 1788, in Clinton Rossiter, ed.,
The Federalist Papers (Penguin, 1961).

William Hanbury, A Complete Body of Planting and Gardening (London, 1773).

James Harrington, The Censure of the Rota (London, 1660).

John Hawles, The grand-jury-man's oath and office explained: and the rights of
English-men asserted. A dialogue between a barrister at law, and a grand-jury-man
(London, 1680).

John Hawles, The Englishman's right: a dialogue between a barrister at law, and a juryman;
plainly setting forth, I. The antiquity, II. The excellent designed use, III. The office and just
privileges of juries, by the law of England (London, 1680; later eds. London, 1732;
London, 1752; London, 1763; London, 1764; London, 1770).

John Hawles, The Englishman's Right. A Dialogue Between a Barrister at Law and a
Juryman; Shewing, I. The Antiquity, II. The Excellent Designed Use, III. The Office and
Just Privileges of Juries by the Law of England (Being a Choice Help for All Who Are
Qualified by Law to Serve on Juries). To Which is Prefixed, An Introductory Essay, On the
Moral Duty of a Judge (Boston, 1772).

Joseph Hawley, in July 6 and 13, 1767, Boston Evening-Post.

Kevin J. Hayes, The Road to Monticello: The Life and Mind of Thomas Jefferson
(Oxford, 2008).

Alan Heimert, Religion and the American Mind: From the Great Awakening to the
Revolution (Harvard, 1966).

Richard H. Helmholz, "Bonham's Case, Judicial Review, and the Law of Nature," Journal
of Legal Analysis 1:1 (2009), 325–54.

James Youngblood Henderson, "The doctrine of aboriginal rights in Western legal tradition," in Menno Boldt and J. Anthony Long, eds., The Quest for Justice: Aboriginal
Peoples and Aboriginal Rights (Toronto, 1985), 185–220.

Samuel Henley, The distinct claims of government and religion, considered in a sermon
preached before the Honourable House of Burgesses, at Williamsburg, in Virginia, March
1, 1772 (Cambridge, MA, 1772).

Gad Hitchcock, A sermon preached before His Excellency Thomas Gage, Esq; governor: the
Honorable His Majesty's Council, and the Honorable House of Representatives, of the
province of the Massachusetts-Bay in New-England, May 25th, 1774. Being the anniversary of the election of His Majesty's Council for said province (Boston, 1774).

The history and proceedings of the House of Commons from the Restoration to the present
time. Containing the most remarkable motions, speeches, resolves, reports and conferences
to be met with in that interval: as also the most exact estimates of the charge of government,
state of the public revenue, the rise and growth of the national debt, expence of the war,
proceedings on ways and means, speeches and messages from the throne, addresses, and remonstrances, also the numbers pro and con upon every division &c. Many of which curious
particulars were never before printed. Collected from the best authorities, compared with
the journals of the House, and illustrated with a great variety of historical and explanatory notes. Together with a large appendix, containing exact lists of every Parliament,

the names of the speakers, their several posts under the government, and other valuable, supplemental pieces (London, 1742–44).

Noah Hobart, *Civil Government, the Foundation of Social Happiness: A Sermon Preached before the General Assembly of the Colony of Connecticut, at Hartford, on the Day of their Anniversary Election, May 10th, 1750* (North London, 1751).

Noah Hobart, *An Attempt to Illustrate and Confirm the Ecclesiastical Constitution of the Consociated Churches in the Colony of Connecticut* (New Haven, 1765).

Noah Hobart, *Excessive Wickedness, the Way to an Untimely Death. A Sermon Preached at Fairfield, in Connecticut, September 7th, 1768. At the Execution of Isaac Frasier* (New Haven, 1768).

William S. Holdsworth, *A History of English Law* (London, 1903, 7th ed., 1956).

Ben Holland, *The Moral Person of the State: Pufendorf, Sovereignty and Composite Polities* (Cambridge, 2017).

Daniel W. Hollis III, "Edward and Charles Dilly," J. K. Bracken and J. Silver, eds., *The British Literary Book Trade, 1700–1820* (Gale Research, 1995), 97–102.

Henry Home (later Lord Kames), *Essays upon Several Subjects concerning British Antiquities: viz. I. Introduction of the feudal law into Scotland. II. Constitution of Parliament. III. Honour. Dignity. IV. Succession or Descent. With an Appendix upon Hereditary and Indefeasible Right* (Edinburgh, 1747).

Henry Home, Lord Kames, *Principles of Equity* (Edinburgh, 1760).

Henry Home, Lord Kames, *The Gentleman Farmer: Being an Attempt to Improve Agriculture, by Subjecting it to the Test of Rational Principles* (Edinburgh, 1776).

István Hont, *Jealousy of Trade: International Competition and the Nation-State in Historical Perspective* (Belknap, 2005).

Theodore Hornberger, "A Note on the Probable Source of Provost Smith's Famous Curriculum for the College of Philadelphia," *Pennsylvania Magazine of History and Biography* 58:4 (1934), 370–77.

Simeon Howard, *A Sermon Preached to the Ancient and Honorable Artillery Company in Boston, New-England, June 7th, 1773. Being the Anniversary of their Election of Officers* (Boston, 1773).

Thomas Bayly Howell, *A Complete Collection of State Trials and Proceedings for High Treason and other Crimes and Misdemeanors, from the Earliest Period to the Year 1783, with Notes and Other Illustrations Compiled by T.B. Howell*, vol. III (London, 1816).

William Howell, "The Declaration of Independence and Eighteenth-Century Logic," *William and Mary Quarterly* 18 (1961), 463–84.

Winthrop S. Hudson, "William Penn's English Liberties: Tract for Several Times," *William and Mary Quarterly* 26: 4 (1969), 578–85.

Daniel J. Hulsebosch, *Constituting Empire: New York and the Transformation of Constitutionalism in the Atlantic World, 1664–1830* (University of North Carolina, 2005).

Daniel J. Hulsebosch, "An Empire of Law: Chancellor Kent and the Revolution in Books in the Early Republic," *Alabama Law Review* 60:2 (2009), 377–424.

David Hume, *Treatise of Human Nature* [1739–40] in *Philosophical Works*, vol. 2 (Edinburgh, 1826).

David Hume, *The History of Great Britain* (Edinburgh, 1754, London, 1762, with subsequent editions).

Francis Hutcheson, *An Inquiry into the Original of Our Ideas of Beauty and Virtue: In Two Treatises* (2nd ed, London, 1726).

Francis Hutcheson, *Short Introduction to Moral Philosophy* (Glasgow, 1747).

Francis Hutcheson, *Two Texts on Human Nature*, ed. Thomas Mautner (Cambridge, 1993).

Francis Hutcheson, *Philosophiae Moralis Institutio Compendiaria, with A Short Introduction to Moral Philosophy*, ed. Luigi Turco (Liberty Fund, 2007).

[Thomas Hutchins and William Smith?] *An historical account of the expedition against the Ohio Indians . . .* (Philadelphia, 1765).

Thomas Hutchinson, *The History of the Colony of Massachusets-Bay, from the First Settlement thereof in 1628, until its Incorporation with the Colony of Plimouth, Province of Main, &c. By The Charter of King William and Queen Mary, in 1691* (Boston, 1764).

Thomas Hutchinson, *Experience Preferable to Theory. An answer to Dr. Price's Observations on the Nature of Civil Liberty, and the Justice and Policy of the War with America* (London, 1776).

Thomas Hutchinson et al., *The Letters of Governor Hutchinson, and Lieutenant Governor Oliver, & c. printed at Boston. And remarks thereon. With the assembly's address, and the proceedings of the Lords Committee of Council. Together with the substance of Mr. Wedderburn's speech relating to those letters. And the report of the Lords Committee to His Majesty in Council* (London, 1774).

Thomas Hutchinson et al., *The representations of Governor Hutchinson and others: contained in certain letters transmitted to England, and afterwards returned from thence, and laid before the General-Assembly of the Massachusetts-Bay. Together with the resolves of the two Houses thereon* (Boston, 1773).

Charles S. Hyneman and Donald S. Lutz, *American Political Writing during the Founding Era, 1760–1805* (Liberty Fund, 1983).

James VI and I, *The True Lawe of Free Monarchies: Or, The Reciprock and Mvtvall Dvtie Betwixt a free King, and his naturall Subiectes* (Edinburgh, 1598). See also *Political Writings* (ed. Johann P. Sommerville, Cambridge, 1994), 62–84.

Thomas Jefferson, *The Papers of Thomas Jefferson*, vol. 1, 1760–1776 (ed. Julian P. Boyd, Princeton, 1950).

Thomas Jefferson, *A Summary View of the Rights of British America: Set Forth in Some Resolutions Intended for the Inspection of the Present Delegates of the People of Virginia, Now in Convention* (Williamsburg, 1774).

Thomas Jefferson, *Notes on the State of Virginia* (Paris, 1785, London, 1787).

Thomas Jefferson Encyclopedia, s.v. "Rice," http://www.monticello.org/site/house-and-gardens/rice.

Merrill Jensen, *The Founding of a Nation: A History of the American Revolution, 1763–1776* (1968, repr. 2004, Hackett).

Charles Coffin Jewett, *A Catalogue of the Library of Brown University* (Providence, RI, 1843).

"Johannes in Eremo," article in the March 26, 1771, *Essex Gazette*.

Samuel Johnson, *Taxation no Tyranny; an Answer to the Resolutions and Address of the American Congress* (London, 1775).

George Johnstone, untitled, in *Georgia Gazette*, no. 93, January 10, 1765.

Journal of the Honourable House of Representatives, of His Majesty's province of the Massachusetts-Bay, in New-England, begun and held at Boston, in the county of Suffolk, on Wednesday the twenty-eighth day of May, Annoque Domini, 1766.

Journals of the Continental Congress for 1774 (ed. Worthington Chauncey Ford et al., Washington, DC, 1904).

Journal of the Convention for Framing a Constitution of Government for the State of Massachusetts Bay . . . (Boston, 1832).

Journals of the House of Representatives of Massachusetts, 1761, 1762 and 1762–63, vols. 38 and 39 (ed. Malcolm Freiberg, Boston, 1967–69).

Journals of the House of Representatives of Massachusetts, 1767 (Massachusetts Historical Society, 1974).

Immanuel Kant, *Zum ewigen Frieden. Ein philosophischer Entwurf* (Königsberg, 1795, tr. Ted Humphrey as *To Perpetual Peace: A Philosophical Sketch*, Hackett, 2003).

Don B. Kates and Clayton E. Cramer, "Second Amendment Limitations and Criminological Considerations," *Hastings Law Journal* 60:6 (2009), 1339–69.

James Kent, *An Introductory Lecture to a Course of Law Lectures, Delivered November 17, 1794* (New York, 1794).

James Kent, *Dissertations: Being a Preliminary Part of a Course of Law Lectures* (New York, 1795).

James Kent, *Commentaries on American Law* (New York, 1826–30).

Ralph Ketcham, *James Madison: A Biography* (University of Virginia, 1971; 1st paperback 1990).

Craig Evan Klafter, *Reason over Precedents: Origins of American Legal Thought* (Greenwood, 1993).

William Knox, *The Present State of the Nation: Particularly with Respect to its Trade, Finances, &c. &c.* (London, 1768).

William Knox, *The Controversy between Great Britain and her Colonies Reviewed: The Several Pleas of the Colonies, in Support of their Right to All the Liberties and Privileges of British Subjects, and to Exemption from the Legislative Authority of Parliament, Stated and Considered; and the Nature of their Connection with, and Dependence on, Great Britain, Shewn, upon the Evidence of Historical Facts and Authentic Records* (London, 1769).

László Kontler and Mark Somos, eds., *Trust and Happiness in the History of European Political Thought* (Brill, 2018).

David B. Kopel, "The Religious Roots of the American Revolution and the Right to Keep and Bear Arms," *Journal of Firearms and Public Policy* 17 (2005), 167–84.

Axel Körner, *America in Italy: The United States in the Political Thought and Imagination of the Risorgimento, 1763–1865* (Princeton, 2017).

Charles I. Landis, "The Juliana Library Company in Lancaster (continued)," *Pennsylvania Magazine of History and Biography* 43:2 (1919): 163–81.

Charles I. Landis and Thomas Penn, "The Juliana Library Company in Lancaster," *Pennsylvania Magazine of History and Biography* 43:1 (1919), 24–52.

Arthur Lee, *An Essay in Vindication of the Continental Colonies of America, from a Censure of Mr. Adam Smith, in his Theory of Moral Sentiments* (London, 1764).

Thomas H. Lee, "Natural Born Citizen," *American University Law Review* 67 (2017), 327–411.

William Leggett, "Rights of Authors," *Plaindealer*, February 11, 1837, repr. in *A Collection of the Political Writings of William Leggett*, ed. Theodore Sedgwick Jr. (New York, 1840).

Daniel Leonard ("Massachusettensis"), "To All Nations of Men," in the November 18, 1773, *Massachusetts Spy*, repr. in Hyneman and Lutz, *American Political Writing*, 1:209–16.

Daniel Leonard ("Massachusettensis"), Letter IX, in the February 6, 1775, *Massachusetts Gazette*.

Lawrence Lessig, *Remix: Making Art and Commerce Thrive in the Hybrid Economy* (Penguin, 2008).

Jacob T. Levy, "Montesquieu's Constitutional Legacies," in R. E. Kingston, ed., *Montesquieu and His Legacy* (New York, 2008), 115–38.

Andrew J. Lewis, *A Democracy of Facts: Natural History in the Early Republic* (Pennsylvania, 2011).

Library Company of Philadelphia, *A Catalogue of Books Belonging to the Library Company of Philadelphia* (Philadelphia, 1741).

Library Company of Philadelphia, *Charter, Laws, and Catalogue of Books, of the Library Company of Philadelphia* (Philadelphia, 1757).

Library Company of Philadelphia, *The charter, laws, and catalogue of books, of the Library company of Philadelphia* (Philadelphia, 1770).

Library Company of Philadelphia, *A Catalogue of the Books, Belonging to the Library Company of Philadelphia; to which is Prefixed, a Short Account of the Institution, with the Charter, Laws, and Regulations* (Philadelphia, 1807).

David Lieberman, *The Province of Legislation Determined: Legal Theory in Eighteenth-Century Britain* (Cambridge, 1989).

William Lincoln, *History of Worcester, Massachusetts: From Its Earliest Settlement* (Worcester, 1837).

John Locke, *Two Treatises of Government: in the Former, the False Principles and Foundation of Sir Robert Filmer, and his Followers are Overthrown. The Latter is an Essay concerning the True Original, Extent, and End of Civil Government* (London, 1689).

John Locke, *Two Treatises of Government* (4th ed., ed. Thomas Hollis, London, 1764).

John Locke, *An Essay Concerning the True Original Extent and End of Civil Government* (Boston, 1773).

Edward Long, *Candid Reflections upon the Judgement Lately Awarded by the Court of King's Bench, in Westminster-Hall, on What Is Commonly Called the Negro Cause, By a Planter* (London, 1772).

Edward Long, *The History of Jamaica: Or, General Survey of the Antient and Modern State of the Island: with Reflections on Its Situation Settlements, Inhabitants, Climate, Products, Commerce, Laws, and Government* (London, 1774).

Nathanael Low, *An astronomical diary; or Almanack for the year of Christian aera, 1767: . . . Calculated for the meridian of Boston, New-England, lat. 42. deg. 25 min. north: but may indifferently serve any part of New-England* (Boston, 1766).

Jean E. Luck, "Science and Knowledge in Bernardin de Saint-Pierre's 'Etudes de la nature' (1784)," PhD diss. Exeter, 2013.

Donald S. Lutz (ed.), *Colonial Origins of the American Constitution: A Documentary History* (Indianapolis, IN: Liberty Fund, 1998).

Andrew Lyall, *Granville Sharp's Cases on Slavery* (Hart, 2017).

Steven J. Macias, "Legal Thought from Blackstone to Kent and Story," in Sally E. Hadden and Alfred L. Brophy, eds., *A Companion to American Legal History* (Wiley-Blackwell, 2013), 484–505.

John Maclaurin, *Dreghorn's Arguments, and decisions, in remarkable cases, before the High Court of Justiciary, and other Supreme Courts, in Scotland* (Edinburgh, 1774).

James Macpherson, *An introduction to the history of Great Britain and Ireland* (Dublin, 1771).

James Madison, *An Oration in Commemoration of the Founders of William and Mary College* (Williamsburg, 1772).

James Madison, *The Writings of James Madison, comprising his Public Papers and his Private Correspondence, including his numerous letters and documents now for the first time printed*, vol. 3, *The Journal of the Constitutional Convention I* (ed. Gaillard Hunt, New York: G.P. Putnam's Sons, 1902).

James Madison, *Federalist Papers* Nos. 51 and 52, February 8, 1788, in Clinton Rossiter, ed., *The Federalist Papers*, (Penguin, 1961).

Pauline Maier, *American Scripture: Making the Declaration of Independence* (New York, 1997).

Frederic William Maitland, "The Body Politic," in Maitland, *Collected Papers* (ed. H. A. L. Fisher, Cambridge, 1911), 3:285–303.

Paul Henri Mallet, *Introduction à L'histoire du Danemarch où l'on traite de la religion, des moeurs, des lois, et des usages des anciens Danois* (Copenhagen, 1755, tr. Bishop Thomas Percy as *Northern Antiquities: or, a Description of the Manners, Customs, Religion and Laws of the Ancient Danes, and Other Northern Nations; Including those of Our Own Saxon Ancestors. With A Translation of the Edda, or System of Runic Mythology, and Other Pieces, From the Ancient Islandic Tongue*, London, 1770).

Massachusetts House of Representatives, January 12, 1768, letter to Dennys DeBerdt, in Samuel Adams, *Writings* (ed. Harry A. Cushing, New York, 1904–8), 1:134–52.

Moses Mather, *America's Appeal to the Impartial World. Wherein the rights of the Americans, as men, British subjects, and as colonists; the equity of the demand, and of the manner in which it is made upon them by Great-Britain, are stated and considered. And, the opposition made by the colonies to acts of Parliament, their resorting to arms in their necessary defence, against the military armaments, employed to enforce them, vindicated* (Hartford, CT, 1775).

Luke Mayville, *John Adams and the Fear of American Oligarchy* (Princeton, 2016).

Spencer W. McBride, *Pulpit and Nation: Clergymen and the Politics of Revolutionary America* (University of Virginia, 2017).

David McCullough, *John Adams* (Simon & Schuster, 2001).

Roy W. McDonald, "Alternative Pleading, I," *Michigan Law Review* 48:3 (1950), 311–28.

Roy W. McDonald, "Alternative Pleading, II," *Michigan Law Review* 48:4 (1950), 429–48.

[Alexander McDougall?] as "Hampden," "The Alarm," in the October 14, 1773, *New-York Journal*.

Paula McDowell, *The Women of Grub Street: Press, Politics, and Gender in the London Literary Marketplace, 1678–1730* (Clarendon, 1998).

Andrew C. McLaughlin, *The Foundations of American Constitutionalism* (New York, 1932).

Jane W. McWilliams, *Annapolis, City of the Severn: A History* (Johns Hopkins, 2011).

"A Mechanic," *To the Worthy Inhabitants of New-York* (New York, 1773).

Ronald L. Meek, *Social Science and the Ignoble Savage* (Cambridge, 1976).

John Stuart Mill, *On Liberty and Other Writings* (ed. Stefan Collini, Cambridge, 1989).

Nicholas P. Miller, *The Religious Roots of the First Amendment: Dissenting Protestants and the Separation of Church and State* (Oxford, 2012).

Peter N. Miller, *Defining the Common Good: Empire, Religion and Philosophy in Eighteenth-Century Britain* (Cambridge, 2004).

John Mills, *Essays Moral, Philosophical, and Political* (London, 1772).

George Richards Minot, *Continuation of the History of the Province of Massachusetts Bay* (Boston, 1798–1803).

Robert Molesworth, *An Account of Denmark, as it was in the Year 1692* (London, 1694).

Michel de Montaigne, "Des Cannibales," in *Essais de messire Michel seignevr de Montaigne, chevalier de l'Ordre du roy, & gentil-homme ordinaire de sa chambre* (Bordeaux, 1580, 185–205, tr. Donald M. Frame as *The Complete Works*, 1943, Everyman's Library, 2003, 182–93).

Montesquieu, Charles de Secondat, *De l'esprit des lois: ou Du rapport que les loix doivent avoir avec la constitution de chaque gouvernement, les moeurs le climat, la religion, le commerce, &c. ; à quoi l'auteur a ajouté. Des recherches nouvelles sur les loix romaines touchant les successions, sur les loix françoises, & sur les loix féodales* (Geneva, 1748, tr. Thomas Nugent as *The Spirit of Laws*, London, 1750, 2nd ed., 1752).

Edmund S. Morgan, *The Birth of the Republic, 1763–89* (Chicago, 1956, rev. ed. 1977).

Edmund S. Morgan, *Puritan Political Ideas, 1558–1794* (1965, Hackett, repr. 2003).

George T. Morrow II, *Of Heretics, Traitors and True Believers: The War for the Soul of Williamsburg* (Telford, 2011).

"Mucius Scaevola," in March 4, 1771, *Boston Gazette*.

"Mucius Scaevola," in November 14, 1771, *Massachusetts Spy*.

James Muldoon, *John Adams and the Constitutional History of the Medieval British Empire* (Palgrave, 2018).

James Murray, untitled, in *Boston Gazette*, March 1, 1765.

John A. Nagy, *Dr. Benjamin Church, Spy: A Case of Espionage on the Eve of the American Revolution* (Yardley, PA: Westholme, 2013).

Caleb Nelson, "Adjudication in the Political Branches," *Columbia Law Review* 107:3 (2007), 559–627.

William Nelson, *The office and authority of a justice of peace.: Collected out of all the books which have hitherto been written on that subject. . . . Digested under alphabetical titles. To which are added presidents of indictments and warrants* (London, 1704).

New York State Bar Association, "Report of the Committee on the Duty of Courts to Refuse to Execute Statutes in Controvention [sic] of the Fundamental Law," presented January 22–23, 1915, in US Congressional serial set, issue 6784, 63rd Congress: 3d session, Senate Documents, 16:3–61.

Brooke N. Newman, "Identity Articulated: British Settlers, Black Caribs, and the Politics of Indigeneity on St. Vincent, 1763–1797," in G. D. Smithers and B. N. Newman, eds., Native Diasporas: Indigenous Identities and Settler Colonialism in the Americas (Nebraska, 2014), 109–50.

William R. Newman, Promethean Ambitions: Alchemy and the Quest to Perfect Nature (Chicago, 2004).

Robert Carter Nicholas Sr., Considerations on the Present State of Virginia Examined (Williamsburg, 1774).

Hezekiah Niles (ed.), Principles and Acts of the Revolution in America... (Baltimore, 1822).

"Observator," No. VIII, The Connecticut Courant, April 30, 1771.

Henry V. S. Ogden, "The State of Nature and the Decline of Lockian Political Theory in England, 1760–1800," The American Historical Review 46:1 (1940), 21–44.

Peter Oliver, Charge to the Jury, December 5, 1770. Founders Online, National Archives, http://founders.archives.gov/documents/Adams/05-03-02-0001-0004-0019.

Peter Oliver, Origin & Progress of the American Rebellion, eds. Douglass Adair and John A. Schuts, Peter Oliver's Origin & Progress of the American Rebellion: A Tory View (Stanford, 1961, reissued 1967).

James Otis, Jr., A Vindication of the Conduct of the House of Representatives of the Province of the Massachusetts Bay: more particularly, in the last session of the General Assembly (Boston, 1762).

James Otis, Jr., The Rights of the British Colonies Asserted and Proved (Boston, 1764).

James Otis, Jr., Considerations on Behalf of the Colonists. In a Letter to a Noble Lord (London, 1765).

James Otis, Jr., A Vindication of the British Colonies, against the Aspersions of the Halifax Gentleman, in his Letter to a Rhode-Island Friend (Boston, 1765).

James Otis, Jr., ("Hampden"), in Boston Gazette, January 6, 1766.

Thomas Paine, "African Slavery in America," Pennsylvania Journal and Weekly Advertiser, March 1775.

Thomas Paine, Rights of Man: Being an Answer to Mr. Burke's Attack on the French Revolution (London, Philadelphia, Boston, Dublin, etc., 1791) in Thomas Paine, Rights of Man, Common Sense and Other Political Writings (ed. Mark Philp, Oxford, 1995).

Thomas Paine, The age of reason. Part the second. Being an investigation of true and of fabulous theology (London, 1795).

Bill Palmer, "Richard Watson, Bishop of Llandaff (1737–1816): A Chemist of the Chemical Revolution," Australian Journal of Education in Chemistry 68 (2007), 33–38.

Moses Parsons, A sermon preached at Cambridge, before His Excellency Thomas Hutchinson, Esq; governor: His Honor Andrew Oliver, Esq; lieutenant-governor, the Honorable His Majesty's Council, and the Honorable House of Representatives, of the province of the Massachusetts-Bay in New-England, May 27th 1772. Being the anniversary for the election of His Majesty's Council for said province (Boston, 1772).

Theodore Parsons and Eliphalet Pearson, *A Forensic Dispute on the Legality of Enslaving the Africans: Held at the Public Commencement in Cambridge, New-England, July 21st, 1773* (Boston, 1773).

John Paul, *A digest of the laws relating to the game of this kingdom* (London, 1775).

William A. Pencak, *Essays in American History* (Lehigh, 2011).

William Penn, *The excellent priviledge of liberty and property being the birth-right of the free-born subjects of England: Containing I. Magna Carta, with a learned comment upon it. II. The confirmation of the charters of the liberties of England ... III. A statute made the 34 Edw. I. ... IV. An abstract of the pattent granted by the King to VVilliam Penn ... V. And lastly, the charter of liberties granted by the said VVilliam Penn to the free-men and inhabitants of the province of Pennsylvania* (Philadelphia, 1687).

Thomas Pennant, *The British Zoology* (London, 1766, 2nd ed., 1768).

Thomas Pennant, *A Tour in Scotland, and Voyage to the Hebrides* (Chester, 1771).

Thomas Pennant, *Arctic Zoology ... Introduction, Class I. Quadrupeds* (London, 1784–85).

Thomas Pennant, *The view of Hindoostan* (London, 1798).

The Pennsylvania, Delaware, Maryland, and Virginia almanack and ephemeris, for the year of our Lord, 1783 (Baltimore, 1782).

"Philanthrop" [Jonathan Sewall?], August 10, 1767, Boston Evening-Post.

[J. Philmore and Anthony Benezet?], *Two Dialogues on the Man-Trade* (London, 1760).

"Philomathes," *The Massachusetts calendar, or An almanac for the year of our Lord 1772* (Boston, 1771).

Steven Pincus, *The Heart of the Declaration: The Founders' Case for an Activist Government* (Yale, 2017).

Arthur W. Plumstead, Introduction to *The Wall and the Garden: Selected Massachusetts Election Sermons, 1670–1775* (University of Minneapolis, 1968).

John G. A. Pocock, *The Ancient Constitution and the Feudal Law: A Study of English Historical Thought in the Seventeenth Century* (Cambridge, 1957).

John G. A. Pocock, *Barbarism and Religion: vol. 4, Barbarians, Savages and Empires* (Cambridge, 2008).

Pierre Poivre, *Voyages d'un philosophe ou observations sur les moeurs et les arts des peuples de l'Afrique, de l'Asie et de l'Amérique* (Yverdon, 1768).

Roscoe Pound, "Hierarchy of Sources and Forms in Different Systems of Law," *Tulane Law Review* 7:4 (1933), 475–87.

Thomas Pownall, *A Treatise on Government: Being a Review of the Doctrine of an Original Contract. More Particularly as it Respects the Rights of Government, and the Duty of Allegiance* (London, 1750).

Thomas Pownall, *Principles of Polity: Being the Grounds and Reasons of Civil Empire* (London, 1752).

Thomas Pownall, *The Administration of the Colonies* (London, 1st ed. 1764, 2nd ed. 1765, 3rd ed. 1766, 4th ed. 1768, 5th ed. 1774).

The Preceptor, May 21, 1772, *Massachusetts Spy*.

[Robert Prescott?], *A Letter from a Veteran, to the Officers of the Army Encamped at Boston* (New York, 1774).

Wilfrid Prest, *William Blackstone: Law and Letters in the Eighteenth Century* (Oxford, 2008).

Richard Price, *Additional Observations on the Nature and Value of Civil Liberty and Free Government* (London, 1777).

Mark Puls, *Samuel Adams, Father of the American Revolution* (Palgrave, 2006).

Jedediah Purdy, "The Politics of Nature: Climate Change, Environmental Law, and Democracy," *Yale Law Journal* 119:6 (2010), 1122–209.

Robert Putnam, "Diplomacy and Domestic Politics: The Logic of Two-Level Games," *International Organization* 42 (1988), 427–60.

Clifford Putney, "Oxenbridge Thacher: Boston Lawyer, Early Patriot," *Historical Journal of Massachusetts* 32:1 (2004), 90-106.

Josiah Quincy Jr., in the February 10, 1772, *Boston Gazette*.

Josiah Quincy Jr., Papers in Daniel R. Coquillette and Neil L. York, eds., *Portrait of a Patriot: The Major Political and Legal Papers of Josiah Quincy Junior* (6 vols., Boston 2005–2014).

Samuel M. Quincy (ed.), *Reports of Cases Argued and Adjudged in the Superior Court of Judicature of the Province of Massachusetts Bay, Between 1761 and 1772* (Boston, 1865).

David Ramsay, *History of the American Revolution* (Philadelphia, 1789).

Thomas W. Ramsbey, "The Sons of Liberty: The Early Inter-Colonial Organization," *International Review of Modern Sociology* 7:2 (1987), 313–35.

Dale Randall, "Dodsley's Preceptor - A Window into the 18th Century," *Rutgers University Library Journal* 22:1 (1958), 10–22.

Ray Raphael, *The Founders: The People Who Brought You a Nation* (New Press, 2009).

Paul de Rapin, *Histoire d'Angleterre* (The Hague, 1724–27, tr. Nicolas Tindal as *The History of England as well Ecclesiastical as Civil*, London, 1725–31).

William Bradford Reed, *The Life of Esther De Berdt* (Philadelphia, 1853).

Sir Thomas Reeve, "Instructions to his Nephew Concerning the Study of the Law," in Francis Hargrave, ed., *Collectanea Juridica. Consisting of Tracts Relative to the Law and Constitution of England* (London, 1791–92), 1:79–81.

John P. Reid, "In the Taught Tradition: The Meaning of Law in Massachusetts-Bay Two Hundred Years Ago," *Suffolk University Law Review* 14 (1980), 931–74.

John P. Reid, *Constitutional History of the American Revolution*, vol. 2: *The Authority to Tax* (University of Wisconsin, 1987).

John P. Reid, "The Jurisprudence of Liberty: The Ancient Constitution in Legal Historiography of the Seventeenth and Eighteenth Centuries," in Ellis Sandoz, ed., *The Roots of Liberty: Magna Carta, Ancient Constitution, and the Anglo-American Tradition of Rule of Law* (Liberty Fund, 1993), 147–231.

John P. Reid, *The Ancient Constitution and the Origins of Anglo-American Liberty* (DeKalb, 2005).

The Report of the Lords Committees appointed to Enquire into the several proceedings in the Colony of Massachusetts Bay, in opposition to the Sovereignty of his Majesty over that Province, and also what hath passed in the House of Lords, relative thereto from the first of January, 1764 (London, 1774).

Geoffrey Robertson, *The Tyrannicide Brief* (Chatto, 2005).

William Robertson, *The History of Scotland, during the Reigns of Queen Mary and of King James VI. Till his Accession to the Crown of England. With a Review of the Scotch History Previous to that Period; and an Appendix Containing Original Papers* (London, 1759).

William Robertson, *The History of the Reign of the Emperor Charles V. With a View of the Progress of Society in Europe, from the Subversion of the Roman Empire, to the Beginning of the Sixteenth Century* (Dublin, 1762–71).

Nicholas A. Robinson, "The Charter of the Forest: Evolving Human Rights in Nature," in D. B. Magrow et al., eds., *Magna Carta and the Rule of Law* (American Bar Association, 2014), 311–77.

David W. Robson, *Educating Republicans: The College in the Era of the American Revolution* (Greenwood, 1985).

Philippe Roger, *L'Ennemi américain. Généalogie de l'antiaméricanisme français* (2002, tr. as *The American Enemy: The History of French Anti-Americanism*, Chicago, 2005).

Bernard Romans, *Concise Natural History of East and West Florida containing an account of the natural produce of all the southern part of British America, in the three kingdoms of nature, particularly the animal and vegetable.: Likewise, the artificial produce now raised, or possible to be raised, and manufactured there, with some commercial and political observations in that part of the world; and a chorographical account of the same.: To which is added, by way of appendix, plain and easy directions to navigators over the bank of Bahama, the coast of the two Floridas, the north of Cuba, and the dangerous Gulph Passage. Noting also, the hitherto unknown watering places in that part of America, intended principally for the use of such vessels as may be so unfortunate as to be distressed by weather in that difficult part of the world* (New York, 1775).

John Rotheram, *A Sermon on the Wisdom of Providence . . .* (London, 1762).

H. Rothwell, "The Confirmation of the Charters, 1297," *English Historical Review* 60 (1945), 16–35, 177–91, 300–315.

Jean-Jacques Rousseau, *Discours sur l'origine et les fondements de l'inégalité parmi les hommes* (Amsterdam, 1755, tr. as *A Discourse upon the Origin and Foundation of the Inequality among Mankind*, London, 1761).

Jean-Jacques Rousseau, *Du contrat social; ou Principes du droit politique* (Amsterdam, 1762, tr. as *A Treatise on the Social Compact: or the Principles of Politic Law*, London, 1764).

Jean-Jacques Rousseau, *Émile, ou De l'éducation* (Amsterdam, 1762).

Benjamin Rush, *An address to the inhabitants of the British settlements in America, upon slave-keeping* (Philadelphia, 1773).

Benjamin Rush, *An oration, delivered February 4, 1774, before the American Philosophical Society, held at Philadelphia. Containing, an enquiry into the natural history of medicine among the Indians in North-America, and a comparative view of their disease and remedies, with those of civilized nations. Together with an appendix, containing, proofs and illustrations* (Philadelphia, 1774).

Benjamin Rush, *The autobiography of Benjamin Rush: his "Travels through life" together with his commonplace book for 1789–1813* (ed. George. W. Corner, Westport, CT, 1948).

Thomas Rutherforth, *Institutes of Natural Law; being the substance of a Course of Lectures on Grotius de Jure Belli et Pacis* (Cambridge, 1754–56).

Jacques-Henri Bernardin de Saint-Pierre, *Voyage à l'Île de France, à l'île Bourbon et au cap de Bonne-Espérance* (Amsterdam, 1773, tr. John Paris as *A Voyage to the Island of Mauritius*, London, 1775, tr. and ed. Jason Wilson as *Journey to Mauritius*, Signal Books, 2002).

Jacques-Henri Bernardin de Saint-Pierre, *Études de la nature* (Paris, 1784).

William Salkfeld, *Reports of Cases Adjudg'd in the Court of King's Bench, with some Special Cases in the Courts of Chancery, Common Pleas and Exchequer, from the First Year of K. William and Q. Mary, to the Tenth Year of Queen Anne. By William Salkeld, Late Serjeant at Law. With Two Tables; the One of the Names of the Cases, the Other of the Principal Matters therein Contained* (London, 1717–24, numerous concurrent and later editions).

Richard A. Samuelson, "The Constitutional Sanity of James Otis: Resistance Leader and Loyal Subject," *Review of Politics* 61:3 (1999), 493–523.

Ellis Sandoz (ed.), *Political Sermons of the American Founding Era, 1730–1805* (2nd ed., Liberty Fund, 1998).

Stephen Sayre, *The Englishman Deceived. A Political Piece: Wherein Some Very Important Secrets of State are Briefly Recited, and Offered to the Consideration of the Publick* (London [perhaps false, in reality New York?], 1768, repr. Salem, MA, 1768).

Isaac Schapira and Mark Somos, "'Bonapartes and Sharks': The Political Philosophy of Herman Melville," *Storia del pensiero politico* 1:2 (2012), 239–74.

David Schultz, "Political Theory and Legal History: Conflicting Depictions of Property in the American Founding," *American Journal of Legal History* 37:4 (1993), 464–95.

Lois Schwoerer, *The Ingenious Mr. Care, Restoration Publicist* (Johns Hopkins, 2002).

Samuel Seabury ("The Farmer" and "The Westchester Farmer"), *Free Thoughts on the Proceedings of the Continental Congress in a Letter to the Farmers* (New York, 1774).

Samuel Seabury ("The Farmer" and "The Westchester Farmer"), *A view of the controversy between Great-Britain and her colonies: including a mode of determining their present disputes, finally and effecually; and of preventing all future contentions. In a letter, to the author of A full vindication of the measures of the Congress, from the calumnies of their enemies* (New York, 1774).

Catherine Sedgewick, "Slavery in New England," *Bentley's Miscellany* 34 (1853), 417–24.

James Sedgwick, *Remarks Critical and Miscellaneous on the Commentaries of Sir W. Blackstone* (London, 1800).

John Selden, "Notes on Fortescue," in Sir John Fortescue, *De laudibus legum Angliæ* (London, 1616).

John Selden, *Mare clausum seu de dominio maris libri duo* (London, 1635).

Lucius Annaeus Seneca, *De clementia* (ed. Susanna Braund, Oxford, 2011).

Jonathan Sewall (Philanthrop), article in January 28, 1771, *Boston Evening-Post*.

Granville Sharp, *A Representation of the Injustice and Dangerous Tendency of Tolerating Slavery or of admitting the least claim of private property in the persons of men, in England* (London, 1769).

Granville Sharp, *A Declaration of the People's Natural Right to a Share in the Legislature; Which is the Fundamental Principle of the British Constitution of State* (London, 1774).

John Shebbeare, *Select Letters on the English Nation: By Batista Angeloni, a Jesuit, Who Resided Many Years in London. Translated from the Original Italian* (Dublin, 1763).

Sheffield Declaration, approved on January 12, 1773, printed in the February 18, 1773 *Massachusetts Spy*.

Richard B. Sher, "Transatlantic Books and Literature Culture," in Eve Tavor Bannet and Susan Manning, eds., *Transatlantic Literary Studies* (Cambridge, 2012), 10–27.

Thomas Sherlock, *Several discourses preached at the Temple Church* (London, 1754).

Suzanna Sherry, "The Founders' Unwritten Constitution," *University of Chicago Law Review* 54:4 (1987), 1127–77.

Samuel Sherwood, *A sermon, containing Scriptural instructions to civil rulers, and all free-born subjects. In which the principles of sound policy and good government are established and vindicated; and some doctrines advanced and zealously propagated by New-England Tories, are considered and refuted.: Delivered on the public fast, August 31, 1774.: With an address to the freemen of the colony. Also, an appendix, stating the heavy grievances the colonies labour under from several late acts of the British Parliament, and shewing what we have just reason to expect the consequences of these measures will be. By the Rev. Ebenezer Baldwin, of Danbury* (New Haven, 1774).

John B. Shipley, "Franklin Attends a Book Auction," *Pennsylvania Magazine of History and Biography* 80:1 (1956), 37–45.

John B. Shipley, "James Ralph's Pamphlets, 1741–1744," *Library* s5-XIX (1) (1964), 130–46.

Clifford K. Shipton, *Biographical Sketches of those who Attended Harvard College in the Classes 1690–1700, with Bibliographical and other Notes*, aka *Sibley's Harvard Graduates*, vols. 4 (Cambridge, MA, 1933), 7 (1945), 11 (1960), 14 (1968), 17 (1975).

Bartholomew Shower, *Cases in Parliament Resolved and Adjudged, Upon Petitions, And Writs of Error* (London, 1698).

Debora Shuger, *Political Theologies in Shakespeare's England: The Sacred and the State in Measure for Measure* (Palgrave, 2001).

Emmanuel Joseph Sieyès, "What is the Third Estate?" [1789] in *Political Writings* (ed. M. Sonenscher, Hackett, 2003).

Eric Slauter, *The State as a Work of Art: The Cultural Origins of the Constitution* (Chicago, 2009).

Eric Slauter, "Reading and Radicalization: Print, Politics, and the American Revolution," *Early American Studies* 8:1 (2010), 5–40.

James Sloss, *A treatise on God's love to the world; Wherein is shewn the perfect agreement betwixt the religion of Jesus, supernaturally revealed in the Gospel, and the religion of nature and reason in its state of integrity before the fall . . .* (London, 1770).

Richard Slotkin, *Regeneration through Violence: The Mythology of the American Frontier, 1600–1860* (Wesleyan, 1973).

Adam Smith, *The Theory of Moral Sentiments* (London, 1759).

Horace W. Smith et al., *Life and Correspondence of the Rev. William Smith, DD* (Philadelphia, 1880).

Maurice H. Smith, *The Writs of Assistance Case* (University of California, 1978).

Pamela H. Smith, *The Body of the Artisan: Art and Experience in the Scientific Revolution* (Chicago, 2004).

Pamela H. Smith, "Making as Knowing: Craft as Natural Philosophy," in P. H. Smith, A. R. W. Meyers, and H. J. Cook, eds., *Ways of Making and Knowing: The Material Culture of Empirical Knowledge* (Bard, 2014).

Thomas Smith, *De republica Anglorum. The maner of gouernement or policie of the realme of England, compiled by the honorable man Thomas Smyth, Doctor of the ciuil lawes, knight, and principall secretarie vnto the two most worthie princes, King Edwarde the sixt, and Queene Elizabeth. Seene and allowed* (London, 1583).

William Smith, *A general idea of the College of Mirania* (New York, 1753).

William Smith, *Discourses on Several Public Occasions during the War in America* (Philadelphia, 1759).

[William Smith and Thomas Hutchins?], *An Historical Account of the Expedition Against the Ohio Indians, in the Year 1764. Under the command of Henry Bouquet, Esq: colonel of foot, and now brigadier general in America.: Including his transactions with the Indians, relative to the delivery of their prisoners, and the preliminaries of peace. With an introductory account of the preceeding campaign, and battle at Bushy-Run. To which are annexed military papers, containing reflections on the war with the savages; a method of forming frontier settlements; some account of the Indian country, with a list of nations, fighting men, towns, distances and different routs. The whole illustrated with a map and copper-plates. Published from authentic documents, by a lover of his country.* (Philadelphia, 1765).

Tobias George Smollett, review of John Gray, *A Comparative View ...*, *Critical Review: Or, Annals of Literature*, 33:462–68 (London, 1772).

Harry M. Solomon, *The Rise of Robert Dodsley: Creating the New Age of Print* (Southern Illinois University Press, 1996).

[John Somers?], *Jura Populi Anglicani: Or, the Subjects Right of Petitioning Set Forth. Occasioned by the Case of the Kentish Petitioners. With a List of the Members of this Present Parliament who Refused the Voluntary Association...* (London, 1701).

Mark Somos, *Secularisation and the Leiden Circle* (Brill, 2011).

Mark Somos, "'A Price would be Set not only upon our Friendship, but upon our Neutrality': Alexander Hamilton's Political Economy and Early American State-Building," in Koen Stapelbroek, ed., *War and Trade: The Neutrality of Commerce in the Interstate System* (Helsinki, 2011), 184–211.

Mark Somos, "Selden's *Mare Clausum*: The Secularisation of International Law and the Rise of Soft Imperialism," *Journal of the History of International Law* 14:2 (2012), 287–330.

Mark Somos, "Bible Interpretation and the Constitution of the Christian Commonwealth in Hobbes's *Leviathan*, Part III," *Storia del pensiero politico* 4:2 (2015), 175–201.

Mark Somos, ed., "George Ticknor's *Progress of Politicks* (1816): An American Reception of German Comparative Constitutional Thought," Max Planck Institute for Comparative Public Law and International Law Working Papers, 2017–20.

Mark Somos, "Harrington's Project: The Balance of Money, a Republican Constitution for Europe, and England's Patronage of the World" in Béla Kapossy, Isaac Nakhimovsky, and Richard Whatmore, eds., *Commerce and Peace in the Enlightenment* (Cambridge, 2017), 20–43.

Mark Somos, "Sigonius' Method: A Sixteenth-Century Italian Source of British Imperial Reform, 1751–1780," in Arthur Weststeijn and Jeremia Pelgrom, eds., *Divergent Discourses on Roman Colonization: Sigonius, Lipsius, and the Development of Roman Colonial Studies* (Oxford, forthcoming).

Michael Sonenscher, *Sans-Culottes: An Eighteenth-Century Emblem in the French Revolution* (Princeton, 2008).

Emma Spary, *Utopia's Garden: French Natural History from the Old Regime to the Revolution* (Chicago, 2000).

Henry Stebbing, *An Enquiry Into the Force and Operation of the Annulling Clauses in a Late Act for the Better Preventing of Clandestine Marriages, with Respect to Conscience: In which the Rights of Marriage Both in and Out of Society are Briefly Discussed Upon the Principles of the Law of Nature* (London, 1754).

Matthew Steilen, "How to Think Constitutionally About Prerogative: A Study of Early American Usage," *Buffalo Law Review* (forthcoming).

Simon Stern, "Between Local Knowledge and National Politics: Debating Rationales for Jury Nullification after Bushell's Case," *Yale Law Journal* 111:7 (2002), 1815–59.

William Stevens, *A discourse on the English constitution; extracted from a late eminent writer, and applicable to the present times* (London, 1776).

William Stevens, *Strictures on a Sermon, Entitled, the Principles of the Revolution Vindicated, Preached before the University of Cambridge, on Wednesday, May 29th, 1776, by Richard Watson, D.D. F.R.S. Regius Professor of Divinity in that University. In a Letter to a Friend* (Cambridge, 1776).

Gerald Stourzh, "William Blackstone: Teacher of Revolution," *Jahrbuch für Amerikastudien* (1970), 184–200.

Benjamin Straumann, *Roman Law in the State of the Nature: The Classical Foundations of Hugo Grotius' Natural Law* (Cambridge, 2015).

Alec Stone Sweet, "Why Europe Rejected American Judicial Review—and Why It May Not Matter," *Michigan Law Review* 101:8 (2003), 2744–80.

Lindsay Swift, *The Massachusetts Election Sermons: An Essay in Descriptive Bibliography* (Cambridge, 1897, repr. from Publications of the Colonial Society of Massachusetts, vol. 1).

Brent Tarter, "The Virginia Declaration of Rights," in Josephine F. Pacheco, ed., *To Secure the Blessings of Liberty: Rights in American History, The George Mason Lectures* (George Mason University Press, 1993), 37–54.

Harold W. V. Temperley, "Debates on the Declaratory Act and the Repeal of the Stamp Act, 1766," *American Historical Review* 17:3 (1912), 563–86.

"Tertius Cato," reply to Mr. Southwick's defense of Thomas Hutchinson, March 28, 1774, *Newport Mercury*.

Oxenbridge Thacher to Benjamin Prat, 1762, *Proceedings of the Massachusetts Historical Society* 20 (1882–83), 46–48.

Oxenbridge Thacher, *The Sentiments of a British American* (Boston, 1764).

Edward Thompson, *Sailor's Letters. Written to his select friends in England, during his voyages and travels in Europe, Asia, Africa, and America. From the year 1754 to 1759* (London, 1766).

Henry David Thoreau, *Walden; or, Life in the Woods* (Boston, 1854).

Robert Thorp, *A Sermon Preached at the Assizes, at Newcastle upon Tyne, Aug 2, 1768* (Newcastle, 1768).

Jeffrey Toobin, "Clarence Thomas Has His Own Constitution," *New Yorker*, June 30, 2016.

John Harvey Treat, *The Treat family: a genealogy of Trott, Tratt, and Treat for fifteen generations, and four hundred and fifty years in England and America, containing more than fifteen hundred families in America* (Salem Press, 1893).

The True Sentiments of America: Contained in a Collection of Letters Sent from the House of Representatives of the Province of Massachusetts Bay to Several Persons of High Rank in this Kingdom: Together with Certain Papers relating to a Supposed Libel on the Governor of that Province, and a Dissertation on the Canon and the Feudal Law (London, 1768).

"T.S.," *A Cool Reply to A Calm Address Lately Published by Mr. John Wesley* (London, 1775).

Richard Tuck, *The Sleeping Sovereign: The Invention of Modern Democracy* (Cambridge, 2016).

Henry St. George Tucker, Sr., *Commentaries on Blackstone's Commentaries, for the Use of Students* (Winchester, 1826).

Henry St. George Tucker, Sr., *Commentaries on the Laws of Virginia: Comprising the Substance of a Course of Lectures Delivered to Winchester Law School* (Winchester, VA, 1831).

Henry St. George Tucker, Sr., *Commentaries on the Laws of Virginia: Comprising the Substance of a Course of Lectures Delivered to Winchester Law School* (Winchester, VA, 1836–37).

St. George Tucker, *Blackstone's Commentaries: with Notes of Reference to the Constitution and Laws of the Federal Government of the United States and of the Commonwealth of Virginia. In Five Volumes, With an Appendix to Each Volume Containing Short Tracts upon such Subjects as Appeared Necessary to Form a Connected View of the Laws of Virginia* (Philadelphia, 1803).

William Tudor, *An oration, delivered March 5th, 1779, at the request of the inhabitants of the town of Boston; to commemorate the bloody tragedy of the fifth of March, 1770* (Boston, 1779).

William Tudor, *The Life of James Otis, of Massachusetts: Containing also, Notices of Some Contemporary Characters and Events, from the Year 1760 to 1775* (Boston, 1823).

Union Library of Philadelphia, *A Catalogue of Books Belonging to the Union-Library-Company of Philadelphia* (Philadelphia, 1754).

Willem Usselincx, *More excellent obseruations of the estates and affairs of Holland* (London, 1622).

[John Vardill?] as "Poplicola," in the December 2, 1773, *Rivington's New-York Gazetteer*.

Emerich de Vattel, *Le droit des gens, ou Principes de la loi naturelle, appliqués à la conduite et aux affaires des Nations et des Souverains* ([Neuchâtel, 1757], London, 1758, with introduction and notes by Béla Kapossy and Richard Whatmore, eds., *The Law of Nations, Or, Principles of the Law of Nature, Applied to the Conduct and Affairs of Nations and Sovereigns, with Three Early Essays on the Origin and Nature of Natural Law and on Luxury* (Liberty Fund, 2008).

Charles Viner, *A General Abridgment of Law and Equity. Alphabetically Digested Under Proper Titles, with Notes and References to the Whole* (23 vols., Aldershot, 1742–53, with index by Robert Kelham, 1758).

Francisco de Vitoria, *De Indis* (1532), in Vitoria, *Political Writings* (ed. Anthony Pagden and Jeremy Lawrance, Cambridge, 1991).

Voltaire (François-Marie Arouet), *La philosophie de l'histoire* (Amsterdam, 1765).

Jeremy Waldron, "Rights and Majorities: Rousseau Revisited," *Nomos XXXII: Majorities and Minorities*, ed. John W. Chapman and Alan Wertheimer, 1990, 44–75.

Andrew S. Walmsley, *Thomas Hutchinson and the Origins of the American Revolution* (New York University, 1998).

William Warburton, *An Enquiry into the Nature and Origin of Literary Property* (London, 1762).

Samuel Ward, Diary, September 12, 1774, in Edmund C. Burnett, ed., *Letters of Members of the Continental Congress* (Washington, DC, 1921), 12–13.

Samuel Ward, *A Modern System of Natural History* (London, 1775–76).

Joseph Warren, *An oration delivered March 6, 1775, at the request of the inhabitants of the town of Boston; to commemorate the bloody tragedy of the fifth of March, 1770* (Newport, RI, 1775).

Mercy Otis Warren ("a Columbian patriot"), *Observations on the new Constitution, and on the Federal and State Conventions* (Boston, 1788).

Richard Watson, *The Principles of the Revolution Vindicated in a Sermon Preached Before the University of Cambridge, on Wednesday, May 29, 1776* (Cambridge, 1776).

Richard Watson, *An Apology for the Bible: In a Series of Letters Addressed to Thomas Paine, Author of a Book entitled, The Age of Reason, Part the Second, being an Investigation of True and Fabulous Theology* (New York, 1796).

Jeff A. Webb, "Leaving the State of Nature: a Locke-Inspired Political Community in St. John's, Newfoundland, 1723," *Acadiensis* 21:1 (1991), 156–65.

Noah Webster, *An Examination of the Leading Principles of the Federal Constitution* (Philadelphia, 1787).

[Paul Wein?], *A Concise Historical Account of all the British Colonies in North-America, Comprehending Their Rise, Progress, and Modern State; Particularly of the Massachusets-Bay (the seat of the present civil war): together with the other provinces of New-England: to which is annexed, an accurate descriptive table of the several countries...* (London, 1775).

Richard Wells, "A few political reflections . . ." in the June 20, 1774, *Pennsylvania Packet*.

John Wesley, *A Calm Address to our American Colonies* (London, 1775).

Samuel West, *A sermon preached before the Honorable Council, and the Honorable House of Representatives, of the colony of the Massachusetts-Bay. Being the anniversary for the election of the Honorable Council for the colony* (Boston, 1776).

[Samuel Wharton, with Edward Bancroft?], *View of the title to Indiana, a tract of country on the river Ohio. Containing Indian conferences at Johnson-Hall, in May, 1765—the deed of the Six Nations to the proprietors of Indiana—the minutes of the congress at Fort*

Stanwix, in October and November, 1768—the deed of the Indians, settling the boundary line between the English and Indians lands—and the opinion of counsel on the title of the proprietors of Indiana ([Philadelphia?], 1775).

Thomas Whately, *The Regulations Lately Made Concerning the Colonies and the Taxes Imposed upon Them, Considered* (London, 1765).

Thomas Whately, *Remarks on The Budget; or a Candid Examination of the Facts and Arguments Offered to the Public in that Pamphlet* (London, 1765).

Thomas Whately, *Considerations on the Trade and Finances of the Kingdom and on the Measures of the Administration since the Conclusion of the Peace* (London, 1766).

Thomas Whately, *Observations on Modern Gardening, Illustrated by Descriptions* (London, 1777).

William Whipple, letter to Joshua Brackett, July 29, 1776, *Proceedings of the Massachusetts Historical Society* 5 (1862), 6.

Nathaniel Whitaker, *A confutation of two tracts, entitled, A vindication of the new churches; and The churches quarrel espoused: written by the Reverend John Wise* (Boston, 1774).

Charles White, *A Treatise on the Management of Pregnant and Lying-in Women, and the Means of Curing, But More Especially of Preventing the Principal Disorders to which They are Liable, Together with Some New Directions Concerning the Delivery of the Child and Placenta in Natural Births, Illustrated with Cases* (London, 1773).

John Wilkes, *The Works of the Celebrated John Wilkes, Esq; Formerly Published under the Title of The North Briton, in Three Volumes* (London, [1765?]).

Abraham Williams, *A Sermon Preach'd at Boston, Before the Great and General Court or Assembly of the Province of the Massachusetts-Bay in New-England, May 26, 1762. Being the Day Appointed by Royal Charter, for the Election of His Majesty's Council for Said Province* (Boston, 1762).

Elisha Williams, *The Essential Rights and Liberties of Protestants. A Seasonable Plea for the Liberty of Conscience, and the Right of Private Judgment, in Matters of Religion, without any Controul from Human Authority. Being a Letter, from a Gentleman in the Massachusetts-Bay to his Friend in Connecticut* (Boston, 1744).

James Wilson, "Comparison of Constitutions," in *Works* (ed. Robert Green McCloskey, Belknap, 1967), 1:326–31.

James Wilson, *Considerations on the Nature and Extent of the Legislative Authority of the British Parliament* (Philadelphia, 1774).

James Wilson, *Lectures on Law* [1790–91] in Wilson, *Collected Works* (ed. Kermit L. Hall and Mark D. Hall, Liberty Fund, 2007).

Joseph Wimpey, *Letters Occasioned by Three Dialogues concerning Liberty; wherein the Author's Doctrine Respecting the State of Nature, is Shewn to be Repugnant to Nature . . .* (London, 1777).

John Wise, *The churches quarrel espoused, or, A reply in satyre, to certain proposals made, in answer to this question, What further steps are to be taken, that the councils may have due constitution and efficacy in supporting, preserving and well ordering the interest of the churches in the country?* (Boston, 1710, 2nd ed. Boston, 1715).

John Wise, *A Vindication of the Government of New England's Churches. Drawn from antiquity; the light of nature; Holy Scripture; its noble nature; and from the dignity Divine*

Providence has put upon it (Boston, 1717; repr., together with *The Churches Quarrel Espoused*, in Boston, 1772).

Steven M. Wise, *Though the Heavens May Fall: The Landmark Trial That Led to the End of Human Slavery* (Da Capo, 2005).

John Witherspoon, *The Dominion of Providence Over the Passions of Men. A sermon preached at Princeton, on the 17th of May, 1776. Being the general fast appointed by the Congress through the United Colonies. To which is added, an address to the natives of Scotland residing in America* (Philadelphia, 1776).

Edwin Wolf, *The Book Culture of a Colonial American City* (Oxford, 1988).

Gordon S. Wood, *The Creation of the American Republic, 1776–1787* (University of North Carolina, 1969).

Gordon S. Wood, *The Americanization of Benjamin Franklin* (Penguin, 2004).

Thomas Wood, *An Institute of the Laws of England; or, the Laws of England, in their Natural Order, according to Common Use. Published for the Direction of young Beginners, or Students in the Law; and of Others that Desire to Have a General Knowledge in our Common and Statute Laws* (London, 1720; 2nd ed. 1722; numerous posthumous editions).

L. Kinvin Wroth and Hiller B. Zobel, Introduction and notes in Wroth and Zobel, eds., *Legal Papers of John Adams* (Belknap, 1965).

"W.Y.," *A Serious Answer to Mr. Wesley's Calm Address to Our American Colonies* (Bristol, 1775).

Edward Wynne, *Eunomus, or, Dialogues Concerning the Law and Constitution of England, with an Essay on Dialogue* (London, 1768).

Craig Yirush, *Settlers, Liberty, and Empire: The Roots of Early American Political Theory, 1675–1775* (Cambridge, 2011).

Charles Yorke, *Considerations on the Law of Forfeitures for High Treason: Occasioned by a Clause, in the Late Act, for Making it Treason to Correspond with the Pretender's Sons, Or Any of Their Agents* (London, 1745).

Arthur Young, *Rural Oeconomy: or, Essays on the Practical Parts of Husbandry* (London, 1770).

[Sir William Young?], *Authentic papers relative to the expedition against the Charibbs, and the sale of lands in the island of St. Vincent* (London, 1773).

Arthur Zilversmit, *First Emancipation: The Abolition of Slavery in the North* (1967).

John J. Zubly, *The Law of Liberty. A Sermon on American Affairs, Preached at the Opening of the Provincial Congress of Georgia. Addressed to the Right Honourable the Earl of Dartmouth: With an Appendix, Giving a Concise Account of the Struggles of Swisserland to Recover their Liberty* (Philadelphia, 1775).

LAWS

Magna Carta

Act for Removing and Preventing All Questions and Disputes Concerning the Assembling and Sitting of this Present Parliament, a.k.a. Parliament Act 1660 (12 Car. II c.1)

Plantation Act or Naturalization Act of 1740 (13 Geo. 2.c.7)
Two-Penny Act of 1755. 6 Laws of Virginia (Hening, 1819) 568
Two-Penny Act of 1758. 7 Laws of Virginia (Hening, 1820) 240.
Tea Act of 1773 (13 Geo 3 c 44)
Boston Port Act of 1774 (14 Geo. III. c. 19)
Massachusetts Government Act of 1774 (14 Geo. III. c. 45)
H.R.4653 (103rd): Mohegan Nation (Connecticut) Land Claim Settlement Act of 1994

CASES

The Case of Swans (1592) Trinity Term, 34 Elizabeth I
Dr. Bonham's Case, 8 Co. Rep. 107; 77 Eng. Rep. 638 (1610)
Bushel's Case (1670) 124 E.R. 1006
Dutton v. Howell (1693)
The City of London v. Wood, 12 Mod. 669, 687 (K. B. 1701)
Mohegan Indians v. Connecticut (1705–1773)
Astley v. Younge, 2 Burr. 807 (1759)
Paxton's Case Gray, Mass. Repts., 51 469 (1761)
King against Taylor (1767), case 76 in Lord John Maclaurin Dreghorn's *Arguments, and decisions* ... 326–29
Millar v Taylor (1769) 4 Burr. 2303, 98 ER 201
Rex v. Richardson (1770–72)
Somersett v Steuart (1772) 98 ER 499
Fabrigas v. Mostyn ([1773] 2 Wm Bl 929, (1773) 20 St Tr 82)
Donaldson v Beckett (1774) 2 Brown's Parl. Cases (2d ed.) 129, 1 Eng. Rep. 837; 4 Burr. 2408, 98 Eng. Rep. 257; 17 Cobbett's Parl. Hist. 953
Brom and Bett v. Ashley (1781)
Miller, et al. v. The Ship Resolution, 2 U.S. (2 Dall.) 19 (1781)
Vanhorne's Lessee v. Dorrance, 2 U.S. (2 Dallas) 304 (1795)
Johnson v. M'Intosh, 21 U.S. (8 Wheat.) 543 (1823)
The Cherokee Nation v. The State of Georgia, 30 US 1 (1831)
Worcester v. Georgia, 31 U.S. (6 Pet.) 515 (1832)
Davis v. Richmond, 512 F. 2d 201 (1975)
Williams v. State of Delaware, 539 A. 2d 164 (1988)
People v. Davis, 958 P. 2d 1083 (1998)
Smothers v. Gresham Transfer, Inc. 332 Or. 83, 23 P.3d 333 (2001)
Lawson v. Hoke, 119 P.3d 210 (Or. 2005)
Liberty Northwest Insurance Corp. v. Oregon Insurance Guarantee Association 136 P.3d 49, 54 (Or. Ct. App 2006)
District of Columbia v. Heller, 554 U.S. 570 (2008)
US v. Rivera-Oros, 590 F. 3d 1123 (2009)
McDonald v. City of Chicago, 561 U.S. 742 (2010)
In re JE, 711 SE 2d 5 (2011)

Klutschowski v. PeaceHealth, 311 P.3d 461 (2013), 354 Or. 150
Teva Pharmaceuticals USA, Inc. v. Sandoz, Inc., 574 U.S. ___ (2015)
Obergefell v. Hodges, 576 U.S. ___ (2015)
Brawner v. Miller, 778 SE 2d 839 (2015)
Horton v. OHSU, 359 Or 168 (2016)
State v. Chipps, 874 NW 2d 475 (2016)

INDEX